SCIENTIFIC INQUIRY INTO HUMAN POTENTIAL

Scientific Inquiry into Human Potential explores the intellectual legacy and contemporary understanding of scientific research on human intelligence, performance, and productivity. Across nineteen chapters, some of the most eminent scholars of learning and psychology recount how they originated, distinguished, measured, challenged, and adapted their theories on the nature and nurture of human potential over decades of scientific research. These accessible, autobiographical accounts cover a spectrum of issues, from the biological underpinnings and developmental nature of human potential to the roles of community, social interaction, and systematic individual differences in cognitive and motivational functioning. Researchers, instructors, and graduate students of education, psychology, sociology, and biology will find this book not only historically informative but inspiring to their own ongoing research journeys, as well.

David Yun Dai is Professor of Educational Psychology and Methodology in the Department of Educational and Counseling Psychology at the University at Albany, State University of New York, USA.

Robert J. Sternberg is Professor in the Department of Human Development in the College of Human Ecology at Cornell University, USA, and Honorary Professor of Psychology at Heidelberg University, Germany.

SCIENTIFIC INQUIRY INTO HUMAN POTENTIAL

Historical and Contemporary Perspectives Across Disciplines

Edited by David Yun Dai and Robert J. Sternberg

NEW YORK AND LONDON

First published 2021
by Routledge
52 Vanderbilt Avenue, New York, NY 10017

and by Routledge
2 Park Square, Milton Park, Abingdon, Oxon OX14 4RN

Routledge is an imprint of the Taylor & Francis Group, an informa business

© 2021 Taylor & Francis

The right of David Yun Dai and Robert J. Sternberg to be identified as the authors of the editorial material, and of the authors for their individual chapters, has been asserted in accordance with sections 77 and 78 of the Copyright, Designs and Patents Act 1988.

All rights reserved. No part of this book may be reprinted or reproduced or utilised in any form or by any electronic, mechanical, or other means, now known or hereafter invented, including photocopying and recording, or in any information storage or retrieval system, without permission in writing from the publishers.

Trademark notice: Product or corporate names may be trademarks or registered trademarks, and are used only for identification and explanation without intent to infringe.

Library of Congress Cataloging-in-Publication Data
A catalog record for this title has been requested

ISBN: 978-0-367-26135-1 (hbk)
ISBN: 978-0-367-26136-8 (pbk)
ISBN: 978-0-429-29165-4 (ebk)

Typeset in Bembo
by Taylor & Francis Books

We dedicate this book to our children:
Vivian and Victor, and
Seth, Sara, Samuel, Brittany, and Melody

DYD and RJS

CONTENTS

List of Illustrations x
Preface xii
Introduction: Historical and Contemporary Perspectives on
Human Potential xv
David Yun Dai and Robert J. Sternberg

PART 1
Evolutionary and Differential Perspectives on Human Potential 1

1 A Journey from Behavioral Ecology to Sex Differences to
   Mitochondria and Intelligence 3
   David C. Geary

2 A Long "Intellectual" Journey 16
   Phillip L. Ackerman

3 Partnership: A Tale by the Tail of the Kite 29
   Nancy M. Robinson

4 Of Human Potential: A Forty Year Saga 41
   Howard Gardner

PART 2
Cognitive and Developmental Perspectives   49

5 Unleashing Clio: Tracing the Roots of My Journey in Cognition   51
Stephen J. Ceci

6 Ignoring Boundaries between Disciplines   60
Fernand Gobet

7 Optimal Expression of Human Potential as the Central Goal of Human Development   75
David Henry Feldman

8 Capitalizing on Chance Opportunities   85
Rena F. Subotnik

9 My Journey from the Humanities to Psychology   96
Ellen Winner

PART 3
Perspectives on Human Creativity   111

10 Human Potential at the Achievement Pinnacle: A Lifelong Preoccupation with History-Making Genius   113
Dean Keith Simonton

11 A Contrarian's Apology and the Changing Contexts of Creativity Research   126
Mark A. Runco

12 Female Teacher/Researcher: My Work in Talent Development Education and in Creativity Education   142
Jane Piirto

13 Business as Unusual: From the Psychology of Giftedness to Changing the World via Innovation   155
Larisa Shavinina

14 Creativity and Cities: A Personal and Intellectual Journey   168
Richard Florida

PART 4
Educational and Social Perspectives   **183**

15 Everything I Needed to Know about Human Intelligence I Learned Before I Even Went to College   185
Robert J. Sternberg

16 Reflections on My Work: The Identification and Development of Creative/Productive Giftedness   197
Joseph S. Renzulli

17 Academic Achievement, Identity, and Hope: Investing in and Over Time   212
Frank C. Worrell

18 Intellectual Roots and Paths   224
Sally M. Reis

19 Learning from Life: How I Became a Wisdom Researcher   235
Judith Glück

Epilogue: The Past, Present, and Future of (Research on) Human Potential   *247*
David Yun Dai

List of Contributors   *266*
Subject Index   *276*
Name Index   *281*

ILLUSTRATIONS

Figures

1.1	The Four Horsemen of the Apocalypse	10
7.1	The universal to unique continuum	81
11.1	A 6P framework on creativity	127
12.1	Piirto Pyramid of Talent Development	145
16.1	Theories underlying the development of creative/productive giftedness	198

Table

10.1	Emergence and duration of long-term topics pursued in my research program	121

PREFACE

The topic of human potential is interesting to people in all walks of life because it is about the possibilities and limits of what one can accomplish in one's lifetime. Most people are curious as to why some people accomplished a lot and others did much less. People are often fascinated by geniuses like Einstein, child prodigies like Mozart, or creative scientists such as Richard Feynman or Marie Curie. Studies of these distinguished individuals clearly provide some answers about the nature and nurture of human potential, but psychologists are always trying to go beyond such cases to find the ultimate sources of mind power.

Toward the end of the last century, Richard Herrnstein and Charles Murray's (1994) book, *The Bell Curve*, stated that human potential is, by and large, a matter of how high your IQ is. The book appeared to cast an ominous shadow on the long-term life prospects of many people who were not higher up in the IQ spectrum. Yet, other scholars have seemed more optimistic: They have argued, for example, that a growth mindset (the belief in your capability for self-improvement; Dweck, 2006) or grit (the unrelenting pursuit of interest and perseverance in the face of obstacles; Duckworth, 2016) can carry one a long way toward achieving one's life ambitions.

Knowledge and understanding of the nature of human potential has profound implications for society and social policy, including how we can strengthen education, select the right employee in work settings, or, more generally, optimize social conditions for the sake of productivity and creativity. The question of human potential happens to be one of the most difficult questions to answer on Earth, as it involves the age-old issue of *"Know Thyself."*

The purpose of the volume is to gather a collection of narratives of distinguished scholars who looked back at, and reflected on, their own intellectual journeys of understanding the nature and nurture of human potential for high-level performance and creative productivity. The volume includes 19 leading scholars specialized in the topics of intelligence, giftedness, talent, expertise, creativity, and wisdom. These scholars represent a wide range of disciplines—from biology, psychology, education, business, and economics, and their scholarly work spans three or more decades. A unique feature of the 19 chapters in this volume is that the authors situate their scientific inquiry in the rich social-historical and personal contexts in which their lives have been embedded. In this way, readers can appreciate how the Zeitgeist of the times in the various past decades have significantly changed the landscape of understanding human potential. Rather than writing about their research technically, with their academic peers as an audience, we asked the authors to develop an *autobiographical perspective* of how they embarked on their respective journeys, how their ideas evolved over time, and what their hindsight is when they look back on their long journeys. More specifically, the authors were asked to:

a   Identify what (events, ideas, and people) triggered a particular line of scholarly and scientific inquiry, and what was the main impetus that has driven their inquiry and brought a unique angle to the field.
b   Highlight changes in the direction of thinking and research that took place over time; what were some turning points, crystallizing events, and findings that led to the changes?
c   Provide reflection or hindsight as to what are some of the most promising ways we should adapt in our approach to understanding human potential.

Given this particular style of writing, on a topic of such a broad appeal, we have sought a broad audience for the volume. First, researchers with a broad spectrum of interests will find this volume informative, as it provides a comprehensive and panoramic view of progress on the issue of human potential. Second, this volume aims to reach out to all educators, for whom cultivating their students' potential to make their lives more fulfilling is one of the most important tasks. The autobiographical and narrative, rather than technical, style of writing makes the topics and issues they discuss more accessible. Quite a number of the authors are teachers turned scholars, whose ways of engagement are congenial to educators' perspectives. Third, this volume is also can be a vital source of information for graduate students and young scholars who are aspiring to conduct research within the areas covered by the volume. The authors, through their narratives, provide an ample survey of the research literature. In addition, the introductory chapter as well as the epilogue provides an overview of the past, present, and future of the field of human potential. Fourth, and finally, general audiences may find this volume intriguing in its own right, as the narratives contained in the volume are also stories and testimonials of what make great accomplishments possible for almost anyone.

We thank Dan Schwartz for his support for this collective project. We also thank our doctoral students, Jessica Murray, Skyla Sun, Yukang Xue, and Panpan Yang, for their editorial assistance. Finally, we dedicate this book to our children, who represent the younger generations to come. Their potential to make new strides and make this world a better place is so much of what motivated and inspired the decades of scholarly work displayed in this volume.

DYD
RJS
May 12, 2020

INTRODUCTION

Historical and Contemporary Perspectives on Human Potential

David Yun Dai and Robert J. Sternberg

> This is what I am driving at—that analogy clearly shows there must be a fairly constant average mental capacity in the inhabitants of the British Isles, and that the deviations from that average—upwards towards genius, and downwards towards stupidity—must follow the law that governs deviations from all true averages.
>
> *Francis Galton* (Hereditary Genius: An Inquiry into Its Laws and Consequences, *1869/1892, p. 32*)

> No person is the master of the whole culture…Each man lives a fragment of it. To be whole, he must create his own version of the world, using the part of his cultural heritage he has made his own through education.
>
> *Jerome Bruner* (After John Dewey, What? *1979, p. 116*)

What makes some individuals accomplish extraordinary feats, from inventing tools and gadgets that improve human conditions, to developing powerful theoretical explanations of the universe or mastering skills at an extraordinary level? This question has fascinated people since the start of civilization. Indeed, what enabled humans (*homo sapiens*) to create a civilization in terms of a dazzling array of cultural creations is still a mind-boggling question. The facts that popular books on this topic can become *New York Times* best sellers (e.g., *Outliers* by Malcolm Gladwell, 2008), and that theoretical ideas such as *emotional intelligence* (Goldman, 1995), *grit* (Duckworth, 2016), or *mindset* (Dweck, 2006) become buzzwords in public discourse, all allude to public fascination with the "secrets" of outstanding accomplishments. Yet, stories of the most recent theoretical advances in this line of scientific inquiry remain to be told.

This book presents a collection of autobiographical accounts of intellectual journeys by a group of leading scholars and researchers who have dedicated three or four decades of their academic careers to understanding the nature and nurture of human potential under the guise of various concepts (genius, child prodigy, giftedness, intelligence, talent, expertise, creativity, wisdom, polymathy, eminent contributions in science, art, and technology, etc.). It aims to trace the evolution of conceptions and theories from historical to contemporary times, and take stock of what has transpired in our understandings as to what make human accomplishments, and hence, civilization, possible.

Defining the Problem

Although the line between the historical and contemporary is not always clear-cut, we can roughly see 1980s as a pivotal period when there was a surge of scholarly work by Ackerman (1988), Bloom (1985), Feldman (with Goldsmith, 1986), Gagné (1985), Gardner (1983), Gruber (1981), Sternberg (1985), Tannenbaum (1983), among many others, that marked a definitive turn in our understanding of underpinnings of human potential in various forms and manifestations of human accomplishments.

The issue of *human potential* concerns possibilities as well as limits of human development—that is, how we identify and specify a set of biological, environmental, and developmental constraints for the realization of human potential, especially contributions deemed as stretching human limits or lifting human civilization to new heights. The range of research and expertise represented in this book reflects the scope of human potential as manifested at different levels, from evolutionary origins and neural systems (i.e., infrastructure of the brain/mind) to psychological processes (e.g., cognition and motivation), from developmental interaction of the person with his or her environment to the synergistic play of a group or community.

As it turns out, it is easier to scientifically map out such constraints for some domains than for others. For example, it is easier to define and determine what enables someone to run a 100-meter sprint within ten seconds than what it takes to make a major scientific contribution or producing a masterpiece of art. In addition to the multitude of targeted phenomena of human accomplishments, the respective importance of natural endowment, environmental experiences, and developmental milestone events (i.e., weights they carry) for these accomplishments has been constantly debated since Galton's (1869) bold proclamation that *nature ultimately prevails over nurture*. The preponderance of historical evidence from archival research (e.g., Lehman, 1953; Simonton, 1999) indicates an extremely skewed distribution of talent and creative productivity. When the criterion of human accomplishments is made more inclusive, for instance, including all professions that more or less involve creative undertakings (Florida, 2002, this volume), 5 to 20 percent of the population are considered gifted or talented (see also Gagné, 2005; Renzulli, 1986). Thus, the scientific discourse on human potential can only be made meaningful and intelligible when boundary conditions (e.g., domain-specificity or context-specificity) for specific knowledge claims are clear. With this in mind, in the following sections, we try to delineate a conceptual landscape along which most researchers (including authors in this volume) have traversed in history, and point out some new directions pursued by contemporary scholars, authors in this volume included.

Capacity, Propensity, and Enduring Individual Differences

Decades ago, Scheffler (1985) identified three ways in which human potential can be conceptualized—as capacity, as propensity or disposition, or as capability. The capacity view assumes that how far one can go in life achievements is capped by one's basic biological makeup. The *capacity* view of human potential is historically very prominent, and elaborated by Galton (1869) 150 years ago (see the quote under the title of this introduction). Spearman (1904) perpetuated this view by declaring that, once and for all, *general intelligence* was objectively defined and measured. Indeed, the notion of a mental capacity that allows some people to achieve marvelous feats but makes others stuck in mediocrity lends itself easily to a psychometric definition of human potential. It is further perpetuated by an IQ-stratified society, bluntly articulated in the book *Bell Curve* (Hernnstein & Murray, 1994). Not surprisingly, it was endorsed by many well-established psychometrically slanted scholars and researchers (Gottfredson, 1997; but see Neisser et al., 1996; Nisbett et al., 2012 for updated reviews on the intelligence controversy; see chapters by Ceci, Feldman, Sternberg, Subotnik in this volume).

A natural offshoot of this capacity view was the invention of *giftedness,* or the notion that a small proportion of children at the top of the general-intelligence continuum can be identified as gifted, who presumably hold the greatest *cognitive capacity* for human achievements. This capacity view implicitly assumes a monotonic relationship between psychometrically measured general intelligence and a gradation of life achievements across domains of cultural importance (Terman, 1925, 1954). However, very early on, scholars and researchers expressed skepticism about the capacity view of human potential. Witty and Lehman (1927), for example, argued for a more distinct role of motivation (drive), a theme picked up by Feldhusen (1986) and Renzulli (1978). In historical hindsight, the capacity view of human potential has long fallen out of favor, as we never know what exactly constitutes this elusive capacity that somehow caps one's achievement. Indeed, contemporary scholars rarely use high IQs exclusively as the core definition of giftedness (see Sternberg & Davidson, 2005; Renzulli, 2005, this volume; see Dai, 2018).

The second conception of human potential Scheffler (1985) identified sees human potential as *propensity* or *disposition*, a tendency to react to and act upon certain classes of situations that is developmentally instigative. This definition does not view human potential as a capacity and is close to *aptitude* as Snow (1992) defined it. Snow's aptitude theory represents a more situated definition of *human potential*: rather than being concerned with long-term predictive efficacy, aptitude as a construct of potential is more proximal, relative to task conditions involved (Snow, 1992; see also Lohman, 2005; Ackerman, this volume). Human potential as dispositional is also in line with the argument advanced by evolutionary psychology for *differential susceptibility* (Belsky & Pluess, 2009). With the emphasis on dispositions or propensities, the locus of human potential was shifted to *the person-situation interaction*, whereby an environmental condition elicits differential adaptive responses, depending on characteristics of the individual. The dispositional or propensity view of human potential also opens doors for a more pluralistic view of human potential. Various forms of child prodigies (Feldman, 1986) or developmental precocity (Lubinski & Benbow, 2006) and polymaths (Root-Bernstein, 2009), differential rates of learning and asymptotic performance (Shiffrin, 1996), and a wide range of talent development trajectories (Gagné, 2005; Ceci et al., 2016) are compatible with this interactionist view. It should be noted that the propensity view of human potential still leans toward the "nature" side of the nature-nurture continuum, given that aptitudes and dispositions are biologically constitutional, albeit developmentally calibrated (Dai, 2017), thus subject to criticism from the nurture camp that emphasizes the primacy of environmental experiences for human accomplishments (e.g., Ericsson, 2006; Howe, Davidson, & Sloboda, 1998). However, the interactionist view of human potential treats the biological and environmental as belonging to one system. With the discovery of epigenesis, the debate between heredity and environment becomes moot. We now know that environment influences how genes are expressed; therefore, heredity and environment have a bi-directional relationship (Gottlieb, 2007). Thus, the propensity to react or act can also be shaped by the environment (Papierno et al., 2005).

Domains, Domain Experiences, and Development of Expertise

The notion of human potential as capacity or propensity can also be construed as *domain-specific*, in that tasks and situations may be distinguished from one another in terms of the type of stimuli, information, or "affordances" involved (Gardner, 1983, this volume). Interestingly, while Spearman (1904) was seeking mathematic certainty of general intelligence "objectively defined and measured," Binet expressed a very different view: "we do not all have intelligence based on the same schemata. Several different kinds of intelligence exist, and the kind that fits one does not fit another. This is a common sense truth" (quoted in Pereira Da Costa et al., 2014, p. 29). Consequently, experiences so engendered are likely increasingly fine-tuned (i.e., adapted) to specific situations or task conditions (VanTassel-Baska, 2005; see also Ceci, this volume). A view of human potential as at least partly domain-specific has further loosened up the hegemony of the capacity view by introducing constructs that implicate the role of extensive learning experiences in formal as well as informal settings, such as deliberate practice (Feldman, 1994, this volume; Ericsson, 2006), or extended problem solving (Bereiter & Scardamalia, 1993).

According to Scheffler (1985), human potential can also be conceptualized as *capability*. This third conception is predicated on a new understanding of ability articulated by Bandura (1993): "Ability is not a fixed attribute residing in one's behavioral repertoire. Rather, it is a generative capability in which cognitive, motivational, and behavioral skills must be orchestrated for numerous purposes" (p. 118). It implies a more malleable, expert-like conception of human potential. In the same vein, Gardner (2003) identified an alternative definition of intelligence, not as a capacity or propensity of some sort, but as "fit execution of a task or role" that carries important adaptive value (Gardner, 2003, p. 48; see also Newell, 1990). This definition is further reinforced by an expertise view of intelligence as contextually bound (Ceci & Liker, 1986; see Ceci, this volume), adaptive (Sternberg, 2019), and developing (Lohman, 2006; Sternberg, 1999; but see Angoff, 1988 for a defense of the distinction between aptitude and achievement).

Domain experiences seen as essential for realizing human potential inevitably bring motivation and personality to the forefront of attention, as the notion of deliberate practice or effortful learning and self-improvement implies intensive, goal-driven activity (Ackerman, this volume). There are two ways of conceptualizing motivation and related personal dispositions (e.g., risk taking) as related to human potential. The first one views motivational factors as *non-intellective* (Tannenbaum, 1983) or as *intrapersonal catalysts* (Gagné, 2005). This conception still treats human potential more like a capacity of some sort, as motivation (e.g., drive) just provides a motor for unleashing this potential (i.e., the capacity) to a certain extent. The other conception treats motivation and related personal dispositions as inherently intellectual and meaning-driven, such as perseverance of interest (i.e., "grit"; Duckworth, 2016), mindset (Dweck, 2006), or the persistent quest for meaning and coherence (Torrance, 1963), exemplified by Charles Darwin and other pathfinders (Gruber, 1981). At a high level of intellectual functioning, the line between motivation, emotion, and cognition is blurred (see Dai & Sternberg, 2004), so is the line between potential and "catalyst".

A Developmental Approach

So far in this review, we have provided an historical account of how early researchers conceptualized and studied human potential. More recently a developmental perspective emerged as a viable alternative, which views human potential is contingent on timely developmental opportunities and experiences (i.e., the right person in the right place at the right time; Simonton, 1999). The idea lends itself to a more dynamic, contextual, and emergent view of human potential (Dai, 2017; Dai & Renzulli, 2008). Moreover, when human development is seen as truly contributing to enhanced human potential rather than merely "unleashing" it, it is inevitable to look into developmental processes and transitions in terms of what is driving the developmental changes as adaptation every step of the way.

The traditional view of individual development tends to emphasize the organismic nature of individual development; that is, the person develops as a whole, with parts coordinated to achieve holistic functions (see Horowitz, 1987; Magnusson, 2001). Indeed, both Piaget (1950) and Werner (1967) alluded to cognitive adaptation as a source of human creativity. In contrast, Vygotsky (1978) put a premium on cultural tools and resources as significantly shaping human development; they lift human competence to a new level that is not achievable when people are left to their own devices (his notion of zone of proximal development or ZPD). More broadly, Stephen Hawking (1996) pointed out a turning point in human evolution, from passing genes (biological evolution) to passing information (cultural evolution) to the next generations. Inevitably, one has to reckon with various new possibilities in human development not due to genetic variations but due to cultural variations and changes (Dai, 2019).

Bruner (1979) cogently argued for the role of culture in individual development (see the quotation at the beginning of this introduction). The central issue for understanding human potential, then, is to delineate the developmental fusion of the biological and cultural (Dai, 2019, in press). Bronfenbrenner and Ceci (1994) brought these two forces together in specific local conditions, what they called "proximal processes" (p. 572), namely, meaningful transactional experiences with specific task and social environments over an extended period. The construct further reinforces the notion of sustained, nonuniversal development through education and training as a necessary condition for high human accomplishments (Feldman, 1994, this volume). Such a developmental view also highlights human agency as an active, purposive force of making meaning and effecting changes (e.g., Bruner, 1990; Gruber, 1981; Csikszentmihalyi, 1993; Moran, 2020), not merely in the form of capacity or disposition. The fundamental conundrum about understanding human developmental potential is that the very personal agency that drives individual development is likely constrained by both environmental and biological forces in an intricate manner. Nevertheless, developmentally engendered individuality introduces a wide range of developmental variations responsible for varied forms of human excellence (Ackerman, this volume; Florida, this volume). Indeed, developmental paths to human excellence are more pluralistic and diverse than monolithic and hierarchical, developmentally probabilistic rather than predetermined (Gould, 1991; see Gardner, this volume), despite domain-general individual differences that may have an evolutionary basis (Feldman, 2003, this volume; Geary, this volume). Such developmental contextualism inevitably brings to attention the nature of social contexts.

Opportunity Structure, Social Interactions, and Ethics

LeVine and White (1986) emphasized the essential role of opportunity structure and culture in unleashing human potential. A broad, common perspective is to conceptualize environments as ranging from impoverished to enriched ones (e.g., Bouchard, 1997). However, more recent efforts have focused on more complex, differentiated environmental conditions (Wachs, 2000). Horowitz (2000), for example, differentiated a range of skill-development opportunities with distinctive affordances and demands, some necessitating minimal experiences to bootstrap a new cognitive structure, and others requiring more intense and sustained educational opportunities and conditions for high-level development, which is often non-universal in nature (see Feldman, this volume).

In the past, human potential was typically seen as residing in the person, only to be unleashed with the environmental stimulation and support. Current thinking has crossed this boundary and made human potential fundamentally *a psychosocial phenomenon*. Concepts such as *distributed intelligence* (Gresalfi, Barab, & Sommerfeld, 2012), a community of professionals engaging in *maximal adaptation* (Dai, 2017, in press) and self-improvement and creative work (Scardamalia & Bereiter, 2006), *collaborative creativity* as involving synergistic power and critical mass (Sawyer, 2012), *cognitive diversity* of a group as breeding excellence (Page, 2008), all lead to unleashed human potential that reflects synergistic power and does not come from any individual alone.

Another significant change since the start of the 21st century is an increasing focus on human potential as socially a double-edge sword. Gardner, Csikszentmihalyi, and Damon (2001) contemplated on the ethics of excellence. Cropley et al. (2010) looked into the dark side of creativity. The paradox of smart people doing stupid things prompted Sternberg (2003) to look into the regulatory power of wisdom and character: how to harness human potential to serve the common good as well as promote optimal development of the individual.

In sum, the criss-crossing of the terrain of human potential from evolutionary, developmental, social-cultural, educational, and social-ethical perspectives constitutes the scope of this line of inquiry, and provides the content and structure of this book.

Rationale for a Narrative (Autobiographic) Approach

This volume attempts to preserve an intellectual legacy in a narrative form typically not systematically documented in the archival literature. The narrative form is distinct and unique in its rich social and personal contexts as to what motivates and sustains a particular line of research, and how ideas from the past have been passed on, modified, or completely transformed.

Einstein (1982) argued that "[k]nowledge exists in two forms—lifeless, stored in books, and alive in the consciousness of men. The second form of existence is after all the essential one; the first one, indispensible as it may be, occupies an inferior position" (p. 80). That knowledge in its rich personal context is more important than knowledge that is more formally presented is consistent with Polanyi's (1958) notion of knowledge as personal, and Bruner's (1996) conception of scientific endeavor as "constructing 'speculative models'" (p. 124). Be it physics or psychology, science is creative rather than merely involves rule-based analytic reasoning. If so, scientists' lived experience of knowing (*as per* Polanyi or Heidegger) becomes essential for understanding how scientific understandings develop and evolve. The narrative taps into a wealth of intellectual, personal, and cultural resources, discourses, and insights not accessible by only looking at barebone scientific arguments and procedures detailed in the archival literature.

Holton (1981) went one step further by studying Einstein and the origins of his scientific creativity; he reached the same conclusion as many psychologists have: Scientific creativity involves hunches, intuitions, convictions, deep metaphors, hypothetical modeling (e.g., thought experiment), and even a sense of aesthetic elegance. If scientific creativity originates in such rich subjectivity of the active mind or intersubjectivity of interacting minds, it follows that only the narrative form can capture active moments of scientific creativity, and there should be no exception when the issue of human potential is concerned. To generate a narrative of intellectual journey or career, we asked the authors to include four elements: context, impetus, evolution, and hindsight.

Origins: Context and Impetus

Contexts, personal as well as social and historical, provide the backdrop for the kind of work one was engaged in. For instance, what (or who) brought specific individuals to the field, and how they started a particular line of work on relevant topics. The narratives the authors provide help situate their decades of work in the context of people (e.g., a family member, a mentor), media (e.g. books and other information channels), and social and personal events (e.g., encounters in education and changes in science and technology) that proved to be critical in shaping their beliefs and values as well as their specific ways of conducting research on a relevant topic.

While context sets the stage, intellectual impetus moves the person in a specific direction. This impetus can come from sheer intellectual curiosity or conviction, as in the case of Einstein, or from some social and practical imperative for improving human conditions, as in the case of Edison. A personal narrative of such impetus will help the reader understand the *deep logic* of a particular line of inquiry, and, subsequently, deeply rooted questions, hunches, beliefs, and values, which can be ontological, epistemological, as well as normative in nature.

Continuities and Discontinuities: Evolution of Ideas

For good or ill, contemporary scholars and researchers inherit an intellectual legacy from the past in terms of core problems, central concepts, methodologies, measurement tools, and instruments. We asked the authors to trace their ideas, models, and approaches to respective origins and retrospectively look at the evolution of their work over time. We assume that the evolution of an intellectual or research tradition works like Neurath's boat (Neurath, 1952). To Neurath, science is fundamentally a social-historical endeavor of constructing models of realities that always retain some old parts while building new ones. Neurath's boat is constantly under construction while functioning as a temporary, functional structure (e.g., floating as it were). Accordingly, some parts of this scientific work (e.g., concepts and propositions) were retained and further refined, and others were discarded as no longer viable or desirable, and still others invented as brand-new ones. Consequently, the reader will see both continuities and discontinuities between the past and present. Far from a unified, coherent model, the evolution of ideas and theories about human potential, at a collective level, would appear not like a wholesale paradigm shift as the term *incommensurability* (Kuhn, 1962) suggests. Instead, we anticipate much heterogeneity even among the contributing group of contemporary scholars for this volume with respect to how they view various forms and manifestations of human potential. However, we also anticipate some critical changes on some issues that redirect the scientific discourse, such as putting epigenetics at the center of scientific discourse on human potential, and finding non-linear, dynamic changes in skill development. The point of taking a more "up and close" look at the evolution of ideas through narrative is to go beyond what Donald Schön (1983) identified as technical rationality (e.g., knowledge as true or false based on statistical arguments) to show a more intricate picture of what is retained, modified, or discarded, and what is newly built at the frontier of knowledge.

Science as a Discourse with Reflection: Historical Hindsight

A more reflective look at the historical perspectives and contemporary changes means being mindful not only of what kinds of insight have been gained over decades of inquiry, but also of meta-level issues of defining the nature of the topic and inquiry itself. For example, we can look at perennial issues, deep ontological assumptions or commitments, as well as changes thereof over time. A related epistemological issue is to determine whether and to what extent reductionism (e.g., a complex phenomenon collapsed into biological and environmental components) and positivism (e.g., making universal claims based on evidence from particular incidents) still work in understanding the nature of human potential. For that matter, a distinct role of value judgment in the behavioral and social sciences has to be reckoned with, since understanding human potential is implicitly or explicitly driven by concerns over improved human conditions and the welfare of civilization (Florida; Glück, both in this volume). We asked the authors to provide their hindsight on what lessons have been gained about the nature and fulfillment of human potential, and how we should go about seeking a deep understanding of possibilities and limits of human development for great accomplishments.

Organization of the Book

To achieve the breadth and depth of the topic at hand, we selectively invited a group of highly accomplished scientists and academics to contribute to this volume. The authors each have 30–50 years of an academic career under their belt, inheriting an intellectual legacy from early generations of scholars and researchers, yet establishing themselves as some of the most authoritative voices in the contemporary scientific discourse on the nature and cultivation of human potential. We also deliberately tried to make the group of contributors as diverse as possible so that they could bring different perspectives and disciplinary backgrounds to bear upon the issues under investigation. They represent a wide range of psychological and social science backgrounds, and their foci cover a spectrum of issues from biological underpinnings of human potential to the role of community and social interaction; from the distinct role of education to systematic individual differences in cognitive and motivational functioning.

The book is divided into four parts. The first part presents chapters from evolutionary and differential perspectives, representing a long tradition in psychology. The second part contains chapters representing cognitive and developmental perspectives. They show how issues of human potential from evolutionary and differential perspectives can be recast in the cognitive and developmental frameworks. The third part presents chapters that provide several personal stories of doing research on human creativity. A wide spectrum of contemporary perspectives reveals a level of complexity of human creativity that go way beyond the initial formulation by Guilford (1950). The fourth part presents chapters that are more or less practically and socially driven; that is, how human potential can be cultivated through education, what is the role of wisdom that guides human action for personal fulfillment as well as the common good. The volume ends with an epilogue that provides a summary and some reflections as to what is fundamentally changed in our understanding of human potential over the past hundred years, and what we are still wrestling with in terms of how we should approach the topic in a way that is scientifically sound yet responsive to social, ethical, and pragmatic concerns.

Acknowledgments

This work was partly supported by a grant to the first author from Army Research Institute for Behavioral and Social Sciences (Grant No. W911NF-17-1-0236). The author was encouraged to freely express his opinions. Ideas presented here, therefore, do not necessarily represent those of the funding agency.

References

Ackerman, P. L. (1988). Determinants of individual differences during skill acquisition: Cognitive abilities and information processing. *Journal of Experimental Psychology: General*, 117, 288–318.

Angoff, W. H. (1988). The nature-nurture debate, aptitudes, and group differences. *American Psychologist*, 43, 713–720.

Bandura, A. (1993). Perceived self-efficacy in cognitive development and functioning. *Educational Psychologist*, 28, 117–148.

Belsky, J., & Pluess, M. (2009). Beyond diathesis stress: Differential susceptibility to environmental influences. *Psychological Bulletin*, 135(6), 885–908. https://doi.org/10.1037/a0017376.

Bereiter, C., & Scardamalia, M. (1993). *Surpassing ourselves: An inquiry into the nature and implications of expertise*. Open Court.

Bloom, B. S. (1985). *Developing talent in young people*. Ballantine Books.

Bronfenbrenner, U., & Ceci, S. J. (1994). Nature-nurture reconceptualized in developmental perspective: A bio-ecological model. *Psychological Review*, 101, 568–586.

Bruner, J. (1979). *On knowing: Essays for the left hand*. Harvard University Press.

Bruner, J. (1990). *Acts of meaning*. Cambridge, MA: Harvard University Press.

Bruner, J. (1996). *The culture of education*. Harvard University Press.

Bouchard, T. J. (1997). IQ similarities in twins reared apart: Findings and responses to critics. In R. J. Sternberg, & E. Grigorenko (Eds.), *Intelligence, heredity, and environment* (126–160). Cambridge University Press.

Ceci, S. J., & Liker, J. (1986). A day at the races: A study of IQ, expertise, and cognitive complexity. *Journal of Experimental Psychology: General*, 115, 255–266.

Ceci, S. J., Williams-Ceci, S., & Williams, W. (2016). How to actualize potential: a bioecological approach to talent development. *Annals of New York Academic Sciences*, 1377, 10–21.

Cropley, D. H., Cropley, A. J., Kaufman, J. C., & Runco, M. A. (Eds.) (2010). *The dark side of creativity*. Cambridge University Press.

Csikszentmihalyi, M. (1993). *The evolving self*. HarperCollins.

Dai, D. Y. (2017). Envisioning a new foundation for gifted education: Evolving Complexity Theory (ECT) of talent development. *Gifted Child Quarterly*, 61, 172–182.

Dai, D. Y. (2018). A century of quest for identity: A history of giftedness. In S. Pfeiffer (Ed.), *The APA handbook on giftedness and talent* (pp. 3–23). American Psychological Association Press.

Dai, D. Y. (2019). New directions in talent development research: A developmental systems perspective. *New Directions for Child and Adolescent Development*, 168, 177–197.

Dai, D. Y. (in press). Evolving Complexity Theory (ECT): A developmental systems approach to giftedness and talent. In R. J.Sternberg, & D. Ambrose (Eds.), *New conceptions of giftedness and talent*.

Dai, D. Y., & Renzulli, J. S. (2008). Snowflakes, living systems, and the mystery of giftedness. *Gifted Child Quarterly*, 52, 114–130.

Dai, D. Y., & Sternberg, R. J. (2004). Beyond cognitivism: Toward an integrated understanding of intellectual functioning and development. In D. Y. Dai, & R. J. Sternberg (Eds.), *Motivation, emotion, and cognition: Integrative perspectives on intellectual functioning and development* (pp. 3–38). Lawrence Erlbaum.

Duckworth, A. (2016). *Grit: The power of passion and perseverance*. Scribner.

Dweck, C. S. (2006). *Mindset: The new psychology of success*. New York: Random House.

Einstein, A. (1982). *Ideas and opinions*. Three Rivers Press. (Originally published in 1954 by Crown Publishers)

Ericsson, K. A. (2006). The influence of experience and deliberate practice on the development of superior expert performance. In K. A. Ericsson, N. Charness, P. J. Feltovich, & R. R. Hoffman (Eds.), *The Cambridge handbook of expertise and expert performance* (pp. 683–703). Cambridge University Press.

Feldhusen, J. F. (1986). A conception of giftedness. In R. J. Sternberg, & J. E. Davidson (Eds.), *Conceptions of giftedness* (pp. 112–127). Cambridge: Cambridge University Press.

Feldman, D. H. (1986). *Nature's gambit: Child prodigies and the development of human potential*. Basic Books.

Feldman, D. H. (1994). *Beyond universals in cognitive development* (2nd ed.). Norwood, NJ: Ablex.

Feldman, D. H. (2003). A developmental, evolutionary perspective on giftedness. In J. H. Borland (Ed.), *Rethinking gifted education* (pp. 9–33). Teachers College, Columbia University.

Florida, R. (2002). *The rise of the creative class*. Basic Books.

Gagné, F. (1985). Gifted and talent: Reexamining a reexamination of the definitions. *Gifted Child Quarterly*, 29, 103–112.

Gagné, F. (2005). From gifts to talents: The DMGT as a developmental model. In R. J. Sternberg, & J. E. Davidson (Eds.), *Conceptions of giftedness* (2nd ed., pp. 98–119). Cambridge University Press.

Galton, F. (1869). *Hereditary genius: An inquiry into its laws and consequences*. Macmillan.

Gardner, H. (1983). *Frames of mind*. Basic Books.

Gardner, H. (2003). Three distinct meanings of intelligence. In R. J. Sternberg, J. Lautrey, & T. I. Lubert (Eds.), *Models of intelligence: International perspectives* (pp. 43–54). American Psychological Association.

Gardner, H., Csikszentmihalyi, M., & Damon, D. (2001). *Good work: When excellence and ethics meet*. New York: Basic Books.

Gladwell, M. (2008). *Outliers: The story of success*. Little Brown and Co.

Goldman, D. (1995). *Emotional intelligence*. Bantam.

Gottfredson, L. S. (1997). Editorial: Mainstream science on intelligence: An editorial with 52 signatories, history, and bibliography. *Intelligence*, 24, 13–23.

Gottlieb, G. (2007). Probabilistic epigenesis. *Developmental Science*, 10, 1–11.

Gould, S. J. (1991). Exaptation: A crucial tool or an evolutionary psychology. *Journal of Social Issues*, 47(3), 43–65.

Gresalfi, M., Barab, S. A., & Sommerfeld, A. (2012). Intelligent action as a shared accomplishment. In D. Y. Dai (Ed.), *Design research on learning and thinking in educational settings: Enhancing intellectual growth and functioning* (pp. 41–64). Routledge.

Guilford, J. P. (1950). Creativity. *American Psychologist*, 5, 444–454.

Gruber, H. E. (1981). *Darwin on man: A psychological study of scientific creativity* (rev. ed.). University of Chicago Press.

Hawking, S. (1996). Life in the universe. Public Lectures. Retrieved October 5, 2019 from www.hawking.org.uk/life-in-the-universe.html

Herrnstein, R. J., & Murray, C. (1994). *The bell curve: Intelligence and class structure in American life*. Free Press.

Holton, G. (1981). Thematic presuppositions and the direction of scientific advance. In A. F. Heath (Ed.), *Scientific explanation* (pp. 1–27). Clarendon Press.

Horowitz, F. D. (1987). *Exploring developmental theories: Toward a structural/behavioral model of development*. Erlbaum.

Horowitz, F. D. (2000). Child development and the PITS: Simple questions, complex answers, and developmental theory. *Child Development*, 71, 1–10.
Howe, M. J. A., Davidson, J. W., & Sloboda, J. A. (1998). Innate talents: Reality or myth? *Behavioral and Brain Sciences*, 21, 399–442.
Kuhn, T. S. (1962). *The structure of scientific revolution*. University of Chicago Press.
Lehman, H. C. (1953). *Age and achievement*. Princeton University Press.
LeVine, R. A., & White, M. I. (1986). *Human conditions: The cultural basis of educational development*. Routledge and Kegan Paul.
Lohman, D. F. (2005). An aptitude perspective on talent identification: Implications for identification of academically gifted minority students. *Journal for the Education of the Gifted*, 28, 333–360.
Lohman, D. F. (2006). Beliefs about differences between ability and accomplishment: From folk theories to cognitive science. *Roeper Review*, 29, 32–40.
Lubinski, D., & Benbow, C. P. (2006). Study of mathematically precious youth after 35 years. *Perspectives on Psychological Science*, 1, 316–345.
Magnusson, D. (2001). The holistic-interationistic paradigm: Some directions for empirical developmental research. *European Psychologist*, 6, 153–162.
Moran, S. (2020). Life purpose in youth: Turning potential into lifelong pursuit of prosocial contribution. *Journal for the Education of the Gifted*, 43, 38–60.
Neisser, U., Boodoo, G., Bouchard, T. J., Boykin, A. W., Brody, N., Ceci, S. J., et al. (1996). Intelligence: Knowns and unknowns. *American Psychologist*, 51, 77–101.
Neurath, O. (1952). *Foundations of the social science*. University of Chicago Press.
Newell, A. (1990). *Unified theories of cognition*. Harvard University Press.
Nisbett, R. E., et al. (2012). Intelligence: New findings and theoretical developments. *American Psychologist*, 67, 130–159.
Page, S. E. (2008). *The difference: How the power of diversity creates better groups, firms, schools, and societies*. Princeton University Press.
Papierno, P. B., Ceci, S. J., Makel, M. C., & Williams, W. W. (2005). The nature and nurture of talent: A bioecological perspective on the ontogeny of exceptional abilities. *Journal for the Education of the Gifted*, 28, 312–331.
Pereira Da Costa, M., Zenasni, F., Nicolas, S., & Lubart, T. (2014). Afried Binet: A creative life in measurement and pedagogy (1857–1911). In A. Robinson, & J. L. Jolly (Eds.), *A century of contributions to gifted education: Illustrating lives* (pp. 23–40). Routledge.
Piaget, J. (1950/2001). *The psychology of intelligence*. Routledge.
Polanyi, M. (1958). *Personal knowledge: Toward a post-critical philosophy*. University of Chicago Press.
Renzulli, J. S. (1978). What makes giftedness? Re-examining a definition. *Phi Delta Kappan*, 60(3), 180–184.
Renzulli, J. S. (1986). The three-ring conception of giftedness: A developmental model for creative productivity. In R. J. Sternberg, & J. E. Davidson (Eds.), *Conceptions of giftedness* (pp. 53–92). Cambridge University Press.
Renzulli, R. S. (2005). The three-ring conception of giftedness: A developmental model for promoting creative productivity. In R. J. Sternberg, & J. E. Davidson (Eds.), *Conceptions of giftedness* (2nd ed., pp. 98–119). Cambridge, England: Cambridge University Press.
Root-Bernstein, R. (2009). Multiple giftedness: The case of polymaths. In L. Shavinina (Ed.), *Handbook on giftedness* (pp. 853–870). Springer Science.
Sawyer, R. K. (2012). *Explaining creativity: The science of human innovation* (2nd ed.). Oxford University Press.

Scardamalia, M., & Bereiter, C. (2006). Knowledge building: Theory, pedagogy, and technology. In R. K. Sawyer (Ed.), *The Cambridge handbook of the learning sciences* (pp. 97–115). Cambridge University Press.

Scheffler, I. (1985). *Of human potential: An essay in the philosophy of education*. Routledge & Kegan Paul.

Schön, D. A. (1983). *Reflective practitioner*. Basic Books.

Shiffrin, R. M. (1996). Laboratory experimentation on the genesis of expertise. In K. A. Ericsson (Ed.), *The road to excellence: The acquisition of expert performance in the arts and sciences, sports, and games* (pp. 337–345). Lawrence Erlbaum Associates.

Simonton, D. K. (1999). Significant samples: The psychological study of eminent individuals. *Psychological Methods*, 4, 425–451.

Snow, R. E. (1992). Aptitude theory: Yesterday, today, and tomorrow. *Educational Psychologist*, 27, 5–32.

Spearman, C. (1904). "General intelligence," objectively determined and measured. *American Journal of Psychology*, 15, 201–292.

Sternberg, R. J. (1985). *Beyond IQ: A triarchic theory of human intelligence*. Cambridge University Press.

Sternberg, R. J. (1999). Intelligence as developing expertise. *Contemporary Educational Psychology*, 24, 359–375.

Sternberg, R. J. (2003). *Wisdom, intelligence, and creativity synthesized*. Cambridge University Press.

Sternberg, R. J. (2019). A theory of adaptive intelligence and its relation to general intelligence. *Journal of Intelligence*, 7(4), 23. https://doi.org/10.3390/jintelligence7040023

Sternberg, R. J., & Davidson, J. (2005). *Conceptions of giftedness* (2nd ed.). Cambridge University Press.

Tannenbaum, A. J. (1983). *Gifted children: Psychological and educational perspectives*. Macmillan.

Terman, L. M. (1925). *Genetic studies of genius: Vol. 1, Mental and physical traits of a thousand gifted children*. Stanford University Press.

Terman, L. M. (1954). The discovery and encouragement of exceptional talent. *American Psychologist*, 9, 221–230.

Torrance, E. P. (1963). *Education and the creative potential*. The University of Minnesota Press.

VanTassel-Baska, J. (2005). Domain-specific giftedness. In R. J. Sternberg, & J. E. Davidson (Eds.), *Conceptions of giftedness* (2nd ed.). Cambridge University Press.

Vygotsky, L. S. (1978). *Mind in society: The development of higher psychological processes*. Harvard University Press.

Wachs, T. D. (2000). *Necessary but not sufficient: The respective roles of single and multiple influences on individual development*. American Psychological Association.

Werner, H. (1967). The concept of development from a comparative and organismic point of view. In D. B. Harris (Ed.), *The concept of development* (pp. 125–148). University of Minnesota Press.

Witty, P., & Lehman, H. C. (1927). Drive: A neglected trait in the study of the gifted. *Psychological Review*, 34, 364–376.

PART 1
Evolutionary and Differential Perspectives on Human Potential

PART I

1

A JOURNEY FROM BEHAVIORAL ECOLOGY TO SEX DIFFERENCES TO MITOCHONDRIA AND INTELLIGENCE

David C. Geary

In 1904, Spearman discovered that performance in school, on various perceptual and cognitive tests, and "common sense" were all positively correlated, and concluded "that all branches of intellectual activity have in common one fundamental function" (p. 285). This function is known as general intelligence or *g*. The nature and origins of intelligence are long-standing interests of mine and the topic of one of my books (Geary, 2005). Recently, I proposed that the basic mechanism underlying *g* is the efficiency of mitochondrial functioning (e.g., cellular energy production) that also explains the relations among *g*, health, and aging. The insight came to me rather quickly, and I put together the theoretical manuscript on the topic (Geary, 2018) over the course of about four weeks. However, the insight was proceeded by several years of reading and thinking about mitochondrial functioning and evolution as related to sex-specific vulnerabilities in cognition and other traits (topic of another book, *Evolution of Vulnerability*, 2015) and can be linked to a decades-long interest in sex differences and their evolution.

In this chapter, I'll detail some of the history behind my interest in sex differences and their evolution, and how this led to a proposal that the efficiency of mitochondrial functioning—the seat of cellular energy production—is the most basic biological mechanism underlying general intelligence (Spearman's fundamental function), which provides an explanation of why intelligence, health, and successful aging in adulthood are interrelated (Geary, 2018, 2019). I understand that this proposal and some of my other ones (especially as related to sex differences) might be controversial, and in fact the question of whether I intentionally try to irritate and offend others has come up. I have to say that I wish that this was the case, but it is not. Topics that might irritate and offend others in the field are often wide open and ready for intellectual exploitation. The general avoidance of such topics also means that much less is known about them, and thus they present the type of ill-structured problem that I find engaging and attractive to think about.

Although I have many collaborators and friends and enjoy working on joint projects of various kinds, I prefer to work alone and am the most content and focused when thinking about some difficult (at least for me) question, often listening to classical music and pacing. In fact, I sometimes find myself a little lost, with "nothing to do", without some interesting question to think about. To be sure, I actually have plenty to do in terms of typical empirical studies but these are more often than not focused on smaller-scale (though useful) questions. Whatever the endeavor, I am keenly aware of the potential to make errors, especially with controversial topics, and would feel quite embarrassed if this were to happen. One result is that I'm actually pretty cautious before publishing ideas that some people might see as well beyond the current empirical evidence. Typically, I've spent a considerable amount of time, often years, thinking about the issue on and off. I generally try to visualize the patterns or relationships (sometimes sketch them) and often mentally simulate how these patterns might change under various conditions, essentially thought experiments to probe the feasibility of what I want to propose. I then read extensively in the area to determine if one point or another is likely to be correct or not. In some cases, I decide that I don't know enough to pursue the question or that my approach is not on track, and at other times decide to continue.

At the end of this incubation and preparation period, I typically have an outline (sometimes on paper but more typically in my head) of how the argument regarding the proposal (examples below) needs to be structured, the literatures that need to be covered, and the questions that need to be addressed to make it a coherent argument. The latter includes consideration of the targeted audience and how they might understand or misunderstand the proposal, given the current Zeitgeist in the field, whatever that might be at the time. The actual writing is usually an alternating mix of frustration and excitement, typically with a persistent low-level of underlying tension that results from dealing with an unsolved and potentially unsolvable (by me) problem. Although I typically have an outline, I often don't know where a deep reading of the associated literatures will lead and whether or not it will be consistent with the proposal I have in mind. This reading often leads to iterative revisions of the proposal and typically results in additional nuance.

I see these types of ill-structured problems as a puzzle to be solved but also as a piece of art, whereby each segment has to be carefully constructed and all of them have to be put together in just the right way to produce a coherent whole that communicates a key message. In the following, I provide a bit of history, starting with graduate school and then my time at the University of Missouri, and the circuitous route that led from an interest to sex differences to sex-specific vulnerabilities and finally to mitochondria and intelligence, health, and aging.

Graduate School

I decided to enroll in the PhD program at the University of California, Riverside (UCR) to study hemispheric specialization, that is, the representation of information in the left- and right-sides of the brain, and its development. As part of the breadth requirements for the PhD, I took a number of courses in physiological and comparative (cross-species) psychology, and these piqued my interest in evolution, especially Krebs and Davies' (1981) *An Introduction to Behavioral Ecology*. The book was actually required reading before the start of one of Lewis Petrinovich's courses in comparative psychology, to get us up to speed before diving into primary articles, and so we never actually discussed it. Nevertheless, I remember reading this book sitting outside of our 40-year-old graduate student housing (temperatures were often > 100 degrees Fahrenheit, with no air conditioning), which was built as "temporary housing" for the air force during WWII (to be torn down after the war). I remember this because I got quite excited about the concepts and research described therein and decided that this was the way to go. It provided a big-picture view of behavior that was otherwise lacking in psychology, but there was not much to be done with it at that time, at least for me.

After completing the required coursework, I spent a year putting together a dissertation proposal that involved the study of sex differences in the hemispheric representation of verbal and spatial information as related to pubertal development, following Waber (1976). The goal was to assess the latter using physician-administered standardized ratings of pubertal development and through the measurement of concentrations of various hormones that change during this time (e.g., testosterone). I was able to convince a reproductive biology lab at UCLA to collaborate on the project (they were interested in the hormone assays as related to pubertal development). My proposal was approved by my dissertation committee and I was ready to go, but the Institutional Review Board (IRB) at UCR refused to approve the project. The reason was that UCR did not have appropriate facilities for the pubertal ratings or the blood draws for the hormone analyses, even though the UCLA lab agreed to send qualified personnel to conduct these. After making some adjustments and submitting appeals, the IRB refused to budge and thus sank my project. I recall being pretty disheartened as a result and considered leaving the program. Fortunately, I was also working with another faculty member, Keith Widaman, on a mathematical cognition study and switched my dissertation project to this area. It is very likely that without Keith's friendship and support I would have left UCR and perhaps the field.

Missouri

After more than 100 applications and only one interview, I landed a one-year teaching position (six classes, plus two in the summer) at the University of Texas at El Paso. Following advances made by Mark Ashcraft and Robert Siegler,

I began my own work on children's mathematical development and the study of children with difficulties learning mathematics; the latter interest emerged from a two-year program and degree in clinical child/school psychology. I continued this work after moving to the University of Missouri, first in Rolla and then in Columbia, because it is an interesting and practically important area of research. I also thought it was a much safer route to tenure than was integrating an evolutionary approach with my interest in sex differences. So, while doing standard cognitive developmental work on children's mathematical development, publishing in appropriate journals, and securing funding from the National Institutes of Health, I was reading on the side to improve my understanding of evolution. Along the way, I met Mark Flinn (Anthropology) who knew most of the major players in the nascent area of sociobiology. He plied me with reading lists.

Except for one short and almost entirely ignored (including by me) article on evolution and cognition, I decided not to publish anything having to do with evolution prior to tenure. The decision was in part due to my relative ignorance of the field, the controversies surrounding sociobiology, and my sense that I had no idea what I would do to support my family if I was denied tenure as a result of pursuing controversial topics. The decision was reinforced by the intense reactions I received from some students, as I started to incorporate these ideas into some of my graduate courses. As just one example, during a lecture on sex differences, a student actually stood up pointed at my notes on the chalkboard (this is before PowerPoint) and yelled "You can't teach this, it's not politically correct!" Needless to say, I continued but after several courses filled with these types of episodes, among other things, I approached their training director and told him I didn't want his "*&%$ing students taking my classes anymore." That was the end of that, although I still get irritated when thinking back on these experiences.

In any case, once tenured, I began to incorporate evolutionary ideas into some of my work, including arguing for a distinction between evolved or biologically primary cognitive abilities (e.g., language, intuitive sense of approximate quantity) and culturally-specific or biologically secondary ones (e.g., reading, symbolic mathematics). This insight came in the context of my frustration with some of my older daughter's schooling, especially the then popular belief that learning to read was essentially the same as language learning, that is, whole language and its counterpart, whole math. I knew there was something wrong with this approach but didn't have a good framework for understanding why. When listening to a lecture by Alvin Liberman (a University of Missouri alum) on language evolution, he offhandedly mentioned that reading was just secondary to language and not important to the gist of his talk. It immediately occurred to me that this was a good way to frame the issue (this is the source of my primary vs. secondary abilities). I thought about the distinction for a while and how it might relate to mathematics and introduced the primary-secondary distinction in my first book, *Children's Mathematical Development* (Geary, 1994), and elaborated on it in an *American Psychologist* article soon thereafter (Geary, 1995). I actually wrote another article before this one that was eventually published in *Behavioral and Brain Sciences* (Geary, 1996), but given the controversial nature of the corresponding topic—evolution, sex differences, and mathematics—it went through multiple reviews, with ten reviewers overall. I argued that there are no sex differences in primary quantitative abilities (e.g., intuitive sense of quantity) and that boys' and men's advantage in some areas of math are secondary to their evolved or primary advantage in spatial abilities, among other things. I have to say that I was pretty naïve when writing this article. I was certainly aware of general social issues regarding these topics but thought a scientific discussion would be more rational and tempered. I was wrong but am thankfully blessed with a good amount of social insensitivity and so continued in this direction.

Male, Female: From Sex Differences to Cognitive Traits

Soon thereafter, a representative from MIT Press approached me about writing a book on sex differences. I didn't know it at the time, but they had been negotiating with Doreen Kimura to write a similar book and thought they had lost her to another publisher; I was their backup. Eventually Doreen went with them and produced her excellent *Sex and Cognition* (1999), but in the meantime they dumped me and offered a couple of free books for the trouble of putting together a book outline and proposal. I had the basic outline ready and was enthusiastic about the project and so approached APA Books, which had published *Children's Mathematical Development*, and they accepted it. I recall someone telling me that I was "crazy for agreeing to write a book about something I knew nothing about." The assessment wasn't entirely true but it wasn't entirely off base either. But I knew enough to know that Darwin's (1871) sexual selection—competition for mates and discriminating mate choices—was the only viable theoretical framework to approach the project; and, besides, what better way to learn than to write a book. Sixteen months later the manuscript for *Male, female* was done and published the following year in 1998 (the 3rd edition should be released in the fall of 2020).

Critical to the downstream point, the writing of the book heightened a preexisting curiosity about sex differences in trait variability, that is, in addition to average sex differences in many traits, males tend to be more variable as a group than females (i.e., more males at the low and high end of many traits). I didn't make too much of it in this first edition but learned that it is related to the condition-dependent expression of traits associated with competition for mates or mate choices. These are traits, such as the peacock's train, that have evolved to be honest indicators (cannot be faked) of male condition, such as overall health, and are more sensitive to environmental stressors than are other traits (Zahavi, 1975). If things go wrong (e.g., poor nutrition) or the male is unhealthy, then these exaggerated traits—ones in which males have an advantage over females—are the first to go. Under these stressful conditions, average trait size shrinks in males, reducing the magnitude of the sex difference, and at the same time males as a group become more variable on the trait; the same process works for females, but often for different traits. I spent a lot of time thinking about this concept and how it might work, and expanded my discussion of it in the second edition (Geary, 2010), but still the explanation was incomplete.

Around that time, I began some collaborative studies with a graduate student I was co-mentoring in the University of Missouri's Interdisciplinary Neuroscience program, Eldin Jašarević. Eldin and I designed several studies to assess whether sexually selected traits are more sensitive to toxins than are other traits. In this case, prenatal and early postnatal exposure to Bisphenol A, working with colleagues in biomedical and animal sciences. In designing the studies, we turned back to behavioral ecology and identified a species of mouse, deer mice (*Peromyscus maniculatus*), in which males compete by means of scramble competition, that is, they expand their range during the breeding season to search for dispersed mates; this approach followed the seminal work of Steve Gaulin and his colleagues (e.g., Gaulin, 1992). Males of this species have better spatial abilities and are more active and less fearful or anxious during the breeding season than are same-species females.

In other words, spatial learning and memory as well as lower anxiety levels are analogous to the peacock's train and are sexually selected traits for males of this species. The first study confirmed sex- and trait-specific deficits following early exposure to the toxin, that is, male but not female deficits in spatial abilities and heightened anxiety (Jašarević et al., 2011). We followed up with a parallel study of a related species (California mouse, *P. Californicus*) in which males do not expand their territory to search for mates (Jašarević et al., 2012), but rather stay near their partner and engage in mate guarding, including extensive territorial marking (urinating to mark their territory). For this species, spatial abilities are not sexually selected but territorial making is, that is, dominant males frequently engage in this marking. Using the same protocol as was used for the deer mice, we showed that early exposure to Bisphenol A had no effect on males' spatial abilities or anxiety but disrupted their territorial marking. So, the deleterious effects of toxin exposure depend on sex, species, and trait, a combination that only makes sense in the context of sexual selection and the evolution of condition-dependent traits that are highly sensitive to environmental stressors.

After the collaborations ended and Eldin moved to the University of Pennsylvania for a post-doctoral position, I continued to obsess over the evolution and expression of condition-dependent traits. After delaying for several years because I knew it would be a difficult and stressful task, I decided to put together a proposal as to how the concept of condition-dependent trait expression might be used to better understand sex-specific vulnerabilities in people. There were already several such reviews for non-human species (Cotton et al., 2004; Johnstone, 1995), and I wanted to apply the same approach to our own species. In my opinion, it is important to review the theory and literature on non-human species before extrapolating to humans, and so I decided to review the broader literature on condition-dependent traits. I began by reading all of the articles on such traits cited in Cotton et al.'s review but didn't stop there. About 500 articles and year later, I had extensive Excel sheets on such traits from arthropods to African elephants. I certainly overdid it but enjoyed the process and learned a lot about condition-dependent trait expression, but hadn't yet done much with humans.

The framework for the review of human studies came from my arguments in *Male, female* about sexually selected traits in men (e.g., height, lean muscle mass, some visuospatial abilities) and women (e.g., language, theory of mind). In other words, I couldn't have put together a proposal on sex differences in human vulnerabilities without first writing *Male, female*. In any case, a year later I had another set of Excel sheets on sex-specific vulnerabilities in people, ranging from growth deficits due to poor nutrition during adolescence to deficits in verbal fluency following chemotherapy. At this point, I had spent two years, on and off, putting together these tables and drafting parts of a manuscript, which was obviously too long for a review article. Fortunately, I had been previously approached by a representative from Elsevier about writing a book on some topic (of my choice) in evolutionary psychology, but I initially declined because I didn't want to commit myself to a publisher's timetable. Eventually though we worked out an agreement that led to another book, *Evolution of Vulnerability* (Geary, 2015), which quickly sold dozens of copies. Despite poor sales, a couple of important insights came from this work.

From *Evolution of Vulnerability* to the *Horsemen of the Apocalypse: In Search of Mechanisms for Sex-Specific Vulnerabilities*

The first came as I was looking through literally 47 single-spaced pages of one-line summaries of condition-dependent traits across 100 species and hundreds of studies. The studies not only covered myriad species, but also many different types of traits, stressors, developmental periods, and study types (e.g., field, experimental). It was essentially a mess that would only make sense to someone who was an expert in this area, which didn't include many psychologists. I had to come up with some simple way to visually convey the idea that all species experience the same types of stressors that can compromise well-being in sex-specific ways. After a couple of false starts, it occurred to me—literally popped into my mind ("Ah, that'll work!")—that the common theme was well captured by the Horsemen of the Apocalypse, which can be concisely and visually represented by Dürer's 1498 woodcut (Figure 1.1); I'm a fan of old woodcuts and try to use them when appropriate.

The key horsemen represent plague (infectious disease), famine, and war (social competition). In other words, these three natural phenomena capture most of the stressors that undermine the well-being of individuals of all species and provide an easy rubric for defining stressors from an evolutionary perspective. If deer mice

FIGURE 1.1 The Four Horsemen of the Apocalypse

produced artists, they too would have come up with something similar to the Horsemen. Of course, predation is also a common threat but if consumed by a predator, the result is death (the fourth Horseman), and not a stressor that has trait- and sex-specific effects. In addition to the first three Horsemen, sexually selected traits are also sensitive to man-made toxins, as we demonstrated with the studies of deer and California mice. The result is we have a universal group of stressors that, in combination with man-made toxins, compromise condition-dependent traits across species. As long as you know something about competition and choice in the species (i.e., sexual selection) you can predict which traits and for which sex the Horsemen will be the most harmful. This is what I attempted to do in *Evolution of Vulnerability*.

The second insight came toward the completion of the book, when I read an article by a biologist, Geoffrey Hill (2014). He proposed that the most basic mechanism underlying the evolution, development, and expression of condition-dependent traits was the efficiency of mitochondrial functioning. Mitochondria are evolutionarily-ancient organelles situated inside of cells, are the primary producers of cellular energy, are important for multiple other biological processes, and result in the generation of cell-damaging reactive oxygen species or oxidative stress. I thought this was a good idea and mentioned it in the book but also thought I didn't know enough about mitochondria to say much else. So, I bought a copy of *Molecular and Cell Biology for Dummies* (Kratz, 2009) as a refresher; we covered this in a physiology course I took as an undergraduate, but I didn't find it particularly interesting at the time. After the refresher and in between other activities, I read various professional reviews and more recent studies on mitochondria and about a year later began working on an expansion of the basic model presented in *Evolution of Vulnerability*, incorporating mitochondrial functioning as related to exposure to the Horsemen and man-made toxins, among other things.

The extension was eventually published in *The Quarterly Review of Biology* (Geary, 2017), but two comments by one of the reviewers left me uneasy but eventually helped to link mitochondria to intelligence. The first was that the centrality of mitochondria could result in greater male vulnerability and variability across all traits, not just sexually selected ones. This is because mitochondrial DNA (mtDNA) are only inherited from mothers and as a result any mutations that compromise female well-being will be eliminated by natural or sexual selection but this cannot happen for males. Mutations that are neutral or beneficial to females will be retained, even if they are harmful to males. It's not that mitochondrial functions (or intelligence) are only determined by mtDNA inherited from mothers. There many nuclear DNA (nDNA) inherited from both parents that influence mitochondrial functions (and intelligence) and can often compensate for deleterious mtDNA in males. Difficulties for some males might be related to the mix of mtDNA and nDNA that contribute to mitochondrial functioning (Lane, 2011).

Whatever the specific mechanisms, this was a good point. I proposed a general across-trait vulnerability for males on top of sex-specific vulnerabilities. I think the solution is that trait vulnerability will vary directly with the amount of cellular energy needed for trait construction and expression and that sexually selected traits tend to be larger and more energy demanding (e.g., courtship displays) and are more vulnerable because of this. Underlying these trait-specific differences is greater male variability in the amount of energy that is typically produced by mitochondria (depending on extent of compensatory nuclear DNA; see Geary, 2018).

In any case, the second comment was regarding Geoffrey Miller's (2000) proposal that general intelligence (efficiency of learning and problem solving in novel contexts) is a sexually selected trait in humans and has evolved largely as a result of female choice (e.g., males displaying their wit to one-up other men and to impress women). My argument in contrast is that cognitive sex differences and associated vulnerabilities are more nuanced, with girls and women being more vulnerable in some areas (e.g., face processing) and boys and men in others (e.g., spatial abilities). I wasn't sure how general intelligence fit into this pattern because the sexes are pretty similar in terms of mean levels of intelligence (although this remains debated), but boys and men are still more variable, as with sexually selected traits.

So, we had a situation where there was more male variability, as with sexually selected traits, but only small or no sex differences at the mean, unlike sexually selected traits. This was a problem and, as is often the case, led to a more or less obsessive preoccupation with this question, on and off for maybe 9 months. The basic issue was the relation between mitochondrial functioning, intelligence, and variation in intelligence and how this might be integrated with my vulnerability model. I knew a bit of the literature on intelligence, having reviewed it in one of my books, *Origin of mind* (Geary, 2005), and was intrigued by and kept up with Ian Deary and colleagues' finding of a consistent relation between intelligence, health, and life span (e.g., Deary et al., 2010). I had also read extensively about the relation between mitochondrial functions and health and how chronic exposure to stressors could gradually undermine these functions and lead to chronic poor health and premature death, while putting together *The Quarterly Review of Biology* article. I thought about trying to write another article focused on intelligence, health, and aging but didn't have the time to do so.

A few months later, at the beginning of Thanksgiving break, I had some down time while waiting for some data to be coded and was able to get started; this was eventually published in *Psychological Review* (Geary, 2018). During the break, I outlined all of the key sections and ideas that needed to be covered and that needed to be plausible for the integration to work, and got started on the writing. I already knew the gist of most of the associated literatures but, one section at a time, did extensive literature searches and reading to ensure the sections were up to date and that I hadn't missed anything. I had to put this down for a few weeks to finish the semester and go on vacation but continued to think about how variation in mitochondrial energy production could influence brain development and functioning in ways that would be expressed as general intelligence.

Testing the Hypothesis

Some of the core ideas that were eventually incorporated into the Neuroenergetics section of the just noted article were worked out while walking around Disney World, and one of them (that subtle variation in mitochondrial energy production is analogous to compound interest and thus could easily result in substantive differences during brain development) came to me while waiting in line to ride on Dumbo with one of my daughters (seriously). When we got back to our room, I emailed one of my graduate students (Felicia Chu) and asked her to write a program to simulate these effects, which I then used to examine how very subtle differences in energy production could result in large differences in neuron generation, depending on how long the process lasted and the number of progenitor cells—I had some familiarity this literature, because I reviewed it in *Origin of Mind*. I recall a sense of relief after this insight, because this was a sticking point, and didn't think much more about it the rest of the trip.

Another sticking point was the finding of more boys and men at the high end of the intelligence distribution. Their over-representation at the low end followed directly from the inability of evolutionary selection to purge mtDNA mutations that were deleterious to males. I assumed (but didn't know) that there must be sex differences in the nDNA that contribute to mitochondrial energy production. I thought an easy solution would be if these genes were located on the X chromosome, following an earlier proposal (Johnson et al., 2009). After diving into this literature, I concluded that it might work for fruit flies but doesn't work for mammals. This was a disappointing dead end but is still briefly discussed in the section Uniparental Inheritance of Mitochondria and Variation in g (Geary, 2018). The reading, however, revealed that there may indeed be sex differences in the nDNA (distributed across chromosomes) that contribute to mitochondrial energy production and could explain the excess of boys and men at the high end of intelligence, as well as some other phenomena (e.g., the maintenance of cognitive abilities in a subset of long-lived men). Once this was worked out, I was able to finish up the manuscript pretty quickly over the remainder of the semester break.

The argument is not that mitochondrial functions are the only factors that influence intelligence, health, and aging, but that they are the lowest common denominator, to use an analogy from mathematics, across all of these domains and thus must contribute to the links between them. I also understand that intelligence itself will be influenced by factors at multiple levels, and that most of the current research is focused on the efficiency of connections among the distributed brain networks that support complex problem solving. I knew I had to integrate this current work with my argument and again tried to visualize the relation and came up with a piping analogy:

> By analogy, consider a system of pipes that transports water from one place to another but can only do so through a circuitous route. The circuity results in several different potential paths, some of which will be more efficient (shorter length) than others. The efficiency (volume) of water movement will also be influenced by water pressure (assuming a constant pipe diameter), independent of path length, such that overall efficiency is a function of path length and water pressure. The system of regions identified in brain-imaging studies as being related to performance on intelligence tests, often measures of fluid intelligence, is analogous to the configuration of the transport pipes .... The water pressure is determined by lower levels of brain functioning; the integrity of neurons and glia that compose these systems and the energy available to maintain them and support their functioning. (Geary, 2018, p. 1032)

At this time, I'm not sure how important mitochondrial functions are, relative to other factors, but they must be a piece of the puzzle; whether they are a minor or major piece remains to be determined.

Hindsight

I never would have imagined that a busted dissertation project on sex differences would eventually contribute to a proposal regarding the biological processes that contribute to intelligence and its relation to health and successful aging in adulthood. Despite its failure, the preparation of the dissertation proposal deepened my understanding of biological sex differences—I still have the associated note cards—and strengthened my interest in the topic, although it would be more than a decade before I got back to it in a serious way. In any case, even if I had been more prescient, anticipation of a potentially fundamental relation between sexual selection and condition-dependent trait expression and the biology of intelligence would not have been possible at the time. This is because the study of condition-dependent traits was still in the early stages in evolutionary biology and the proposal that these were direct indicators of mitochondrial functioning is very recent (Hill, 2014) and still remains to be fully vetted by biologists.

In all, the merging of these aspects of sexual selection with intelligence could have only happened with wide reading in both areas and a desire to simplify things. I often wonder if my desire to simplify is intensifying as I get older, because of age-related reductions in working-memory capacity and thus an inability to consider more than one or two things at a time. In any event, I think the outcome is related to a combination of persistence, wide-ranging interests and curiosity, an at-times obsessive and often stressful focus on a specific topic (with a lot of reading and reflection), but at the same time attempting to understand how these specific issues fit within a bigger, evolutionarily-informed picture.

Acknowledgments

I thank Mary Hoard, Eldin Jašarević, and Yin Xia for comments on an earlier draft.

References

Cotton, S., Fowler, K., & Pomiankowski, A. (2004). Do sexual ornaments demonstrate heightened condition-dependent expression as predicted by the handicap hypothesis? *Proceedings of the Royal Society of London B: Biological Sciences*, 271, 771–783.

Darwin, C. (1871). *The descent of man, and selection in relation to sex*. London: John Murray.

Deary, I. J., Weiss, A., & Batty, G. D. (2010). Intelligence and personality as predictors of illness and death: How researchers in differential psychology and chronic disease epidemiology are collaborating to understand and address health inequalities. *Psychological Science in the Public Interest*, 11, 53–79.

Gaulin, S. J. C. (1992). Evolution of sex differences in spatial ability. *Yearbook of Physical Anthropology*, 35, 125–151.

Geary, D. C. (1994). *Children's mathematical development: Research and practical applications*. American Psychological Association.

Geary, D. C. (1995). Reflections of evolution and culture in children's cognition: Implications for mathematical development and instruction. *American Psychologist*, 50, 24–37.

Geary, D. C. (1996). Sexual selection and sex differences in mathematical abilities. *Behavioral and Brain Sciences*, 19, 229–284.
Geary, D. C. (1998). *Male, female: The evolution of human sex differences*. American Psychological Association.
Geary, D. C. (2005). *The origin of mind: Evolution of brain, cognition, and general intelligence*. American Psychological Association.
Geary, D. C. (2010). *Male, female: The evolution of human sex differences* (2nd ed.). American Psychological Association.
Geary, D. C. (2015). *Evolution of vulnerability: Implications for sex differences in health and development*. Elsevier Academic Press.
Geary, D. C. (2017). Evolution of human sex-specific cognitive vulnerabilities. *The Quarterly Review of Biology*, 92, 361–410.
Geary, D. C. (2018). Efficiency of mitochondrial functioning as the fundamental biological mechanism of general intelligence (g). *Psychological Review*, 125, 1028–1050.
Geary, D. C. (2019). The spark of life and the unification of intelligence, health, and aging. *Current Directions in Psychological Science*, 28, 223–228.
Hill, G. E. (2014). Cellular respiration: The nexus of stress, condition, and ornamentation. *Integrative and Comparative Biology*, 54, 645–657.
Jašarević, E., Sieli, P. T., Twellman, E. E., Welsh, T. H. Jr, Schachtman, T. R., Roberts, R. M., Geary, D. C., & Rosenfeld, C. S. (2011). Disruption of adult expression of sexually selected traits by early exposure to Bisphenol A. *Proceedings of the National Academy of Sciences of the United States of America*, 108, 11715–11720.
Jašarević, E., Williams, S. A., Roberts, R. M., Geary, D. C., & Rosenfeld, C. S. (2012). Spatial navigation strategies in *Peromyscus*: A comparative study. *Animal Behaviour*, 84, 1141–1149.
Johnstone, R. A. (1995). Sexual selection, honest advertisement and the handicap principle: Reviewing the evidence. *Biological Reviews*, 70, 1–65.
Johnson, W., Carothers, A., & Deary, I. J. (2009). A role for the X chromosome in sex differences in variability in general intelligence? *Perspectives on Psychological Science*, 4, 598–611.
Kimura, D. (1999). *Sex and cognition*. MIT Press.
Kratz, R. F. (2009). *Molecular and cell biology for dummies*. Hoboken, NJ: John Wiley & Sons.
Krebs J. R., & Davies, N. B. (1981). *An introduction to behavioural ecology*. Blackwell Science, Ltd.
Lane, N. (2011). Mitonuclear match: Optimizing fitness and fertility over generations drives ageing within generations. *Bioessays*, 33, 860–869.
Miller, G. F. (2000). *The mating mind: How sexual choice shaped the evolution of human nature*. Doubleday.
Spearman, C. (1904). "General intelligence," objectively determined and measured. *American Journal of Psychology*, 15, 201–292.
Waber, D. P. (1976, May 7). Sex differences in cognition: A function of maturation rate? *Science*, 192, 572–574.
Zahavi, A. (1975). Mate selection—A selection for a handicap. *Journal of Theoretical Biology*, 53, 205–214.

2

A LONG "INTELLECTUAL" JOURNEY

Phillip L. Ackerman

Relatively early in college, I decided that I wanted to pursue psychology as a profession, and set my sights on getting into graduate school to attain a PhD. The path I didn't take was to get good grades in college. The other path available was to seek entry into the honors program in psychology. Perhaps through a lack of oversight, the honors program at the University of Virginia (UVa) had no GPA requirements, only that a student have an advisor and a thesis plan. By the time I applied for the program, I had clear interests in psychological testing and statistics/methodology, and an idea for a thesis project. The thesis plan was to develop a set of personality-trait measures for use in the selection of dormitory resident advisors (RAs)—a straightforward application of testing principles, in that the measure used at the time was an off-the-shelf multitrait personality inventory, for which only a single scale out of 10 that were administered had a correlation with RA performance that was (barely) statistically above zero. After nine months of background work and preparations for the initial try-out of my new personality measure, an Assistant Dean decided that the concurrent sample of RAs would no longer be made available for completing the assessments. That probably had a lot to do with the fact that the extant selection procedure, though relatively poor, had been originally established by *that* particular Assistant Dean.

"Constancy of the IQ"

So, I was left to start another honor's thesis project from scratch, with one year less to complete it than my original plan. After some discussions with my advisor, Doug Mook, it was decided that I would do an extensive literature review, rather than an empirical study—which would remove the problem associated with obtaining a field sample. The topic I selected was the "Constancy of the IQ"—something that had all the elements of testing and statistics/methodology that held my interests. The downside to this plan was something my father (who was an I/O psychology professor) passed on to me after I had started the project and came to appreciate the amount of literature on the topic. He said: "There are two topics you should not consider for your work because of the massive number of papers on each—one was the Rorschach Test, the other was IQ". He, of course, was quite correct about the difficulty in reviewing the literature on IQ testing. Some years before I started my project, a psychologist had created a Bibliography on Human Intelligence (Wright, 1968). That report had 6,786 entries, including books, journal articles, and dissertation abstracts, all concerned in one way or another with human intelligence. In those days—which preceded computerized records, one had to depend on such aids, and also do iterative look-ups of periodic cumulative versions and monthly updates of Psychological Abstracts in order to find articles listed on the topics of interest.

Each discovery of a potentially relevant article title meant a trip to the "stacks" of the library, and a lot of handwritten note-taking (as coin-operated duplicating machines were only just coming into university libraries, and they were few in number and expensive to use). Thankfully, UVa had both a world-class library and "open stacks", which meant that even a lowly undergraduate could wander the collections with great freedom. I spent countless hours reading the historical and current literature on human intelligence in general, and on sources of change and variability in intelligence, to ultimately create a BA Honors thesis (which turned out to be longer than both my Master's thesis and PhD thesis manuscripts). Topics in the thesis included theories of intelligence, childhood and adult development, nature versus nurture, and various attempts at improving IQ. The most important conclusion was that, contrary to assertions by people like Spearman, intelligence can be a dynamic construct in many ways. IQ measures mask both normal and unusual development, because they focus on the relative standing of individuals in a population, rather than on absolute levels of performance. Effects of environmental deprivation, for example, showed clear deleterious effects on intellectual development, and aging has myriad effects that result in both positive and negative influences. The thesis was not particularly groundbreaking, but the experience of reading the historical literature on intelligence provided the essential foundation I have depended on for the past several decades.

Matriculating in the quantitative/measurement psychology program at the University of Illinois provided numerous opportunities to develop my quantitative skills and to explore different contexts for the study of individual differences in intellectual abilities. Learning about factor-analytic techniques from Ledyard Tucker (who had been one of L. L. Thurstone's main graduate assistants from 1935 to 1946, and who later spent years working as the first Director of Statistical Analysis at ETS), and about intelligence theory and assessment applications from Lloyd Humphreys (who had significantly contributed to the Army Air Forces Aviation Psychology Research Program during World War II) were similarly instrumental in developing quantitative and substantive expertise, respectively.

It was a somewhat serendipitous event that provided the basis for my first foray into empirical research on intellectual abilities. In the late 1970s and early 1980s, impressed with the efforts attempting to link research and theory of information processing and learning with constructs associated with intellectual abilities (largely associated with Earl Hunt and Robert Sternberg), the program manager at the Office of Naval Research mandated that several grantees would incorporate the study of process-ability relations into their research programs, something that several of them had no great desire to do. Anyway, one such researcher, Walter Schneider, was confronted with the need to incorporate such individual-differences considerations into his studies of learning. A shared office with one of his research assistants led to discussions of what kinds of research might be conducted to answer questions of the relations between automatic and controlled information processing and individual differences in intellectual abilities. None of the students in the Experimental Psychology program were interested in such an endeavor, and so I was hired as a research assistant with a relatively unstructured mandate to figure out how individual differences in abilities were related to learning (acquisition of automatic information processing skills) and performance on tasks that required controlled information processing.

Information Processing and Intellectual Abilities

At first, the idea of correlating ability measures with performance on tasks requiring controlled processing and automatic processing seemed like a relatively straightforward enterprise. Cattell's theory, for example, proposed that fluid intellectual abilities (Gf) were most highly associated with processing novel content, and crystallized intellectual abilities (Gc) were most highly associated with existing knowledge and skills. I figured that all I had to do was use a set of measures to assess Gf and Gc and administer them to participants who were performing controlled and automatic information-processing tasks. The practical downside to this approach, from an empirical perspective, is that it combined two different approaches (the experimental and correlational, Cronbach, 1949), in the most taxing manner. The experimental approach to researching "learning" was typically to study a small number of participants for a long period of time. The correlational approach to researching individual differences in abilities was to get a large number of participants for a relatively short period of time. Combining these approaches meant testing a lot of participants for a long period of time—something that has historically stressed the resources of most laboratories and the patience of most researchers.

After several series of studies, which initially served as the basis of my PhD thesis, and follow-up articles, I came to several conclusions about the role of intellectual abilities and individual differences in information processing task performance. First, like several other researchers working in the area (e.g., Carroll, 1980; Kyllonen, 1985), I concluded that intellectual abilities do not account for a lot of variance in performance on basic information processing tasks. Instead, the "content" (verbal, numerical, spatial) of the task appeared to be much more highly related to respective content abilities than is the underlying processing (e.g., controlled vs. automatic processing). Second, when it comes to learning and skill acquisition, the hypotheses based on Cattell's theory were too simplistic—in particular traditional Gc measures are far too broad to capture individual differences in the acquisition of narrow information-processing skills (Ackerman, 1986, 1987). Fundamentally, it appeared that, for relatively straightforward information-processing tasks that proceeded from controlled to automatic processing, the abilities that were most associated with individual differences in performance were first broad content abilities, followed by perceptual-speed abilities, and then finally, when highly skilled performance was attained, individual differences in performance were most highly associated with psychomotor abilities (e.g., see Ackerman, 1988). Although broad content abilities had been well studied in the literature since early in modern psychology and were dominant in Thurstone's Primary Mental Ability framework (Thurstone, 1938), perceptual speed and psychomotor abilities had been relatively neglected in both research and application since around the 1950s. The finding of the importance of these abilities in my basic empirical research led me to a more in-depth examination of both perceptual speed and psychomotor abilities.

Perceptual Speed and Psychomotor Abilities

One of the many times I turned to the historical literature in my career was in the investigation of perceptual-speed and psychomotor abilities. Although perceptual-speed ability tests had been created as early as the beginning of the 20th century (e.g., see Whipple, 1914 for a review), most of the literature on research and applications was scattered in several different places, including a modest contribution to overall scores in some traditional IQ tests. What makes some of these tests particularly interesting is that they involve short-term learning tasks (e.g., the Digit-Symbol test in the Wechsler Adult Intelligence Scale), which makes them fundamentally different from other components of the tests. Drawing on the extant research in the area[1] and current theory, I created a taxonomic classification of such tests, and determined that there were at least four different underlying factors of perceptual speed ability, namely: scanning, memory, pattern recognition, and complex factors. This approach was found to be a highly useful in determining which perceptual-speed measures were most likely to be related to individual differences in performance on a variety of learning tasks, from simple information-processing tasks to more complex assessments of job performance (e.g., see Ackerman & Cianciolo, 2000).

For tests of psychomotor ability, the challenge was a bit different, though the history of such measures was as extensive as that of perceptual speed measures. Several vocational ability batteries (e.g., the GATB) contained at least one measure of psychomotor ability (e.g., steadiness, dexterity) and many narrower occupational ability tests (e.g., the Purdue Pegboard Test) had been in use for many decades. These measures had been investigated in a variety of contexts, but the majority of psychomotor ability assessments relied on specific apparatus-based tests, such as the classic measures of Rotary Pursuit, Tapping, Maze Tracing, and the Mirror-Star Drawing Test. Returning to the experience of the military in using psychomotor abilities for predicting occupational performance, it was clear that such tests had substantial utility and promise, but they were removed from large-scale screening assessments—not because of any insufficiency of the tests, but because they were expensive to use and maintain when testing was distributed in many locations, rather than in a centralized place (Fleishman, 1956). Because of the ready availability of personal computers and the introduction of touch-sensitive computer monitors in the late 1990s, it was possible for us to create psychomotor assessments that were analogous to many that had been previously only available with custom apparatus, along with stop clocks and electromechanical counters. In a series of studies, where we managed to dig-up old apparatus tests to administer alongside our computerized tests, we found that we could capture both reliable and valid psychomotor ability variance with the new computerized assessments (Ackerman & Cianciolo, 1999, 2000); which ultimately has made it possible for many more researchers and applied psychologists to assess these abilities.

Complex Task Performance

Examining individual differences in basic information-processing tasks as a means toward better understanding human intelligence turned out to be a relatively unproductive avenue of research, mainly because such tasks did not have much common variance with traditional measures of intellectual abilities (e.g., see Carroll, 1980). So, in the late 1980s, in collaboration with Ruth Kanfer, we created a more complex learning task, called the Kanfer-Ackerman Air Traffic Control Task. It was a rudimentary low-fidelity task, but it required about five to six hours of task practice before most learners became highly skilled in performance (Ackerman, 1988). In addition to providing a much-improved platform for assessing individual differences in skill acquisition, the task was an excellent vehicle for examining influences other than intellectual abilities on learning and performance, including motivation and personality traits (e.g., Kanfer & Ackerman, 1989). These investigations addressed a variety of different issues, including aptitude-treatment interactions, goal setting, massed-vs-spaced practice, and other topics, as individual differences in performance were examined with respect to cognitive (ability), affective (personality), and conative (motivation) determinants of performance. Based on the success of these investigations, and with the advent of more powerful computers and software, we scaled-up the research to use a mid-fidelity air traffic control simulation platform (called TRACON, for

Terminal Radar Approach Controller). One of the most important characteristics of this task is that even though learners improve in performance over a period of 18–25 hours of time-on-task, the task has continually high demands on general and spatial intellectual abilities (something that contradicted extant theories of ability-skill relations over time—see Ackerman, 1989; Henry & Hulin, 1987). The TRACON software platform was sufficiently realistic in critical ways that it served as an excellent analog for real-world performance of air traffic controllers (ATCs), when we used it for development and laboratory validation of a battery of ability tests for selection of ATCs—a battery that is still in use today (Ackerman & Kanfer, 1993).

Typical vs. Maximal Performance

Over the years, our efforts to determine the trait determinants of individual differences in performance suggested that the standard laboratory approach that implicitly (or explicitly) assumed that learners continually gave their maximal attention to the assigned task was substantially incomplete, at best. Learners vary in their degree of effort allocated to a task based on innumerable other influences (e.g., sleep deprivation, fatigue, insufficient motivation). It occurred to me that there is a fundamental mis-match between conditions of high-stakes ability testing, for example, and the criteria that we aim to predict (e.g., course grades, occupational performance). That is, we use measures of "maximal" performance on ability tests to predict assessments of "typical" performance in the real world. Historically, assessments of typical behavior have belonged to the personality domain, while assessments of intellectual abilities have been based on maximal performance (Binet & Simon, 1905; Cronbach, 1960; see Ackerman, 1996 for a review). To assess individual differences in abilities in a more "typical" context, we adopted two approaches. The first was to develop a self-report measure that attempted to assess "Typical Intellectual Engagement", and the other was to start examining crystallized intellectual abilities in a manner that concentrated on "current" knowledge rather than "historical" knowledge. Historical crystallized intelligence was identified by Cattell as that which had been acquired long before it is assessed—it is the hallmark of general information tests on traditional IQ tests, and is a significant portion of the math and vocabulary sections of college and graduate school selection tests (i.e., material that was learned in high school). Current crystallized intelligence represents the depth and breadth of knowledge that an individual possesses. It was expected that a large portion of an individual's knowledge repertoire, including occupational and non-occupational knowledge would not be common to a standard K-12 school curriculum. Most critically, crystallized intellectual abilities represent something that is less reactive to high-stakes testing, because it is acquired over long periods of education and experience. Thus, it was expected to better represent "typical" intellectual capabilities, in comparison to maximal intellectual performance.

Domain Knowledge

My early research combining learning experiments (long periods of practice) with individual-differences assessments (large samples of participants) represented the kind of research enterprise that is daunting to conduct, yet provided good returns on the investment of time and effort. In somewhat the same manner, attempting to assess the depth and breadth of domain knowledge for areas that are not common to a standard K–12 curriculum, was a tall challenge. Fortunately, I received substantial assistance in the form of retired Advanced Placement (AP) and College Level Examination Program (CLEP) tests of academic domain knowledge from the Educational Testing Service (ETS). My students, most notably Eric Rolfhus and Margaret Beier, and I created several additional tests covering topics such Music, Business, Current Events, Technology, and Health. We created over 20 tests of domain knowledge, and to save time, we administered the tests in the same format used for one-on-one intellectual ability testing. That is, we started with the easiest items, and then moved on to the next domain to be sampled when the examinee got three items-in-a-row wrong. This helped maintain interest on the part of the examinees and allowed us to assess knowledge across a large number of different areas. Even with 20 or so academic and non-academic domains sampled, we still only scratched the surface of the repertoire of most adults, because we were unable to develop tests of a wide variety of occupational specialties.

Initial research based on assessment of the depth and breadth of domain knowledge in samples of participants ranging from 18-year-olds to 70-year-olds provided a wealth of information about the nature of crystallized intellectual abilities and established several important findings. The first major finding was that middle-aged adults tend to perform better on most domain knowledge tests, when compared to younger adults. If we give adults credit for what they know—both traditional assessments of historical Gc and a generous sampling of domain knowledge, and combine these assessments with measures of Gf, we found that, rather than declining intellectual abilities after individuals reach age 18–21, intellectual abilities, on average, tended to increase at least into middle age (Ackerman, 2000; Beier & Ackerman, 2001, 2003). The second major finding is that trait complexes (groups of related personality, motivation, and interest traits; see Ackerman & Heggestad, 1997; Snow, 1963) have significant and meaningful relations with individual differences in the depth and breadth of domain knowledge, pointing to the notion that there are facilitative and impeding traits for acquisition and maintenance of crystallized intellectual abilities. The third major finding was not expected, but nonetheless, significant. Large gender differences were found for most of the knowledge domains that we have investigated. These findings spurred several investigations where we could account for much of the gender differences by including trait complexes as predictors (Ackerman et al., 2001). Follow-up studies extended these results to the examination of college-student success, especially in STEM areas, and to adolescents and their enrollment patterns for elective courses (such as AP and honors courses). Together, these results were found to support the proposition that "investment" of cognitive resources over a long period of time, though the direction and level of effort toward knowledge and skill acquisition, give rise to the differentiation of the individual's repertoire of domain knowledge and skills.

Re-framing Adult Intelligence

Most recently, I have returned to the issues of adult intellectual development, but this time with the goal of re-framing the construct of adult intelligence in a way that provides improved construct validity over existing measures, and especially with attention to predicting adult performance on intellectually-demanding tasks, such as occupational performance. The approach is both theoretically driven and application oriented. It takes account of my framework of trait complexes that are facilitative or impeding of knowledge and skill acquisition over the adult lifespan, basic research on learning, and changes in the content of ability demands in the developed world (Ackerman, 2017).

Briefly, the approach I am advocating stands in contrast to approaches that propose that adult intelligence can be reduced to relatively context-free assessments of working memory or abstract reasoning (e.g., Raven's Progressive Matrices Test). Such measures have repeatedly been found to be poor predictors of performance on intellectually demanding real-world tasks. Those researchers who argue for Working Memory "Capacity" as the essence of adult intelligence have fooled themselves, mainly because they fail to validate their measures against real-world criteria. Instead, they live inside a bubble where they only seek "criterion" validation with other relatively context-free measures, such as individual differences in performance on abstract-reasoning tests.[2] Such investigations may have some relevance for impairments that take place in old age, or as a function of neural injuries, but they likely hold little value for predicting occupational performance or the depth and breadth of an individual's expertise. (Surely, few such researchers would risk going under the scalpel of a brain surgeon who had high working memory capacity performance or high Raven's scores, yet had little experience or expertise in doing brain surgery ...)

On reflection, I think that the source of the fundamental problems with most experimental psychologists who venture into the area of intelligence, is that they are unable to move beyond the approach described by Cronbach (1949), in that they are only interested in the variation that they create in the laboratory. So, they use the most basic symbols as stimuli (such as letters, numbers, and simple words), or novel abstract symbols, in the blind hope that there are no salient individual differences in familiarity with the stimuli that might influence how the participants perceive, recognize, or operate with them. Of course, such hopes are rarely justified—for example, the standard *Stroop test* (Stroop, 1935) which has been the subject of thousands of studies, provokes no conflicts in naming colors of color words printed in different colors for illiterate participants or for those who are not familiar with the language used for the stimuli. It isn't so much that using simple and arbitrary stimuli is pointless—the real difficulty comes when one tries to generalize results to real-world behaviors, without an explicit empirical evaluation. Doing good individual-differences research is hard, especially when evaluating external validity, and even more so for participants sampled beyond the college student population. Doing experimental research with arbitrary symbols and college student participants is easy, but the price to be paid is a lack of generalizability.

In contrast to those who advocate for the centrality of working memory in determining intelligence, Wechsler's (1939) development of the Bellevue Scales (later the Wechsler Adult Intelligence Scales—WAIS), has proved to be an essential tool for evaluating IQ in adult samples. But, the historical utility of the WAIS is mainly for making clinical diagnoses, not in the prediction of academic or occupational performance. The Wechsler tests, and adult extensions of other traditional measures of IQ (e.g., the Stanford-Binet) paint a rather bleak picture of adult intelligence—with declines in average performance indicated for adults as early as in their mid-20s. Based on my earlier research on adult age and domain knowledge, along with other studies that have examined the persistence of learning and skills in middle-to-old age, I have endeavored to re-conceptualize adult intellect and development. In addition, following in the footsteps of researchers like Demming and Pressey (1957), I have tried to consider what adult intelligence actually means in the early part of the 21st century—a period in which the advent of technological advances in and out of the workplace has fundamentally changed the strategies for solution of intellectual problems.

The main argument I have made is two-fold. First, at least some of the content of traditional IQ tests for adults, which can be traced back at least to the early 1900s, is largely irrelevant for today's adults. For example, Binet determined that, in an attempt to reduce the correlation of his tests with socio-economic status, his intelligence tests for children would be designed so that they did not involve reading or writing. A child might therefore have no pre-school exposure or experience with such skills and still, at least theoretically, the child could perform quite well on the Binet tests. Such design features are still common to one-on-one IQ tests, over 100 years after Binet's original scales were published, even for adult assessments, such as the most recent versions of the WAIS. But for most, if not nearly all adults in the modern developed parts of the world, lacking reading and writing skills is especially limiting, in terms of a capability to solve intellectually-demanding problems. Thus, reading and writing are critical components of adult intelligence but are not assessed by the extant gold-standard intellectual-ability tests.

Other intellectual capabilities are also important to various areas of adult cognitive functioning, but are not assessed in a substantial manner by these intelligence tests, such as critical thinking, working with technology, finding information on the Internet, comprehension for complex topics and sustained mental effort over extended periods of time, and previously mentioned domain-specific knowledge. Items and scales on the traditional IQ tests may be directly relevant or at least highly related to knowledge and skills needed for academic performance of children and adolescents (such as common cultural knowledge, basic computational math, memory for digits, or even working memory) but many of these skills have become anachronistic as solely intellectual tasks, when a computer or smartphone is within arms-reach of the individual who needs to solve a particular real-world or even academic problem. Although adults who were born in the Baby Boomer cohort or earlier cohorts were encouraged or required to learn their times-tables and mentally calculate basic math problems (e.g., figuring a tip at a restaurant, or making change at a cash register), later generations of students turned to hand calculators, and then to their smartphones to solve such problems. Does that make more recent cohort members less intelligent than their elders, at least in terms of numerical abilities (an idea that directly conflicts with Flynn's theory)? A typical high-school student with a graphical calculator can solve algebra and geometry problems that a similarly situated high-school student in 1965 might be expected to struggle to solve. I would argue that questions of which cohort is more or less intelligent are not directly answerable; the typical intellectual knowledge and skills of the cohort groups are *different*, and thus not comparable—not necessarily better or worse.

The second argument I make is that there is a vast under-explored area of *criteria* for adult intelligence that lies between college/university performance, on one hand, and clinical diagnoses of age-related impairments such as dementia, on the other hand. There simply are too few specifications of the criteria for adult intellectual performance, which in turn, renders an attempt to validate measures of adult intellect nearly impossible. Job performance represents one domain, but it is likely to be different across occupations that differ widely in terms of their knowledge and skill demands (e.g., the intellectual demands of an air traffic controller job are likely to be different in content and process from the jobs of a lawyer or accountant). Another domain pertains more to performance outside of the workplace, in day-to-day interactions with technology or real-world problem solving. A functional taxonomy of intellectual-criterion tasks is needed in order to serve as the focal criteria for validation of any old or new intelligence assessment measures. So, there clearly is much work to do in the field of intelligence assessment, that in turn, may better inform our knowledge of adult-intellectual development across the lifespan.

Hindsight

When I started my research career, I followed the Zeitgeist of the time. Most basic researchers in the field of intelligence were looking for the information-processing building blocks that could account for individual differences in intellectual abilities. In hindsight, most of us who conducted research in this area came away with interesting insights, but little in the way of assessment instruments that could be used for application purposes. It was probably a necessary path to take, in order to come to the realization that intellectual capabilities reflect a much more contextually-driven set of operations, especially for adults. It took a long time for me to recognize the wisdom of people like Ferguson (1956), who advocated for a perspective that concentrated on transfer of training, rather than novel learning, because for adults, and even for children, new learning is normally built upon existing learning, and to consider Binet's description of the "pedagogical method" of intelligence assessment, which takes account of the individual's knowledge and skills. Although Binet had good reasons for avoiding the pedagogical method in assessing young children, this was a major design factor that was a poor choice for assessing older adolescent and adult intelligence.

Similarly, like many psychological researchers, I spent quite a lot of time and effort conducting studies on college/university students and presenting them with tasks that were stripped of any external contexts (e.g., by using simple letters, numbers, and spatial figures as stimuli). After conducting many studies, I ultimately realized that young adults, especially those attending a university with selective admission standards, had limited similarities to middle-aged and older adults. Once I had that realization, I found the importance of not just domain knowledge, but also that individual differences in personality, interests, self-concept, and motivational traits had much more important influences in the development and expression of intellectual competence.

In looking back on my career, it is clear to me that the path starting with a year and a half spent in the library as an undergraduate provided a foundation that I have benefitted from on many occasions. Drawing on the long history of theory and research on IQ and intelligence has been valuable in many ways, from providing data for reanalysis for answering current research questions, to suggesting new/refined assessment instruments for applications in selection. Not every theory proposed or every study conducted in the first half of the 20th century was a success, but many times even in the failures, there was very frequently a lesson learned, one that was informative and inspirational. People often complain that psychology is not a cumulative science in the way that physics or chemistry may be. But at least in the field of intelligence, the accumulated experience and insights of the early investigators provides a rich record available for all to consider, if they only have the luxury of time and effort to consider it.

Notes

1 One source of research that I have repeatedly found to be absolutely invaluable, when evaluating the existing database of ability assessments and the empirical basis for their construct and criterion-related validity, is the work of the U.S. Army Air Forces Aviation Psychology Research Program. The work described in these reports was innovative, even

from the perspective of current research, and the scope of the validation work conducted by these researchers is without parallel in the history of ability research and application. Two massive volumes from the series of reports provide descriptions of hundreds of tests, both in paper-and-pencil format (Guilford & Lacey, 1947) and with tailored apparatus tests ranging in complexity from simple tapping plates to rotary pursuit and complex coordination – which involved matching lights with simultaneous hand and foot controls (Melton, 1947), which were evaluated with samples of hundreds or thousands of examinees.

2 I first encountered the fallacy of attempting to establish raising intelligence by only using only IQ test scores to index the success of the intervention, in my BA thesis. In 1940, Wells and her colleagues announced that they had raised intelligence of preschoolers, by examining only the change in IQ test scores after the intervention. Ultimately, the claims were refuted by people such as McNemar and Goodenough, because the "effects" were attributable to regression-to-the-mean statistical artifacts. But I was impressed that the error in Wells' attribution could have also been easily discovered by observing the effects (or lack thereof) of their intervention on academic performance, something that researchers who think the IQ score is an acceptable criterion measure rarely consider.

References

Ackerman, P. L. (1986). Individual differences in information processing: An investigation of intellectual abilities and task performance during practice. *Intelligence*, 10, 101–139.

Ackerman, P. L. (1987). Individual differences in skill learning: An integration of psychometric and information processing perspectives. *Psychological Bulletin*, 102, 3–27.

Ackerman, P. L. (1988). Determinants of individual differences during skill acquisition: Cognitive abilities and information processing. *Journal of Experimental Psychology: General*, 117, 288–318.

Ackerman, P. L. (1989). Within-task intercorrelations of skilled performance: Implications for predicting individual differences? *Journal of Applied Psychology*, 74, 360–364.

Ackerman, P. L. (1996). A theory of adult intellectual development: process, personality, interests, and knowledge. *Intelligence*, 22, 229–259.

Ackerman, P. L. (2000). Domain-specific knowledge as the "dark matter" of adult intelligence: gf/gc, personality and interest correlates. *Journal of Gerontology: Psychological Sciences*, 55B(2), 69–84.

Ackerman, P. L. (2017). Adult intelligence: The construct and the criterion problem. *Perspectives on Psychological Science*, 12(6), 987–998.

Ackerman, P. L., & Cianciolo, A. T. (1999). Psychomotor abilities via touchpanel testing: Measurement innovations, construct, and criterion validity. *Human Performance*, 12, 231–273.

Ackerman, P. L., & Cianciolo, A. T. (2000). Cognitive, perceptual speed, and psychomotor determinants of individual differences during skill acquisition. *Journal of Experimental Psychology: Applied*, 6, 259–290.

Ackerman, P. L., & Heggestad, E. D. (1997). Intelligence, personality, and interests: Evidence for overlapping traits. *Psychological Bulletin*, 121, 219–245.

Ackerman, P. L., & Kanfer, R. (1993). Integrating laboratory and field study for improving selection: Development of a battery for predicting air traffic controller success. *Journal of Applied Psychology*, 78, 413–432.

Ackerman, P. L., Bowen, K. R., Beier, M. B., & Kanfer, R. (2001). Determinants of individual differences and gender differences in knowledge. *Journal of Educational Psychology*, 93, 797–825.

Beier, M. E., & Ackerman, P. L. (2001). Current events knowledge in adults: An investigation of age, intelligence and non-ability determinants. *Psychology and Aging*, 16, 615–628.

Beier, M. E., & Ackerman, P. L. (2003). Determinants of health knowledge: An investigation of age, gender, abilities, personality, and interests. *Journal of Personality and Social Psychology, 84 (2)*, 439–448.

Binet, A., & Simon, Th. (1905/1973). *The development of intelligence in children*. Translated by Elizabeth Kite. Arno Press.

Carroll, J. B. (1980). *Individual difference relations in psychometric and experimental cognitive tasks*. (Tech. Rep. No. 163). Chapel Hill: University of North Carolina, The L. L. Thurstone Psychometric Laboratory.

Cronbach, L. J. (1949). *Essentials of psychological testing*. Harper.

Cronbach, L. J. (1960). *Essentials of psychological testing* (2nd ed.). New York: Harper & Brothers.

Demming, J. A., & Pressey, S. L. (1957). Tests "indigenous" to the adult and older years. *Journal of Counseling Psychology*, 4(2), 144–148.

Ferguson, G. A. (1956). On transfer and the abilities of man. *Canadian Journal of Psychology*, 10, 121–131.

Fleishman, E. A. (1956). Psychomotor selection tests: Research and application in the U.S. Air Force. *Personnel Psychology*, 9, 449–467.

Guilford, J. P., & Lacey, J. I. (Eds.) (1947). *U.S. Army Air Forces Aviation Psychology Program Research Reports: Printed classification tests*. Report No. 5. U. S. Government Printing Office.

Henry, R. A., & Hulin, C. L. (1987). Stability of skilled performance across time: Some generalizations and limitation on utilities. *Journal of Applied Psychology*, 72, 457–462.

Kanfer, R., & Ackerman, P. L. (1989). Motivation and cognitive abilities: An integrative/aptitude-treatment interaction approach to skill acquisition. *Journal of Applied Psychology—Monograph*, 74, 657–690.

Kyllonen, P. C. (1985). *Dimensions of information processing speed* (AFHRL-TP-84–56). Brooks Air Force Base, TX: Air Force Systems Command.

Melton, A. W. (Ed.) (1947). *Army Air Forces Aviation Psychology Program Research Reports: Apparatus Tests*. Report No. 4. Washington, DC: U.S. Government Printing Office.

Snow, R. E. (1963). *Effects of learner characteristics in learning from instructional films*. Unpublished doctoral thesis. West Lafayette, IN: Purdue University.

Stroop, J. R. (1935). Studies of interference in serial verbal reactions. *Journal of Experimental Psychology, 18(6)*, 643–662.

Thurstone, L. L. (1938). Primary mental abilities. *Psychometric Monographs*, 1.

Wechsler, D. (1939). *The measurement of adult intelligence*. The Williams & Wilkins Co.

Whipple, G. M. (1914). *Manual of mental and physical tests. Part I: Simpler processes*. Warwick & York.

Wright, L. (1968). *Bibliography on human intelligence*. Public Health Service Publication No. 1839. U.S. Government Printing Office.

3

PARTNERSHIP

A Tale by the Tail of the Kite

Nancy M. Robinson

A partnership, sadly interrupted in 1981, has played a defining role in my life for 70 years. Hal Robinson and I met in 1950 in Maud Merrill's class on intelligence at Stanford just as we were beginning graduate study. Maud became our beloved mentor and, because of the inherently fascinating areas of her interest and because of her kind guidance, exerted a strong influence on our lives. This memoire is a "two-fer", an account of a partnership that persisted even after one of its members was gone.

Beginnings

In 1949, with questionable wisdom but encouraged by the Veterans' Administration, which needed psychologists, Stanford's psychology faculty abruptly decided to establish a clinical psychology program. Lacking evidence how best to select applicants, they decided to accept up to 30 students and weed out those that didn't make the grade. Hal and I, both final-quarter undergraduates, were invited to apply. Only a handful of us survived the first, highly stressful year.

During high school in Houston, I don't think I heard or had a fresh idea during my four years there. Working with a counselor in a career guidance agency, however, I developed the intention to become, like her, a developmental psychologist, possibly an academician. Arriving soon after at Stanford, barely age 17, I scurried to learn to think and write critically. Hal had arrived at Stanford via a more complex route, enrolling at Pomona after four war years in the South Pacific as a Marine, trying a joint Pomona-Stanford program leading to a law degree but soon deciding that field wasn't for him. He worked a year for the California Association of Manufacturers (ironic for the son of a union organizer/ railroad telegrapher) and returned to finish his bachelor's degree as expeditiously as possible, using the remainder of his GI Bill funding.

We married at the end of that first year and eventually completed our PhDs, becoming parents along the way. Hal finished first, taught for a couple of years at San Francisco State and undertook odd jobs to get us on our financial feet. In 1959, we were off to the University of North Carolina, where, during the first few years, nepotism rules precluded my holding a campus job. This is where Hal's creativity, with a healthy dose of chutzpa, took over. Our complementary roles became our pattern of collaboration. It was some years later that a friend, describing that collaboration, commented that even high-flying kites need tails for stability, a kindly statement taken as such by both of us.

Getting Started: The "Other End" of the Normal Curve

There existed then no introductory textbook in child-clinical psychology. Lacking mastery of a field before jumping into it never bothered Hal—I was the one tasked with tracking down what more we needed to know. He saw where we were going; I filled in the blanks. We decided to begin with the field, now called *intellectual (or cognitive) disability*, that was suddenly bursting into its own. The choice was over-determined. Hal had a sister who had been institutionalized at age 5 (mistakenly, as it was discovered 25 years later) when his newly widowed mother abandoned her five young children to fend for themselves in a series of separate foster homes. Mental retardation was supposed to be Chapter 1, but it turned into a central focus, for me one that lasted 30 years.

Hal developed the outline for the book as well as each chapter's outline. For each topic, he included a preceding chapter to equip the reader with enough basic knowledge about the topic (e.g., genetics) to understand how it applied to the emerging field of *mental retardation*. I wrote the initial drafts, to be passed back and forth until we were satisfied. How much more peaceful our lives would have been in the age of computers on which one could keep one's critical markups hidden! The original textbook and its revision ten years later comfortably put our children through college and made our names in the field.

Eventually, I did join the UNC faculty but meanwhile Hal kept developing programs that needed staffing for a year until someone could be properly recruited. He never got me into anything I couldn't handle, but neither was I ever fully prepared, so life was always something of a scramble. By this time, we had four children. In the South it was easy to find and afford quite wonderful full-time housekeepers/nannies. (If you haven't read or seen *The Help*, you should.)

The partnership we established worked well for us despite, and because of, its challenges. Hal developed high-flying interests and saw opportunities that no one else did. I frankly was doubtful about some of his visions, but he was, with amazing frequency, right about them. I would get busy developing the background we needed and executing the plans, thoroughly in awe of where we arrived.

Our major accomplishment during our 1959–1969 years in Chapel Hill was the establishment of the Frank Porter Graham Child Development Center (FPG), one of the dozen research centers funded by NICHD in the mid-1960s. The Center is still going strong. Its original mission was to combat what was then known as *familial retardation*, essentially multi-generational low functioning in families with few resources, little education, and dim prospects. Its intervention thrust was very early day care through preschool, beginning when the mother returned to work, and including black and white families, low-income and middle-income families. Pediatricians, psychologists, and educators were involved. At this time, Chapel Hill and UNC were both highly segregated. Not until 1968 did UNC admit its first undergraduate black student, appropriately (for UNC) a star basketball player on his way to the USA Olympic team. Living in North Carolina during the Civil Rights movement was also thrilling and empowering because our nonviolent picketing and petitioning, in addition to establishing FPG, did make a difference. It was exactly what Dr. King dreamed about.

Hal had grand architectural ideas for FPG, envisioning a mini-village of octagonal buildings housing care for multiple age groups. Like the Center, the elementary school into which the children graduated, was named after a former governor and president of UNC whom Hal encountered by chance and described as the finest human he ever expected to meet. Alas, the built Center, which fortunately Hal never saw, was maximally uninspiring, but the thrust of the original mission emerged as the Abecedarian Project. The intervention model was translated by Craig Ramey[1] into other research settings and the "Abecedarian" curriculum has had international application under the direction of Joseph Sparling. The original intervention and comparison groups are now in their 40s, demonstrating remarkable long-time effects in life achievement and even measurable brain-function in such tasks as decision making.

The results of our pilot intervention were stunning on their own. After two years, for the children from low-income families, the differences in IQ between the Center children and community case-matched controls were a whopping 30 points. Those for children from middle-class families were less impressive, but the presence of those children as playmates may have contributed to the success of those from lower-income families.

Launching FPG had advocacy from the UNC president, the governor, a couple of U.S. senators, and Harold Howe III, who headed an educational think tank nearby. They all supported the integration of both students and staff. Suddenly, all these supporters were replaced and "Doc" Howe left for D.C. to become Commissioner of Education. Hal concluded that a big-name outsider would have more clout in working through these politics and accepted a faculty position for which he'd been recruited at the University of Washington. Jim Gallagher, though not a Southerner, was in the U.S. Office of Education and wise in policy and politics. He became Center Director—a wise choice indeed.

By 1969, it was clear that early childhood education abroad was something about which we in the United States needed to know much more. Supported by the

Carnegie Corporation, we assembled an American team with Urie Bronfenbrenner (Cornell), Julius Richmond (Harvard), and Martin Wolins (UC Berkeley), and set about recruiting collaborators abroad. We soon found that everyone we invited was as eager as we were to learn from one another. We became a team from a dozen countries spanning both sides of the Iron Curtain. One of our meetings, at the Villa Serbelloni on Lake Como, coincided with the first moon landing, memorably celebrated by those of us from all twelve countries. During a sabbatical year in Paris, Hal and I edited nine short books describing implicit contracts between families and state for the care of young children as well as writing an overview with Martha Darling, then an early child-care specialist at the Organization for Economic Co-operation and Development (OECD). Three totalitarian countries were omitted from the book series: Russia, because the authors refused to publish what the state censors permitted; Cuba, because those authors were willing to comply with the censors; and Yugoslavia, because they tried to write by committee and the effort fell apart.

About that time, I decided that I needed a job with some stability and lucked into one leading the psychologists and educators at UW's Child Development and Mental Retardation Center (CDMRC). During my 14 years there, my research focused mainly on following children who had been exposed to or born with risky conditions such as low birth weight and maternal illnesses. These were straightforward longitudinal studies of value but not much inventiveness, and I missed the excitement of our partnership.

The Gifted End of the Curve

Meanwhile, in 1973, Hal had new interests and considered two possibilities. One idea focused on maternal effects of the hormone and neuropeptide, oxytocin. Two barriers stood in the way of that route. Hal would need to spend a lot of time exploring fields outside the realm of psychology, and UW at that time had no lab equipped to assay the substance. He did a bit of pilot work but decided to pass it by. How vindicated he would feel were he alive today!

As a natural outgrowth of our exposure to the work of Lewis Terman through Maud Merrill, his disciple, we also had both been harboring an interest in giftedness. I'd even taught a course in the subject at UNC, prompted by America's new attention to talent development after Sputnik. Pursuing this interest was considerably more feasible. Hal had former graduate students in need of jobs and he (correctly) thought a grant from the Spencer Foundation could be available. Specifically, he wanted to follow children identified as precocious in the very early years (2½ to 5), at least to first grade and possibly much longer. He had available a campus preschool, which he developed for gifted youngsters.

In addition to that study, Hal's brave willingness to stride ahead with new ideas birthed a program of very early entrance to the UW for exceptionally bright students, maximum age 14. He returned from Baltimore visiting his good friend, Julian Stanley, who talked proudly about the very young students he'd admitted to Johns Hopkins. "If Julian can start a program, so can we!" Hal said, and set about doing it. Not until some years later, during a visit by Julian to our campus, did I discover that (a) Julian didn't *have* a program but *was* the program, (b) most of Julian's students were older than those he talked most about, and (c) his students didn't even know one another!

The first few students Hal recruited included our youngest daughter, who went from a self-taught year of algebra straight into calculus, bolstered by a weekend reading her TA's trigonometry text. The initial youngsters succeeded in UW courses without extra preparation, but the next few needed tutoring in math. It soon became obvious that a transition year of preparation in university level academic skills would be a good idea. Hal put together such a year's curriculum, accepted some extremely young students (one was age 8), and gave it a try. He also added an assessment and short-term counseling clinic for bright youngsters and involved several of his graduate students who were interested in giftedness for dissertation research. The Center for Capable Youth was off and running. As Hal had predicted, the field of developmental disability had hit a conceptual plateau, so he and I began to make plans for me to spend part-time in the new Center.

Crisis, Loss, and Change

But then, on a trip to Mexico to celebrate our 30th anniversary, Hal died scuba diving. He wasn't highly experienced. The 40-foot dive he'd signed up for turned out to be a 90-foot dive. Having depleted his air supply, he apparently rose to the surface too quickly and was hit by the bends. This, alas, was the fatal result of his intrepid spirit, a dreadful outcome past my imagining.

Because of international red tape, I had a few days in Mexico to think things through. Our children were of course devastated, but their educations were well launched. Two had completed their studies; one was in medical school; and the 16-year-old "EEPer", as the accelerated students were called, was a junior at Reed College after two years at UW.

In any university, a major project like the one Hal had initiated disappears if the professor behind it is no longer there. I knew UW would be no different. What Hal had begun was unique and too significant to let go, so I marched into the Dean's office and announced that I wanted to undertake the Center's directorship. It was rocky going at first. There was no funding aside from EEPers' modest tuition for the Transition School year and the clinic's assessment fees. Moreover, Tom James, head of the Spencer Foundation, terminated the grant for Hal's study, but it still needed to be finished. I inherited all of Hal's responsibilities except teaching his courses. Unlike Upper Campus, where the Center was located, my salary had always been soft money, as was true of 90% of the Medical School faculty. I took a lesson from Hal and ignored these "slight" problems for the moment.

Like many other psychology departments, this one was strongly biased toward honoring theoretical rather than applied research, and not about to make things easy for me. Hal might have been rash about some things, but naïve he was not. He had seen to it that the Center's space belonged not to the Department of Psychology, but an administrative step higher up. The Dean under whom responsibility for the Center fell was Ron Geballe, a physicist who could not possibly have been more supportive. He helped me navigate all kinds of university hurdles that naturally occurred because no one had anticipated having very young students on campus. (Could EEPers be admitted as regular students without graduating from high school? Could an EEPer so admitted participate in PAC 12 sports? Live in a dorm? Get a Pell Grant? Declare a major? Work in a lab where some monkeys might have Simian HIV?) Ron also helped me obtain modest grant funding from the Murdoch Foundation (Intel money). Years later, after he retired, he taught physics in our Transition School for several years.

Further guidance was generously forthcoming from Julian Stanley and from David Lubinski, Julian's disciple, who were (and David is) always there with encouragement and advice. How much they taught me about mentoring!

Hal's sister, a public-school counselor, took a year's leave to get the Transition School in order. She and Hal had been exceptionally close all their lives, and she was as devastated by his loss as I was. Hal's graduate students quickly brought me up to date on current research. When I broke Hal's intended news to parents that the preschool space was needed for the Early Entrance Program, they incorporated the school and moved it into the community, where it is now an excellent pre-K to 8 school for gifted students, one of five such independent schools we are lucky to have in this area.

I gradually eked out a half salary from the Center budget, but continued half-time at my former job, every year receiving promises from the Administration to find funds for the other half. It was obvious, however, that I wasn't going anywhere else. Not only was I devoted to keeping Hal's work alive, but I found the field of giftedness and the students themselves to be exceptionally rewarding. "Somehow" those funds didn't materialize until my retirement 20 years later.

I felt responsible for short-changing neither of my two roles at opposite ends of the normal curve, so disciplined myself to leave campus by 11 PM every night. Nobody home but me. I shed a few of my responsibilities at CDMRC such as editing the archival journal in mental retardation and heading the clinical psychology internship. Eventually, it dawned on me that I could exist on a half salary. In 1988, I gave up my coveted parking space behind the School of Medicine and forsook mental retardation.

My Research in Giftedness

The Early Entrance Program of course has served as a target of numerous studies. Research with a variety of Center colleagues yielded more targeted studies than anything else I touched.

The participants in Hal's longitudinal study not only yielded very interesting information about the high degree of stability of ability in the early years, but also served as a reservoir of subjects for subsequent research on a variety of topics.

With NIMH funding, we studied the psychological effects of having a gifted sib, subgroups being pairs of sibs in which zero, one, or both had been designated as eligible for special school programs.

For some years, we received information about the highest-scoring 7th–8th grade students in Washington State who had enrolled in the Johns Hopkin Talent Search. I sent each of them a letter listing 20-plus ways they might create a better educational match for themselves than their regular classes were likely to provide, including, of course, our fast-paced summer classes and the Early Entrance Program. This large group gave us entry to studying the correspondence of verbal-math patterns and interests of extended family members in verbal vs. math-science realms.

How does one go about finding very young gifted children who are not yet in school? In his longitudinal study, Hal had used local newspapers and radio media as well as contacts with pediatricians, preschools, and Head Start teachers. Indeed, virtually all the children nominated by their parents were precocious. My colleagues and I used this approach in identifying very young children, studies that were more fun than anything else I undertook. These included mathematically precocious children whom we found as they were graduating from preschool or kindergarten, providing biweekly half-day math programs to half the group, randomly chosen. Phil Dale and I recruited toddlers with precocious language by 20 months of age and, with Catherine Crain-Thoreson followed them to age 6.

In addition, in return for serving on a research advisory board for a humongous study of the effects of continuing, through third grade, Head-Start-like services to post-Head-Starters, Rich Weinberg and I gained access to the data for the children who did best in school, compared with the others. Sharon and Craig Ramey headed the study. Despite exquisite matching of experimental and control schools and meticulous care in execution, school districts ruined the study out of admiration for the intervention services, which they then provided to their *non*-served schools. Before long there was no detectable difference between the two groups. That didn't stop Rich, the Rameys, and me from looking at families of children who did best, most of whom would have been eligible for gifted programs had such been available in their schools.

It doesn't always work, however, to piggyback free on other people's data, especially to borrow the services of statisticians who are in love with complex analytic models. Case in point: In the verbal-math study, we gathered information not only about math-science interests vs. verbal interests of extended family members but also about their musical backgrounds. Because the needed analyses were much simpler, I couldn't talk the statistician into examining associations of music with dominant math vs. verbal ability!

Similarly, the author of a national day care study who approached me about using family and day-care data to predict high achievement, was overly in love with fancy analyses. I couldn't persuade her statistician that we already had abundant evidence about factors relating to high achievement. I had other questions requiring only an ANOVA or even a chi-square, but they were having none of it. As I predicted, the manuscript was rejected (the only one of mine ever turned down). It was their database, after all, and old-fashioned me didn't have the skills required. (I may be the only person you know with only a flip top phone.)

Hindsight: What Have I Learned?

About kites and tails: Kites do need tails, but tails need kites as well. What would the Center have become if Hal had lived? I can only guess:

- Our accelerated daytime programs would have morphed into a residential school; students would have come from far and wide and admission would have been even more selective.
- Hal would have eventually become bored even with the most highly gifted students, turned running the programs over to me, and perhaps proceeded with his interest in oxytocin, arriving there earlier than anyone else. Or with some new ideas I've never dreamed of.
- Before long, we'd have written a book. Or several.

And, too

- When partners play complementary roles and one is lost, the other moves toward the middle. I was determined to keep Hal's dream alive, but in smaller steps I could manage alone.
- One day when bemoaning the probability that I'd never impact the field as had Hal and Julian, I realized that it was enough, instead, to aspire to asking important questions. Although there are other programs of early entrance to universities, none is a copy of ours. Among them are one that has become essentially a challenging high school and several that accelerate only one or two years. Some are at colleges that lack the rigor and/or scope to challenge very bright students. Many colleges or universities do take pity on occasional local students who clearly need acceleration, but they don't provide the peer group, transition experiences, or counseling we do. We are still pointing the way to possibilities.

What did we learn from the studies of students enrolled in the Early Entrance Program?

- A combination of test scores on measures such as the ACT and SAT, grades, conversations (not written recommendations) with teachers, and interviews with applicants and their parents are effective in selecting students who are out of place in middle school, eager for challenge, and mature both socially and in managing their lives. Clues to students who will do well are remarks made at the end of a day-long visit such as telling us how unhappy they are in middle school (those who were happy don't need us!) and how right the day's experience felt. Those who subsequently don't do well during the transition year and leave for high school almost invariably are those with warring or otherwise disturbed parents whose issues have been hidden from us.

- Although we didn't require individual testing for admission, I did administer WISC's for a while, finding that successful applicants were almost all scoring 145 or above.
- Acceleration works; even radical acceleration works well for very bright students who are relatively mature for their age, as are most gifted students, even though not as far ahead as they are intellectually. They have thrived academically and socially and are happy with their decision to take the leap, some responding that they should have accelerated even more.
- Comparing EEPers with groups matched for test scores (regular age students), qualified young applicants who decided to go to high school, and regular-age National Merit finalists, our students were most like the last of these groups at entry and as adults. Their academic and occupational attainment certainly did not suffer from their youth.
- Their peer group is essential to the well-being of these teenagers, but after a couple of years, about half of the students' friends are regular-age UW students.
- My successor established a second early entrance program at the UW, an Academy that substitutes for the last two high school years. I knew that there were already such successful programs elsewhere, but I was afraid that a less-radical competitor would kill applications for the EEP itself. I was wrong. Both are going strong at UW.
- It was more difficult for the boys to find girlfriends than vice versa, but the addition of the Academy provided additional dating possibilities.
- Rates of marriage—stable marriage—and adult life satisfaction are high. Several marriages are of two EEPers or a former EEPer and an Academy student.
- Both peer group and supportive staff constitute long-term resources for many students.
- We don't have any Nobelists (yet), but we do have Rhodes Scholars, winners of many other academic honors, and high frequencies of advanced degrees, the major exception being UW graduates recruited by nearby Microsoft and tech startups (some of which ex-EEPers have started themselves). These techies insist that they learn more on the job than they would in graduate school.
- I've saved the above point for last. As many readers are aware, there is division in among those of us who strive to enable optimal talent development

of gifted students. Some believe we should aim toward producing elite leaders who are paradigm-shifters, publicly recognized for their significant impact. Others (of whom I am one), believe that optimal talent development so seen denies the talents of most gifted students. A teacher is lucky in a lifetime to encounter one or two elite game-shifters. Yet, without opportunity and challenge, many gifted youngsters would wither or simply get by, never attaining the best of which they are capable. We need excellence in all fields—superb practitioners, investigators, performers, whatever. We need more tails than we do kites! Constant game-changing might produce more chaos than a healthy society can endure.

- Contrary to expectations of lay observers, for very bright students, special classes are less likely to lead to intolerance than is making them suffer through endless days of boredom. To quote an EEPer: "Being in regular classes was like watching a slow-motion movie six hours a day". This situation did nothing to endear her classmates to her or vice versa. My criterion of a non-elitist is someone who can sit next to a stranger on a bus, whatever that person's background, and appreciate a genuinely interesting conversation.

From the several studies of very young, precocious children?

- Not only are parents virtually always right about their children's precocity, but when we confirm their reports using standardized assessments, we have also validated the tests! Voila! Test results reflect real life!
- Our society aches for early intervention for the very young in marginalized families. Hal and I reviewed the numerous experimental programs of the mid-1960s while developing Frank Porter Graham. It soon became obvious that not only do socioeconomic differences emerge by 18 months to 2 years, as was already known, but that if we don't intervene by then, it's too late. The programs with largest and longest lasting results all began by age 2. Giftedness can be destroyed at an early age and even ages 3–4 are late to start fixing it. We need to keep alert to students with unrealized potential whatever their age but left-behind children need something different than do those who have profited from the wisdom and resources of dedicated parents.
- Over time, the very young children we studied showed a high degree of stability within their groups in intellectual abilities and specific strengths. This was true of those in Hal's original study, the early talkers, and the math-precocious. Individual changes over time clustered around the mean of their group, not the mean of their age cohort.
- Few early talkers became early readers, but except for one dyslexic 6-year-old, they learned very rapidly to read well once they started. Math-precocious children remained so, but those who experienced our multi-modal approach not only displayed higher math scores at the study's end but showed higher correlations among measured cognitive domains.

- Alas, the most highly math-precocious youngsters were all male. (Maybe things have now changed?)

And the family studies?

- Don't believe "what everybody knows!" Every single study I'd found in the literature—mostly "sympathetic" interviews with parents—demonstrated deleterious effects of having a gifted sibling. With our approach, with 366 pairs with 0, 1, or both identified as gifted, there were very few group differences, but each difference we did find was positive! Gifted children are, if anything, a gift to their siblings, according to both the sibs and the mothers.
- As I and my geneticist colleagues expected, relatives of high-math students showed evidence of math-science interest and talent, with relatives of high-verbal students showing more verbally oriented interests and talents. The closer the relationships, the stronger the effects.
- With respect to the post-Head Start studies, the overall group's test scores look pretty much like those of unselected populations. The highest attainers tended to come from families who, while only a smidgeon higher in income, seemed to be somewhat more planful and child-oriented. They had fewer children, for example, their parenting practices were more responsive and flexible, and the children were more socially skilled than were the comparison group.

And finally

I have a confession: Even at age 89, 70 years after this tale began, I still suffer from Imposter Syndrome. I've received just about every award from the National Association for Gifted Children for which I'm eligible. I am grateful but don't understand the pedestal on which I'm placed. As I read the roster of paradigm-changers included in this volume of autobiographies, I'm awed but I appreciate the company! And it wouldn't have happened without Hal.

Note

1 Ramey, C. T. (2018) The Abecedarian approach to social, educational, and health disparities. *Clinical Child and Family Psychology Review, 21,* 527–544.

References

Chamrad, D. L., Robinson, N. M., Treder, R., & Janos, P. M. (1995). Consequences of having a gifted sibling: Myths and realities. *Gifted Child Quarterly, 39,* 135–145.

Dale, P. S., Crain-Thoreson, C., & Robinson, N. M. (1995). Linguistic precocity and the development of reading: The role of extra-linguistic factors. *Applied Psycholinguistics, 16,* 173–187.

Janos, P. M., Robinson, N. M., & Lunneborg, C.E. (1989). Academic performance and adjustment status of early college entrants, non-accelerated peers, and college classmates. *Journal of Higher Education, 60,* 495–518.

Robinson, N. M. (2003). Two wrongs do not make a right: Sacrificing the needs of academically talented students does not solve society's unsolved problems. *Journal for the Education of the Gifted, 26,* 251–273.

Robinson, N. M., Abbott, R. D., Berninger, V.W., & Busse, J. (1997). Developmental changes in mathematically precocious young children: Matthew and gender effects. *Gifted Child Quarterly, 41,* 145–159.

Robinson, N. M., Lanzi, R. G., Weinberg, R. A., Ramey, S. L., & Ramey, C. T. (2002). Factors associated with high academic competence in former Head Start children at third grade. *Gifted Child Quarterly, 46,* 281–294.

Robinson, H. B., & Robinson, N. M. (1971). Longitudinal development of very young children in a comprehensive day care program: The first two years. *Child Development, 42,* 1673–1683.

4

OF HUMAN POTENTIAL
A Forty Year Saga

Howard Gardner

Scholars typically begin their work by building on the contributions of their own teachers as well as on the achievements of those whose works they have studied. I was no exception—I began by studying the works of Jean Piaget in developmental psychology. And when I began to carry out empirical studies, I used Piagetian methods to study the artistic development of children, which Piaget had neglected because of his focus on logical and scientific thinking.

Through a series of plans and accidents, I conducted research at two different sites: Harvard Project Zero, where I was studying the development of cognitive and symbolic skills in children, particularly those employed in the arts; and the Veterans Administration Hospital in Boston, where I studied the breakdown of symbolic and artistic capacities in individuals with acquired brain damage. Being (for whatever reason) more of a book-writing than an article-writing scholar, I wrote books on artistic development in children (Gardner, 1973a), on Piaget's theory (Gardner, 1973b), and on the breakdown of cognitive capacities under conditions of brain damage (Gardner, 1975).

Had I not gone through my old files from a few years ago, I would have forgotten that in 1976 I had outlined a book called *Kinds of Minds*. In that never-to-be-written book, I planned to describe the kinds of cognitive capacities that I'd seen developing in children and the ways in which those cognitive capacities break down under conditions of brain damage. As the grandiose title signaled, I was prepared to argue that human beings can foreground different kinds of minds—e.g. the scientific mind, the artistic mind, the mechanical mind, etc.

I put that project aside, at least for a while. Then, in 1978–1979, I had one of those experiences that end up being life-changing. A Dutch foundation, the Bernard Van Leer Foundation approached the Harvard Graduate School of Education, where I was a non-faculty researcher, living on (or off) "soft money".

The Foundation was prepared to offer the school a very generous grant—ultimately well over one million dollars over a five-year period—to answer a broad and amorphous question: "What is known about the nature and the development of human potential?"

The Dean of HGSE, who happened to serve on the board of the foundation, was also looking for ways to cover some of my salary (and that of one other junior member of the school). And so he asked whether, with the support of a few key senior faculty members, we would be willing to lead a "Project on Human Potential". At the time, with an eye toward Berkeley, Malibu, and Esalen, I quipped "Human potential is more of a 'west coast' term than an 'east coast' term" and yet I was quite happy to accept a leadership position and to devote some years of my life to exploring this wide-open and mind-opening question.

"Human potential" turned out to be somewhat of an inkblot test. Philosopher Israel Scheffler probes the meaning of the term in a thoughtful book called *Of Human Potential* (Scheffler, 1985). Anthropologist Robert LeVine and sociologist Merry White looked at human potential as it is conceptualized and realized across a variety of cultures and cultural settings; their conceptualization and conclusions are reported in *Human Conditions: The Cultural Basis of Educational Development* (LeVine & White, 1986).

In my case, generous support from the Foundation allowed me, aided by several excellent researchers, to carry out a far-ranging examination of the social scientific and natural scientific evidence about various human cognitive capacities—as it were, the research needed to lay out and support a systematic argument about "Kinds of Minds".

Very briefly, in *Frames of Mind* (Gardner, 1983), I developed the idea that intellect should be conceptualized as pluralistic. Rather than thinking of individuals as "smart" or "dumb" across the board, one can accrue considerable evidence, from a range of disciplines, that intellect is better conceived as consisting of a number of relatively independent computational devices; I elected to call these "multiple intelligences" (which I soon abbreviated as "MI"). And so, an individual might be strong (or weak), say, in her logical abilities, and that assessment simply does not allow us to predict performance on spatial tasks, musical tasks, use of the body to solve problems, or capacity to understand the motivations of other people.

Of all of my scholarly work, MI had by far the most immediate and, at least so far, the greatest long-term impact. While few psychologists have embraced the theory (due to their allegiance to the concept of general intelligence, abbreviated as g), my formulation has seemed plausible to biologically-oriented scholars. And it has attained and maintained popularity within education and with the general educated public—both in the United States and abroad. While researchers have rarely followed up my work directly, I think it has held up pretty well in the intervening decades (for reviews see, Gardner, Kornhaber, & Chen, 2018; Davis,

Christodoulou, Seider, & Gardner, 2011; Gardner, 2006; Kornhaber, Fierros, & Veenema, 2004; Shearer, 2009).

From the vantage point of several decades, I believe that I have a clear idea of how the view of human potential captured in my writings of the 1980s represented a scholarly advance—as well as the ways in which it was limited.

In comparison to other scholarship on intelligence, I drew on a far wider set of disciplines (neurology, genetics, anthropology) and had a much more capacious view of intellect—not only solving school-style problems, but also creating products that are valued in one or more cultural settings. I was not tied to a particular kind of test in a formal setting—indeed, I was strongly biased toward ordinary (and on occasion extraordinary) behaviors in natural settings. I was much more open to the kinds of abilities that were valued in pre-historic times (hunting, gathering, fishing, farming) and to the ways in which scholastic settings have also called on different abilities in different settings at different historical periods. Of course, my examples and evidence still drew heavily on Western research in recent decades. But when I was criticized for cultural bias, I responded, "Well, I am sure that my work is influenced by my own background and the society in which I have lived, but it is far less biased than work on intelligence undertaken by most other scholars".

But today, with the advantage of hindsight, access to new research, and considerable knowledge of what has happened in the world since the late 1970s, I would point several limitations. And these limitations, in turn, suggest how—looking forward—one might formulate "human potential" more capaciously.

1. While I was trained across the social sciences (in a field that encompassed sociology and anthropology), I was thinking and writing very much as a psychologist. And while psychologists have important things to say about human nature and human potential, we scarcely have a monopoly of wisdom on that topic. Today: In writing about human potential, I would pay far more attention to differences across cultures and across historical eras.
2. Even within psychology, I had a fairly narrow conception. Almost all of my work on intelligence/potential focused on human cognition—though I had a much broader view of cognition than many of my peers. When I spoke about interpersonal and intrapersonal intelligences, I was fixed on "knowing" about self and others, and not on more affect-laden or personality aspects of human nature. (In this way, my work differs from the well-known work of Daniel Goleman (2006)). Today: I would avoid the almost exclusive valorization of cognition. However, defined or delineated, I would pay more attention to social, emotional, and personality factors. These are often called "non-cognitive". I don't like that rejection, but I am content to refer to them as "soft skills".
3. Also, and importantly, my view of human intelligence was pointedly amoral. Any intelligence can be used for benign purposes or malignant

purposes: one can use language to write exquisite poetry or to instigate ethnic cleansing.

I have certainly atoned for this omission. For over twenty years, with many colleagues, I've been studying the nature of ethical and moral thinking, across the life span, and across many different professions. In this work, we have focused on what it means to use intellectual (and other) strengths in ways that are positive for the wider community. While we recognize that what is "good" can be complex and controversial, we avoid the postmodern trap of refusing to pass judgment on issues of character and behavior (Gardner, Csikszentmihalyi, & Damon, 2001; Gardner, 2010; see also thegoodproject.org).

4. More so than almost any other work in cognition at the time, I searched for relevant evidence from biology—particularly from neuroscience (the representation of different capacities in the human cortex) and from genetics (the extent to which different capacities may be heritable). But in the intervening decades, we have learned a great deal more about the biology of human potential—and so an informed study of the intelligences today would delineate what we do know, what we expect to know, and what remains wrapped in mystery (Shearer & Karanian, 2017). I suspect that the division into eight or nine intelligences is not sufficiently fine-grained from a neuroscientific point of view, but it captures the insight clearly for educators and non-specialists.

5. Understandably, in a wide-ranging study of intellect, I focused on the human capacities that pervade the species. Individuals with special talents or specific deficits occupied only a small part of the radar screen. But in the succeeding decades, with colleagues like David Feldman and Lynn Goldsmith (1991), and Ellen Winner (1997), we've taken a much closer look at talent, expertise, prodigiousness, creativity, leadership, and genius, as well as individuals and groups that exhibit flagrant deficits in various areas (Gardner 1993; 1995; 1997; 2006, Chapter 3). Humans differ from one another at least as much as do snowflakes or bacteria—and we need to survey that entire canvas in any account of human potential (Rose, 2016)

6. Even though the Project on Human Potential was carried out in a school of education, none of the principals had been trained in that area—we were drawn from the social sciences and the humanities. Accordingly, much of our writing about education was incidental, rather than focal. Both because of my longevity in a school of education and because of the unparalleled interest in my work among educators, I've devoted a great deal of time to thinking about how best to realize human potential—which I would now immediately pluralize as "human potentials".

Any bias that I may have had toward explanations of human potential in terms of genetic contributions has been greatly countered by my (and others') increased knowledge of the large differences in educational outcomes both within and across nations and cultures. Relatively few of those differences seem due strictly to individual differences in individual human genomes. Rather, as I have come to put it, how much one achieves within or across intelligences is a joint product of how *important* that capacity is in the society where one happens to live, how highly *motivated* one is to develop that capacity, and how *skilled* are the teachers and the technologies of education available in one's culture—or, nowadays, across the globe.

Which brings us up to the 21st century: In what has been termed the era of *homo sapiens*, we have assumed that the species is basically fixed (Harari, 2015). Once Neanderthal had become extinct, for whatever reason, our ancestors came increasingly to dominate the natural world and to make the planet ours—for better or for worse.

And of course, we have witnessed *the better*: I would valorize the emergence of religious and moral codes; the invention of writing; the domestication of animals; the mastery of farming and hunting; wide access to written materials; the emergence of machines, electronics, and digital technologies—the list goes on.

But of course, we have also encountered *the worse*: almost everything just listed has been put not only to good but to malignant use. As an example, religion has motivated murderous crusades while also fostering humane treatment of the old, the lame, and the sick. And of course, we have had slavery, warfare, genocide, mass pestilence, and lesser forms of chicanery and less flagrant sins. Even globalization—initially lauded as the culmination of the Enlightenment, if not the End of History—can foster ugly forms of tribalism, nationalism, and warfare.

But in recent decades, it has become increasingly clear that *homo sapiens* represents but a chapter in the history of the planet, and not its glorious culmination. From the angle of science and medicine, we can for the first time make significant alterations in the human genome—enhancing or extinguishing traits, or even creating new ones, temporarily or permanently, and enhancing our lifespan, some say infinitely. Human potential becomes the terrain of what biologists and geneticists can conjure up—and what the rest of the population will allow or even encourage.

From another angle—that of technology, computer science, robotics, and artificial intelligence—we can begin by enhancing (or, again, eliminating) certain already existing human traits (Harari, 2015). Or, to go further, we can create entities that surpass the species in cognitive capacities (as well as other traits). So much so, indeed, that we may eventually choose or be forced to cede human problem solving and product creating capacities to entities that we can only dream about—or, that we used to relegate or elevate to the realm of science fiction.

Accordingly, when we change the definition of what it means to be human, or when we create entities—biological or computational—that far exceed what used to be meant by the species and its potential(s), we are likely to need an entirely different set of concepts and explanations.

Indeed, in using the term "we" I am already anticipating that the new species is a linear descendant of ours—but that assumption in itself might be fallacious. Entire lines of evolution have disappeared (where are the dinosaurs or the species that existed before the Cambrian explosion?), and each biological species has its point of origin.

I salute the new experts—the biologists and the computer scientists—who may create new species and new conceptions of post-human potential. But in doing so, I hope that we do not neglect the amazing achievements of our own species. We did not simply invent writing: we enabled Plato to document what Socrates thought and said; we enabled Shakespeare to portray the enduring features of human beings and Virginia Woolf to capture the experiences of the moment. We did not simply create the first musical instruments and figure out how to write musical scores: we enabled Mozart to compose exquisite music, Yo-Yo Ma to perform it on the cello, and Renee Fleming to sing it. And it was human beings who created enduring institutions (churches, schools, and civic offices) and enduring processes (legal systems, constitutions, and Bills of Rights). While a scholarly work necessarily focuses on those findings that can be generalized, human potential as we know it is realized in some way in each and every person. And while we still can, we should admire the heights of human potential…and make sure that whatever happens next can preserve and build on those achievements.

Acknowledgments

This article was originally published in a special issue on "Rethinking Human Potential: A Tribute to Howard Gardner" of the *Journal for the Education of the Gifted* (Volume 43, Issue 1, March 2020). The permission to reproduce it in this book was obtained May 19, 2020 from the Copyright Clearance Center (Order No. 4832040467177; Invoice No. RLNK503551177)

References

Davis, K., Christodoulou, J., Seider, S., & Gardner, H. (2011). The theory of multiple intelligences. In Sternberg, R. J., & Kaufman, S. B. (Eds.), *Cambridge handbook of intelligence*. Cambridge University Press.
Feldman, D., & Goldsmith, L. (1991). *Nature's gambit*. Teachers College Press.
Gardner, H. (1973a). *The arts and human development*. Wiley.
Gardner, H. (1973b). *The quest for mind*. Knopf.
Gardner, H. (1975). *The shattered mind: The person after brain damage*. Knopf.
Gardner, H. (1983). *Frames of mind: The theory of multiple intelligences*. Basic Books.
Gardner, H. (1993). *Creating minds*. Basic Books.
Gardner, H. (1995). *Leading minds*. Basic Books.
Gardner, H. (1997). *Extraordinary minds*. Basic Books.
Gardner, H. (2006). *Multiple intelligences: New horizons*. Basic Books.

Gardner, H. (2010). *Good work: Theory and practice*. http://thegoodproject.org/pdf/GoodWork-Theory_and_Practice-with_covers.pdf.

Gardner, H., Csikszentmihalyi, M., & Damon, W. (2001). *Good work: When excellence and ethics meet*. Basic Books.

Gardner, H., Kornhaber, M., & Chen, J. (2018). The theory of multiple intelligences: Psychological and educational perspectives. In Sternberg, R. J., *The nature of human intelligence* (pp. 116–129). Cambridge University Press.

Goleman, D. (2006). *Emotional intelligence: Why it can matter more than IQ*. Bantam.

Harari, Y. (2015). *Sapiens: A brief history of humankind*. Harper.

Kornhaber, M., Fierros, E., & Veenema, S. (2004). *Multiple intelligences: Best ideas from research and practice*. Allyn and Bacon.

LeVine, R., & White, M. (1986). *Human conditions: The cultural basis of educational developments*. Routledge and Kegan Paul.

Rose, T. (2016). *The end of average*. HarperOne.

Scheffler, I. (1985). *Of human potential*. London: Routledge and Kegan Paul.

Shearer B. (2009). *Multiple intelligences at 25: Assessing impact and future of multiple intelligences for teaching and learning*. Teachers College Press.

Shearer, B., & Karanian J. (2017). The neuroscience of intelligence: Empirical support for the theory of multiple intelligences? *Trends in Neuroscience and Education* 6, 211–223.

Winner, E. (1997). *Gifted children: Myths and reality*. Basic Books.

PART 2
Cognitive and Developmental Perspectives

PART 2

5

UNLEASHING CLIO[1]

Tracing the Roots of My Journey in Cognition

Stephen J. Ceci

When I accepted the editors' invitation to write about the context, impetus, and evolution of my thinking about cognition, I envisioned something quite unlike what I ended up writing here. I set out planning to trace the intellectual history of my current ideas, focusing on papers that influenced my thinking when I was in graduate school. Naturally, there were many such papers, with developments in parallel processing models of thinking and reasoning, and especially the debate over the importance and pervasiveness of general intelligence. When I sought reasons for my interest in these papers, however, I began to appreciate currents that ran through my childhood and interacted with and catalyzed my later interest in these domains (thinking, reasoning, memory, and intelligence). This chapter is a highly personal story, as you will see, one that required unleashing Clio, the muse of my personal history. I am not sure readers will learn much of value from following me on this personal journey, but I feel I gained insight into why I became immersed in the type of cognition that takes place in everyday contexts.

Early Life Events Set the Stage for My Later Interests

When I was very young, sometime around the age of nine (I think), an event occurred that would later prove influential in my academic interests: I was arrested. A group of teenage boys and I used to play baseball on a street corner at night; I was much younger than they were, so I suspect that I perceived it as an honor of sorts to be included in their nighttime street activities. We must have been loud because an elderly man sometimes called the police to complain. He was an ex-officer himself so his calls got immediate response. When a police car would approach our corner and an officer emerge, we would disperse into a maze of alleys to evade him. Perhaps dodging the police was a thrilling game to us—I am guessing because my memory is very hazy. One night someone hit a ball that broke a window in the old man's house, and he called his former colleagues on the police force again. In a short time, a number of police cars simultaneously blocked egress from all of the alleys. Five of us were apprehended, handcuffed, and put in the back seats of several of the police cars and taken to jail. I do not remember what happened next except being released to my mother late at night and walking home with her, the police station being several miles from our house. Some months later, I appeared in court with my four teenage codefendants. I do not recall what happened to the older boys, but I was sentenced to reimburse the cost of the replacement glass and ordered to attend a summer camp sponsored by the police department.

Contrary to what you might expect, I actually liked being at this camp. I got to do things that city kids rarely did, such as canoeing, archery, and camping; we learned card games like Pinochle and board games; and the camp served foods that, while initially foreign to me, I liked very much. (My dietary preferences changed as a result of this camp experience and to this day they are unlike the rest of my family's.) However, for the purpose of this chapter, the most important consequence of attending this camp is that I met several boys whose paths would later cross with mine. One of them was someone whose uncle owned a sub shop not far from where I lived.

One day a couple years after my arrest, the owner of the sub shop approached me while I was playing pinball in his shop. He said he heard from his nephew who had been at camp with me that I had a very good memory. I don't know if I had an exceptional memory; it was better than my friend's memory but, based on true memory prodigies I later studied, it is not remarkable. At any rate, he asked me to study and recall strings of digits in forward order, which I did. He would read a string of numbers to me and then wait a minute and ask me to recall them in the same order. I assume that I recalled enough digits in correct order to satisfy him because he offered to pay me what seemed like a lot of money to memorize numbers. After committing the numbers to memory, I would walk to a vegetable/fruit stand about a mile away and repeat the numbers to a man who worked there. The sub shop owner was a bookie whom people gave money to in hope of winning the daily number, or they placed bets on horseraces or other sporting events. Every day some people would bet 50 cents or a dollar on 3-digit combinations usually based on a child's birthdate or license number or simply their "special number". If they won, the bookie would pay them 500-to-1, which if you think about it, was a bad wager because there are 1,000 3-digit numbers between 000 and 999. (There were several methods used to determine the daily winning number, all of which were essentially random, such as taking the winning horse that day in third race and using the third digit from its win, place, and show payoffs; other methods also were used at various times.) If bookies were careful not to overextend themselves by holding too much money on a single number, they could make a handsome living.

Bridgett Davis provides a fascinating account of her mother's bookmaking business in Detroit in the 1960s and 70s (Davis, 2019), which fully accords with my own experience as a numbers runner in the 1960s.

Sometimes the bookie I worked for took in too much money on a single number or horse. When this happened, he would "lay-off" some of the money to a higher-level bookie, called a "bank". The man who owned the fruit stand to whom I repeated the numbers was such a bank. He was the person to whom the sub shop owner would lay-off or transfer bets that were larger than he wanted to risk having to pay. As noted, the pay-off for picking the winning daily 3-digit number was 500-to-1. So, if this bookie held $25 on a winning daily number, say "437", he had to pay bettors who wagered the $25 on the winning number $12,500. Although no single bettor waged $25 on a single number, collectively, a group of bettors might bet $25 on the same number, and if it was a winner, then the bookie had to come up with $12,500 by the end of the day. For the sub shop owner, $25 was larger than he was comfortable holding on a given number, so to minimize his exposure he would transfer some of the $25 to a larger bookie, the bank.

It was against this backdrop that each day the bookie would read a list of numbers to me and I would spend a minute or two memorizing them and then walk a mile to the fruit stand and repeat them to the bank and hand over the cash that went with the numbers. For instance, I might repeat $16 on 437; $10 on 057, $7 on 928, and $5 on 621, and hand over $38. The reason the numbers had to be memorized and not written on paper is because if the police caught people carrying "paraphernalia" related to the numbers racket, they'd arrest them and the paper slips would be used as evidence of book-making. (One of my own uncles experienced this unhappy outcome and served two years in a state penitentiary, although in his case the police not only confiscated paper slips and an adding machine but also had a wiretap recording him discussing numbers.)

My job with the bookie segued into better-paying jobs for other bookies and banks around town. One particular bank, an elderly woman named Esther, employed me over a period of many years that extended well into my undergraduate years at college. Several days each week I would leave campus after a class or lab and drive to bars, restaurants, and smoke shops to collect horseracing bets that the bookies wanted to lay-off on Esther. I did this on those afternoons each week when I didn't have labs or tests. Esther employed others to collect the money on the days I didn't. The money was good and the job was easy if you didn't mind carrying many hundreds of dollars in cash, which I didn't.

Esther sometimes ended up holding more money on a horse than *she* wanted to risk. If the horse was, say, 20-to-1, and she was holding $1,000 on it, she might self-insure by sending someone—a different type of "runner"—to the racetrack to actually wager some of the $1,000 on the horse in question. So, if it won, Esther would not be responsible for paying the full amount. Sometimes I was the runner who took money to the track and wagered it on the horse in question; if it won, I would bring the winnings to Esther. There were several other runners who would take money from Esther to the racetrack and bet it, and I knew of other runners doing the same thing for another bank in town.

I discovered that not all runners would bet the money they took from the bank to the track. Some would actually "book" the bet themselves. For example, instead of wagering on a 20-to-1 horse that the bank wanted to lay-off at the track, a runner might book the bet themselves, that is, not bet the money, if they thought the odds at post-time were overrated. This gave them a big personal profit if the horse in question did not win. Of course, when the horse in question did win, they were out of pocket a large sum of their own money. Some of these individuals were seemingly good at deciding when to wager the bank's money on a horse and when not to. Although I did not have any hard data, I knew that some runners had affluent lifestyles, so I assumed they won more than they lost because for many of them being a runner was their only or main job.

Little by little, I learned how runners determined whether to wager the money from banks at the track or book the bet themselves and pocket the money when the horse lost. Based on their analysis of a race, they might conclude that the horse in question was overvalued by the betting public (who establish the actual post-time odds). If they felt that a horse was overvalued, they might not wager the bank's money on it. For example, if a horse was 3-to-1 at post-time, but the runner felt it really had a much lower chance of winning, say, only a 5-to-1, then he (they were all men) might pocket the money and assume that over many such decisions he would make money by not wagering on over-valued horses. Conversely, if a runner thought a horse was undervalued (its true chances of winning were better than what the general public believed), he might wager even some of his personal money on it. Because I was curious how runners analyzed (i.e., handicapped) races, I sometimes probed them about how they did this. It was obvious that handicapping was quite complicated, involving many variables, not all of which were equally important. Every time I thought I understood their decision process, I would discover that I did not, as I explain below. Another reason I had trouble grasping the handicapping process is that different runners sometimes came up with different decisions on the same horse, indicating there was not a single agreed-upon mental model that they all shared. I never got to the bottom of the handicapping process when I left this world to start graduate school in my early 20s. But this experience left its imprint.

During my graduate school days, I was drawn to research on memory, including feats of exceptional memory (see below). I was also drawn to feats of everyday cognition. No doubt these interests were seeded by my experiences with bookies. Not long after receiving my PhD, I returned to racetracks and started interviewing handicappers to determine what their mental models looked like; how they analyzed races and how they assessed real odds (as opposed to the betting public's assessment, which established official post-time odds). I no longer was limited to only my intuitions, because I had acquired in graduate school a cognitive and statistical toolbox that I could employ to analyze these questions. A sociologist named Jeff Liker became fascinated listening to me talk about these questions, so I invited him to join me in a formal study of racetrack handicappers. This was the beginning of a study that took us several years to complete because it involved lots of trips to Philadelphia-area racetracks to interview handicappers, ask them to handicap experimental racing programs that we designed to systematically manipulate variables, ask them to predict post-time odds a day in advance of the actual public wagering which establishes the official odds, etc. When Jeff Liker and I finally finished the analyses, we realized these handicappers fell into two classes: although both were highly knowledgeable, one group was more expert than the other. We discovered that the top experts were supremely talented and seemingly successful. Their mental models involved combinations of many variables, with differential weights and non-linearity.

We had a sense of this complexity from our interviews with experts (for details, see the Appendix in Ceci & Liker, 1986), but it took systematic experimental manipulation of racing data to confirm it. We derived a statistical measure to reflect complexity in handicapping races that was based on up to seven variables, some of which interacted with others. Less expert handicappers had developed models that were not as complex and they were less accurate in predicting post-time odds and in picking winners than were those who were more expert; and the reason for their lower success was tied to their less complex models.[2] One of our findings was that the b coefficient that reflected complexity in handicapping, and was predictive of success at the track, was unrelated to IQ. In the early 1980s, this finding went against the dominant psychometric Zeitgeist that held that everything complex was saturated with general intelligence, g. Many held that most cognitive performances, and certainly all complex behaviors, were predicted by measures of general intelligence, such as IQ scores. Because of our failure to find a correlation between IQ and mental complexity at the track, it was difficult to publish our findings. The premier journal in our field at that time (*Psychological Review*) rejected our manuscript with diametrically split reviews, and so did another journal. Finally, the *Journal of Experimental Psychology: General* accepted our paper and it was published the following year (Ceci & Liker, 1986).[3]

No sooner had I finished the study of racetrack handicappers, than I began studies of Brazilian bookies and street vendors (Ceci & Roazi, 1994; Schliemann, Carraher, & Ceci, 1996), stock market analysts (Ceci & Ruiz, 1992), and card counters at casinos (Ceci, DeSimone, & Johnson, 1992). These studies of gamblers were sprinkled across my main area of research, which had always been memory, especially children's memory. Yet both my main research and my work with gamblers were influenced by chance events. In the case of my memory research, the chance event was a request from a judge that set me on a path that I continue to hew today. Had the judge not called me when he did, my memory research would have taken a different course. This seems indisputable.

These anecdotes suggest how chance encounters and random stochastic processes may have influenced who I became as a researcher. Growing up amidst gamblers, bookies, and banks (including an uncle in prison for running numbers), affected my thinking in two ways that I was not to become aware of for many decades: first, it taught me that sometimes very smart people who happened to be poorly educated and who scored low on IQ tests could nevertheless be very complex in their thinking. Some of the most complex handicappers we studied were abysmal on various subtests of the *Wechsler Adult Intelligence Scale* (WAIS), such as vocabulary; they were not formally educated beyond elementary school and would stare blankly when asked to define IQ words such as "espionage", Second, it made me realize that cognitive complexity was context-specific. Concerning the latter, most of the expert handicappers I encountered did not reason nearly as complexly about their social lives or about planning their pension as they did at handicapping races. The most blatant illustration of this context-specificity was our discovery of a low correlation between experts' WAIS arithmetic performance and seemingly similar arithmetic they had to do at the track. Unlike the base 10 system used on the WAIS, at the track everything to be calculated is in 5ths. For example, the determine how fast a horse "closed" (i.e., ran the final stretch of a prior race against horses comparable to those in an upcoming race), the expert would note that the time at the start of the stretch was, say, $1:29^{4/5th}$ and the time at the finish of the race the final time was $1:57^{1/5th}$ sec thus, 27 and 2/5th closing speed. Hence, accuracy doing mental arithmetic at the track bore little resemblance to doing it on the WAIS. This led to a lengthy study of the link between formal education and performance on IQ tests. Wendy Williams and I found that for each year of missed or extended education there was a corresponding decrement/increment in IQ; even missing school due to illness or summer vacation was associated with changes in performance on tests: two children with the same IQ at age 13 ended up with different IQs by age 18 if one dropped out of school before graduation (Ceci, 1991; Ceci & Williams, 1997). The context of test-taking was strongly influenced by the schooling context. There were many other instances of context-specificity that we came across.

In one study conducted by my lab members of a card counter named "Bubbles", who was banned from casinos, we documented his ability to perfectly recall a deck of cards, each presented at a 1 sec rate. We filmed him (because we felt no one would believe it otherwise!) accurately recalling up to 22 digits forward and backward! (If you do not realize how remarkable a feat it is to recall 22 digits backward, check the WAIS tables and you will discover that recalling even a third of that number is off-the-chart.) Yet, notwithstanding Bubbles' unbelievable memory for digits and playing cards, his memory for words, colors, and sentences was just average (Ceci, DeSimone, & Johnson, 1992).

Thus, as my thinking evolved, I began to realize that these beliefs based on my childhood experiences motivated me to develop a conceptual framework that highlighted context-specificity and the orthogonality of various forms of cognitive complexity; my theory was an attempt to explain how general and specific factors joined to determine everyday cognition (Ceci, 1996). Urie Bronfenbrenner and I found that even very micro-level cognitive processes, such as temporal calibration (coordinating your internal clock with a wall clock), were heavily influenced by the context. Some contexts foster more complex calibration than others; we found that the efficiency with which someone engaged in multicausal reasoning was tied to aspects of the physical and social setting, with videogames eliciting greater complexity than laboratories for what appears to be the identical problem-solving task (Ceci & Bronfenbrenner, 1985). Like the work with gamblers, this work also showed the danger of assuming that the panoply of someone's cognitive ability can be captured from a snapshot of them in one setting, usually a lab.

So being steeped in my early environment prepared me in ways that went beyond my awareness at the time to think about phenomena in certain ways that would decades later shape my research. In graduate school, I learned experimental designs and statistical approaches that permitted me to document how individuals can be more complex in some contexts than others, even when the thought processes in the two contexts seem formally isomorphic. Observing runners at lunchtime as they decided whether they would lay-off a bank's coverage on a horse at the track or book the bet themselves seemed as complicated as what my professors were doing in their labs later that afternoon. I am making no claim that the two groups shared the same IQ scores, but I am claiming they were both supremely complex in their thinking, despite the handicappers' sometimes unimpressive IQs.

I have already discussed the difficulty my colleagues and I had publishing some of our work when we started. At the time, it seemed as if we were in a small minority in thinking along these lines. Soon I discovered a growing group of researchers making similar findings and theorizing in similar, albeit not identical, ways. (Bob Sternberg was a leading figure in this new way of thinking about general intelligence.) Although g has not disappeared from modern thinking about intelligence, it has been dethroned as the core of cognition. I'd like to think my childhood arrest and exposure to gamblers played a small role in this shift.[4]

Hindsight: Looking Back on How My Research Has Evolved

When I was starting out as a psychologist, I recall reading in one of the volumes of *A history of psychology in autobiography,* which was edited by C. Murchison, a chapter written by the great psychologist, Edward Chace Tolman. In these volumes, each contributor was asked to think retrospectively about the programmatic nature and evolution of their research. Tolman, I remember, bristled at being asked to reflect on the evolution of his ideas and he wrote that when he was a young psychologist, he wasted more time than he should have worrying about the programmatic nature of his evolving work. He said that, as an old man, he realized that one should aim to be able to look back on a career and not ask about the evolution of one's work but whether it was fun doing it. When I read this statement as a young man, I was not sure what Tolman meant, but now that I am pretty old myself, I think I do understand. When I was pre-tenure, I strove to build a portfolio of interrelated studies that had a critical mass; I followed up each study with the next one in the program. However, many decades ago I ceased trying to be programmatic for the sake of being programmatic. And I ceased constraining my thoughts into the next step in the evolution of the research question I had previously been working on. I tackled questions that grabbed my interest without regard to whether and how they fit in with prior work. At times, the studies seemed to come out of nowhere. I simply did not consider whether they fit into a program. The reason I tackled most questions is because at the moment I thought about them they intrigued me. That alone was my justification. I know others feel similarly, and my easiest example comes from Ulric (Dick) Neisser, the late cognitive psychologist who some credit with launching the modern cognitive science revolution in the late 60s. I was visiting Emory University to give a talk and at the time Dick Neisser was on the faculty there. He was fascinated by several newly-published studies that were very far outside his "program" of scholarship, so much so that I remember asking another cognitive scientist to explain to me what Dick saw as the common denominator among these studies that fascinated him. The response of this colleague is one I still remember vividly: Dick Neisser loved studies that "pissed on the altar". Any study that debunked sacred cows drew his attention and sometimes led to his immersion in research spawned by this newly-discovered work. Neisser never seemed to consider how or if it fit into his research program. I am no Dick Neisser. But I did learn a lot from being his colleague for several decades (after he returned to Cornell). And, like Urie Bronfenbrenner, Dick's appetite for diverse research rubbed off on me.

To conclude, I did what I did because at the time it fascinated me; that was the sole rhyme and reason. If in retrospect someone can trace common conceptual threads across my diverse studies, I cannot claim to have been consciously aware of such threads at the time I launched these studies. My closing thought is that no one should take my historical legacy any more seriously than that of a someone who spent the bulk of his career meandering into and out of ideas without much thought about they were connected.

Notes

1 Clio is the Ancient Greek muse of history and creativity.
2 Without going into the statistical "weeds", picking winners is less important than assessing true odds and predicting post-time odds. For example, if someone picked the favorite in every race, he or she would have won 37% of the time but they would have lost money over the long haul. Alternatively, if someone is able to pick undervalued

horses that win only 5% of the time, it can be very lucrative. It all comes down to identifying gaps between post-time odds and true odds, the latter which entails deep analysis of the past performance data of all horses competing in a given race. Past performance data are published in the daily racing form, and also in the unofficial Early Form that is sold a day in advance of the race to give serious handicappers more time to analyze races.

3 This article eventually came to be highly cited, and several years ago in its anniversary issue, *MENSA Research Journal* selected it as one of the five most influential studies of intelligence in the past 30 years, an acknowledgement that surprised us in view of MENSA's equating of IQ scores with general intelligence.

4 I discovered during my years as a professor that about 10% of my colleagues grew-up under straitened circumstances. I once assumed that my upbringing was unusual among members of the academy, given that neither of my parents went beyond 10th grade. Yet, many colleagues traveled their own nonmodal routes to becoming professors, including one who was an emancipated minor at age 16 and lived alone in welfare housing on food stamps and attended night school to get her GED before going to college on a scholarship. Another woman who left home at age 15 and was raised by nuns and friends' parents before getting a scholarship to college. Another was the son of a lower working-class family whose father pumped gas for a living. And lots of other non-traditional routes that might surprise those who imagine that all faculty came from ascendant families. We often did not.

References

Ceci, S. J. (1991). How much does schooling influence general intelligence and its cognitive components?: A reassessment of the evidence. *Developmental Psychology*, 27, 703–722.

Ceci, S. J. (1996). *On intelligence: A bio-ecological treatise on intellectual development* (2nd ed.). Harvard University Press.

Ceci, S. J., & Bronfenbrenner, U. (1985). Don't forget to take the cupcakes out of the oven: Prospective memory, time-monitoring and context. *Child Development*, 56, 152–164.

Ceci, S. J., & Liker, J. (1986). A day at the races: IQ, expertise, and cognitive complexity. *Journal of Experimental Psychology: General*, 115, 255–266.

Ceci, S. J., & Roazi, A. (1994). Context and cognition: Postcards from Brazil. In R. J. Sternberg, & R. K. Wagner (Eds.), *Intellectual development* (pp. 26–49). Cambridge University Press.

Ceci, S. J., & Ruiz, A. (1992). The role of general intelligence in transfer: A case study. In R. Hoffman (Ed.), *The psychology of expertise*. Springer-Verlag.

Ceci, S. J., & Williams, W.M. (1997). Schooling, intelligence, and income. *American Psychologist*, 52(10), 1051–1058.

Ceci, S. J., DeSimone, M., & Johnson, S. (1992). Memory in context: A case study of "Bubbles P"., a gifted but uneven memorizer. In D. J. Hermann, H. Weingartner, A. Searleman, & C. McEvoy (Eds.), *Memory improvement* (pp. 169–186). Springer-Verlag.

Davis, B. M. (2019). *The world according to Fannie Davis: My mother's life in the Detroit Numbers*. Little, Brown and Company.

Schliemann, A. D., Carraher, D. W., & Ceci, S. J. (1996) Everyday cognition. In J. E. Berry, P. B. Dasen, & T. S. Saraswathi (Eds.), *The handbook of cross-cultural psychology* (2nd ed.) Vol. 2: Basic Processes and Developmental Psychology. Allyn & Bacon.

6

IGNORING BOUNDARIES BETWEEN DISCIPLINES

Fernand Gobet

My research has focused on the psychology of expertise, with many excursions in other fields such as the acquisition of language, intelligence, cognitive training, philosophy, computational modeling, and artificial intelligence. Although my undergraduate studies were carried out in an unexceptional department, I had the good fortune of working around the time of my PhD with two of the founders of modern cognitive psychology: Adriaan de Groot and Herbert A. Simon. Both had an unorthodox approach to psychology and methodology and ignored boundaries between disciplines—two characteristics I have inherited. I started my career within the classic expertise research tradition, which paid little attention to individual differences and instead emphasized the role of practice. In the last 15 years or so, I have been increasingly interested in combining the cognitive and psychometric approaches to expertise and talent. There were several reasons behind this intellectual change, the main one being that my PhD students collected data, both quantitative and qualitative, that systematically supported the role of talent. The main lessons I have learned in my career is that the future of the psychology of expertise lies in multi-disciplinary research and that most theories in psychology are poorly specified, which is a serious barrier to progress.

Contexts

As a child, I wanted to become a scientist, although of course I only had the faintest idea of what this meant. My parents bought their first (black and white) TV to watch the landing on the moon live—what an experience for a seven-year old child! I also vividly remember a movie about the life of Marie Curie, which I saw when I was about ten years old.

Unfortunately, my interest in science was severely dented when I was in what is called secondary school in Switzerland (equivalent to Grades 6–8 in the US). On two occasions, I had prepared a large binder with detailed information for my science class—one about biology and the other about astronomy—which went well beyond the call of duty. My teachers paid little attention to them, which disappointed me deeply. At the same time, I was excelling in Latin and ancient Greek. As these topics were very rewarding, I decided to follow a classics track rather than a scientific track, to the great despair of several of my teachers. Of course, this meant less exposure to scientific topics.

A First Career in Chess

At about the same time, at the age of 13, I won an important scholastic chess competition, which covered all the French- and Italian-speaking cantons of Switzerland. This success attracted much attention—there was much interest in chess after the Fischer-Spasski world championship in 1972, which obviously was very gratifying for a young boy. So, my interest and motivation switched from science to chess. The fact that most of my science teachers were rather uninspiring was another factor behind this change. The preference of chess over studying was to last until the end of high school, and in fact well into my time at the university.

With hindsight, it is clear that I already had much interest in the questions of thinking and expertise during these formative years. First, being a precocious child—I entered secondary school two years earlier than most of my classmates—meant that I was considered as "intelligent", which raised my interest in what intelligence was. Second, playing chess—the most intellectual of games—at a competitive level and successfully not only against teenagers but also against adults labeled me as a smart boy. It also meant that I had many discussions with friends about why I was so good at chess and also about what it would take to become Grandmaster. So, the question of talent vs. practice was never very far. Living in a country that was backwards from a chess point of view—for example, in comparison with what was then the Soviet Union—made it plainly clear that the environment is essential in developing expertise: a chess culture, the presence of strong players and coaches, a rich technical chess literature—all this was lacking in Switzerland. At the same time, there was little doubt in my and my colleagues' minds that some players were more gifted than others—Bobby Fischer being a prime example.

At my peak, I was one of the best players in Switzerland—with the title of an International Master—but never reached world class level. Had I kept playing chess professionally rather than moving to science, I probably would have become a (weak) Grandmaster. My chess career gave me the opportunity to play against several of the very top players in the world—first-hand encounters with exceptional experts. Were these superstars really different from me?

My impression was that, by keeping practicing—practicing very hard, admittedly—I could reach the level of most the top players I had played against. In fact, I had beaten several of them, such as Grandmaster Vlastimil Hort, who at his peak was a candidate to the world title. I even had a winning position against former world champion Boris Spasski, although I did not see the winning move and managed to lose the game at the end (see Gobet, 2018, for details). A few players seemed beyond reach, however. World champion Gary Kasparov, who played the Swiss national team in simultaneous games, winning most of them, was clearly in a different league. Losing against him in such circumstances was painful, but many years later gave me the opportunity to write a paper on the link between pattern recognition and search in chess (Gobet & Simon, 1996).

Studying at the University

When choosing my field of study at the University, I was constrained by my chess career. For practical and financial reasons, I considered only the University of Fribourg, a fairly unremarkable university that had the advantage of being local. My own inclination, and indeed the social pressure at the time, was to study medicine. But this would have been too time consuming and would have meant the end of my chess career. I briefly considered studying Greek and Latin, given my strength in these languages and my penchant for the kind of problem solving that is involved in translating from these languages into French. However, the prospect of spending the rest of my life studying dead languages did not appeal to me.

For a while, I played with the idea of becoming a philosopher. However, one of the first philosophy books I stumbled across was not encouraging, to say the least. Written by Józef Maria Bocheński, a Polish Dominican and logician who had been an influential professor of philosophy at the University of Fribourg, it emphasized that philosophy students should master at least English, German, French, Italian, Russian, Latin, ancient Greek, and Hebrew. This was a bit too much for me, even with my classics background. Either Bocheński was wrong or he meant his advice tongue in cheek: I am now in a Philosophy Department in spite of having forgotten most of my Latin and Ancient Greek!

In the end, I decided to study psychology, which allowed me to combine a relatively light program of study with my interests in intelligence, thinking, problem solving, and expertise. There was also some practical motivation: studying psychology might help understand my own thinking and thus improve in chess. (It did not.) Finally, the fact that the department was small and relatively new was somehow attractive to me.

Very rapidly, within two or three months of study, I came across the seminal research carried out by Adriaan De Groot on chess players' thinking (De Groot, 1965) and Herbert A. Simon and William G. Chase on chess players' perception and memory (Simon & Chase, 1973). These studies were mentioned in a class taught by Jean Retschitzki, a new professor in the Psychology Department who was doing research on computer modeling and awale (an African game). As he had spent a postdoc period at Carnegie Mellon University, he knew Simon's work.

At the beginning, I found it difficult to sympathize with Simon's research. For example, MAPP (Memory-aided Pattern Perceiver), the computer program he had developed with Gilmartin (Simon & Gilmartin, 1973) to explain chess players' memory, looked too naïve to my eyes. By contrast, I was fascinated by De Groot's 463-page book, which I read from cover to cover, taking copious notes in the process. Using protocol analysis, De Groot performed a very detailed analysis of the way chess players, including world champions Alexander Alekhine and Max Euwe, were thinking while trying to find the best move in a position unknown to them. For a semi-professional chess player and a budding cognitive psychologist, this was material from Heaven! Because of his deep understanding of chess, and despite the complexity of his analyses, De Groot had an undeniable influence on me.

My intense interest in chess psychology did not stop me from slowly drifting into clinical psychology, psychopathology, and psychoanalysis, topics on which many courses were offered at the University of Fribourg. In particular, I devoted much time studying cognitive-behavior theory, which was the main strength of the Department. All the classes in clinical psychology were taught in German; at that time, my German was much better than my English, a consequence of the fact that I had read numerous chess books in German and that most of my teammates in the Swiss national team were Germanophone.

I had extensive exposure to Jean Piaget's ideas, as many of my teachers had been his students. My impression of his work was mixed. I was impressed by his theoretical developments and his emphasis on the interaction between nature and nurture. He actually was brilliant, if not always fair, in criticizing the extreme views of nativism and empiricism. Unfortunately, Piaget's research was taught in a very calcified and dogmatic way, which did not encourage the development of new ideas or the design of experiments exploring and potentially contradicting his theories. Whether this was due to the nature of Piaget's empirical and theoretical work or to the style of my teachers is an interesting question. Probably both.

My *mémoire de licence* (roughly equivalent to a Master's) managed to combine my interests in chess psychology and clinical psychology. It applied the concept of learned helplessness (i.e., learning that one cannot control one's environment) to chess players, using an elegant experimental design (the "triadic design") that had been originally developed with rats and dogs, among others by Martin Seligman. The aim of my study was to establish whether skill modulates the negative effects of learned helplessness. There were three groups. With the first group, players were shown chess problems and had to quickly choose the best move from two alternatives; all problems had an objective solution (one move was better than the other) and feedback was veridical, with a wrong choice eliciting an unpleasant beep from the computer. With the second group, learned helplessness was induced by presenting chess problems that had no objective solutions (the two proposed moves yielded the same outcome); each player in the second group was randomly paired with a player in the first group, receiving the same feedback; this controlled for the frequency and order of positive and negative feedback. The third group acted as a control group: players did not receive any problems during the treatment phase. The sample was very strong, with the highest skill level including most players of the Swiss national team. In addition to a mood questionnaire, the effect of the manipulation was measured by two post-tests: the first consisted of problems requiring a rapid solution and was similar to the manipulation; the second, akin to De Groot's (1965) task, consisted of a single position where players had to find the best move while thinking aloud. The results showed that the learned-helplessness group was more depressed and performed worse with the short-problem posttest, but not with the long-problem posttest—thus the effect was proportional to the degree of similarity between manipulation and posttest. The mid-strength players were the most sensitive to the manipulation.

After graduation, my intention was, in order, to become a chess Grandmaster, to finish my PhD at around 35 (which was not uncommon at the time in Switzerland and in many European countries), and then either to enjoy a chess career or to practice as a clinical psychologist. A memorable discussion with my brother Tobie convinced me that I should give precedence to my PhD. Still, the main plan was to pursue a chess career later. At 27, I had barely started my PhD, had no scientific publications, and was more interested in chess than in psychology. Only a miracle could save my scientific career!

Collaborating with Herbert A. Simon

In part inspired by a colleague who had just obtained a PhD fellowship from the Swiss National Science Foundation, I decided to apply for a similar fellowship to work on my PhD in the United States. My intended mentors were Herbert A. Simon (Carnegie Mellon University in Pittsburgh, Pennsylvania) for six months and Dennis Holding (University of Louisville, Kentucky) for the same duration. I had read Holding's (1985) book on chess psychology, which I had bought for a small fortune, and was rather sympathetic to his critique of Simon's research.

The first weeks of my stay at Carnegie Mellon were a series of shocks. First a cultural shock, of course. Next, a linguistic shock, as my knowledge of (American) English was quite limited, which meant that I struggled a lot at the beginning, both within and outside Carnegie Mellon. Finally, an intellectual shock. I had moved from an average university in Switzerland to collaborate with a Nobel Prize winner in a world-class university. Although I had good knowledge of my specific research area (chess players' knowledge and memory), I had obvious weaknesses in several aspects of psychology and statistics, which meant that I had to spend time to correct them. Also, perhaps foolishly, I took several classes in artificial intelligence (AI), causality, and logic in the Department of Philosophy. And of course, I had to work on my PhD, which included both data collection and computer modeling. No surprise then that I was working and studying nearly all my waking hours. In doing so, I was following Simon's advice that one should work 80 hours a week!

During my stay at Carnegie Mellon, the focus was on understanding the mechanisms underpinning chess players' perception and memory and on collecting data supporting those mechanisms. The overall aim was to revise chunking theory (Simon & Chase, 1973) so that it could account for a number of recalcitrant empirical results, such as experts' rapid encoding into LTM. Incidentally, this is why Simon had accepted hosting me in spite of my meagre academic pedigree. He had anticipated that my chess expertise would be beneficial in addressing the criticisms leveled at chunking theory.

Empirically, I carried out three classes of experiments. The first showed that the exact location of patterns on the chess board was important and sensitive to mirror-image changes. This invalidated a hypothesis proposed by Holding that a chunk could encode the same constellation of pieces placed on different places on the board. Thus, chunks are encoded perceptually and not conceptually. The second line of research confirmed that experts' memory is remarkable indeed: masters were able to recall several boards presented in quick succession. The third set of experiments replicated and extended Chase and Simon's detailed analyses aiming at understanding the structure of chunks. A much larger sample and presentation by computer ensured more reliable results than in the original study, which had only three participants. The results in the main supported Chase and Simon's conclusions, but also showed that they underestimated the size of chunks. They proposed an upper boundary at around four to five pieces, while the new results identified chunks that were much larger, sometimes more than fifteen pieces.

The theoretical contribution was to show that some chunks evolve into larger structures, which we called templates. These structures allow rapid encoding into LTM. The new theory—template theory—was implemented in the CHREST computer model, which did a good job at accounting for the main empirical results (Gobet, 1993; Gobet & Simon, 2000).

I was sympathetic to computational modeling before going to Carnegie Mellon but lacked hands-on experience. The truth is that Simon completely converted me to information-processing psychology, modeling using architectures based on EPAM (Elementary Perceiver and Memorizer), and computational modeling in general. The secret to successful science was simple for Simon: to collect detailed data and to explain the mechanisms in play using mathematical or computational models. My visit to Carnegie Mellon, which was meant to last six months, finally lasted for six years. I never went to Louisville to visit Dennis Holding.

When working with Simon, I had relatively little interest in the question of talent and practice, although I discussed it briefly in a chapter for a German book

(Gobet, 1996). My view had not changed since my time as a semi-professional chess player: practice plays an essential role in developing expertise, but talent is present as well. Although I was according more importance to practice than talent, my view was not as extreme as that described in Ericsson, Krampe, and Tesch-Römer (1993). I remember a discussion of that paper in our small EPAM group (mostly Simon, Howard Richman, Jim Staszewski, and me), where we noted that measures of variability were rarely reported in that paper.

Collaborating with Adriaan De Groot

In 1991, while still living in Pittsburgh, I visited Adriaan de Groot in Groningen (The Netherlands), a visit that was followed by several more visits over the years to Schiermonikoog, the small Frisian island where he lived. The intention was to obtain data on chess players' eye-movements, which Simon had mentioned to me, to carry out simulations with CHREST. It took some negotiation skills to convince de Groot, as he had the intention to publish a book about these data; but finally, he gave his permission, with the condition that I would help him finish the book—which of course I accepted.

Simon had warned me that de Groot was a complicated man. As much as Simon was searching for parsimonious accounts of empirical data, so de Groot was emphasizing their complexity and their irreducibility to simple explanations. De Groot had a strong background in mathematics and philosophy of science and was very influential in teaching methodology for psychology and education departments in Dutch universities. His book on methodology (De Groot, 1969) is still very much worth reading. In it, he argues that interpretative approaches can be used together with more quantitative approaches.

The book that came out of our collaboration—*Perception and Memory in Chess* (De Groot, Gobet, & Jongman, 1996)—illustrates how quantitative and qualitative approaches can be happily married. After a philosophical introduction, the question of perception and memory in chess is approached using mathematical analysis based on information theory, experimental methods, eye movement recordings, computational modeling with CHREST, and detailed analyses of retrospective verbal protocols. Thus, my goal of modeling eye-movement data with CHREST was reached, but, perhaps more importantly, De Groot's "softer" approach led me to appreciate the richness of verbal protocols—sometimes compared with the eye-movement records. I remember some fascinating discussions we had on numerous topics, including philosophy, psychology, and, of course, chess. The last chapter of our book gives a flavor of our conversation, our common views, but also our disagreements.

Impetus and Logic of Research

The impetus behind my work has been made clear in the previous sections. Looking back at my career, I do not think that there is a strong internal logic in my research—some paths were planned but others were not anticipated at all. However, it is possible to identify two different overarching and in part contradictory forces.

On the one hand, there are clear constants: I have followed several research avenues in a very consistent, almost stubborn way. First, the CHREST architecture, which I developed for chess in my PhD thesis, led me to model phenomena in several other domains of expertise (e.g., Go, physics, and programming) and in domains beyond expertise, including language acquisition, concept formation, and implicit learning. Next, my interest in expertise has remained unabated since my undergraduate time, for more than three decades. Over the years, my many interests—both conceptual and methodological—allowed me to look at expertise from different vantage points and even different fields. This was best illustrated in my book *Understanding Expertise* (Gobet, 2016), which advocated for a multi-disciplinary study of expertise, including psychology, neuroscience, sociology, genetics, sociology, philosophy, and AI. Finally, I have kept a deep interest in modeling (using a variety of techniques) and in the methodology of modeling.

On the other hand, my research has been very pragmatic. I use the tools available to answer the questions I am interested in, which means that I have mastered, to various extents, a good number of methodologies. Importantly, I let my PhD students formulate their own questions and choose their own methods, with sometimes some nudging from me. To take three examples: Guillermo Campitelli used verbal protocols and brain imaging; Christopher Connolly, interviews; and Giovanni Sala, meta-analyses. In some cases, I was learning these methodologies at the same time as the students, often trailing behind them. Every so often, the questions reflected my move to new academic environments. For example, my interest in modeling the acquisition of syntactic structures was greatly helped by the fact that, when I moved to Nottingham from Pittsburgh, I stayed for several weeks in the house of Julian Pine, an expert in language acquisition. This led to a long-term collaboration and a flurry of publications (e.g., Freudenthal, Pine, Aguado-Orea, & Gobet, 2007).

My many interests allowed me to address similar questions in different fields of psychology. The best example is perhaps my research on the acquisition of syntactic categories. Curiously, just as my views were moving from nurture to nature in the field of expertise (see below), my research on the acquisition of syntactic categories with Julian Pine was criticizing nativist views and adducing evidence, both empirical and computational, for the essential role of the environment. Specifically, we found that typical errors occurring early in children's acquisition of language can be explained by a fairly simple learning mechanism that picks up regularities in the language they are exposed to, with the additional assumption that the likelihood of learning is higher at the beginning and particularly the end of utterances. Importantly, the modeling does not imply the absence of individual differences. Indeed, one of the parameters in the model could reflect differences in the rate at which one's first language is acquired. With our approach, which clearly refutes extreme nativist views such as Chomsky's, language can be considered as a kind of expertise (Gobet et al., 2001).

Evolution

With a few exceptions—e.g., expertise has remained a constant focus of attention over the years—my scientific interests have fluctuated during my career. My interest in the nature/nurture question was strong when I was a chess player, faded away when I was at Carnegie Mellon, and then became strong again, as a result of interactions with several PhD students who addressed the issue directly or indirectly. Intuition was a significant question as a chess player, was in the background at Carnegie Mellon and Nottingham, but has since been at the fore of my interests, not least because of its importance in philosophy (Gobet, 2017). I devoted considerable efforts to understand the mechanisms of high-level perception and memory at Carnegie Mellon and Nottingham, but less so since. Computer modeling, including methodological issues, has remained a strong interest since my Carnegie Mellon years.

Importantly, my view has changed on a key topic: the respective roles of talent and practice in the acquisition of expertise. As a PhD student and chess player, I saw practice as the key factor, although I recognized the role of talent. A favorite topic of discussion among chess players was how far a player with little talent could progress with the right type and amount of practice. My view was that such a player would be able to reach the level of a professional player (i.e., to become an International Master), but not the level of a Grandmaster. Some of my colleagues disagreed, arguing that the improvement would stop earlier. If anything, the balance tilted even more in the direction of practice during my stay at Carnegie Mellon, even though the question nature/nurture was not one of my main interests at the time. Traditionally, cognitive psychology has had a bias against talent and preferred studying practice and learning, although the role of talent was recognized at least by some researchers—for example, Simon and Chase (1973) explicitly mentioned talent in their famous paper about the acquisition of skill.

From Artificial to Human Intelligence

My conversion was rather slow and started when I was at the University of Nottingham. A first important moment was related to teaching. My class on Intelligent Systems, which introduced AI to psychologists, had a relatively low attendance and was facing axing by the Department, which is rather ironic, with hindsight, given the current popularity of AI. I was thus asked to revamp this module to make it more popular, which I did by adding considerable material (more than half the content of the module) about standard psychometric research on intelligence. In preparing the revised class, I learnt a lot about intelligence research and realized that some of my previous sources, which were rather critical with respect to psychometric approaches (e.g., Gould, 1981), were not telling the entire story. The two texts I used for the class (Mackintosh, 1998; Sternberg, 2000) were influential in my new way of thinking about intelligence and the nurture/nature debate.

Collaborating with PhD Students

The second reason for my conversion is that several PhD students forced me to review my position and move much more to the nature side of the nurture-nature debate. The first was Guillermo Campitelli, an Argentinean psychologist who was also a chess player and a chess coach, with a strong interest in deliberate practice. Before moving to Nottingham to work on his PhD, he collected data under my supervision on the role of deliberate practice in chess. His was one of the very first experiments to combine measures of deliberate practice with markers of talent (handedness and starting age). The results clearly showed that deliberate practice is not sufficient for reaching high levels of expertise (Gobet & Campitelli, 2007). Deliberate practice explained only about 24% of the variance in skill, and there was considerable variability, one player needing more than 23,000 hours to reach master level while another player needed only about 3,000 hours (an 8:1 ratio). Starting age correlated with skill, even after deliberate practice had been partialed out. Finally, handedness differentiated players and non-players, but there was no correlation between handedness and skill.

The second major blow against the kind of predominance of deliberate practice argued for by Ericsson et al. (1993) was provided by Merim Bilalić. Among other experiments he performed (e.g., Bilalić, McLeod, & Gobet 2007), he carried out a longitudinal study on children practicing chess, collecting a high density of data (IQ test, measures of deliberate practice, and measures of personality and motivation). Key findings were that (a) IQ plays a large role at the beginning of learning to play chess and (b) the influence of IQ remains at later stages, even after deliberate practice and motivation have been partialed out.

The third PhD student behind my conversion was Philippe Chassy. Contrary to Campitelli and Bilalić, Chassy believed that the main contributing cause to expertise was talent, not practice. Although his PhD thesis was focused on emotions, he also investigated possible mechanisms at the genetic and neural levels for the development of expertise and linked them to notion of chunking (e.g., Chassy & Gobet, 2010).

Two further PhD students were interested in intelligence, albeit in different ways. Toby Staff focused on the acquisition of expertise in sports. His key hypothesis was that children who successfully learn skills in sports are also more intelligent. He also collected data on deliberate practice, showing that athletes representing Great Britain track and field team at the 2012 Olympics acquired expertise in about seven years on average, significantly less than the ten years postulated by the deliberate practice framework (Staff, Gobet, & Parton, 2019).

Giovanni Sala addressed intelligence through the issue of far transfer. His first aim was to collect data showing that teaching chess leads to educational and cognitive benefits. I had always been skeptical about the possibility of far transfer. Earlier in my career, at the beginning of my PhD, I had worked for two years on a project on the effects of learning the programming language LOGO, which found no evidence of far transfer. Later, together with Guillermo Campitelli, I carried out a review of the literature on the effects of chess instruction and found that there was little evidence that it improved academic performance and cognition.

Ethical approval for Sala's experiments was taking ages, so I suggested he carry out a meta-analysis on the putative benefits of chess instruction. After chess, he also investigated music, working-memory training, video game training, exergames, and brain training (for reviews, see Sala et al., 2018; Sala & Gobet, 2019). The results were consistent across domains: once study design (mostly, active vs. passive control groups) and publication bias are taken into account, there is no evidence for far transfer. The findings also show that intelligence and working memory are not easily malleable, contrary the view commonly held in the field of cognitive training. The fact that chess players and musicians tend to have a higher level of intelligence than the population at large can be explained by the hypothesis that more intelligent individuals choose these activities. Indirectly, the findings provide support for the hypothesis of innate intelligence and talent. The findings are also consistent with CHREST—while learning is a powerful mechanism, it is domain specific, and its effects do not generalize to other domains.

Two further PhD students contributed to my change of heart with respect to the question of talent and practice, this time with qualitative research. Christopher Connolly was interested in transition expertise: how can some individuals make several successful transitions during their career? Using semi-structured questionnaires, he interviewed individuals who had transitioned from expert roles in their field to different roles in the same field (e.g., a solo violinist becoming head of a music department). The domains of expertise covered sports, music, and business. The interviews contained statements showing that the individuals having carried out successful transitions were very intelligent indeed, for example, being able to generalize their expert knowledge beyond the primary domains, through inductive and inferential mechanisms. In addition, several of them excelled in different domains (e.g., a sports person trained as a lawyer) and several of them displayed high social intelligence.

The other qualitative PhD student, Morgan Ereku, chose a rather exotic topic: dating skills and, more specifically, pick-up artists. The interviews further documented the importance of deliberate practice: pick-up artists practice their skills for hundreds, if not thousands of hours. They use training techniques that are in line with deliberate practice, including repeating the same actions again and again in order to get rid of weaknesses. But again, the interviews also revealed the obvious fact that talent (e.g., physical attractiveness) matters in dating.

Hindsight

During my PhD and postdoctoral years at Carnegie Mellon University, there was a palpable sense of excitement: computational modeling seemed to have made a quantum jump with Allen Newell's (1990) idea of Unified Theories of Cognition, realized in the SOAR cognitive architecture; cognitive psychology was uncovering striking new phenomena; the budding field of cognitive neuroscience showed great promises; and research into expertise was making great strides.

Thirty years after, I feel a sense of anticlimax. There has not been much quantifiable progress in psychology—definitively no overarching theoretical framework of the kind proposed by Newell that would put some order in the mass of data psychologists have been collecting. And of course, the replication crisis has led to a crisis of confidence: psychologists used to think that their great strength consisted of their skill in collecting reliable data, but that illusion has now dissipated with the realization that many key results in psychology are not replicable. Similarly, in part due to methodological issues, cognitive neuroscience has failed to live up to its promises.

Methods for Theory Building in Psychology

More specifically, I do not think that there has been much theoretical progress in expertise research. The key theoretical ideas have remained more or less the same, and most theories are seriously unspecified. For example, old and incorrect theories such as deliberate practice and Dreyfus and Dreyfus's five-stage theory still dominate the field (see Gobet, 2016, for a discussion of the limitations of these theories). With respect to the question of nature and nurture, the best that has been proposed is that there are interactions between innate talent and practice, but the proposed mechanisms (if any) lack detail. In that respect, the contrast with AI, which had been often derided by psychologists in the past, is striking. AI sets targets—which sometimes seemed preposterous at the time, such as beating the world champion in chess—and meets them. Psychology should perhaps set similar targets and reach them.

New methods are needed for making theory development in psychology more efficient. I have been obsessed with this aim for many years. A first idea stemmed from the realization that too much information is lost by averaging data, which is nearly always done in psychology. For example, people use different strategies and their knowledge differs in important ways, which is obvious when verbal protocols are collected to understand problem solving. What is the meaning of averages in such cases? Individual Data Modeling (Gobet & Ritter, 2000) aimed to fully use the information held in data to develop a detailed computational model simulating the behavior a single participant (or several participants analyzed individually) across a large number of experiments in a variety of domains (e.g., perception, learning, and decision making). Parameters, which include qualitative parameters such as strategies, can be averaged across models. A second idea was to import methods from software engineering (agile development methods) to optimize the development of computational models (Lane & Gobet, 2012). The key insight was to systematically and continuously evaluate the soundness of the implementation by running batteries of tests going from low-levels aspects of the code to the goodness of fit of the model with the data.

A third idea, which I have been ruminating on for more than twenty years, is to use AI to (semi-)automatically develop theories in psychology and other sciences. More specifically, the Genetically Evolving Models in Science (GEMS) project uses evolutionary computation to evolve theories that account for a set of experimental results (Lane, Sozou, Gobet, & Addis, 2016). While the method is limited to simple experiments at the moment, the idea is to improve it further to the point that it can be used to develop models of expertise and talent. This project, which is at the intersection between psychology, neuroscience, computer science and philosophy of science also means that I am finally back to my early interest in philosophy.

The Need for Multi-Disciplinary Research

I have been increasingly convinced that multi-disciplinary research is necessary for understanding expert behavior, as was clearly indicated in the title of my last book on expertise (Gobet, 2016). This is due to the complexity of the subject matter, the variety of explanatory mechanisms, and the interaction between these mechanisms. In addition, several phenomena have been studied in different disciplines with a lack of knowledge of what previous work had been done in other disciplines, which is not an efficient use of the available resources. A good example is expert intuition, which has been intensively but independently studied in psychology, philosophy, and AI.

Different disciplines address issues related to expertise from different angles and at different levels of analysis, which can be very productive. For example, psychology has developed powerful methods for collecting and analyzing data, philosophy provides effective tools for sharpening arguments, and AI have developed valuable techniques for carrying computer simulations. Unfortunately, multi-disciplinarity in expertise research is rare; it is also hard, not the least because it raises difficult problems of communication. In my case, although I had several brilliant collaborations, I also faced many failures.

Envoi

Trying to understand expertise has been, over the last 30 years, a fascinating voyage of discovery. It has led me to live in three different countries and work in six different universities; it has forced me to consider many new questions, to employ different levels of analysis, and to learn novel methodologies. In my quest, I have been navigating across disciplines, as documented above. Such a voyage had pleasant moments but also costs and difficult times. But by far its most rewarding aspect is that it gave me the opportunity to meet remarkable colleagues and students and to create strong and durable friendships.

Author Note

Funding from the European Research Council (ERC-ADG-835002—GEMS) is gratefully acknowledged. I'm thankful to Christopher Connolly, David Dai, Giovanni Sala, Robert Sternberg, and Andrew Waters for comments on an earlier version of this chapter.

References

Bilalić, M., McLeod, P., & Gobet, F. (2007). Does chess need intelligence? A study with young chess players. *Intelligence*, 35, 457–470.

Chassy, P., & Gobet, F. (2010). Speed of expertise acquisition depends upon inherited factors. *Talent Development and Excellence*, 2, 17–27.

De Groot, A. D. (1965). *Thought and choice in chess* (first Dutch edition in 1946). Mouton Publishers.

De Groot, A. D. (1969). *Methodology. Foundations of inference and research in the behavioral sciences.* Mouton.

De Groot, A. D., Gobet, F., & Jongman, R. W. (1996). *Perception and memory in chess: Heuristics of the professional eye.* Van Gorcum.

Ericsson, K. A., Krampe, R. T., & Tesch-Römer, C. (1993). The role of deliberate practice in the acquisition of expert performance. *Psychological Review*, 100, 363–406.

Freudenthal, D., Pine, J. M., Aguado-Orea, J., & Gobet, F. (2007). Modelling the developmental patterning of finiteness marking in English, Dutch, German and Spanish using MOSAIC. *Cognitive Science*, 31, 311–341.

Gobet, F. (1993). A computer model of chess memory. In W. Kintsch (Ed.), *Fifteenth Annual Meeting of the Cognitive Science Society* (pp. 463–468). Erlbaum.

Gobet, F. (1996). Expertise und Gedächtnis [Expertise and memory]. In H. Gruber, & A. Ziegler (Eds.), *Expertiseforschung. Theoretische und methodische grundlagen.* Westdeutscher Verlag.

Gobet, F. (2016). *Understanding expertise: A multi-disciplinary approach.* Palgrave.

Gobet, F. (2017). Three views on expertise: Philosophical implications for rationality, knowledge, intuition and education. *Journal of Philosophy of Education*, 51(3), 605–619. doi:10.1111/1467-9752.12253

Gobet, F. (2018). *The psychology of chess.* Routledge.

Gobet, F., & Campitelli, G. (2007). The role of domain-specific practice, handedness and starting age in chess. *Dev Psychol*, 43, 159–172.

Gobet, F., & Ritter, F. E. (2000). Individual data analysis and Unified Theories of Cognition: A methodological proposal. In Taatgen, N., & Aasman, J. (Eds.), *Proceedings of the Third International Conference on Cognitive Modelling* (pp. 150–157). Universal Press.

Gobet, F., & Simon, H. A. (1996). The roles of recognition processes and look-ahead search in time-constrained expert problem solving: Evidence from grandmaster level chess. *Psychological Science*, 7, 52–55.

Gobet, F., & Simon, H. A. (2000). Five seconds or sixty? Presentation time in expert memory. *Cognitive Science*, 24, 651–682.

Gobet, F., Lane, P. C. R., Croker, S., Cheng, P. C. H., Jones, G., Oliver, I., & Pine, J. M. (2001). Chunking mechanisms in human learning. *Trends in Cognitive Sciences*, 5, 236–243.

Gould, S. J. (1981). *The mismeasure of man*. Norton.

Holding, D. H. (1985). *The psychology of chess skill*. Erlbaum.

Lane, P. C. R., & Gobet, F. (2012). A theory-driven testing methodology for developing scientific software. *Journal of Experimental and Theoretical Artificial Intelligence*, 24(4), 421–456.

Lane, P. C. R., Sozou, P. D., Gobet, F., & Addis, M. (2016). Analysing psychological data by evolving computational models. In A. Wilhelm, & H. Kestler (Eds.), *Analysis of large and complex data* (pp. 587–597). Springer.

Mackintosh, N. J. (1998). *IQ and human intelligence*. Oxford: Oxford University Press.

Newell, A. (1990). *Unified theories of cognition*. Harvard University Press.

Sala, G., & Gobet, F. (2019). Cognitive training does not enhance general cognition. *Trends in Cognitive Sciences*, 23(1), 9–20.

Sala, G., Aksayli, N. D., Tatlidil, K. S., Tatsumi, T., Gondo, Y., & Gobet, F. (2018). Near and far transfer in cognitive training: A second-order meta-analysis. *Collabra: Psychology*.

Simon, H. A., & Chase, W. G. (1973). Skill in chess. *American Scientist*, 61, 393–403.

Simon, H. A., & Gilmartin, K. J. (1973). A simulation of memory for chess positions. *Cognitive Psychology*, 5, 29–46.

Staff, T., Gobet, F., & Parton, A. (2019). Investigating the period of practice needed to acquire expertise in Great Britain 2012 track and field Olympic athletes. *Journal of Expertise*, 2, 148–163.

Sternberg, R. J. (Ed.) (2000). *Handbook of intelligence*. Cambridge University Press.

7

OPTIMAL EXPRESSION OF HUMAN POTENTIAL AS THE CENTRAL GOAL OF HUMAN DEVELOPMENT

David Henry Feldman

I took an IQ test while in middle school in Ford City, Pennsylvania where I grew up. I didn't know anything about it before, but I was told that it would help determine if I was eligible for a special Saturday event, the Joe Berg Science Program. After taking the test I was curious about a vocabulary word I had no idea how to define and looked it up. The word was "apocrypha".

Apocrypha, as I learned, referred to a set of writings between the Old and the New Testaments. As a Jewish boy, I was schooled only in the Old Testament and so had not read nor heard about the apocrypha. It certainly made me angry to be expected to know a fairly obscure word from another religion, and if this were a straightforward story, say, like Bob Sternberg's (1988; also this volume), the experience might have sent me on a career bent on reforming intelligence.

For better or worse, while I was not happy about missing the vocabulary word (and was not selected for the science program), it didn't affect me in a major way (to be sure, though, I still remember it after more than 60 years). I wasn't all that eager to give up my Saturday mornings (TV, then sports) and I wasn't interested in science, having only had one class (biology) in my small, rural school. In fact, I wasn't much interested in school at all.

Although I did well, or at least got good grades, I was not a good student. I never studied more than the absolute minimum, didn't read on my own at all, and didn't give a thought to what I would do after high school other than go to college, which all middle-class Jewish boys were expected to do in those days.

Fortunately, I had a brother four years older who took me aside after my junior year and gave me a stern warning that if I didn't do something about it, I was likely to be stuck in our little Allegheny mountain mill town for the rest of my life. Jerry was in his third year at the University of Rochester as a math and physics student and had been a fiercely gifted kid, having read everything in every library within 20 or 30 miles of Ford City while a teenager (and was a real handful for his teachers in school).

Jerry gave me a stack of paperback books and told me to start reading them; I believe Dostoevsky's *The Brothers Karamazov* was one of them. He also arranged for me to work in a psychology lab at his university that summer. I spent six weeks cleaning out rat cages at the Medical School and eating lunch with the doctors in the hospital cafeteria. I also got a taste of what college life might be like.

A Personal Revelation or "Crystallizing Experience" in College

When it came time to apply to college, I applied to Rochester. Apparently with the help of some lobbying from Jerry at the admissions office, I was admitted for the Fall term of 1960. A profoundly important event occurred shortly thereafter, during my first class at Rochester. It was a large required Western Civilization course taught by Hayden White, a young charismatic instructor. I was stunned. I sat in the front row and thought I saw God. At that moment, I had what Howard Gardner and Joe Walters (Walters & Gardner, 1986) decades later called a "crystallizing experience" and knew I would be a university professor.

I nearly flunked out my first semester, including a D+ in Professor White's course. All those years when I had skated by were catching up to me. I had no study skills and had never been tested among a group of talented students, many of whom had wonderful preparation at the secondary school level. It was the juxtaposition of knowing that I was destined to be a professor against the reality of nearly flunking out that started a remarkable process of self-discovery that is at the center of this essay.

For some reason, I was undaunted by my failure to do well in college. I was upset about it, for sure, but it did not lead me to rethink my options. I simply assumed that I would somehow figure out what I needed to do to succeed in academia and set about doing it. You already know the end of the story, so you know that I achieved my goal, but the process was anything but straightforward.

Although my grades gradually improved, they were never stellar, certainly not competitive for a good graduate program. I majored in history more or less by default. I worshipped Professor White (who died recently, by the way) and the History Department at Rochester was supposed to be a good one (whatever that meant). I did try a math and a chemistry course my first year to see if I could do science, and the results were unequivocal: not a chance.

When I got to my senior year, I had to decide what to do after college. I knew what I wanted to do but wasn't sure that my record would get me there. As a senior, I did get an A in a seminar taught by Professor White and he agreed to write a letter for me, but my grades were a problem (my situation was similar to my friend and colleague Sid Strauss from Tel Aviv University who said, when asked how he did in school, that he was the valedictorian of the bottom third of his class).

Graduate School Years

So I decided to hedge my bets by applying for corporate jobs and was invited to Cincinnati to interview for an entry position at Procter and Gamble. The other hedge, which was more of a back door plan than a hedge, was to apply to MAT programs in teacher education with the idea that, once I was in a good graduate school by the back door, I would be able to talk my way into a good history graduate program. I turned down Procter and Gamble when I was admitted to Stanford's MAT program in Social Studies.

After teaching social studies to seniors at Castro Valley High School for a year, I had nothing in place for the next year. My plan to switch to the History graduate program was a nonstarter. I also tried Political Science there and at Berkeley with the same discouraging results. With the Vietnam War heating up, my new wife and I had only camp counselor jobs in Sturbridge, Massachusetts waiting for us and a loose plan to apply for social-work jobs (Diane was a psych major) in New York (she was from Long Island).

While at Camp Robinson Crusoe (I was default Boating Counselor), I worked with a young man, Hampton Howell III, who had just graduated from Harvard College. Hamp and I found we had a lot to talk about, and at some point, he mentioned a program at Harvard that he thought I might be interested in: Human Development. At Hamp's urging, I went into Cambridge for an interview with a Professor Jerome Kagan(!) in William James Hall.

I don't remember the interview much, but I think I recognized a graph sitting on the floor in Kagan's office and remarked that it looked like Fels Study data (which I had read about in a psychology course at Rochester). Whether this had anything to do with it or not of course I don't know, but on the day before registration at Harvard in September of 1965 I got a call saying I was admitted to the master's program in Human Development.

We cancelled our social-work applications and I enrolled at Harvard the next day. This was the beginning of my career as a developmental psychologist: courses with Robert White and Gerald Lesser, lectures by Erik Erikson, Larry Kohlberg, Talcott Parsons, B.F. Skinner, and Shep White, among many others, crystallized a new sense of direction for me and I applied for PhD programs in child and human development, as well as in developmental psychology for Fall, 1966.

I was fortunate(!) to be admitted to Stanford's Child Development PhD program to study with Pauline Sears in Education and with Robert Sears in Psychology. I am not proud of this exactly, but I completed the program and got my degree from Stanford in two and a half years, thus never getting the kind of world-class training that was available there.

I found that there was a powerful force in me driving me to get out into the world and do my work. Of course, I had only the vaguest idea then of what that meant. Whatever it was, it was not what either Pat or Bob Sears was doing. I had taken a summer course at Stanford with Peter Droz from Geneva and learned about Piaget. I was stunned at the power and grandeur of Piaget's theory and knew that cognitive development a la Piaget would be where I would start.

As it happened, there was no one at Stanford at the time who was doing cognitive-developmental research in the Genevan tradition, so I found myself on my own as far as a research topic and methodology were concerned. In the Fall of 1968, I did a study in the San Francisco schools on 270 Black, Asian, and White children based on Piaget's spatial-reasoning tasks, wrote it up, and asked Eliot Eisner (an art education professor who had just arrived at Stanford) to chair my dissertation committee—and handed him a complete draft.

Entering Academia

In January of 1969 I arrived in Minneapolis to take a position as Assistant Professor of Special Education and Educational Psychology, with a focus on intelligence, gifted education and creativity. Although not primarily what I did in my graduate studies at Harvard and Stanford, I had written papers and reviews of creativity versus intelligence research while still a graduate student.

After two years of productive work at Minnesota, I applied for an outrageously early promotion and was turned down, at which point I told my Chairman Maynard Reynolds that I quit. It was winter in 1971 and I had, again, no job and no prospects.

As it happened, my next-door neighbor in Minneapolis was Joe Glick, a wonderful cognitive developmentalist, who was just finishing his remarkable book with Michael Cole and others, *The Cultural Context of Thinking and Learning* (Cole, Gay, Glick, & Sharp, 1971). Joe and I walked to work together every day and when he heard that I quit my job, he suggested that I apply to Yale, where they were looking for developmental psychologists with an interest in education.

I spent the next three years at Yale in Psychology, with a joint appointment in Education, and became a developmental psychologist by doing it. Colleagues like Bill Kessen and Ed Zigler were models to emulate in terms of the methodological sophistication of their research programs more than the specific topics they were studying. It was also at Yale that I was able to work with very talented students at both the undergraduate and graduate levels, and to have a student (Sam Snyder) work directly with me on his dissertation.

The years in New Haven (1971–1974) were pivotal for me in terms of solidifying my major areas of interest. I turned 30 at Yale and, for the first time, felt that I knew the kind of work I needed to be doing. That work was a combination of a developmental approach to creativity and giftedness, on the one hand, and macro theory and research on the development of expertise, on the other, both within a cognitive development framework.

Unfortunately, the areas that I chose to study, perhaps even more the ways that I chose to study them, were not within the accepted parameters of the Yale

Psychology Department and I was let go after three years, never having done a single experiment while in New Haven. What I did do, with Sam Snyder, was lay the groundwork for what is now called Nonuniversal Theory (Feldman, 1980), some conceptual work on creativity, and also some early empirical work on transitions in cognitive development (Feldman, 1974; Snyder & Feldman, 1978).

Three Pivotal Events

By the time I left New Haven for Boston and Tufts, where I have now been for 45 years, I had a clearer and more coherent sense of the work I was put on this Earth to do. Soon after arriving at Tufts, three pivotal events occurred: I soon became friends and a close colleague of Howard Gardner; I began writing *Beyond Universals in Cognitive Development* (Feldman, 1980); and started the ten-year case study of child prodigies that resulted in *Nature's Gambit: Child Prodigies and the Development of Human Potential* (Feldman & Goldsmith, 1986).

Through Howard Gardner I began working on a Social Science Research Committee intended to rejuvenate the fields of giftedness and creativity research. After three tumultuous years I was named head of the Committee and was able, again with Howard Gardner's support, to refocus the Committee on extreme giftedness and creativity with a cognitive developmental and contextual approach. Along the way new members were brought in to work with the Committee, among them Mihaly Csikszentmihalyi. Csikszentmihalyi, in working with the committee, constructed a broad systems framework to guide the creativity research field that was the basis for a collaborative effort among Howard Gardner, Csikszentmihalyi and me and published as a book (Csikszentmihalyi, 1988; Feldman, Csikszentmihalyi, & Gardner, 1994).

The use of the term "human potential" in the title of the book on child prodigies *Nature's Gambit: Child Prodigies and the Development of Human Potential* and much of the content of that book were my first efforts to put into words what I now think of as a kind of secular faith based on the belief that it should be the right of every person to be able to express their full human potential; and it is the responsibility of society to make that goal a reality.

I had been introduced to the notion of human potential a few years earlier when working with Howard Gardner on the Van Leer Human Potential Project at Harvard, the work that led to Howard's famous book *Frames of Mind* (Gardner, 1983), among other important contributions.

I went on to publish a second edition of *Beyond Universals* (Feldman, 1994) and continued (with my students) to do research on the development of expertise in broad cultural domains like aesthetic reasoning, teaching, chess, and other fields. I also wrote several chapters and articles trying to articulate a developmental approach to giftedness and creativity based on the cognitive-developmental framework in both *Beyond Universals* and *Nature's Gambit* mentioned earlier.

Nature's Gambit and Evolutionary Basis of Human Abilities

Increasingly, I introduced an evolutionary component into my theoretical writing about giftedness and creativity. The earliest instance of this line of thought was in *Nature's Gambit*, where I proposed that nature had hedged its bets in human evolution by endowing each of us with both broad, general intellectual capabilities as well as capabilities to master specific cultural domains (*g* or IQ, on the one hand, and talent for chess or athletics or music, on the other).

A child prodigy, I claimed, was a child endowed with at least average and often well above-average IQ (as I had found in my subjects), as well as a powerful ability to master the challenges of a specific domain, such as music, chess, writing, or math. I extended this observation to the rest of us, arguing that we each have a combination of general intellectual ability that helps us be able to adapt to many environments as well as one or more specific abilities that can only be expressed in certain very specific contexts (following Bruner's article about early development in monkey species; Bruner, 1971).

Prodigies are a rare combination of general and specific abilities, but we all share some form of the same evolutionary gambit (thus the title *Nature's Gambit*). The more general ability I labeled an evolutionary *gift*, the more specific ones I labeled an evolutionary *talent* (see Feldman, 2016, 2019a, 2019b).

I am pleased to see that the scholarly field of gifted studies has moved toward a focus on the development of talent and human potential, using frameworks similar to the one I have been proposing. In particular, the "talent development" movement in the field seems highly concordant with my perspective, although the evolutionary component is not included in current examples (e.g., Subotnik, Olszewski-Kubilius, & Worrell, 2011, 2019). Others have taken an explicitly developmental perspective and proposed educational policies to develop full potential (e.g. Dai, 2010, 2019; Gagné & McPherson, 2016).

Since arriving at Tufts, I have been teaching courses on creativity and on cognitive development, both with a Piaget-inspired theoretical emphasis and both focused on large-scale change, major creative achievements on the one hand, major cognitive-development transformations on the other. As with the research, the two areas were approached mostly independently, albeit with a common developmental emphasis. One of the things I have been trying to do in the past decade or so is to bring the two areas together in both my teaching and my scholarship. And as it happens, one of them (my teaching) was to play a major role in my scholarship on the development of human potential.

What is a Good Theory of Cognitive Development?

Since about 2005 I have been using a set of criteria for evaluating macro-cognitive developmental theory and research that I borrowed and then elaborated from the late Bill Kessen at Yale. Bill had proposed that theories should be evaluated in terms of their claims and the empirical support for those claims about *Beginnings,*

Stages or States of Development, and *Transitions*. I added *Ends* as a fourth criterion and have asked my students to analyze various frameworks aiming to explain broad changes in cognitive development: Piaget, Vygotsky, NeoPiagetians, Dynamic Systems, Theory Theory, Modular Theories, Nonuniversal Theory, Multiple Intelligences and a few others. Students used the acronym BEST to help them remember the criteria.

After a few years using BEST in my courses, it occurred to me that my own theory, Nonuniversal Theory, was underspecified with respect to the BEST criteria. So much of my work on expertise had been focused on levels and transitions in nonuniversal domains that Beginnings and Ends for the theory as a whole were unmarked. I hadn't noticed the problem because there are numerous domains encompassed in the theory, each domain having a beginning or Novice level and an End or Master level. As long as I thought about each domain and not about the theory as a whole, things seemed to be ok.

Eventually, I tried to think about the beginning of the beginning in Nonuniversal Theory: what does the newborn bring with her or him into the world that is not already there in the Beginnings claims of other theories? Since the theory is mainly about the development of expertise and mastery in (primarily) nonuniversal domains, it seemed reasonable to assume that human beings are naturally predisposed to seek to develop their full potential in a field that is uniquely right for each person. And that they are able to know when their experience supports the effort at achieving full potential and when it does not. As a newborn, of course, babies are not aware that they should be archaeologists or weather forecasters or novelists, but they can be aware of conditions that foster growth in areas that help point them in the direction of a uniquely satisfying way to fulfill their potential. I imagined a kind of internal gyroscope that indicates whether things are going in the right direction from the very beginning.

One of the questions about the literally hundreds of culturally constructed domains encompassed within Nonuniversal Theory is why the domains were created in the first place (see Figure 7.1 for a universal-unique continuum). It made sense to me that domains exist at least in large part to provide the circumstances for developing unique potential. And when a domain that someone needs does not exist adequate to this purpose, it may be necessary to try to create one. As Olympic gymnast Olga Korbutt once remarked, "If gymnastic didn't exist, I would have invented it".

With a viable Beginnings claim for Nonuniversal Theory in hand, it was necessary to construct an End for the theory as well. For this purpose, I proposed the claim that each human being is capable of knowing the extent to which each

Universal___Pancultural___Cultural___Disciplined___Idiosyncratic___Unique

FIGURE 7.1 The universal to unique continuum

of us has been able to achieve our potential to contribute to a field or domain (or invent one in unusual cases) in our unique ways.

This End does imply that everyone has the potential to be a great master in a field, but that each of us will be able to judge if we were able to make full use of the unique qualities and abilities that make us who we are. That judgment might come early in life (e.g., for an Olympic gymnast like Olga Korbutt) or late (for a philosopher or poet). Ideally, the judgment each of us makes is that we made the best use of our gifts and talents possible. Sometimes that did not yield eminence or honors or other forms of recognition that we might have hoped we would receive, but it would recognize that, given the life we led and the opportunities that we did or did not receive, we did the best that we could have done.

Having added a Beginning and End to the theory as a whole gave it an integrity and coherence that was not evident before. The theory had been about the development of expertise in the numerous culturally available domains available at any period of time. What the theory did not deal with was *why* someone would want to master one or another of these domains. With the Beginning claim in place, it is a natural thing for human beings to seek, engage in, and achieve fulfillment of their unique potential through the development of expertise.

In thinking about Nonuniversal Theory as a motivational as well as a cognitive developmental framework, I wondered if there were motivational theories that were similar and remembered that I had read Abraham Maslow's work as an undergraduate (Maslow, 1943). I reviewed Maslow's theory and it is in some ways very close to the Nonuniversal Theory's claim of Beginnings, placing self-fulfillment as the highest and most distinctly human motive. What was different, though, was Nonuniversal Theory's assumption that the drive for self-fulfillment (expression of unique human potential in my framework) was at the peak of a pyramid of other motives, implying that all of the other motives had to be satisfied before one could turn to self-fulfillment. Nonuniversal Theory assumes that the drive for self-fulfillment guides development from the outset, giving direction when possible to all of the other motives. It serves an organizational, self-defining, and evaluative function as well as a drive for self-fulfillment.

It was at this point that I began to realize that I had not only been constructing a theoretical framework and empirical research program about the development of expertise, a framework that celebrates the great diversity of possible domains within which expertise can be developed, but a kind of spiritual embrace of an ideal. The ideal is that we should live in a world where every person should have the opportunity to develop and fulfill the unique potential to contribute to society found in each of us. It stresses the notion that self-realization is an ideal and a right. Like Piaget's ideal that everyone has a naturally curious mind that seeks to understand its world, and Vygotsky's ideal that everyone has a natural desire to form relationships with people close to her or him and become part of a culture, Nonuniversal Theory's ideal is that everyone has a natural desire to develop their unique potential in a way that is satisfying and fulfilling.

Reflection and Hindsight

I also realized that the theory is as personal for me as it is scholarly. As should have been clear from the early parts of this chapter, it was not obvious for many years what my path would be and what my work was really about. The probabilities of my being able to fulfill what I believe to be my unique potential to contribute to the study of development were not large. I was an indifferent student, was never encouraged to seek graduate education, had no clear idea of what field I wanted to study, was turned down several times to study developmental psychology and the fields I tried to pursue before I found human development. And although I have had a successful career in academia, the parts of my work that are most important to me are still largely ignored in the field, or worse (I'm sure I share this lament with many others).

What has sustained me through the mostly discouraging experiences and affirmed me in the fewer encouraging ones is a faith that I had and have important work to do. If I have an unusual gift it is that my belief in the importance of the work I would do was never shaken. I have been determined to do the work I believed was my best work and did it mostly independent of the usual forms of recognition and reward in my field. Sometimes I have been rewarded, more often not.

I am grateful for the opportunity to do my work and do it the way that I needed to, and that work gave me the chance to fulfill what to me feels like my unique potential. Whatever its fate in the academic marketplace, I know that I have done the very best that I could and am satisfied that I was able to say who I am through my discipline, my domain, and my writing. I believe that I have achieved the End that I propose for Nonuniversal Theory, not completely because I believe I still have work to do, but because I have had the all too unusual privilege of doing exactly what I needed to do in this world and do it my way. Me and Frank Sinatra.

References

Bruner, J. S. (1971). The nature and uses of immaturity. *American Psychologist*, 27, 1–22.
Cole, M., Gay, J., Glick, J. A., & Sharp, D. (1971). *The cultural context of learning and thinking*. Basic Books.
Csikszentmihalyi, M. (1988). Society, culture, and person: A systems view of creativity. In R. J. Sternberg (Ed.), *The nature of creativity* (pp. 325–339). Cambridge University Press.
Dai, D. Y. (2010). *The nature and nurture of giftedness*. Teachers College Press.
Dai, D. Y. (2019). New directions in talent development research: A developmental systems perspective. *New Directions for Child and Adolescent Development*, 168, 177–197.
Feldman, D. H. (1974). Universal to unique: A developmental view of creativity and education. In S. Rosner, & L. Abt (Eds.), *Essays in creativity* (pp. 45–85). North River Press.
Feldman, D. H. (1980). *Beyond universals in cognitive development*. Ablex.
Feldman, D. H. (1994). *Beyond universals in cognitive development* (2nd ed.). Ablex.

Feldman, D. H. (2016). Two roads diverged in the musical wood: A co-incidence approach to the lives of Nyiregyhazi and Menuhin. In G. McPherson (Ed.), *Musical prodigies: Interpretations from psychology, education, musicology, and ethnomusicology* (pp. 115–133). Oxford University Press.

Feldman, D. H. (2019a in press). Commentary on the special issue: Human potential for the 21st century. *Journal for the Education of the Gifted.*

Feldman, D. H. (2019b, October). *Confessions of a lifelong (but not lifespan) developmentalist.* Presidential Address, Society for the Study of Human Development, Portland, Oregon.

Feldman, D. H., & Goldsmith, L. T. (1986). *Nature's gambit: Child prodigies and the development of human potential.* Basic Books.

Feldman, D. H., Csikszentmihalyi, M., & Gardner, H. (Eds.) (1994). *Changing the world: A framework for the study of creativity.* Praeger.

Gagné, F., & McPherson, G. (2016). Analyzing musical prodigiousness using Gagne's integrative model of talent development. In G. Mcpherson (Ed.), *Musical prodigies: Interpretations from psychology, education, musicology, and ethnomusicology* (pp. 3–114). Oxford University Press.

Gardner, H. (1983). *Frames of mind.* Basic Books.

Maslow, A. H. (1943). A theory of human motivation. *Psychological Review,* 50, 370–396.

Snyder, S. S., & Feldman, D. H. (1978). Internal and external influences on cognitive developmental change. *Child Development,* 48, 937–943.

Sternberg, R. J. (1988). *The triarchic mind: A theory of human intelligence.* Penguin Books.

Subotnik, R. F., Olszewski-Kubilius, P., & Worrell, F. C. (2011). Rethinking giftedness and gifted education: A proposed direction forward based on psychological science. *Psychological Science in the Public Interest,* 12, 1–54.

Subotnik, R. F., Olszewski-Kubilius, P., & Worrell, F.C. (Eds.) (2019). *The psychology of high performance: Developing human potential into domain-specific talent.* American Psychological Association.

Walters, J., & Gardner, H. (1986). The crystallizing experience: Discovering an intellectual gift. In R. J. Sternberg, & J. E. Davidson, (Eds.), *Conceptions of giftedness* (pp. 306–331). Cambridge University Press.

8

CAPITALIZING ON CHANCE OPPORTUNITIES

Rena F. Subotnik

Four interconnected themes have influenced my intellectual development and productivity. Happily, the factors I describe make my story one that can be replicated by others. Generous guiding lights, most particularly Abraham Tannenbaum and Robert Sternberg, helped shape my thinking about giftedness and talent development, and opened doors of career opportunity I didn't even know existed. These experiences promoted my interest in high performance in domains, with a focus on psychosocial skills. Finally, thanks to participation in writing teams, I've been able to communicate ideas that have helped me to feel as if I've led a productive career.

Guiding Lights

I graduated from City College of New York in the 1960s with a minor in education, typical for my cohort of first-generation women. My intentions were to apply for a Master's degree in teaching. On registration day at Teachers College, Columbia University, I stepped into the first open door I encountered, the office for special education, seeking directions on where I needed to go. At the desk closest to the door, Dr. Abraham Tannenbaum greeted me warmly and successfully distracted me from my path out the door by asking about my own education up until that point. I was a product of New York City's long-standing gifted-education programs, including Hunter College Elementary School, Special Progress in junior high school (7–9th grade in two years), and the Bronx High School of Science. His response was, "I want you in my gifted education Master's program".

Professor Tannenbaum was in the midst of finalizing his psychological model on transforming potential into transformative creativity (Tannenbaum, 1983) and shared his progress with the class. His class presentations were electrifying and the discussions rich, so much so that I still treasure the notebook I kept for each course. In light of our studies of gifted education's history, his arguments for a new look at the field made perfect sense. Terman's *Genetic Study of Genius* at mid-life (Terman & Oden, 1959) highlighted the outcomes of his high-IQ study participants, differentiating those who were satisfied and productive from those who were not. Analyzing those outcomes led Tannenbaum and my classmates to view childhood giftedness based on IQ as an insufficient guarantee of generativity in adulthood. Tannenbaum's model acknowledged the role of general ability, although how high the needed IQ cutoff could be would vary by domain. The rest of his formula for transforming ability into high-level accomplishment included special domain abilities, non-intellective factors, environmental supports, and chance. On one of his unforgettable riffs, he commented that a high IQ could lead to good cocktail conversation, but contribution to human welfare or beauty required narrowed focus, creativity, and personal skills. This fed my lifelong fascination with domain talents and opened me up to deep admiration of the Bloom and his colleagues' *Developing Talent in Young People* (Bloom, 1985) when it came out, and later, Piirto's wonderful *Understanding Those Who Create* (Piirto, 1992). Finally, Professor Tannenbaum was the first to introduce me to the role of chance factors in fulfillment of potential. He was always careful to distinguish between "dumb luck" and capitalizing on chance opportunities to meet a mentor, demonstrate one's talent, or face a challenge constructively. His classes were laced with stories about well-known individuals like Leonard Bernstein, who capitalized on an opening to conduct the New York Philharmonic when a visiting conductor fell ill.

After Teachers College, I pursued life as a gifted education teacher in Seattle Public Schools, eventually choosing to seek a PhD at the University of Washington. With the PhD in hand, I achieved my dream of being hired at Hunter College, an institution with a Masters in gifted education and a PreK-12 laboratory school for 1,200 gifted students. Soon after I got there, however, I encountered understandable but personally difficult tension within my department over support for gifted education and the laboratory school. The selective school and the major were considered elitist under the auspices of a higher education institution that in recent years was committed to open admissions and inclusion.

The president of Hunter College when I arrived was Donna Shalala. She invited me to her office to offer some funding to conduct a study of alumni of Hunter College Elementary School. Her motivation was to find out, for potential fundraising purposes, where they were today and what they were doing. She wisely viewed this as an opportunity for me to get some publications and be successful at the college. A couple of years later, my first book came out, reporting on this retrospective study of 10 years of Hunter College Elementary School graduates at mid-life (Subotnik et al., 1993). My grad students and I were able to find over 300 alumni who filled out a slightly revised version of Terman's mid-life questionnaire. Like Terman, we discovered that, in spite of the fantastic selectivity of the population (97–99th percentile on individual IQ test), the accomplishments of the participants were not especially notable, much to the disappointment of the development department. I came to the conclusion that identifying only for very high IQ, even with a special education, did not differentiate this population from their similarly high to middle SES neighbors who attended New York City private schools. With my hat in the ring for promotion and tenure, a not very supportive department chair sent my book to Robert Sternberg, someone whom she and I considered a rock star. I think my department chair was disappointed with his reaction, which was very positive and began a long connection between us. Sternberg's Triarchic Theory (Sternberg, 1985), particularly its focus on creativity and practical intelligence, was central to my evolving views.

Around the same time as the promotion ordeal, I was contacted by Prof. Franz Monks in Nijmegen to make a contact for him at the Juilliard School for one of his clients. During my appointment with the Juilliard admissions director, and after providing her with Franz' questions and contact information, I discovered, serendipitously, that she had an interest in Hunter College Elementary school for her daughter. This connection led to long conversations about identifying and developing academic and musical talent. Through her intervention, I was given the green light to collect data on these topics at the Juilliard Pre-College, the Saturday institution that catered to prodigious musical talent too young for the conservatory (and no, her daughter didn't end up applying to Hunter College Elementary School).

After I began publishing and presenting on this topic, Robert Sternberg proposed including music talent development as a component of Yale's contribution to the National Research Center on the Gifted and Talented. I was to be the lead on this project in partnership with Linda Jarvin, one of his colleagues. Sternberg's model of developing expertise, from abilities to competencies, and competencies to expertise (Sternberg, 1998), was the framework upon which Linda and I organized our data collection. We wanted to show how conservatory instruction changed over time from admission to post graduation. As a result of working with this elite population, we added another stage to the expertise model and called it SP/A, or Scholarly Productivity/Artistry, to incorporate the work of composers (Scholarly Productivity) as well as performers (Artistry). Sternberg invited Linda and me to write up this work in *Conceptions of Giftedness*, which brought notice from scholars around the world who were not familiar with this work (Subotnik & Jarvin, 2005). Sternberg also suggested that we team up with Franz Monks and Kurt Heller to put out a new edition of the *International Handbook on Giftedness and Talent* (Heller et al., 2000). Although the work of recruiting contributors and editing was demanding, especially with so many authors whose first language wasn't English, it also exposed me to some outstanding international scholarship that led to friendships and collaborations over the years. As you can see, my guiding lights led me to opportunity. One opportunity led to another, sometimes unexpectedly and sometimes intentionally. I never knew at the time where a next step would take me; the important thing was to take the step and throw myself completely into making it a successful one.

Chance Opportunities

In my view, so much of what makes it easier and more plausible for people to capitalize on chance occurrence is access to insider knowledge, a version of what Sternberg and Wagner (1986) call practical intelligence. Many people seem to have this intelligence, yet many novice performers and creative producers assume that talent wins out over all other factors in career trajectories. Over time, we all become more cynical in response to setbacks, opening us up to increased recognition of the role played by insider knowledge or "connections". If we want a more equitable landscape for talent development, this insider knowledge or practical intelligence can be made more widely accessible and taught explicitly.

I experienced the role of chance and insider knowledge on my first day as a fully certified teacher in the Seattle Public Schools. One of the experienced staff generously welcomed me and shared some wisdom. "You might think that the principal is the most influential person to please around here, but you need to get the school secretary and custodian on your side, and your life here will be much more pleasant". Although I considered myself generally respectful of others, this information was invaluable because, as a novice, I didn't recognize how much I needed these two individuals for supplies, communications, and other important tasks inside and outside of the classroom.

In 2009, after becoming a full professor at Hunter College, an American Association for the Advancement of Science (AAAS Congressional Fellow), and a senior staff member at the American Psychological Association (APA), I considered whether I had achieved what I'd set out to do and could start winding down my professional life. After some follow-up conversations with my husband and a financial advisor, I received an email from the editor of *Psychological Science in the Public Interest* (PSPI), a highly impactful journal published by the Association for Psychological Science. The experience reminded me of a TV program that was popular when I was a child called *The Millionaire*. The plot each week involved a functionary representing a wealthy individual who, out of the blue, delivered a check for $1M to a family. The invitation to write about giftedness for PSPI was an equivalent experience: Here was another chance to take the next step in my own growth trajectory. Maybe it was easier to take the plunge this time, given what had come before, but I made another decision that's been a source of joy and pleasure—accepting this opportunity and forming a team with two dear colleagues.

I was offered an entire issue to address in depth my ideas about the topic of giftedness, requiring only that I assemble of a team of outstanding scholars to formulate the work with me. I couldn't think of more perfect scholars to invite than Paula Olszewski-Kubilius and Frank Worrell. The opportunity also came with support in the form of $5K, which was used to fund writing and research meetings of the team, as we were so widely dispersed geographically (Paula Olszewski-Kubilius at Northwestern and Frank Worrell at Berkeley). To top it off, the offer came with an opportunity to publish a short version of the article in *Scientific American*, should the magazine choose to take it on. To meet our obligations to PSPI and our own objectives, we reviewed the literature on eminence, talent development, high performance, creativity, and giftedness and in a number of domains. We took a developmental, domain-specific, and psychosocial perspective in building a model (which we ended up calling the Megamodel to tip our hats to all the models and theories we drew from). Not only did *Scientific American* publish a brief version of the article (Subotnik et al., 2012), but it also republished the piece two more times over the years (Subotnik et al., 2015, 2019a). Sometimes, Paula, Frank, and I would want to pinch ourselves with this good luck. We tried to figure out who might have recommended us for this great honor. Looking at the list of associated editors, it's possible that Sternberg may have been the source, although we have never confirmed that supposition to this day.

Taking the unexpected opportunity offered by PSPI changed the direction of my life. Since the publication of *Rethinking Giftedness and Gifted Education* (Subotnik et al., 2011) in *Psychological Science in the Public Interest,* we've accrued international attention to what many people told us was a comprehensive analysis of the literature on eminence, high ability, giftedness, talent, and creativity in domains.

Focusing on Domains, Psychosocial Development, and Insider Knowledge

As far back as my years as a doctoral student at the University of Washington, I hoped to explore domain talent, particularly in math and science, and chose my mentor, Betty Kersh, head of mathematics education, accordingly. After much back and forth, we determined that, for my dissertation, the best combination of my concerns would be to study creative problem formulation in elite science talent. The population I would work with was Westinghouse (subsequently Intel, and now Regeneron) Science Talent Search winners; that is, winners of the most prestigious award for science research earned by U.S. adolescents. Focusing on the creative process they used in selecting a research question for the paper they submitted to the competition, the study was designed to be mixed method—quantitative cross-sectional analysis supported by interviews. By chance, in the year of my study's winners, 1983, my alma mater, Bronx Science, had a record 21 semifinalists. When I contacted the principal, asking if I might interview the 21, he was very accommodating. Having access to these 21 made contacting the others far easier and expeditious. My growing insider knowledge helped me to understand the power of word of mouth in collecting study subjects.

Although I was interested in the initial outcomes for completing my dissertation, my plan was to conduct a longitudinal follow up of the participants to see if those who generated their own problem to solve were more likely to remain in the science pipeline. The follow up data collections showed me that several of my earlier assumptions were wrong. For one thing, those who were given a research problem to pursue as part of an apprentice-type project conducted by a university or hospital lab were more likely to remain in science and to be successful ten years later than those who had generated their own question for the Talent Search. The latter group, while showing the traditional signs of early creativity, missed out on the mentoring and insider knowledge they would have gotten had they been in an apprenticed lab situation. Those who worked diligently in labs learned the values of the environment and were introduced to the culture and gatekeepers in the field, including professors at universities where they might pursue their studies and have special attention (Subotnik et al., 1993).

Another very surprising outcome from the longitudinal study was highlighted when comparing equally talented music students with Westinghouse winners. Given the prestige of the award, Westinghouse winners had a better shot at admission to the college of their dreams. Many chose Harvard. Four years later, out of the Westinghouse finalists who attended Harvard, only one was still a science major. Those who enrolled at high quality institutions with a focus on undergraduate education and building on students' already acquired skills were more likely to remain science majors.

Music students, in contrast, picked their higher education institution based on the teacher they wanted to work with. Each summer before conservatory, they would take master classes with various teachers, check them out, and hope to be noticed. Admission to conservatory is based not only on audition, but also the willingness of a teacher to take on a student. Once the match is made, the idea is to assess the abilities of the student and move on from their current development. Aiming for Harvard, where graduate students were a priority in science labs, showed that gifted adolescents in science and their families ignored insider knowledge about the most promising path to pursuing science careers.

Working in the longitudinal and retrospective arena of Hunter Elementary School and the Westinghouse winners also reinforced for me the importance of taking a developmental view of giftedness. What may seem like the strengths and abilities needed at one stage of life will often take a back seat to other skills and abilities that are needed later. This view of giftedness was made more evident to me in *Developing Talent in Young People* (Bloom, 1985), where Bloom and his team differentiated the teachers/mentors and opportunities that his study population of elite thinkers and performers required at different stages of their lives.

The conservatory and Westinghouse experiences reverberated often during my career. I understood deeply that talent has to be developed actively and rigorously at each stage, and that psychosocial skills and insider knowledge are malleable to instruction and increasingly important to successful careers. At the conservatory, even mundane guidance about how to dress for certain occasions and how to introduce a piece to an audience is not left to chance. Of course, individuals will put their personal stamp on some of these activities but knowing what has worked in the past is advantageous even in rebelling against tradition.

Writing Partnerships

When I was a child, I used to spend hours writing and illustrating little books of stories I made up or dreamt about. Once I encountered formal writing instruction, however, I received a lot of criticism. I don't know whether I froze up in response because I was used to having things come easily, or whether the criticism came with little constructive guidance. In either case, the fear of expressing myself in writing continued through graduate education. I must have been good enough at tests, class participation, and asking research questions to have been passed along, but my writing continued to be judged as mediocre. It wasn't until my dissertation that I received successful intervention. A kind member of my committee provided "tracked changes" on my manuscript and explained his decisions in each case. With much effort, I caught on and approached writing with less trepidation. Unfortunately, enough performance fear remained that I continued to miss out on several opportunities due to procrastination. I found that the best way to overcome my fears was to work with others. Optimally, we would talk through ideas (something I was never short of!) and then break the work into pieces, assign first drafts of small chunks to each participant and then swap. This was best done in person. Using this process, I got through my first book and a couple of early peer-reviewed articles.

My productivity increased dramatically when I worked collaboratively. Since the mid-1980s, I have been fortunate to have joined forces with creative, brilliant, dependable, and enjoyable scholars, including Karen Arnold, Linda Jarvin, and most recently, Paula Olszewski-Kubilius and Frank Worrell. One lesson for me in the often-lonely world of scholarship is that, with some caveats, good collaborators are all around us.

In the early 1990s, I organized several scholars exploring longitudinal research as a means to understand giftedness as it evolved from childhood or adolescence into adulthood. We were interested in prediction and the impact of opportunity and personal characteristics on outcomes later in life. Among those most active in this group was Karen Arnold, who followed Illinois high school valedictorians for over a decade (Arnold, 1995). My work studying Westinghouse Science Talent Search winners was a parallel effort in that we started with 1983 high school seniors. We enjoyed our conversations and began to generate a number of projects, including editing a collection of longitudinal work in gifted education for an edited volume called *Beyond Terman: Contemporary Longitudinal Studies of Giftedness and Talent* (Subotnik & Arnold, 1994). The 1990s was also a period when concerns about the development of gifted women were growing. We conducted interviews with our respective longitudinal participants and as well as cross sectional quantitative analyses of males and females at each stage of data collection resulting in a collection called *Remarkable Women* (Arnold et al., 1996).

Karen lived in Boston, so getting together in person was an effort. We made it work every two or three months by picking someplace we both wanted to go and spent two or three days of conceptualizing, writing, and editing for several hours in the morning followed by hiking, walking, or touring in the afternoon. It was thoroughly enjoyable and we both went home from those meetings with enough material to build on without facing writer's block.

Karen was approaching tenure and promotion and needed to generate more solo publications. In the meantime, I was busy writing up my data from the Juilliard Pre-College study, and Sternberg's invitation to team up with Linda Jarvin came at the right moment. This work became a passion project for both Linda and me. We expanded the work I had started with the Juilliard Pre-College program to a more systematic study of psychosocial skills development at three prestigious classical music conservatories in the U.S.—Juilliard, The Curtis Institute, and the New England Conservatory of Music. This work would have been too big for one person to manage, but with Linda, Bob, and a doctoral student at Yale, Eric Moga, we were able to conduct, transcribe, and analyze over 80 interviews with students and faculty in strings, voice, and wind instrument departments. We published several papers on this (Subotnik et al., 2003; Jarvin & Subotnik, 2010). Linda and I developed a talent development model (Scholarly Productivity/Artistry or SP/A) that has influenced others in the performance area and set the stage for another experience of enjoyable partnership. Linda, who is now president of the Paris School of the Arts, and I are recently reunited in a new endeavor called TAD (see below).

The third and most long-lasting writing partnership I've experienced has been with Paula Olszewski-Kubilius and Frank Worrell. The team got together in response to the invitation from *Psychological Science in the Public Interest* that I described above. We have similar and complementary interests in talent development in the arts and academics, our approach to the writing process, our views of gifted education, and what we want to contribute to the field. We are friends, supporters, cheerleaders, and nudges to one other. We add a day or two together at professional functions as well as make special trips across country to get some collaborative writing done. Our work has evolved from model building (the Megamodel) to exploring and extending different components of our model that are of particular interest, including psychosocial skills and insider knowledge. We are always on the lookout for opportunities to do exciting new and not so new projects together, whether writing or presenting. My productivity has increased geometrically since we started our collaboration and I anticipate the generativity will continue until and even beyond my retirement from APA.

This writing trio continues to publish and has recently spun off in two different configurations. One is as a component of a high-performance psychology group made up of scholars from sports, arts, developmental, counseling, school, and educational psychology. The group has generated four projects and completed two thus far. One is an article that provides a more balanced view of the benefits of competition for young people than is traditionally offered in the education literature. It was published in the *Review of General Psychology* (Worrell et al., 2016). A second is an edited book on the psychology of high performance published by APA (Subotnik et al., 2019). The third is a study on gatekeepers in different domains and is in revision for the *Review of General Psychology*. Finally, a longer-term project explores benchmarks of psychosocial skills across domains. The first article exploring the basics of the project was published in *New Directions in Child and Adolescent Psychology* (Olszewski-Kubilius et al., 2019).

Yet another outgrowth of this trio is international in nature. We have joined a group called TAD, sponsored by the Karg Foundation in Germany and led by Prof. Franzis Preckel from the University of Trier. TAD includes scholars from Europe (including Linda Jarvin) and the US interested in talent development. The work is a spinoff of our Megamodel that focuses on the individual contributions to talent development more than environmental factors, with the idea of developing a research agenda measuring personal factors in three domains: mathematics, visual arts, and music.

Summary of Reflections on Human (including My Own) Potential

It is of great satisfaction to me that the preponderance of work in the high potential research and practice arenas is focused on domains of talent and taking a developmental perspective that privileges human agency equally, if not over genetic or inherited dispositions. I am proud that my colleagues and I have contributed to these changes through our publications and presentations. In the coming years, I hope that we will also build a strong foundation for the contributions of psychosocial skills and insider knowledge to talent trajectories. Based on this chapter contribution, I offer the following considerations (and insider knowledge) for working in the arena of human potential.

- Research or program inputs and outcomes need to be sensitive to domains and development. For example, talent domains such as mathematics, chess, gymnastics, and string performance can be identified earlier than other domains. That means, for these domains, identification can take place earlier than in others such as social sciences. Further, an 11-year old string player who has been working intensely for seven years at his or her instrument, needs different instruction and support than an 11-year old just starting to play a clarinet (because that instrument requires more fully developed lung capacity to begin than does violin). An 11-year old student gifted in mathematics may require more acceleration than an 11-year old history buff, whose exposure to, and experience with, serious history study may be just launching.

- Sort out what is neglected yet important in talent development. Currently, psychosocial skills and insider knowledge are neglected contributions to talent development in academic domains. These skills and information are typically inculcated by coaches or agents in the performance world. Who could play this role for academically talented students? More widespread access to these important factors could help equalize outcomes between more advantaged and disadvantaged talented youth. Certainly, those who participate in mentorship, internship, or apprenticeship programs may get this exposure (although even then the mentors need to be apprised of the fact that this is part of their responsibility). It also becomes important for talent developers, such as educators and parents, to make inroads into outside of school expertise that may be very useful on this front.
- Another area highlighted in talent development models including the Megamodel, is identifying the specific abilities that need to be cultivated early in the domain talent trajectories, and that when exhibited make a person a good "investment" in intensive instruction, coaching, mentoring, and other support. Some work has been conducted in mathematics and in dance, but everything else is ripe for refinement.
- Creative productivity happens in teams as well as a result of solo effort. That is reflected as well in research conducted in the field. For me, the turning point was finding great writing and research partners. The team literature promotes creating a team of experts to create an expert team (Salas et al., 2008). That means linking with those from whom you learn, people who are peers and who complement your own skills and knowledge. It's not, however, useful to try to force-fit relationships with those whom you respect but strongly disagree with. Those deep disagreements can be left to critics and peer reviewers.

I haven't always taken the time to recognize those who helped me along the way, but this chapter provides me with the opportunity to thank a few people, particularly Robert Sternberg, for his influence on my opportunities and ideas. We never know where chance will take us, but from my experience, there are no regrets, and only deep gratitude for the joyful career I've had thus far. It is incumbent upon us as senior scholars, like those generous souls I have mentioned here, to make chance opportunities available to up and coming professionals in our midst.

References

Arnold, K. D. (1995). *Lives of promise: What becomes of high school valedictorians*. Jossey-Bass.
Arnold, K. D., Noble, K. S., & Subotnik, R. F. (Eds.) (1996). *Remarkable women: Perspectives on female talent development*. Hampton Press.
Bloom, B. J. (Ed.) (1985). *Developing talent in young people*. Ballantine Books.

Heller, K. S., Mönks, F. J., Subotnik, R. F., & Sternberg, R. J. (Eds.) (2000). *International handbook of giftedness and talent* (2nd ed.). Pergamon.

Jarvin, L., & Subotnik, R. F. (2010). Wisdom from conservatory faculty: Insights on success in music performance. *Roeper Review, 32*, 78–87.

Olszewski-Kubilius, P., Subotnik, R. F., Davis, L. C., & Worrell, F. C. (2019). Benchmarking psychosocial skills important for talent development. In Subotnik, R. F., Assouline, S. G., Olszewski-Kubilius, P., Stoeger, H., & Ziegler, A. (Eds.), *The Future of Research in Talent Development: Promising Trends, Evidence, and Implications of Innovative Scholarship for Policy and Practice. New Directions for Child and Adolescent Development,* 168, 161–176.

Piirto, J. (1992). *Understanding those who create.* Dayton: Ohio Psychology Press.

Salas, E., Cooke, N. J., & Rosen, M. A. (2008). On teams, teamwork, and team performance: discoveries and developments. *Human Factors: The Journal of the Human Factors and Ergonomics Society, 50*, 540–547.

Sternberg, R. J. (1985). *Beyond IQ: A triarchic theory of intelligence.* Cambridge University Press.

Sternberg, R. J. (1998). Abilities are forms of developing expertise. *Educational Researcher, 27*(3), 11–20.

Sternberg, R. J., & Wagner, R. K. (Eds.) (1986). *Practical intelligence: Nature and origins of competence in the everyday world.* Cambridge University Press.

Subotnik, R. F., & Arnold, K. D. (Eds.) (1994). *Beyond Terman: Contemporary longitudinal studies of giftedness and talent.* Ablex.

Subotnik, R. F., & Jarvin, L. (2005). Beyond expertise: Conceptions of giftedness as great performance. In R. J. Sternberg, & J. E. Davidson (Eds.), *Conceptions of giftedness* (2nd ed., pp. 343–357). Cambridge University Press.

Subotnik, R. F., Duschl, R., & Selmon, E. (1993) Retention and attrition of science talent: A longitudinal study of Westinghouse Science Talent Search winners. *International Journal of Science Education, 15* (1), 61–72.

Subotnik, R. F., Olszewski-Kubilius, P., & Worrell, F. (2011). Rethinking giftedness and gifted education: A proposed direction forward based on psychological science. *Psychological Science in the Public Interest 12*(1), 3–54.

Subotnik, R. F., Olszewski-Kubilius, P. & Worrell, F. (2015, January). Nurturing the young genius: Renewing our commitment to gifted education is key to more innovative, productive and culturally rich society. *Scientific American Mind,* 32–39.

Subotnik, R. F., Olszewski-Kubilius, P., & Worrell, F. C. (Eds.) (2019). *The psychology of high performance: Developing human potential into domain-specific talent.* American Psychological Association.

Subotnik, R. F., Jarvin, L., Moga, E., & Sternberg, R. J. (2003). Wisdom from gatekeepers: Secrets of success in music performance. *Bulletin of Psychology in the Arts, 4,* 5–9.

Subotnik, R. F., Kassan, L., Summers, E., & Wasser, A. (1993). *Genius revisited: High IQ children grown up.* Ablex.

Tannenbaum, A. J. (1983). *Gifted children: Psychological and educational perspectives.* Macmillan.

Terman, L. M., & Oden, M. H. (1959). *The gifted group at mid-life: 35 years' follow up of the superior child. Genetic studies of genius* (vol. 5). Stanford University Press.

Worrell, F. C., Knotek, S. E., Plucker, J. A., Portenga, S., Simonton, D. K., Olszewski-Kubilius, P., Schultz, S. R., & Subotnik, R. F. (2016, July 25). Competition's role in developing psychological strength and outstanding performance. *Review of General Psychology.* Advance online publication.

9

MY JOURNEY FROM THE HUMANITIES TO PSYCHOLOGY

Ellen Winner

Before I became a psychologist, I was a student of literature, and then of painting. I grew up in a family steeped in the humanities (my father a professor of Slavic literature, my mother a cultural anthropologist—and, yes, I would call this form of anthropology part of or at least very close to the humanities). I never thought of myself as a social scientist, let alone a natural or physical scientist. I did not begin doctoral studies in psychology until six years after graduating from Radcliffe College (then the women's part of Harvard) as an English major. At the start of my freshman year in college I registered for four year-long survey courses, each in one of the areas in which I contemplated majoring: English literature, philosophy, art history, and psychology. I chose the art history course because it was the closest I could get to studio art. At my college interview with a Radcliffe dean, the previous year, I had said I was interested in art. Her reply was sharp: "Radcliffe girls don't have time for art". The psychology class was taught by Jerome Bruner and George Miller (called Social Sciences 8), and I had no idea how lucky I was to be taking a course from these giants—who deserve credit for having co-founded cognitive psychology,

I loved all of my freshman year courses except for art history, which was taught in a dull way and required extensive memorization. At the end of the year, I decided on English as my major (or "concentration", to use the Harvard lingo), all the while planning to go to art school to study painting after receiving my BA. I did just that, attending the School of the Museum of Fine Arts in Boston. But I stayed for only one year, unsure that I was cut out for the life of a painter. Perhaps I felt I was not good enough; perhaps I felt I needed more structure; perhaps it felt too solitary; perhaps I was worried about making a living. I am quite sure that all of these concerns were percolating.

Then I wondered what to do with my life. I knew I did not want to go to graduate school in literature because I said to myself that I did not want to write books about books. Also, perhaps to differentiate myself from my parents, I did not see myself as an academic. I remember going through the Harvard course catalogue, looking at the various departments, and alighting on clinical psychology as a career—something not just academic but also practical. Perhaps the wonderful lectures by Bruner and Miller influenced this choice, but I have no conscious awareness of this. I think that I was always attracted to psychology because of my fascination with novels—where the psychology of fictional characters was laid bare. In addition, I always liked to try to solve other peoples' psychological problems (and had in fact sought professional help after college in solving some of my own)!

Soon thereafter, while I researched clinical psychology programs, I was looking for a summer job to pay the rent. I chanced upon a research assistant position in "the psychology of art" at Project Zero at the Harvard Graduate School of Education. I had vaguely heard of Project Zero but did not know that it was a research organization studying the arts from a cognitive perspective. This position sounded ideal, given that my two interests were then psychology and art! I submitted my CV through the Harvard Employment Office, but never heard back. Apparently, the Employment Office had screened me out of consideration, assuming that I did not qualify for a position in psychology after having taken only one psychology course. Undeterred, I made a phone call to Project Zero and reached the secretary (that was the term used then). She (yes, then they were almost always "shes") told me that a final hiring decision was about to be made, but that if I got my CV over right away, I might get an interview with the research director/investigator, Howard Gardner.

The next day I was invited for an interview. As I entered the main office of Project Zero, I saw someone bent over a file cabinet. His hair was messy and he looked like a graduate student. But when I said that I was looking for Dr. Gardner (expecting an eminent graying professor), that person stood up and introduced himself as Howard Gardner, co-director of Project Zero. I was a little surprised. During a lively interview, I mentioned that I had written my senior thesis on three kinds of metaphor in the poetry of William Butler Yeats. At that point, I had a premonition that I would be offered the job. And when Howard went on to tell me that he had just received an NSF grant to study the development of metaphoric language in childhood, I realized why the topic of my thesis had hit the jackpot.

But there was a problem. Howard asked for a two-year professional commitment. I was intent on only giving him one year, while I applied to doctoral programs in clinical psychology. Howard asked me to think about it overnight, which I did. The next morning, I called him and accepted the position, realizing that this two-year position would strengthen my graduate-school application. My decision changed the course of my life, both professionally and later personally.

And that two-year commitment expanded quite a bit since I never left Project Zero and, in fact, quite a number of years later (nine to be exact), Howard and I, who worked so well together, and shared so many interests, got married.

The day I was hired, Howard handed me a box of typed-up interviews querying young children about their conceptions of the arts. My job was to make sense of this and write it up. I was thrilled at this challenge, and fascinated by children's strange conceptions about art. The youngest children, ages four to seven, focused on how works were physically produced—the actions required. It was only at adolescence that participants thought about art-making as cognitive, as a product of the mind. This study became my first journal article, "Children's Conceptions of the Arts", with me as second author (Gardner, Winner, & Kircher, 1975). I began to learn about qualitative coding and quantitative data analysis, though in those days we brought punch cards over to the computer center with instructions on which analyses we wanted. Many, many years later, I published an experiment called "Seeing the Mind Behind the Art" and am now writing a paper on when children distinguish art artifacts from non-art artifacts. That first assignment got under my skin.

Within a few months I realized that research in the developmental psychology of the arts appealed to me far more than becoming a clinician. Two years later, I enrolled in the Harvard Psychology Department, where I received my PhD in developmental psychology in 1978, working with psycholinguist and social psychologist, Roger Brown. Roger was a brilliant writer and thinker who was also very versed in the arts and humanities. Perhaps it was not a coincidence that Howard and I were both lured into psychology by our contact with Jerome Bruner, and that, later, Roger Brown was the doctoral advisor for both of us (I describe the research I carried out under Roger Brown's direction later on in this chapter). Over the years after graduate school, Howard and I developed a close friendship with both Bruner and Brown. After completing doctoral work, I was offered a position as an assistant professor in the psychology department of Boston College. I accepted. I had no desire to leave Boston because I wanted to retain my connection to Project Zero, where I had received an appointment as Research Associate.

If asked to describe my research style, I would mention collaborating, synthesizing, and wandering.

Collaborating

I love collaborating on research, and most of my studies have been conducted with undergraduate and graduate students, as well as sometimes with colleagues at Project Zero and Boston College. I like tossing around ideas about research design and data analysis with my collaborators. But when it comes to writing books, I like to work alone. True, I have co-authored three arts education books (mentioned later on), but my strong preference is to write as a solo author.

Synthesizing

I like to synthesize. When I arrived at Boston College in 1978, I was asked to teach a course on the psychology of art. I looked in vain for a textbook on the topic but found none. I thus created the readings for my course from articles and excerpts of books, and after teaching this course for several years, decided to write the missing textbook, which I entitled *Invented Worlds: The Psychology of the Arts* (Winner, 1982). Here I synthesized and critically analyzed the existing research on the psychology of visual arts, music, and literature. I examined the development of each of these art forms both in terms of production and perception and examined what we know about adult cognition in each of these art forms. I also devoted chapters to special topics such as the neuropsychology of the arts and the relationship between artistic creativity and psychopathology. The book became a standard text in the small field of psychology of art and was translated into Chinese and Korean.

And then, 36 years later, I wrote another synthesis on the psychology of art, entitled *How Art Works: A psychological exploration* (Winner, 2018). I selected a set of long-standing philosophical questions about the arts (e.g., can art be defined, why do we disparage forgeries, does literature make us more empathic, why do we enjoy experiencing negative emotions from art) and examined how the empirical evidence from psychological experiments (including my own) can help resolve these questions. Whereas the earlier text drew almost entirely on the published literature by other scholars, my recent book draws heavily on research carried out in the aforementioned Arts and Mind Lab. I've helped to launch a field—serving as president of APA's Division 10 (Society for the Psychology of Aesthetics, Creativity and the Arts) in 1995–96, and recently joining the advisory board of the Max Planck Institute of Empirical Aesthetics in Frankfurt.

Wandering

Instead of spending my career focusing on the ramifications of one central question, burrowing deeper and deeper, I have wandered from one research topic to another. While my research has always focused on the arts writ large—figurative language (metaphor and irony), drawing, music, and theater—within this broad area my research has been quite varied, and I will try to give some sense of this below. Here are some of the topics I have studied over the course of my career, some conducted at Project Zero, others conducted through my Arts and Mind Lab at Boston College.

Child as Artist

My earliest research examined the developmental course of metaphor and drawing. I started with metaphor when I was a graduate student working with Roger Brown. Roger was a kind and brilliant doctoral mentor. He provided wonderfully incisive comments, written in pencil in his scrawling but beautiful handwriting, on anything I gave him.

At that point in his career, Roger had just published *A First Language* (Brown, 1973), documenting the emerging syntax and semantics of three children, Adam, Eve, and Sarah. As part of my dissertation, I analyzed the language of Adam to address the question of whether metaphoric language emerges early in language acquisition, or only after "literal" language had been nailed down. This child's speech, in conversation with his mother and with a language researcher, was recorded over a total of 112 hours at ages 2, 3, and 4. I wanted to know whether this child created *deliberate* metaphors in his spontaneous speech.

I pored over the mimeographed transcripts of Adam's speech from age 2 to 4, seeking to distinguish his mistakes (misnomers, over extensions), from deliberate metaphors. When Adam used an unconventional name for an object, which he had previously named literally, I counted this as a deliberate metaphor. When he used an unconventional name accompanied by the transformational action of pretend play, I also counted this as a deliberate metaphor.

Adam produced two kinds of metaphor. One kind grew out of symbolic play. An object was transformed through pretend action (e.g., at age 2, Adam held a horn like an eggbeater, made turning motions with his hand, and then said "mixer"). At three, he took a ball on a string and held the string to his chin, saying "Look, my beard". I call these "pretend action" metaphors.

This child also made metaphorical renamings without any pretend action. All he needed to do was notice a resemblance and verbalize it. For example, seeing two irons facing each other, he described these (at age 3) as the boy and the mommy talking to each other. At the same age he referred to hair as "dark woods" and at four, he described a red balloon on a green tube as an apple on the tree. I call these "perceptual metaphors".

The kinds of metaphors that Adam produced changed with age. The most common form of metaphor uttered at age two were pretend action metaphors. These decreased sharply after age two. In striking contrast, perceptual metaphors increased with age so that by the age of four, three quarters of his metaphors were perceptual ones.

During 112 hours of recording, Adam created many metaphors and far fewer mistakes. Out of all the 266 unconventional utterances he made, 79% were metaphors and 21% were mistakes—typically overextensions of a word (such as calling all long thin objects snakes; all round objects balls, etc.). I called the paper I wrote on this "New Names for Old Things" (Winner, 1979). While a great deal had been written about children's early overextension, this was the first study (to my knowledge) that made the case for early metaphor and demonstrated how to distinguish metaphor from overextension.

These findings were based on the language of just one child. So, I next designed an experiment with 45 children ages 3, 4, and 5 to find out whether I could elicit metaphoric renamings from them (Winner, McCarthy, & Gardner,

1980; see also Mendelsohn, Robinson, Gardner, & Winner, 1984). For comparative purposes, we also included a group of 8- and 10-year-olds and adults. We played a game in which the adult and the child or adult took turns coming up with pretend names for a series of objects. Sometimes we let the children (and adults) play with the objects before offering a pretend name (the child action condition); sometimes they watched the experimenter performing a pretend action on an object (like making a block hop like a frog) (experimenter action condition); and sometimes we just let them look at the object (the perceptual condition).

The experimenter action condition proved very easy even for 3-year-olds and yielded many metaphoric renamings. Metaphoric renamings in the other conditions increased with age. When we asked judges to rate the metaphors for quality, we found that metaphors judged to be superior were higher for the older children than for the 3-, 4-, and 5-year-olds. However, it is noteworthy that one quarter of the metaphors produced by preschoolers (ages 3, 4, and 5) were judged to be apt and appealing. For example: a dishwashing tool with strips of orange sponge attached to a plastic handle was called a windmill (age 3), a tree with fall leaves (age 4), and a palm tree (age 5). This experiment showed that preschool aged children are surprisingly competent at creating new metaphors. Most of the metaphors produced in this experimental study were based on similarities of shape, as were most of Adam's perceptual metaphors.

Given the centrality of novel metaphoric thinking in great poetry and revolutionary scientific inventions, one might assume that metaphorical thinking is highly sophisticated, and out of the purview of the young child. But, in fact, this mode of thinking comes naturally to the young child. Perhaps this is not surprising, if we think about what developmental psychologists, parents, and early childhood educators know to be true of preschool children—that they are impulsive and uninhibited rather than systematic and careful; that they explore and play, trying to find out as much as they can about the world around them, without fearing making wrong hypotheses about the world that have to be revised. They are adventurous in their thinking, in their questions, and in their art making—just think about the playful paintings of the four-year-old compared to the more cramped and stereotypical drawings of the 10-year-old. These proclivities are just the kinds of characteristics that make creativity possible, and the invention of a metaphor is a profoundly creative act.

There is evidence to suggest that novel metaphoric language declines in middle childhood—perhaps due to a desire to follow the rules and use language "correctly". We described this developmental trajectory as a "U-shaped curve", starting out high, then declining, and rising again only in those who go on to become writers, especially poets (Gardner & Winner, 1982).

Out of this research grew a book that I titled *The Point of Words: Children's Understanding of Metaphor and Irony* (Winner, 1988). Here I explored what we know about children's use of the two major forms of poetic language—metaphor and irony. I developed a theory for why the ability to make sense of metaphor emerges so much earlier than does sensitivity to irony. Metaphor requires only the ability to perceive similarities across domains, while irony requires something more sophisticated—the ability to recognize something about the listener's mind. If I say "great job" to someone who has dropped a tray of dishes, I know that my listener will not think I am mistaken and will not think I am lying, but will recognize that in fact I mean the opposite of what I said. Recognizing that a speaker means the opposite of what she said, and that the speaker is not lying but instead intends the listener to know she means the opposite, requires a theory of mind beyond the ken of the 2- and 3-year-old.

We also described a U-shaped curve in children's drawings (Gardner & Winner, 1982). Early drawings are playful and imaginative, with no concern for realism, and they bear a striking resemblance to 20th century Abstract Expressionism. But by the age of 8 or 9 or 10, children become preoccupied with realism, leading to more conventional, stereotyped drawings. We found that even acclaimed artists passed through what we called a "literal" stage, with their adult drawings often far more similar to their early childhood than middle childhood works.

My studies of early childhood visual art led me to wonder about the oft-hear, disparaging claim "My kid could have done that". To be sure, the paintings of 4-year-olds look on the surface a lot like Abstract Expressionist paintings by Willem DeKooning, Hans Hoffman, or Sam Francis, to name just a few. Could people tell the difference? To find out, we carried out a series of studies comparing responses to Abstract Expressionist paintings vs. to paintings by preschool children as well by elephants, monkeys, and apes. We found that even people admitting to no knowledge about modern art were able to distinguish these two classes of paintings at a rate significantly above chance, and that people make this discrimination on the basis of perceived intentionality. Thus, we concluded that non-art experts are quite able to read intentionality in completely non-representational markings, inferring a mind behind the art. When a computer scientist used our items to find out whether a deep learning machine could do this—namely, distinguish child scribblings from acclaimed mid-20th century masterpieces, he found the same above-chance rate of success, and even found that the machine made the same kinds of errors as humans did.

Giftedness

My study of artistic development led me to the study of talent in the arts. In my book, *Gifted Children: Myths and Realities* (Winner, 1996a), I expanded the definition of giftedness (which usually refers only to the academically gifted) to include children with high ability in the arts. No matter what the area of high ability, children deemed to be gifted show three characteristics: an early ability to learn rapidly in a domain; what I have called a "rage to master" (intense drive);

and the desire to march to their own drummer, often needing little or no adult scaffolding.

These findings were based on case studies I carried out of a number of highly gifted children, and also on a synthesis of existing research on the question of giftedness. It turns out is that children who are highly gifted in an art form face many of the same problems faced by academically gifted children: they do not easily find a peer group, and they do not easily fit into school. These children show signs of high ability from an early age and cry out for challenge. Parents are often accused of pushing such children, but more often than not, these children are pushing their parents. Children like this make difficult demands on our educational system, particularly child prodigies—those who are profoundly gifted, years ahead of their chronological peers. And there is no easy solution, especially considering that children who are profoundly gifted in one area need different kinds of advanced courses from those gifted in another area. I have been gratified to find that my term "rage to master" is now often referred to often without attribution, telling me that this term somehow has stuck and made its way into popular discourse.

My study of child prodigies led me to strongly oppose what I call "the ten thousand hours myth"—the claim first articulated in the research literature by Anders Ericsson (Ericsson, Krampe, & Tesch-Römer, 1993) that intensive deliberate practice is *sufficient* to account for all high accomplishment, and thus there is no need to posit innate talent. I have called this view old wine in new bottles—the old wine is the behavioristic (Skinnerian) school of psychological analysis; the new bottle is the term deliberate practice (Winner, 1996b).

Art Education

My study of artistic development also led to an interest in art education. In 1987, I joined a research team at Harvard Project Zero called Arts PROPEL, a project carried out in collaboration with the Educational Testing Service and the Pittsburgh Public Schools. Our goal was to develop a framework for arts education that would lead to deep understanding in the arts as well as to an authentic method of assessment. We worked in three areas of the arts—visual arts, music, and imaginative writing. I directed the visual arts component. With teachers from the Pittsburgh schools as well as some arts teachers in the Boston area, we developed sample long-term projects (called Domain Projects) that involved students first in PROoduction (making of a work of art), but then also in PErception (looking closely at their own and others' works, including works by major artists) and refLection (thinking critically about the steps from first to final draft) (hence the acronym PROPEL). This project resulted in a four-volume handbook, for which I was the editor in chief (Camp & Winner, 1993; Winner, 1993; Winner & Simmons, 1993; Winner, Davidson, & Scripp, 1993).

The major thinkers in progressive arts education of the mid-20th century—Victor D'Amico (D'Amico, 1942), Victor Lowenfeld (Lowenfeld, 1947), Henry

Schaeffer-Simmern (Schaefer-Simmern, 1948), among others—had expressed views consistent with what we came up with. What we added was the concept of *domain projects*, the idea that arts education should include production, perception, and reflection, and that student work should be kept in what we called *"process-folios"*. Process-folios were to contain not just finished works but all of the drafts of each work and the journal reflections that accompanied the making. Teachers were to use the process-folios as a way to formatively (and summatively) assess student learning.

Because of my interest in arts education, I was intrigued by the frequent claims—among arts advocates and the popular media—that studying the arts improves children's academic performance. I was somewhat skeptical of such claims, aware that transfer of learning is something that has been extremely difficult to demonstrate. I decided to explore this question systematically. In collaboration with Lois Hetland (then a doctoral student in the Human Development Program at the Harvard Graduate School of Education), I directed a three-year project called REAP (Reviewing Education and the Arts Project). We searched exhaustively for research since 1950, published and unpublished, that examined the relationship between some form of arts education and some form of non-arts, academic outcome, and that reported quantitative outcomes. We published ten separate meta-analyses on these studies in a double issue of *The Journal of Aesthetic Education* (Winner & Hetland, 2000).

Our findings were clear to us, but evoked controversy in the arts-education world. We reported plenty of evidence for a positive correlation between arts study and academic performance, but no evidence of a causal link. For example, when we examined the studies that had an experimental or quasi-experimental design, we could find no evidence that studying the arts led to higher test scores or grades.

Many arts teachers and artists have applauded our work, because they have long distrusted the attempt to justify the arts in terms of the arts' effects on basic academic skills such as math and reading. Arts teachers have told us that the consequence of such justification is that arts teachers feel that it is more important for arts teachers to train spatial, verbal, or math ability than to foster understanding in the arts. One music teacher told us that music teachers have begun to feel that they have to teach the physics of sound rather than the aesthetics of sound because they fear that music must raise test scores in order to remain secure in the school curriculum.

However, many in the arts-policy world were upset by our findings and angered by our publishing them. While they have not been able to point to clear evidence that the arts do in fact raise academic skills, they have voiced the fear that our research will be used to cut the arts from schools. Our response to them was that the best way to strengthen the arts in our schools is to change the conversation. We need to stop justifying arts courses in terms of their compensatory "bonus" effects and instead focus primarily on their "core" effects.

And this stance led us to carry out an ethnographic, qualitative study of what is actually taught in visual arts classes. Our reasoning was that if we want to determine whether what is learned in arts classes transfers outside of the art class, we first have to figure out what is really learned in studio art classes.

If you ask someone what students learn in visual arts classes, you are likely to hear that they learn how to paint, or draw, or throw a pot. Of course, students learn arts techniques in arts classes. But what else do they learn? Are there any kinds of general thinking dispositions that are instilled as students study arts techniques?

We determined to describe the kinds of thinking skills, or habits of mind, being taught in the "parent domain" of the art form in question. Only then does it make sense to ask whether one or more of these skills might transfer to learning in another domain of cognition outside of the arts.

In order to determine the habits of mind that emerge from serious visual art study, we undertook a qualitative, ethnographic study of "serious" visual arts classrooms. We observed and videotaped 38 visual arts classes from the Walnut Hill School for the Arts and the Boston Arts Academy. We selected these schools because we wanted to start with the best kinds of arts teaching. These were schools for students with interest and talent in an art form, where students spend at least three hours a day working in their chosen art form, and where teachers are practicing artists. As a crucial part of the study, we interviewed teachers after each class to find out what they intended to teach and why.

After coding videos of teaching (two independent coders achieved high inter-rater reliability), we found six potentially generalizable habits of mind being taught at the same time as students were learning the *craft* of painting and drawing and were connecting their own art-making with that of the art world. I list these alphabetically so as not to suggest any hierarchy of importance. Our claim is that these habits of mind are central components of "thinking like an artist". These are not the kinds of thinking skills picked up by standardized math and verbal tests, but nonetheless these are very important skills to have.

Engage and Persist

Teachers in visual arts classes present their students with projects that engage them, and they teach their students to stick to a task for a sustained period of time. Thus, they are teaching their students to *focus and develop inner-directedness*. As one of our teachers said, she teaches them to learn "how to work through frustration".

Envision (Mental Imagery)

Students are constantly asked to *envision what they cannot observe directly* with their eyes. Sometimes students were asked to generate a work of art from imagination rather than from observation. Sometimes they were asked to imagine possibilities in their works. Sometimes they were asked to imagine forms in their drawings that could not be seen because they were partially occluded. And sometimes they are asked to detect the underlying structure of a form they were drawing and then envision how that structure could be shown in their work.

Express (Personal Voice)

Students are taught to go beyond craft to *convey a personal vision* in their work. As one of our drawing teachers said, "…art is beyond technique…I think a drawing that is done honestly and directly always expresses feeling".

Observe (Noticing)

"Looking is the real stuff about drawing", one of our teachers told us. The skill of careful observation is taught all the time in visual arts classes and is not restricted to drawing classes where students draw from the model. Students are taught to look more closely than they ordinarily do and to see with new eyes.

Reflect (Meta-cognition/Critical Judgment)

Students are asked to become reflective about their art making and we saw this reflection take two forms.

> *Question and Explain.* Teachers often ask students to step back and focus on an aspect of their work or working process. Teachers' open-ended questions prompt students to reflect and explain, whether aloud or even silently to themselves. Students are thus stimulated to develop meta-cognitive awareness about their work and working process.
> *Evaluate.* Students in art classes get continual training in evaluating their own and others' work. Teachers frequently assess student work informally as they move around the room while students are working, as well as more formally in critique sessions. Students are also asked to make evaluations themselves—they are asked to talk about what works and what does not work in their own pieces and in ones by their peers. Thus, students are trained to make critical judgments and to justify these judgments—shades of Arts PROPEL.

Stretch and Explore

Students are asked to try new things and thereby to extend beyond what they have done before—to explore and take risks. As one painting teacher said, "You ask kids to play, and then in one-on-one conversation you name what they've stumbled on".

Transfer of learning from one domain (arts) to another can never be assumed. These skills must first be clearly taught and learned in the visual arts. These skills may or may not be used by students outside of the context in which they were learned. If skills do transfer, they may only do so when teachers explicitly teach for transfer—helping students to see how a skill learned in setting A can be drawn on in Setting B or D or Z. The study of transfer of learning from one domain to another has a long and vexed history, and one should never assume that a skill that "sounds" general is in fact generalized. Only careful research can tease apart those skills that generalize from those that do not, and the circumstances under which transfer occurs. But transfer of learning to non-arts areas should never be used as a justification for the importance of arts education.

We published our findings in three books, all with the words Studio Thinking in their titles (Hetland, Winner, Veenema, & Sheridan, 2007, 2013; Hogan, Hetland, Jacquith, & Winner, 2018). We elected to begin this qualitative study in the visual arts, but the same kind of study can and should be done in any art form in which one seeks to answer what is learned and what might transfer. And I am happy to report that one of my former doctoral students, Thalia Goldstein, is carrying out this kind of study with theater, and another, Jill Hogan, has carried out such a study with high school orchestra and band classes.

Did we change the conversation away from test scores? I hope so. I know that many art teachers in the US—as well as some abroad—have adopted the studio-thinking framework. But I often still come upon claims about how the arts enhance academic learning. This shows how hard it is to get people to stop repeating "fake news", because it often "feels right" and is repeated without thinking much about the evidence needed to support such a claim.

Hindsight

When I began working at Project Zero, research in the psychology of the arts was almost non-existent. Now, while not (yet) a central area of psychology, the field of the psychology of the arts has grown considerably, with an APA journal devoted to this area (*The Psychology of Aesthetics, Creativity, and the Arts*, begun in 2006), as well as *Empirical Studies of the Arts*, (begun in 1983), and with a Max Planck Institute in Frankfurt dedicated to the study of Empirical Aesthetics. And yet, there are still too few job openings for psychologists who study the arts. This was true when I was in graduate school, and this is what my graduate students face today.

My humanist background at home and in school shaped my research career, leading me to focus on the somewhat unusual topic of the psychology of the arts, rather than on those topics regularly found in the tables of contents of psychology textbooks—memory, attention, language, reasoning, etc. I have no regrets. I have been extremely fortunate to have taught in a department that valued courses and research in the psychology of the arts and to have talented students who have helped to expand the field. It is my hope that we have helped to nudge the field of the psychology of art closer the mainstream of psychology.

Acknowledgments

I wish to thank my major funders throughout my career: the National Science Foundation, the National Institutes of Health, the National Endowment for the Arts, the Dana Foundation, the Spencer Foundation, the J. Paul Getty Trust. And a special shoutout to the Bauman Foundation and to Patricia Bauman and John Bryant for their foresight and faith.

References

Brown, R. (1973). *A first language: The early stages.* Harvard University Press.
Camp, R., & Winner, E. (Eds.) (1993). *Arts PROPEL: A handbook for imaginative writing.* Harvard Project Zero and Educational Testing Service.
D'Amico, V. (1942). *Creative teaching in art.* International Textbook Company.
Ericsson, K. A., Krampe, R. Th., & Tesch-Römer, C. (1993). The role of deliberate practice in the acquisition of expert performance. *Psychological Review*, 100(3), 363–406.
Gardner, H. & Winner, E. (1982). First intimations of artistry. In S. Strauss (Ed.), *U-shaped behavioral growth.* Academic Press.
Gardner, H., Winner, E., & Kircher, M. (1975). Children's conceptions of the arts. *Journal of Aesthetic Education*, 9, 60–77.
Hetland, L., Winner, E., Veenema, S., & Sheridan, K. (2007). *Studio thinking: The real benefits of visual arts education.* Teachers College Press.
Hetland, L., Winner, E., Veenema, S., & Sheridan, K. (2013). *Studio thinking 2: The real benefits of visual arts education* (2nd ed.). Teachers College Press.
Hogan, J., Hetland, L., Jacquith, D., & Winner, E. (2018). *Studio thinking from the start: The K-8 art educator's handbook.* Teachers College Press.
Lowenfeld, V. (1947). *Creative and mental growth: A textbook on art education.* MacMillan.
Mendelsohn, E., Robinson, S., Gardner, H., & Winner, E. (1984). Are preschoolers' renamings intentional category violations? *Developmental Psychology*, 20, 187–192.
Schaefer-Simmern, H. (1948). *The unfolding of artistic activity.* University of California Press.
Winner, E. (1979). New names for old things: The emergence of metaphoric language. *Journal of Child Language*, 6, 469–491.
Winner, E. (1982). *Invented worlds: The psychology of the arts.* Harvard University Press.
Winner, E. (1988). *The point of words: Children's understanding of metaphor and irony.* Harvard University Press.
Winner, E. (Ed.) (1993). *Arts PROPEL: An introductory handbook.* Harvard Project Zero and Educational Testing Service.
Winner, E. (1996a). *Gifted children: Myths and realities.* Basic Books.
Winner, E. (1996b). The rage to master: The decisive case for talent in the visual arts. In K. A. Ericsson (Ed.). *The road to excellence: The acquisition of expert performance in the arts and sciences, sports and games* (pp. 271–301). Lawrence Erlbaum.
Winner, E. (2018). *How art works: A psychological exploration.* Oxford University Press.
Winner, E., & Hetland, L. (Eds.) (2000). The arts and academic achievement: What the evidence shows. *Journal of Aesthetic Education*, 34 (3–4).

Winner, E., Davidson, L., & Scripp, L. (Eds.) (1993). *Arts PROPEL: A handbook for music.* Harvard Project Zero and Educational Testing Service.

Winner, E., & Simmons, S. (Eds.) (1993). *Arts PROPEL: A handbook for the visual arts.* Harvard Project Zero and Educational Testing Service.

Winner, E., McCarthy, M., and Gardner, H. (1980). The ontogenesis of metaphor. In R. Honeck and R. Hoffman (Eds.), *Cognition and figurative language.* Erlbaum.

PART 3
Perspectives on Human Creativity

10

HUMAN POTENTIAL AT THE ACHIEVEMENT PINNACLE

A Lifelong Preoccupation with History-Making Genius

Dean Keith Simonton

Quick question: What attribute do the following seven persons have in common that is utterly uncommon? Aristotle, Ludwig van Beethoven, Emily Dickinson, Thomas Edison, Galileo Galilei, Pablo Picasso, and Leo Tolstoy. Need a hint? They also share exactly the same rare characteristic with another seven: Julius Caesar, Catherine the Great, Winston Churchill, Steve Jobs, Nelson Mandela, Mao Zedong, and Muhammad. If you still need help, it's permissible to Google those names that might be unfamiliar to you. Don't worry, a lengthy and detailed Wikipedia article on each and every one is absolutely guaranteed. You're right! They all went down in history for their distinctive contributions to the annals of human civilization. As such, they all represent the pinnacle of what individuals can achieve. They are the gold medalists in creativity or leadership. Each can be considered a bona fide genius in their chosen area of achievement. Hence, any scientist who wanted to investigate the apex of human potential in a given area could do no better than to use these luminaries as research "participants".

Yet scientific analysis of such historic celebrities is exceptional rather than routine. Most researchers confine themselves to more ordinary and contemporary exemplars of talent and giftedness. To be sure, from time to time, some investigator may conduct a case study of a particular notable. Or the researcher might depart from their normal practice to conduct a multiple-case inquiry into several such illustrious figures. But I know of only one scientist who ever devoted an entire research program to studying such folk, namely, me. How did that oddity happen? Well, that's a long story, one that actually harks back to my elementary school years.

Context

Born into a working-class home where the father was a high-school dropout who labored away at an assembly line job, my initial prospects were not very promising. Yet my dad hated his employment, and thus hoped that his first-born and only son would do better than he did. So when an elementary school teacher suggested that my family purchase an encyclopedia to serve as a constant reference source for my subsequent education, they made the financial sacrifice to make it happen (buying the 1947 revision of the 19-volume *World Book Encyclopedia*). Although initially the volumes were way over my head with respect to my reading skills, the entire set was amply illustrated. Turning the pages, I was curious about all of the strange faces, often with exotic clothing and hairdos, who looked nothing like anybody I knew. As my reading skills improved, and as the pages became more worn, I gradually came to realize that these individuals were all favored with biographical entries precisely because of their supreme accomplishments. The photos, paintings, and sculptures featured famous scientists, philosophers, creative writers, visual artists, and composers as well as eminent monarchs, politicians, military leaders, revolutionaries, entrepreneurs, and religious figures.

By the time I reached high school, this wonder was channeled into diverse directions that fleshed out the bare-bones biographies. For example, I used my hard-earned cash working at a car wash to purchase a set of 54 volumes that contained all of the supposed *Great Books of the Western World*, from Homer to Freud and encompassing undoubted masterpieces of science, philosophy, and literature (Hutchins, 1952). I then began its 10-year reading program. Another big purchase was the complete set of "University Prints, Boston" that included thousands of unbound reproductions of the greatest art of the world, including painting, sculpture, and architecture. Like the reading program, I developed the daily habit of going through at least one wad of these prints each day (e.g., the Italian painter Giotto was covered by a collection of more than two dozen prints, a half dozen in splendid color). Although these were both personal hobbies, I also engaged in various high school extracurricular activities that cultivated my patently encyclopedic interests. These included acting in three drama productions (one as the lead actor) and serving as captain of the knowledge-bowl team—leading the team to a televised victory on "Scholar Quiz". I even had one of my artworks—a pastel still life—prominently displayed in the Principal's office. At the same time, I did well in my formal coursework, becoming the class salutatorian and receiving top honors in science, social studies, and English.

All seems well and good, except for a Catch-22. When I applied to college, I couldn't major in everything under the sun. Focus became essential. During the admissions interview at my first choice, Occidental College, I was specifically asked what my plans were. My immediate specific answer was history. The interviewer was startled, saying that from my transcripts and test performance they had assumed that I would become some science major. Indeed, I had been identified as scientific talent for a special metropolitan program way back in junior high school! So I quickly corrected myself, saying that I really wanted to major in chemistry. Whatever reservations I might have had about the impulsive switch were assuaged by the interviewer's reminder that this liberal-arts college required all entering students, no matter what their majors may be, to take a two-year course in the history of civilization. Because this course was instructed by a team of professors ranging from the sciences to the arts and humanities, I could enjoy the best of both worlds. No matter what was going on in my specialized chemistry lectures and labs, I would continue learning about the ultimate achievements in world history, from science to politics and from antiquity to the present day. And we read primary sources, too, from the *Epic of Gilgamesh* to the *Tale of Genji* to the *Autobiography of Malcolm X*. Great class!

Do you discern the hidden time bomb? What happens after this phenomenal survey course is completed at the end of my sophomore year? Will I rest satisfied with all of the far more specialized upper division courses required to complete a chemistry major? Do I really want to become a chemist, or at least a high school chemistry teacher, which was one of my original aspirations? I was stuck. And then a miracle happened.

Impetus

The schedule for completing my chemistry major was crammed full of required courses. But it did have one slot open for an elective in my second year. For some reason I cannot recall—maybe it was because the last two volumes of the *Great Books* were exclusively devoted to William James and Sigmund Freud—I decided to take an introductory class in psychology. I was absolutely blown away. Besides the fact that the subject was far more intrinsically interesting than my chemistry courses, I learned for the first time that psychologists researched topics that were more directly connected with my lifelong fascinations. In particular, researchers in that discipline actually investigated topics related to genius, creativity, leadership, and talent. Yet those investigations were conducted in a totally scientific manner, in line with my strong affinity with science. To get more specific, consider the following three examples of topics treated at length in my textbook (viz. Hilgard & Atkinson, 1967):

1. The classic longitudinal study of intellectually gifted children initiated by Lewis M. Terman (1925–1959), including an extensive discussion of why not all high-IQ kids grew up to earn biographical entries in *Who's Who in America* or *American Men of Science*—two obvious eminence criteria at the time.
2. The series of studies conducted at UC Berkeley's Institute for Personality Assessment and Research (IPAR), which included direct and extensive

assessments of eminent architects, creative writers, and mathematicians (e.g., MacKinnon, 1965).
3. Harvey C. Lehman's wide-ranging research on the relation between age and superior contributions to science, philosophy, literature, the visual arts, and music composition, as well as the age at which athletes in major individual sports are most likely to win championships (e.g., Lehman, 1953). These encompass the peaks of actualized human potential in multiple domains.

Although not rigorous research by any means, the textbook also discussed scientific discovery using the introspective reports of Walter B. Cannon, Friedrich Kekule, and Henri Poincaré as well as creative episodes associated with A. H. Becquerel, Alexander Fleming, and Albert Einstein—all scientists of the highest caliber.

My life as a chemistry major was thus doomed, and by the end of my junior year I had switched totally over to a psychology major. This shift was consolidated when I took, as my very next class, an upper-division course in social psychology. That's when I learned that psychologists also studied leadership, another topic of interest since childhood. Moreover, I began to think of both genius and creativity as having a strong socio-psychological aspect. Creative genius, especially, constituted a special form of sociocultural leadership—the exertion of wide-spread and enduring personal influence over a whole civilization. That assertion certainly applies to the seven eminent creators listed in this chapter's first paragraph.

For that reason, I chose to apply for admission into a graduate program in social psychology, but one housed in an interdisciplinary unit, namely, Harvard's Department of Social Relations, which included sociology and cultural anthropology along with the less behavioristic subdisciplines of psychology. Although the department soon fell apart, reorganizing into more traditional units, I was still able to pursue my interests. Yet once again I found myself in a quandary. Both my undergraduate honors thesis and my graduate master's thesis relied on the usual research participants—the student volunteers who happen to be enrolled in a lower-division psychology course. But these individuals were serving as extremely distal proxies for the persons I really wanted to investigate, to wit, the creators and leaders who have made history.

I couldn't even resort to the methodology used at IPAR for my doctoral dissertation. Besides lacking the resources available to that institution, I wished to address hypotheses that required that the subjects be deceased! For instance, I was interested in the relationship between age and achievement, including the developmental location of the first, best, and last major contribution to civilization. But the last work, and sometimes even the best work, cannot be known until the career is definitely complete, thereby ruling out the addition of any superior masterwork, including something that might be published posthumously. Copernicus's magnum opus, *On the Revolutions of the Celestial Spheres*, was published right before his death, while Wittgenstein's landmark *Philosophical Investigations* came out after he passed away. Another severe difficulty was my curiosity about the sociocultural context of creativity and leadership. After all, I was thoroughly familiar with the rise and fall of world civilizations. Ancient Athens experienced Golden Ages in art, literature, philosophy, and politics that came and went while leaving plenty of more ordinary Athenians behind for centuries thereafter. Yet the sociocultural milieu changes very slowly, and in any single generation appears relatively static. That reality requires a research sample that spans a considerable duration, at least several centuries. The culture of Renaissance Italy differs appreciably from contemporary Italy, but that Renaissance started about 600 years ago! Thus, I was stuck once more.

One day I was browsing unbound issues of journals in the library, when I came across an article published in a 1971 volume of the *Journal of Cross-Cultural Psychology*. *JCCP* is a well-respected journal today, but back then it was a lowly start-up. In fact, that was just the second volume, having started publication in the year I entered graduate school. The specific issue did not look very impressive because the articles were still printed in low-budget typescript. Even so, the article's title in the table of contents instantly caught my eye: "Creativity: A Cross-Historical Pilot Survey" (Naroll et al., 1971). The study examined the "causes of creative florescences in particular periods of time" (p. 181) in four civilizations: China, India, Middle East, and Europe. The creative activity in each civilization was determined by counting the number of eminent creators in each period, and the hypothesized causes were political fragmentation, democratic government, wealth, geographic expansion, and external challenge. Only a "pilot survey", by the authors' own admission, the methods employed were extremely crude. I thought I could do much better. The eventual result was my 1974 doctoral dissertation, the first unique expression of my own creative career.

Evolution

That dissertation contained three main studies, two of which are worth mentioning here (Simonton, 1974). The first was a follow-up of Lehman's (1953) work on age and achievement, in which I examined a sample of 420 creative writers representing the world's major literary traditions, from the ancient Greeks to modern Europe and from the British Isles to Japan. Among other findings, I showed that not only that poets tend to produce their best work at younger ages than do prose writers, but also that this age difference was a cross-cultural and transhistorical universal (Simonton, 1975a). The second major investigation used a sample of more than 5,000 eminent creators of Western civilization to examine the fluctuations in creative activity across 127 generations (Simonton, 1975b). I then demonstrated that creative activity in most domains was a positive function of role-model availability, political fragmentation, and imperial instability but a negative function of political instability, such as assassinations, *coups d'etat*, and military revolts.

It should be noted that these two investigations dramatically differ in methodology. On the one hand, the age and literary achievement study used the individual creative writer as the unit of analysis, and then conducted a fairly standard even if highly complex multiple regression analysis (the complexity coming from the 16 two-way interaction terms involving both qualitative and quantitative variables). On the other hand, the generational inquiry aggregated the creative individuals into larger 20-year periods, and then applied dynamic time-series analysis adapted from econometrics, an uncommon method for psychologists at the time. Both of these approaches can be seen throughout my career. For instance, generational time-series were later used for Chinese, Japanese, and Islamic civilizations (e.g., Simonton, 1988a, 1997b, 2018b).

Although the dissertation launched my research program in two divergent directions, the two studies converge on another distinctive point: Both investigations relied upon historiometric methods. These are techniques that apply objective quantitative measurements and correlational statistics to biographical and historical data in order to test scientific hypotheses about genius and related phenomena (Simonton, 2014b). Although obviously inferior to mainstream methodologies in many ways, particularly in comparison with laboratory experiments, historiometry has an asset shared by none other: All subjects uniquely exemplify the phenomenon of scientific interest rather than serve as remote stand-ins for the phenomenon. This asset produces another advantage: Unlike the participants in most research methods, such as experiments or surveys, the subjects are not anonymous and thus interchangeable. On the contrary, the subjects in historiometric research are identifiably unique and accordingly constitute what have been called "significant samples" (Simonton, 1999a). That means that subsequent researchers can study the exact same notables, just adding new variables and introducing the latest statistical methods.

To illustrate, the second volume of Terman's (1925–1959) longitudinal study actually contains a retrospective study by one of his graduate students, namely, Catharine Cox (1926). The subjects are not intellectually gifted children but rather 301 of the most eminent creators and leaders in Western civilization from the Renaissance to the late 19th century. Because she identified each of her geniuses, and provided both estimated IQ scores and the raw data for each one as well, it was possible for me 50 years later to define some additional measures to replicate and extend her findings regarding the relation between intelligence and achieved eminence (Simonton, 1976a; see also Walberg, Rasher, & Hase, 1978). More than 30 years later, unpublished data on the physical and mental health of a subset of these 301 was found in an archive, and subsequently used for yet another follow-up inquiry (Simonton & Song, 2009). Nothing prevents future research on these exact same creators and leaders—people like Isaac Newton, René Descartes, Miguel de Cervantes, Michelangelo Buonarroti, Wolfgang

Amadeus Mozart, Napoleon Bonaparte, Horatio Nelson, Abraham Lincoln, and Martin Luther!

The ease with which historiometry supports such replication-and-extension research also shows up in my work on outstanding political leadership. This work started with European hereditary monarchs, and then continued for a much longer duration with presidents of the United States. In the former case, I took advantage of two previous historiometric studies published by the very person who coined the term "historiometry" (Woods, 1909, 1911). His first investigation assessed several royal families on two individual difference variables, namely, intelligence and morality (Woods, 1906), while his second rated rulers from these families on leadership effectiveness (Woods, 1913). Combining these two data sets, and adding some new data, I published a pair of inquiries into the underlying causes of extraordinary political leadership for 342 monarchs in 14 European nations (Simonton, 1983, 1984). Although these monarchs inherited their positions, only a rare few attained the distinction of Austria's Maria Theresa, England's Elizabeth I, France's Louis IV the Great, Prussia's Frederick the Great, Russia's Peter the Great, Spain's Charles V, Sweden's Gustavus Adolphus, and Turkey's Suleiman the Magnificent. In any event, besides gauging the impact of genetic and environmental factors on monarchal eminence, the investigations also determined the extent to which eminence as a monarch was a matter of being "the right person" versus being at "the right place at the right time".

Even before the two monarch studies, I took an interest in US presidents, publishing an exploratory study combining data from various sources (Simonton, 1981). But that fascination soon expanded immediately afterwards (Simonton, 1986a). A major impetus came when I had tenure as Visiting Research Psychologist at IPAR in 1985. Then I discussed the possibility of adapting one of their standard personality measures, namely the Gough Adjective Check List, as an observer-based instrument that could be applied to biographical extracts (Gough & Heilbrun, 1965). The outcome was an influential study that assessed 39 presidents on 14 personality dimensions (Simonton, 1986b). Over the course of the next 20 plus years I would conduct follow-up investigations that added both new variables and new presidents (e.g., Simonton, 1988b, 2006). This research program led to the persistent replication of a specific 6-variable equation that predicts presidential greatness, replications conducted by others as well (e.g., Cohen, 2003; for review see Simonton, 2012). In a nutshell, the greatest presidents rate higher in intellectual brilliance, serve more years in the White House, function longer in the capacity of wartime commander-in-chief, avoid major scandals in their administration, and, most strikingly, are more likely to have been assassinated in office!

I hasten to add that the exact replication of cases can apply to units of analysis at either bigger or smaller levels than individual creators or leaders. In the former case, multiple generational analyses have been based on Sorokin's (1937–1941) impressive tabulations of fluctuations in Western philosophical positions from the ancient Greeks to the early 20th century (e.g., Klingemann, Mohler, & Weber,

1982; Martindale, 1975; Simonton, 1976b, 1976c). In the latter case, single products rather than persons can serve as the unit of analysis, where the products are again identifiable as masterpieces or would-be masterpieces. Illustrations include compositions in the classical repertoire (e.g., Kozbelt & Meredith, 2010; Meredith & Kozbelt, 2014; Simonton, 1980a, 1980b, 1989a, 2015), award-nominated motion pictures (Cerridwen & Simonton, 2009; Pardoe & Simonton, 2008; Simonton, 2009), and William Shakespeare's sonnets (Simonton, 1989b, 1990) and plays (e.g., Derks, 1994; Simonton, 1986c, 2004). Anyone who seeks to replicate these studies can do so using precisely identical samples.

Well, I think my time is up. Nonetheless, the above narrative has only partially covered the evolution of my historiometric work. Worse still, I have completely ignored my published mathematical models, computer simulations, laboratory experiments, psychometric inquiries, meta-analyses, interviews, and single-case studies. So I will just resign myself to referring to Table 10.1, which offers a schematic overview of my research program from 1975 to the present day. As is readily seen, my general tendency has been to diversify the range of topics, while retaining several key topics throughout my career. One critical aspect of this diversification is my expansion from focusing on environmental influences ("nurture") to incorporating potential genetic factors ("nature"). Most striking, perhaps, are three novel contributions: a mathematical model of talent development (Simonton, 1999b), the introduction of meta-analytic methods for estimating total genetic effects on talent (Simonton, 2008), and a research agenda for integrating the concept of talent with the role of deliberate practice in the acquisition of domain-specific expertise required for exceptional performance (Simonton, 2014a). Taken together, these contributions should raise the nature-nurture debate to a much higher level of sophistication.

A final central development over the years has been my increasing concern with theory. For instance, I have elaborated Campbell's (1960) blind-variation and selective-retention theory of creativity into a far more precise and comprehensive framework (e.g., Simonton, 1997a, 2003, 2011, 2013). Hence, not all of my research is empirical, and much of my empirical research is theoretically driven. Interestingly, the delay between theoretical prediction and empirical evaluation can sometimes take decades. In particular, my 1985 model of the nonlinear relation between IQ and exceptional leadership did not undergo empirical test until 2017 (Antonakis, House, & Simonton, 2017; cf. Simonton, 1985). But the positive results made it worth the wait!

Hindsight

As a "distinguished professor emeritus", I am naturally inclined to look back over the past several decades to reflect on what I have and have not accomplished.

On the positive side, my research program has certainly been productive: 14 books (11 sole authored, one edited, one co-edited, and one author-reprint

TABLE 10.1 Emergence and duration of long-term topics pursued in my research program

Years published	Topics investigated
1975–2019	Career landmarks in the arts and sciences (adding a mathematical model in 1984)
1975–2019	Sociocultural context of creativity: civilizations of Europe, Islam, China, and Japan
1975–2019	Scientific creativity and discovery: both empirical research and theoretical models
1976–2019	Intelligence or IQ: eminent creators, US presidents, and European monarchs
1976–2019	Family environment, including birth order and socioeconomic background
1976–2018	Education and training, with special interest in domain-specific expertise acquisition
1977–2019	Psychopathology in both leaders and creators, with emphasis on latter
1978–2018	Multiple discovery and invention, via empirical and mathematical analyses
1980–2018	Classical music, particularly the computer content analysis of musical themes
1981–2018	Presidential leadership: personality, biography, and historical context
1983–2009	William Shakespeare: computer content analyses of both plays and sonnets
1985–2019	Eminent psychologists: the foundations for exceptional influence on the field
1985–2018	BVSR creativity: Donald Campbell's original 1960 theory extensively developed
1991–2018	Genetic contributions, including both emergenic inheritance and epigenetic growth
1992–2018	Eminent women: Japanese writers, Presidential First Ladies, and psychologists
1998–2015	Eminent African American creators, leaders, performers, and athletes
2002–2014	Cinematic creativity and esthetics: awards, box office, and critical acclaim
2002–2018	Comtean hierarchy of the sciences: empirical and theoretical analyses
2005–2018	Openness to experience: both multiple-case and single-case studies (B. F. Skinner)

Note: Many of these topics will converge and interact in a single publication, exemplifying Gruber's (1989) "networks of enterprise" (e.g., Simonton, 2003, 2018a).

collection), 155 book chapters in edited volumes (54 in handbooks), 55 entries in 29 different encyclopedias, and 350 contributions (174 full articles and 176 shorter pieces) to 134 different journals, annuals, and other periodicals. Not only has my research appeared in top-tier journals, but their editors singled out 46 of my publications as lead articles in such prestigious venues as *Psychological Review, Psychological Bulletin, Perspectives on Psychological Science, Journal of Personality and*

Social Psychology, and the Journal of Applied Psychology. Moreover, judging from the citations received, I certainly can't complain about being overlooked: More than 425 publications have been cited at least once, 273 have been cited ten times or more (i.e., the $i10$ index), and my h-index stands at 79, meaning that 79 of my publications have been cited 79 or more times. My books and articles have also won major awards. All this despite the fact that in graduate school I was actively discouraged from pursuing this line of work because the output would be unpublishable in top journals (Simonton, 2002).

On the negative side, my research program is of the kind that will always be more admired than imitated. Few if any are going to follow in my footsteps; not even my graduate students did so. Indeed, although some of my best students might have published a historiometric study or two while under my mentorship (most notably Damian & Simonton, 2015), they then got a postdoc in which they retooled themselves in more mainstream methodologies and substantive topics (but see Simonton & Ting, 2010). In today's highly competitive job market, their choices make perfect sense. I don't know if I would have landed an academic position today doing what I do now. Yet alongside this practical reality is my own personal creative style. Because I'm not much of a collaborator, 93% of my publications are single authored. I follow the pattern of the "lone scientist" in the days before Big Science. Nowadays publications are more often churned out by big laboratories and collaborations generating lengthy author lists.

At the onset of this chapter, I said that I am the only research psychologist to ever commit the entire length of a career to the scientific study of eminent creators and leaders. Will that distinction always be the case? I don't know. But what I can say is that if anyone in the future wants to investigate the same topics shown in Table 10.1, they will likely use my major findings as the starting point. That's enough for me.

References

Antonakis, J., House, R. J., & Simonton, D. K. (2017). Can super smart leaders suffer too much from a good thing? The curvilinear effect of intelligence on perceived leadership behavior. *Journal of Applied Psychology*, 102, 1003–1021.

Campbell, D. T. (1960). Blind variation and selective retention in creative thought as in other knowledge processes. *Psychological Review*, 67, 380–400.

Cerridwen, A., & Simonton, D. K. (2009). Sex doesn't sell—nor impress: Content, box office, critics, and awards in mainstream cinema. *Psychology of Aesthetics, Creativity, and the Arts*, 3, 200–210.

Cohen, J. E. (2003). The polls: Presidential greatness as seen in the mass public: An extension and application of the Simonton model. *Presidential Studies Quarterly*, 33, 913–924.

Cox, C. (1926). *The early mental traits of three hundred geniuses*. Stanford University Press.

Damian, R. I., & Simonton, D. K. (2015). Psychopathology, adversity, and creativity: Diversifying experiences in the development of eminent African Americans. *Journal of Personality and Social Psychology*, 108, 623–636.

Derks, P. L. (1994). Clockwork Shakespeare: The bard meets the regressive imagery dictionary. *Empirical Studies of the Arts*, 12, 131–139.
Gough, H. G., & Heilbrun, A. B., Jr. (1965). *The Adjective Check List manual*. Consulting Psychologists Press.
Gruber, H. E. (1989). Networks of enterprise in creative scientific work. In B. Gholson, W. R. Shadish, Jr., R. A.Neimeyer, & A. C. Houts (Eds.), *The psychology of science: Contributions to metascience* (pp. 246–265). Cambridge University Press.
Hilgard, E. R., & Atkinson, R. G. (1967). *Introduction to psychology* (4th ed.). Harcourt, Brace, & World.
Hutchins, R. M. (Ed.) (1952). *Great books of the Western world* (54 vols.). Encyclopaedia Britannica.
Klingemann, H.-D., Mohler, P. P., & Weber, R. P. (1982). Cultural indicators based on content analysis: A secondary analysis of Sorokin's data on fluctuations of systems of truth. *Quality and Quantity*, 16, 1–18.
Kozbelt, A., & Meredith, D. (2010). A note on trans-historical melodic originality trends in classical music. *International Journal of Creativity and Problem Solving*, 20, 109–125.
Lehman, H. C. (1953). *Age and achievement*. Princeton, NJ: Princeton University Press.
MacKinnon, D. W. (1965). Personality and the realization of creative potential. *American Psychologist*, 20, 273–281.
Martindale, C. (1975). *Romantic progression: The psychology of literary history*. Hemisphere.
Meredith, D., & Kozbelt, A. (2014). A swan song for the swan-song phenomenon: Multilevel evidence against robust end-of-life effects for classical composers. *Empirical Studies of the Arts*, 32, 5–25.
Naroll, R., Benjamin, E. C., Fohl, F. K., Fried, M. J., Hildreth, R. E., & Schaefer, J. M. (1971). Creativity: A cross-historical pilot survey. *Journal of Cross-Cultural Psychology*, 2, 181–188.
Pardoe, I., & Simonton, D. K. (2008). Applying discrete choice models to predict Academy Award winners. *Journal of the Royal Statistical Society: Series A (Statistics in Society)*, 171, 375–394.
Simonton, D. K. (1974). *The social psychology of creativity: An archival data analysis*. Unpublished doctoral dissertation, Harvard University.
Simonton, D. K. (1975a). Age and literary creativity: A cross-cultural and transhistorical survey. *Journal of Cross-Cultural Psychology*, 6, 259–277.
Simonton, D. K. (1975b). Sociocultural context of individual creativity: A transhistorical time-series analysis. *Journal of Personality and Social Psychology*, 32, 1119–1133.
Simonton, D. K. (1976a). Biographical determinants of achieved eminence: A multivariate approach to the Cox data. *Journal of Personality and Social Psychology*, 33, 218–226.
Simonton, D. K. (1976b). Do Sorokin's data support his theory?: A study of generational fluctuations in philosophical beliefs. *Journal for the Scientific Study of Religion*, 15, 187–198.
Simonton, D. K. (1976c). The sociopolitical context of philosophical beliefs: A transhistorical causal analysis. *Social Forces*, 54, 513–523.
Simonton, D. K. (1980a). Thematic fame and melodic originality in classical music: A multivariate computer-content analysis. *Journal of Personality*, 48, 206–219.
Simonton, D. K. (1980b). Thematic fame, melodic originality, and musical zeitgeist: A biographical and transhistorical content analysis. *Journal of Personality and Social Psychology*, 38, 972–983.
Simonton, D. K. (1981). Presidential greatness and performance: Can we predict leadership in the White House? *Journal of Personality*, 49, 306–323.

Simonton, D. K. (1983). Intergenerational transfer of individual differences in hereditary monarchs: Genetic, role-modeling, cohort, or sociocultural effects? *Journal of Personality and Social Psychology, 44*, 354–364.

Simonton, D. K. (1984). Leaders as eponyms: Individual and situational determinants of monarchal eminence. *Journal of Personality, 52*, 1–21.

Simonton, D. K. (1985). Intelligence and personal influence in groups: Four nonlinear models. *Psychological Review, 92*, 532–547.

Simonton, D. K. (1986a). Presidential greatness: The historical consensus and its psychological significance. *Political Psychology, 7*, 259–283.

Simonton, D. K. (1986b). Presidential personality: Biographical use of the Gough Adjective Check List. *Journal of Personality and Social Psychology, 51*, 149–160.

Simonton, D. K. (1986c). Popularity, content, and context in 37 Shakespeare plays. *Poetics, 15*, 493–510.

Simonton, D. K. (1988a). Galtonian genius, Kroeberian configurations, and emulation: A generational time-series analysis of Chinese civilization. *Journal of Personality and Social Psychology, 55*, 230–238.

Simonton, D. K. (1988b). Presidential style: Personality, biography, and performance. *Journal of Personality and Social Psychology, 55*, 928–936.

Simonton, D. K. (1989a). Shakespeare's sonnets: A case of and for single-case historiometry. *Journal of Personality, 57*, 695–721.

Simonton, D. K. (1989b). The swan-song phenomenon: Last-works effects for 172 classical composers. *Psychology and Aging, 4*, 42–47.

Simonton, D. K. (1990). Lexical choices and aesthetic success: A computer content analysis of 154 Shakespeare sonnets. *Computers and the Humanities, 24*, 251–264.

Simonton, D. K. (1997a). Creative productivity: A predictive and explanatory model of career trajectories and landmarks. *Psychological Review, 104*, 66–89.

Simonton, D. K. (1997b). Foreign influence and national achievement: The impact of open milieus on Japanese civilization. *Journal of Personality and Social Psychology, 72*, 86–94.

Simonton, D. K. (1999a). Significant samples: The psychological study of eminent individuals. *Psychological Methods, 4*, 425–451.

Simonton, D. K. (1999b). Talent and its development: An emergenic and epigenetic model. *Psychological Review, 106*, 435–457.

Simonton, D. K. (2002). It's absolutely impossible? A longitudinal study of one psychologist's response to conventional naysayers. In R. J. Sternberg (Ed.), *Psychologists defying the crowd: Stories of those who battled the establishment and won* (pp. 238–254). American Psychological Association.

Simonton, D. K. (2003). Scientific creativity as constrained stochastic behavior: The integration of product, process, and person perspectives. *Psychological Bulletin, 129*, 475–494.

Simonton, D. K. (2004). Thematic content and political context in Shakespeare's dramatic output, with implications for authorship and chronology controversies. *Empirical Studies of the Arts, 22*, 201–213.

Simonton, D. K. (2006). Presidential IQ, openness, intellectual brilliance, and leadership: Estimates and correlations for 42 US chief executives. *Political Psychology, 27*, 511–639.

Simonton, D. K. (2008). Scientific talent, training, and performance: Intellect, personality, and genetic endowment. *Review of General Psychology, 12*, 28–46.

Simonton, D. K. (2009). Cinematic success, aesthetics, and economics: An exploratory recursive model. *Psychology of Creativity, Aesthetics, and the Arts, 3*, 128–138.

Simonton, D. K. (2011). Creativity and discovery as blind variation: Campbell's (1960) BVSR model after the half-century mark. *Review of General Psychology*, 15, 158–174.
Simonton, D. K. (2012). Presidential leadership: Performance criteria and their predictors. In M. G. Rumsey (Ed.), *Oxford handbook of leadership* (pp. 327–342). Oxford University Press.
Simonton, D. K. (2013). Creative thought as blind variation and selective retention: Why sightedness is inversely related to creativity. *Journal of Theoretical and Philosophical Psychology*, 33, 253–266.
Simonton, D. K. (2014a). Creative performance, expertise acquisition, individual-differences, and developmental antecedents: An integrative research agenda. *Intelligence*, 45, 66–73.
Simonton, D. K. (2014b). Historiometric studies of genius. In D. K. Simonton (Ed.), *The Wiley handbook of genius* (pp. 87–106). Wiley.
Simonton, D. K. (2015). Numerical odds and evens in Beethoven's nine symphonies: Can a computer really tell the difference? *Empirical Studies of the Arts*, 33, 18–35.
Simonton, D. K. (2018a). Creative genius as causal agent in history: William James's 1880 theory revisited and revitalized. *Review of General Psychology*, 22, 406–420.
Simonton, D. K. (2018b). Intellectual genius in the Islamic Golden Age: Cross-civilization replications, extensions, and modifications. *Psychology of Aesthetics, Creativity, and the Arts*, 12, 125–135.
Simonton, D. K., & Song, A. V. (2009). Eminence, IQ, physical and mental health, and achievement domain: Cox's 282 geniuses revisited. *Psychological Science*, 20, 429–434.
Simonton, D. K., & Ting, S. S. (2010). Creativity in Eastern and Western civilizations: The lessons of historiometry. *Management and Organization Review*, 6, 329–350.
Sorokin, P. A. (1937–1941). *Social and cultural dynamics* (vols. 1–4). American Book.
Terman, L. M. (1925–1959). *Genetic studies of genius* (5 vols.). Stanford University Press.
Walberg, H. J., Rasher, S. P., & Hase, K. (1978). IQ correlates with high eminence. *Gifted Child Quarterly*, 22, 196–200.
Woods, F. A. (1906). *Mental and moral heredity in royalty*. Holt.
Woods, F. A. (1909, November 19). A new name for a new science. *Science*, 30, 703–704.
Woods, F. A. (1911, April 14). Historiometry as an exact science. *Science*, 33, 568–574.
Woods, F. A. (1913). *The influence of monarchs: Steps in a new science of history*. Macmillan.

11

A CONTRARIAN'S APOLOGY AND THE CHANGING CONTEXTS OF CREATIVITY RESEARCH

Mark A. Runco

The changes that are inherent in scientific theories may come as a surprise to scholars and their audiences. That is because there is a common assumption that the sciences focus on things that are stable. Certainly, most things studied by the sciences, from universes to molecules, only change at a rate that is far beyond human perceptual capacities. Yet everything changes. Gergen (1973) brought this point home when he accused social psychology of being history instead of science, the idea being that research findings only represent how things are at one point in time. This point actually applies to all of psychology, not just social psychology, and behavioral scientists should recognize that they are investigating how things are at one point in time. Changes need to be taken into account, built into theories, and underscored when the limitations of research findings are reported. Thus it is admirable that one of the themes of the present volume is that scientific findings and assumptions change and, for that reason, that it is a good idea to be explicit about the contexts of research.

The certainty of change and variations among and between contexts is quite clear in the creativity research. That is why "press" (an abbreviation of environmental pressures but sometimes just labeled "places") has been recognized in creativity theories at least since Rhodes' (1961) famous article described "the 4Ps". Rhodes identified four strands in the creativity research, including *person* (or personality), *process, product,* and *"press"*. The last of these was a term frequently used throughout psychology at that time when explaining the impact of environments or contexts on behavior and thinking.

Another theme of the present volume is that creative potential is important. My work suggesting that there is no more important topic in the field is summarized in this chapter. This chapter also explores why the attention given to creative potential has varied over the years. As we will see in this chapter, some of that variation is due to the fact that the field of creative studies was not viewed as scientific until 30–40 years ago—but then everything changed. When it did change the research on creativity became more objective, but topics such as potential were relegated. That occurred because potential is not a topic that lends itself to objective study. Potential, unlike a creative product or manifest action, is latent and far from manifest. Creative potential is not easily measured, and measurement is a requirement of any scientific subject matter.

This chapter thus supports two of the themes of this volume, namely that (a) scientific findings are not stable and variations in scientific results reflect context, and (b) creative potential is among the most important topics in the research. As we shall see, these two themes are interwoven.

Creative Potential

About ten years ago I revised Rhodes' (1960) 4P framework such that it included *potential* as a 6th P. A fifth P had already been nominated by Simonton (1995). That was *"persuasion"*, which is a good label for research exploring how creative things and people change the way that others think. So persuasion was a 5th P and "potential" then proposed as a 6th. The 4P framework was also revised such that it was hierarchical (see Figure 11.1).

Hierarchical Framework:
Perspectives on Creativity

Creative Potential
Person
   Creative styles
   Personality traits
Process
   Cognitive (intrapersonal)
   Socio-historical
Press
   Distal
     Evolution
     Zeitgeist
     Culture
   Immediate
     Places
     Setting

Creative Performance
Products
   Ideas
   Designs
   Inventions
Persuasion
   Inter-personal
   Systems
     Individual-Field-Domain
   Interactions
     Individual x Environment
     State x Trait

FIGURE 11.1 A 6P framework on creativity

The reason for this revision shows the importance of context, as promised just above, but before going into detail about that, the entire hierarchical framework should be described. It is a very simple hierarchy, with two general categories for creativity research, namely Potential and Performance. Personality, Press (or place), and Process (three of the other original categories proposed by Rhodes (1961)) are subsumed under Potential. Product, Persuasion, and Person X Environment interactions are subsumed under Performance. The category labeled Potential thus includes approaches where the creativity is latent and possible but not entirely guaranteed nor manifest (Runco, 2003). The Performance category, on the other hand, includes expressions of creativity that have occurred and are manifest rather than latent. All socially recognized creativity, where there is a creator but also an audience, fits under Performance because to have been recognized by an audience the creativity could not be latent and must have been expressed. Otherwise an audience may not see it, let alone recognize it as creative.

I selected Potential and Performance as the most general categories for the hierarchy because of context. This particular context involved a trend in the field—a trend that was surprising and disappointing. That trend started about 30 years ago and emphasizes socially recognized creativity. As noted above, socially recognized creativity is that which involves an individual expressing a creative idea but also some audience reacting appreciatively to it. This is quite different from creative ideas that are personal, where an individual solves a problem for him- or herself and the idea is not shared so not socially appreciated. This kind of personal creativity may merely allow one person to adapt to hassles and day-to-day problems, with no audience whatsoever. Still, it may be original and effective, if only for that one individual. It thus satisfies the two requirements of the standard definition of creativity (Runco & Jaeger, 2012). Admittedly research on socially recognized creativity is quite informative, but if the field focuses entirely on it, much would be overlooked. In fact, the most important topics for the field will be overlooked. The most important topics all assume that there is such a thing as potential, where there is the possibility of creativity but it was not yet manifest. These are important topics because creative potential may be universal, and if we don't value creative potential, even though it is by definition latent, most creativity (i.e., the creative potential that each and every person has) will be ignored. Additionally, potential is important in all efforts to support or enhance creativity. It is for this reason that these efforts and programs are best described as efforts to "fulfill creative potential". Guilford (1975) seemed to share my thinking about creative potential. He wrote, "if by any approach we could lift the population's problem solving skills by a small amount on the average, the summative effect would be incalculable" (p. 53).

Why was there a trend toward socially recognized creativity surprising? I called it disappointing because an emphasis on socially-recognized creativity relegates creative potential, but why is it also surprising?

Creativity Need Not Be Social

Fortunately, creativity research often shows respect for contrarianism. This is fortunate because I have found myself in a contrarian position more than once during my career. Several professors told me that I should not do a dissertation on creativity, for example, but I went ahead and did one. The reason I was told to choose a different topic is quite relevant because my PhD is in cognitive psychology, and at that point in time, in the early 1980s, cognitive psychology was becoming increasingly rigorous, and proud of it. For years, cognition had been viewed as unfit for scientific study and was dismissed because thinking could not be observed and could only be inferred. This is one reason Behaviorism was so popular: the method of introspection, used in the very first schools of psychology, had failed, and Behaviorism offered more objective methods and topics. Behaviorism focused on observable behaviors that needed no inferences (Epstein, 1990; Runco, 2019a, 2019b). Eventually methods were developed such that the cognitive research included controls and experimental rigor, and although inferences from the data were still often required, they were strong and convincing.

A good example of research focusing on observable behavior is that of Epstein (1990). He worked with B. F. Skinner, the two of them arguing that creativity was not amenable to scientific study and that it was more reasonable to investigate insight instead. Their research, summarized by Epstein (1990), does indeed make very few assumptions. Epstein and Skinner were able to manipulate insight in pigeons using reinforcers and subsequently observed insightful problem solving. The wording here is critical: They observed insight; they did not need to infer that it had occurred. This can be contrasted with research on divergent thinking (summarized by Runco & Acar, 2019). In this research a divergence of thought is not observed. Instead, ideas produced by an individual when problem solving are recorded and the process that supposedly lead to them, and connects them, is inferred. If a person receives an open-ended problem like "name things that are square", just to use a very simple divergent thinking task as an example, and that person responds with "a baseball diamond" and "a chessboard", little divergence is suggested. The diamond and the chessboard are both used for playing games. If a person responds with "a square meal" and "a square root", more divergence is suggested. But in both cases the divergence, or lack thereof, must be inferred.

The cognitive sciences did eventually develop methods that relied on few inferences. They also received a push from advances in human factors research, investigations by the military, Piaget's (1950) studies of cognitive development, and perhaps most importantly, strides made in artificial intelligence (AI), which was exploring and testing quite interesting models of cognition. Nobel Laureate Herb Simon went into some detail about the creativity of AI (Simon, 1988) and cited several impressive examples of programs that could indeed solve classic scientific problems. Yet in every case the computers had to be programmed, so a human was required, and the relevant information provided to them. This led to a rebuttal from Mihaly Csikszentmihalyi (1988), which focused on the fact that computers and digital agents cannot find meaningful problems for themselves, nor are they intrinsically motivated. This same debate is alive and well as I write this chapter (Miller, 2019), though it takes a different form. Consider, for example, the fairly recent shift away from the *Turing Test*, which for years was central to AI (and challenged a computer to pass as a human in a conversation) to the *Lovelace Test* (which challenges a computer to generate an original idea).

The respect given to cognitive psychology, which was quite obvious in the context of the early 1980s, influenced my thinking as I chose a dissertation topic. Even with professors saying that creativity was not scientific enough, I was convinced that there were objective methods that could be used to study creativity, so I went ahead with my dissertation on divergent thinking. The same reasoning (albeit less contrarianism) a few years later supported by decision to found the *Creativity Research Journal*. Both my dissertation and the CRJ reflected my belief that it was possible to do objective, scientific research on creativity.

Domain Differences and the Art Bias

The professors who dismissed the possibility of a good dissertation on creativity probably held the *art bias*, which was another problem for people studying creativity. The art bias is apparent when a person believes that creativity is only important for the arts, or that only artistic individuals are creative. The art bias is tied to the belief that the arts, and therefore all creativity, depends on aesthetics and other highly subjective processes. The art bias was quite strong when the field of creative studies was young, and in fact it is still apparent, though not so much in the academic research (Cropley, 2014). It is a huge problem in education because when teachers hold the art bias, they are likely to only see and support the creativity of artistically talented students and miss the creativity of students who are creative outside of the arts.

My contrarianism was apparent in my pushing ahead with a dissertation on creativity, even though I was working on a PhD in cognitive psychology. True, there were several indications that creativity was important outside of the arts. The clearest data that were contrary to an art bias may be those showing domain differences in creativity. "Domain differences" refers to the theory and now sizable body of findings that creativity in one field or discipline (e.g., science, or the performing arts, or athletics) is distinct from creativity in all other fields or disciplines (Baer, 1991; Plucker, 1998; Runco, 1986a). This view was rare but apparent in the 1930s (cf. Patrick, 1935, 1937, Patrick, 1938) but gained momentum at the Institute for Personality Assessment and Research (cf. Barron, 1995; Helson, 1999; MacKinnon, 1962). No doubt some domains overlap, but a body of within-subject research shows that creative performance in any one domain is typically largely uncorrelated with creative performances in other domains.

The idea of domain differences has spurred an enormous amount of research but the domains identified have changed quite a few times, and in fact some important changes in context could be charted just by surveying the research domains. One of the notable advances in this area occurred when Howard Gardner published *Frames of Mind*, in 1983, for it marshaled evidence from various fields (e.g., experimental psychology, developmental psychology, the brain sciences) to show that it was wiser to acknowledge domains rather than focusing only on one general intelligence ("g"). That 1983 volume pointed to seven domains (verbal-symbolic, mathematical, inter-personal, intra-personal, bodily-kinesthetic, musical, and spatial). A few years later, Gardner (2000) added the naturalistic domain and discussed the possibility of an existential domain. Gardner was also clear that, contrary to speculation, a spiritual domain was not supported by data (at least using the criteria Gardner carefully set out in his work, such as the possibility of experimentally separating domains by performances and seeing clear cross-cultural differences and clear developmental trajectories). Importantly, Gardner's theory was not focused on creativity, but it certainly applied to creativity.

Creativity in the Moral Domain

Early in the 1990s I met Gardner, along with Mihalyi Csikszentmihalyi and William Damon, when they did a sabbatical at Stanford University's Center for the Advanced Study of the Behavioral Sciences. To be clear, I was there for just two days, at their invitation, while they were there for months. They were working on an important new idea that suggested an enormously important advance. The efforts of Gardner et al. led to a number of publications on humane creativity and eventually led to the volume, *Good Work* (Gardner et al., 2008). This still strikes me as enormously important in that it signaled that creativity was valuable and useful on a very broad sociocultural level and could be used to solve some of the most important problems facing humanity.

Not long after I was approached by Howard Gruber. Like Gardner et al., Gruber was a big name in creative studies, in part due to his fascinating study of Charles Darwin (Gruber, 1981), his theory that insights are not all that fast but are instead protracted over time, his advancing case study methodologies (Gruber & Wallace, 1993), and his applying this method to the cognitive developmental psychologist Jean Piaget (Gruber, 1996). In the early 1990s he too had turned his attention to a topic that is as important as humane creativity. He referred to it as "creativity in the moral domain". It was quite easy to convince me to devote a special issue of the *Creativity Research Journal* to that topic. That volume included Gruber and Wallace's own notable articles and ideas but about 10 other perspectives on creativity in the moral domain. The paper that is probably the most commonly cited is Robert McLaren's (1993) very influential article titled "The Dark Side of Creativity". It described how creativity could be used towards immoral, unethical ends. McLaren was a colleague of mine at California State University, Fullerton, and as bright as they come. Still, I was surprised about the popularity of the concept of "the dark side" until finally I realized, with disappointment, that the concept of a dark side of creativity is more sensational and thus attention-grabbing than is the concept of moral creativity. Certainly, there are books and articles that acknowledge both moral and immoral creativity, including the volume I co-edited with Cropley, Cropley, and Kaufman, but even it was titled *"The Dark Side of Creativity"* (Cropley et al., 2010).

I must admit to more contrarianism at this point because my chapter in that volume is entitled, "There Is No Dark Side of Creativity" (Runco, 2010). My argument was that creativity is an expression of various cognitive and extra-cognitive processes that serve humans quite well, and that malevolent creativity is not a special kind of creativity but is instead just a process that itself is unladen by values of any sort but, in some unfortunate instances, directed by immoral values. In other words, creativity can go in various directions. Some people have values that direct their creativity to benevolent ends while others have different values and these direct the very same process to malevolent ends. If parsimony is used, as it should be for a scientific theory, creativity is one thing and the dark side involves something outside of it, namely, immoral or malevolent values.

Values are an enormously important part of creativity, and like the idea of potential, too often overlooked. As a matter of fact, one suggestion I have often offered when asked how creative potentials can be fulfilled involves values. Put briefly, if children are around creative adults, they will probably infer that creativity is an admirable and valuable thing. If they internalize this view and the idea that creativity is valuable, they are likely to invest in creativity and are likely to attempt to behave more creatively themselves.

This discussion of values as they related to the fulfillment of potential is related to another critical part of the theory of moral creativity. Both creativity and morality involve *intentionality*. That is, in fact, the point of emphasis in the article I contributed to the Wallace and Gruber (1993) special issue of the *Creativity Research Journal,* which was devoted to Creativity in the Moral Domain. There I explored a definition of creativity that depended on two things—one, intentions, and the other, unconventionality. The second of these may be manifested as nonconformity, contrarianism, and rebelliousness. In this light creativity is curtailed by conventions, dogma, tradition, and conformity. The conclusion in that article was that creativity and morality are not opposites, even though the former is often unconventional and the latter often conventional. Further, creativity (both malevolent and benevolent) is tied to intentions. Admittedly, that does mean that serendipity and fortunate accidents are uncreative, given that they may not be intentional, but Louis Pasteur was no doubt correct when he said, "fortune favors the prepared mind". You might say that values can lead the person to look for creative ideas, and even if a discovery is serendipitous, intentionality was involved in the process.

The work on morals is enormously important, and probably more important today than ever before. After all, the problems facing humanity are more pressing and global (e.g., climate crises) than ever before. Moral creativity may also help with the political problems that now face USA and much of the world, with democracy under systematic attack (Maddow, 2019). This is why much of my own writing explores the value of creativity for the solving of political problems (Runco, 2017, 2020). Several ongoing empirical investigations are assessing political creativity among adolescents and should be published in the near future.

Creativity is Not a Rock

There is a kind of convergence in my thinking, with both intentions and the concept of potential apparent in my work on the theory of *personal creativity* (Runco, 1996). The theory of personal creativity will be reviewed below and will explain why I mentioned surprises above. In addition, contrarianism is again apparent. I have already mentioned that, early in the 1980s, I was told not to do a dissertation on creativity because creativity was more art than science—but I moved ahead, confident that there was a way to be objective about creativity, so it could be studied with scientific methods. That was the underlying aim of my early empirical work: I tried to contribute to the small body of research that demonstrated objectivity in studies of creativity. Most of my work was correlational, which does have limitations (e.g., no evidence of cause and effect), but it was a step in the right direction. It was justified by the belief about objectivity. The point is that I put a great deal of thought into supporting a science of creativity. Little did I know how well that science would develop. In fact, the surprise mentioned twice above was that the science of creativity grew and grew—and went too far! In my eyes, it became too objective. This extremely objective view of creativity adopted theories and methods that actually mislead people about creativity. They may even be the norm these days, which means I am now fighting the opposite battle, now arguing that creativity is not well understood with maximally objective methods. I once gave a talk, "Creativity is not a Rock", the thesis of which was that methods that work in the hard sciences do not necessarily apply, across the board, to creativity. That includes geology, which is why I mentioned the rock. Surprisingly, early on in my career I did my best to show that creativity could be objectively studied. Late in my career I remained a contrarian but with the opposite intent. Creativity research had gone too far towards objectivity (Runco, 1999).

Examples of misleading theories that focus too much on objectivity include product theories and theories that posit that creativity must be defined in terms of social recognition. Recall here Simonton's (1988, 1995) idea of persuasion. That is a useful approach, but much of this work is focused on genius and not on creative potential. There is also the Systems Theory of Csiksentmihalyi, which I was happy to include in the Inaugural issue of the *Creativity Research Journal* in

1988 and which was thus influential 30 years ago. This systems theory describes how an individual may have an idea, and the most attractive ideas are then being adopted by others working in the same field. If the field itself adopts the idea (or method, or concept, or insight), it may become a part of the entire domain. At that point it may influence newcomers to the field. This is not itself an objectionable view, but it has been taken too far in theories that argue very explicitly that there is no creativity without social recognition. Kasof's (1995) attributional theory exemplifies the extreme and misleading theory of social recognition. It requires attributions by people other than the creator or else there is no creativity. In fact, Kasof went so far as to suggest that people who want to be creative should invest in "impression management" techniques so they are more likely to influence the judgments and attributions of others! Kasof's attributional theory was presented as a featured article in the *Creativity Research Journal*, along with a number of commentaries. My own commentary on attributional theory suggested that impression management would result in a "displaced investment". Such behavior is displaced in the sense that the creator would be better off investing time into the creative work rather than investing in things outside of it, such as the impressions of others. The convergence mentioned above is apparent because personal creativity was not only a reaction to theories requiring social recognition. Personal creativity also includes intentions, just as did creative morality (Runco, 1993).

Many of the same issues plague the product approach to creativity. Very likely the attraction of product approaches to creativity is that products can be seen, measured, counted. It is in that sense that they are amenable to objective study. But products do not inform us about the processes that lead to the outcome. They only really inform about the product, and all else, including an explanation of the creative process, must be inferred. Further, such inferences are always a look backwards. We might identify an unambiguously creative product, but how did it come about? To answer that we must look to the past, and that information is not always reliable or even available (Runco et al., 2010). True, product research is useful, but it is certainly not be the best way to get at process, and without identifying the process, we do not have much of an explanation (Jay & Perkins, 1997).

Processes must be studied if we are to best understand how to fulfill creative potential. Efforts to fulfill creative potential must target the mechanism that is responsible for creative behavior. That mechanism involves various processes. Educators are unlikely to get very far if they merely show their charges highly creative individuals or unambiguously creative products and leave it at that. At best the students may be impressed by the creativity. They may be inspired and they may want to be creative. This is not far from the internalization of values mentioned above; but by itself, it is unlikely to pay dividends. Students must also learn methods and practice the process. Procedural knowledge should be included in any effort to fulfill creative potentials.

More on the Science of Creativity

Earlier I used the term "optimal objectivity" for studies of creativity. The product approach and social theories that require social recognition tend to go too far. They only examine creative products, not the underlying processes, and they require social recognition, which precludes personal creativity. Social theories also disregard one of the tenets of science, namely, parsimony. They conflate social impact, fame, and recognition with creation, which is far from parsimonious. Social recognition is not required for personal creativity.

In the theory of personal creativity, something new and effective is brought into existence. My own suggestion for the processes leading up to such creation involves intentions, as well as the construction of an original interpretation. The latter is something that is well recognized in cognitive psychology where top-down information processing and perception allow the construction of meaning. The resulting new idea or insight may be shared with others, but it need not be, which is why the focus is on personal creativity. If the new idea or insight is shared, there may be a reaction, but the new idea may be ignored, or examined and dismissed, or perhaps appreciated. Such appreciation, and any recognition that may be bestowed on the idea, is the result of processes that are independent of the actual creative processes used by the creator. Reactions come after creation. Thus, insight is one thing, but impact is quite another (Runco, 1995). It is misleading to conflate the two.

The latest version of the theory of personal creativity does acknowledge social recognition (Runco & Beghetto, 2018). It refers to *primary creativity*, which is essentially the personal creativity outlined above, but also *secondary creativity*, which is the creativity required by an audience as they construct their own interpretation of the idea put forth by the initial creator. Hence creators use the process relying on the construction of new interpretations, and if they share their new idea, an audience may use the same process. If they do, they too are creative. Still, the creativity by the individual does not depend on the creativity or attribution by an audience. Note how the social recognition follows the creator's own work. As such it is easy to see how primary creativity is distinct from secondary creativity.

Contrarianism is apparent in that this theory was started as a reaction to (i.e., rejection of) socially recognized creativity. Contrarianism is also apparent my criticisms of the Big C/little c dichotomy so often used in the literature (Runco, 2014). The Big C/little c dichotomy implies that there are two kinds of creativity. One is related to famous creativity and one is related to everyday or personal creativity. Interestingly, Merrotsy (2013) did a literature review to determine the origin of the dichotomy and did not find much! He ended up concluding that Big C/little c dichotomy may have been borrowed from studies of culture, where there is also a Big C/little c dichotomy. Worse than the unknown origin is the fact that the Big c/little c dichotomy implies that the two kinds of creativity may be independent of one another when in fact they may be inextricable. It is quite possible that the capacity to construct original interpretations, which is a critical aspect of personal creativity, is vital also to eminent and world-class creativity, though eminent creativity may also involve expertise, persistence, and other things—things that often come after the actual creation and are not causally important to it. In this light, the Big C/little c creativity distinction is actually a false dichotomy. True, it is very frequently cited in the creativity research, but these citations may be perpetuating a myth. This may be harmful if, say, the dichotomy is shared with educators or students. They should be told that personal creativity can lead to significant instances of creativity, even eminent creativity. They should not be told that students' creativity is of one sort, while famous creators' talents were of a completely different sort, as the Big C/little c distinction implies. One final point: there are better terms for Big C (eminent, world-class) and little c (personal, everyday) creativity.

Divergent Thinking

This is a good place to say a bit more about the research on divergent thinking. That is because the ideas that are a result of divergent thinking may very well be important to creators of all levels and domains. Certainly, what constitutes an idea may vary. Ideas are not always verbal, for example, though often when they are studied or quantified the focus is on verbal ideas. That is just convenience; it is difficult to operationalize ideas that take other forms. Realistically, there are likely to be musical ideas, kinesthetic ideas, intrapersonal ideas, and so on, as well as verbal ideas. Put differently, it may be that ideas are preverbal (cf. Tweney, 1996) and only midway through the cognitive creative process are symbols brought in so the gist of the idea can be communicated. This is merely a hypothesis, but regardless, there is a huge amount of research on ideas and divergent thinking and there is no reason to think that it only applies to a limited segment of the human population.

Recall that this chapter refers to context and change. It contains many examples of how academic and social contexts have changed, and the creativity research has followed along. One thing has not changed all that much: the fact that ideas are valuable. This is evidenced by the fact that J. P. Guilford is often cited as being instrumental in giving the creativity research a huge push forward (Plucker, 2001). Admittedly several other contextual events also pushed the interest in creativity, including Sputnik and the concern over USA falling being in science and technology, but Guilford detailed the reasons to study creativity in his famous APA Presidential Address, and he provided various methodologies. True, his statistical approach was subjective and was quickly rejected by Undheim and Horn (1977) and others, but the statistical problems were with the general structure-of-intellect model and not Guilford's conception of divergent thinking (or what he called divergent production). Divergent thinking has been studied, with a bit of variation, ever since Guilford proposed it.

The research on divergent thinking has undergone some changes. That dissertation I was not supposed to do was on divergent thinking. I was interested in the overlap of the indices taken from divergent thinking tests and adopted a statistical method that allowed me to control one of them (fluency, or the number of ideas produced) while examining another (originality, or the statistical novelty of the ideas). Then I examined the reliability of the residuals. I took those residuals to represent pure originality or originality that was not dependent on fluency and ideational productivity. Results indicated that, in the more talented segment of my sample, originality was reliable after fluency was statistically controlled. This was an important finding because many examiners look only to fluency, and the data indicate that this practice is a mistake. It is a mistake because of theory, as well. Originality is a part of nearly all definitions of creativity. It is a prerequisite. Fluency is not. There are also experimental manipulations that indicate that it would be a mistake to rely on fluency. These investigations (cf. Acar, Runco, & Park, in press; Runco, 1986b; Runco et al., 2005) use explicit instructions that require examinees to direct their thinking toward fluency, or originality, or perhaps flexibility (where the individual taps diverse conceptual categories). Results indicate that increased fluency does not lead to increased originality. The explicit instructions can change one index (fluency, or originality, or flexibility) while not changing the others. If the indices were dependent on one another and originality or flexibility dependent on fluency, such selective changes would not be possible. Recently, computerized scoring of divergent- thinking tests has replicated the results of my dissertation and reconfirmed that originality is reliable even after fluency is controlled (Dumas & Runco, 2018).

While the research on divergent thinking and ideation suggests that some things have remained fairly stable over the years (i.e., a respect for ideas as part of creative cognition), the use of computerized scoring indicates that there have been important changes resulting from technological advance. The computer methods have added much to the research on divergent thinking, in part because they relate ideation to models of semantic memory and associative networks. Computerized scoring methods can, for instance, calculate distances between ideas produced, which is very much like the idea of remote associates from theories of creativity (Mednick, 1962). In addition, there is a parallel between ideational flexibility, from theories of divergent thinking, and semantic or conceptual variety. So, while theories of divergent thinking point to the value of flexible ideation, computer methods can calculate how many different conceptual categories are used as an individual produces ideas. In short, computer methods have changed the actual testing as well as the scoring, with clear-cut implications for creative cognition (Acar & Runco, 2014; Hass, 2015).

Dare to be a Radical but Don't be a Damn Fool

This chapter identified contrarianism as a reaction to several of the contexts that have influenced thinking about creativity but changed over the years. One scientific context assumed that creativity was not an appropriate topic for objective and scientific investigation, and then, less than 20 years later, the field went too far toward objectivity, or at least depended too much on product investigations and a definition that included social recognition. At one point in my career I reacted to one scientific context and argued that creativity could be studied scientifically; 20 years later I had to write about the misleading nature of social recognition and the need to study creativity with a science that was not overly objective.

This chapter has said a bit about the art bias, which is a problem when it misleads educators (who may assume that creativity is only expressed in the arts), but this should not be taken to imply that the arts should be disregarded by the research on creativity. The arts are unambiguously creative and as such highly informative. There is much to learn from studies of the arts. What comes to mind right now, given what was said just above about contexts changing and the field going from one extreme to the other, is the lyric, "nine mile skid on a 10 mile ride" (Jerry Garcia, "He's Gone"). The field of creativity certainly has a huge amount of momentum! But we must keep in mind that even though scientific study is of utmost importance, some parts of creativity are personal, and the emotional, aesthetic, personal aspects are not easy to quantify. Creativity is a unique human capacity and as such requires a unique brand of science, with objective methods—but not the same entirely objective methods that are used with the hard sciences.

Contrarianism can also be taken too far, so care must be taken when offering recommendations for the fulfillment of potential. One recommendation points to *ego strength* (i.e., self-confidence and grit) and standing up for oneself. Creativity does require originality, and originality in turn requires non-conformity, contrarianism, and even rebellion. At the same time, recommendations must include suggestions to exercise discretion. Here, discretion is much like "choosing your battles", or more precisely, knowing when to rebel and when to act in a conventional manner. There is much to be said for fitting in and getting along with other people, and fitting in often requires conventional behavior, not rebellion. People need to be aware of laws and rules, and often should follow them—for safety and consideration of others. Thus, what is most important is to exercise discretion. People should be mindful of their immediate contexts and make mindful decisions about when to conform and when to rebel, when to rely on routine, tradition, and convention, or when to try something new, express originality, and break with the past. This all suggests that *post-conventional* thinking is good for creativity (Runco & Charles, 1997), for it is defined in terms of an awareness of conventions, combined with a capacity to think for oneself. This view also supports a quotation Frank Barron once shared with me and has been one of the most useful things I have heard in nearly 40 years of work on creativity: "Dare to be a radical but don't be a damn fool".

References

Acar, S., & Runco, M. A. (2014). Assessing associative distance among ideas elicited by tests of divergent thinking. *Creativity Research Journal*, 26, 229–238.
Acar, S., Runco, M. A., & Park, H. (in press). What should people be told when they take a divergent thinking test? A meta-analytic review of explicit instructions for divergent thinking. *Psychology of Aesthetics, Creativity, and the Arts*.
Baer, J. (1991). Generality of creativity across performance domains. *Creativity Research Journal*, 4, 23–40.
Barron, F. (1995). *No rootless flower*. Hampton Press.
Cropley, A. J. (2014). Is there an "arts bias" in the *Creativity Research Journal*? *Creativity Research Journal*, 26, 368–371.
Cropley, D. H., Cropley, H. J., Kaufman, J. C., & Runco, M. A. (Eds.) (2010). *The dark side of creativity*. Cambridge University Press.
Csikszentmihalyi, M. (1988). Solving a problem is not finding one: A reply to Simon. *New Ideas in Psychology*, 6, 183–186.
Dumas, D., & Runco, M. A. (2018). Objectively scoring divergent thinking tests for originality: A re-analysis and extension. *Creativity Research Journal*, 30, 466–468.
Epstein, R. (1990). Generativity theory. In M. A. Runco & R. S. Albert (Eds.), *Theories of creativity* (pp. 116–140). Sage.
Gardner, H. (2000). *Intelligence Reframed: Multiple Intelligences for the 21st Century*. Basic Books.
Gardner, H., Csikszentmihalyi, M., & Damon, W. (2008). *Good work*. Basic Books.
Gergen, K. (1973). Social psychology as history. *Journal of Personality and Social Psychology*, 26, 309–320.
Gruber, H. E. (1981). *Darwin on man: A psychological study of scientific creativity*. University of Chicago Press.
Gruber, H. E. (1993). Creativity in the moral domain: Ought implies can implies create. *Creativity Research Journal*, 6, 3–15.
Gruber, H. (1996). The life space of a scientist: The visionary function and other aspects of Jean Piaget's thinking. *Creativity Research Journal*, 9, 251–265.
Gruber, H. E., & Wallace, D. (1993). Creativity in the moral domain. *Creativity Research Journal*, 6, 1–200.
Guilford, J. (1975) Creativity: A quarter century of progress. In I. Taylor & J. Getzels (Eds.), *Perspectives in creativity* (pp. 37–59). Aldine Publishing Company.
Hass, R. W. (2015). Feasibility of online divergent thinking assessment. *Computers in Human Behavior*, 46, 85–93.
Helson, R. (1999). Institute of Personality Assessment and Research. In M. A. Runco & S. Pritzker (Eds.), *Encyclopedia of creativity* (pp. 71–79). Elsevier.
Jay, E., & Perkins, D. (1997). Creativity's compass: A review of problem finding. In M. A. Runco (Ed.), *Creativity research handbook* (vol. 1, pp. 257–293). Hampton Press.
Kasof, J. (1995). Explaining creativity: The attributional perspective. *Creativity Research Journal*, 8, 311–366.
Maddow, R. (2019). *Blowout: Corrupted democracy, rogue state Russia, and the richest, most destructive industry on earth*. Random House.
MacKinnon, D. W. (1962). The nature and nurture of creative talent. *American Psychologist*, 17, 484–495.
McLaren, R. B. (1993). The dark side of creativity. *Creativity Research Journal*, 6, 137–144.
Mednick, S. (1962). The associative basis of the creative process. *Psychological Review*, 69, 220–232.

Merrotsy, P. (2013). A note on Big C creativity and little c creativity. *Creativity Research Journal*, 25, 474.
Miller, A. (2019). *The artist in the machine: The world of AI-powered creativity*. The MIT Press.
Patrick, C. (1935). Creative thought in poets. *Archives of Psychology*, 26, 1–74.
Patrick, C. (1937). Creative thought in artists. *Journal of Psychology*, 5, 35–73.
Patrick, C. (1938). Scientific thought. *Journal of Psychology*, 5, 55–83.
Piaget, J. (1950). *The psychology of intelligence*. Harcourt Brace.
Plucker, J. A. (1998). Beware of simple conclusions: The case for content generality of creativity. *Creativity Research Journal*, 11, 179–182.
Plucker, J. A. (2001). Introduction to the Special Issue: Commemorating Guilford's 1950 presidential address. *Creativity Research Journal*, 13, 247.
Rhodes, M. (1961). An analysis of creativity. *Phi Delta Kappan*, 42, 305–310.
Runco, M. A. (1986a). The generality of creative performance in gifted and nongifted children. *Gifted Child Quarterly*, 31, 121–125.
Runco, M. A. (1986b). Maximal performance on divergent thinking tests by gifted, talented, and nongifted children. *Psychology in the Schools*, 23, 308–315.
Runco, M. A. (1993). Moral creativity: Intentional and unconventional. *Creativity Research Journal*, 6, 17–28.
Runco, M. A. (1995). Insight for creativity, expression for impact. *Creativity Research Journal*, 8, 377–390.
Runco, M. A. (1996). Personal creativity: Definition and developmental issues. *New Directions for Child Development*, 72, 3–30.
Runco, M. A. (1999). Creativity need not be social. In A. Montuori & R. Purser (Eds.), *Social creativity* (vol. 1, pp. 237–264). Hampton.
Runco, M. A. (2003). You can't understand the butterfly without (also) observing the caterpillar: Comment on Mumford. *Creativity Research Journal*, 15, 137–141.
Runco, M. A. (2010). Creativity has no dark side. In D. H. Cropley, A. J. Cropley, J. C. Kaufman, & M. A. Runco (Eds.), *The dark side of creativity* (pp. 15–32). Cambridge University Press.
Runco, M. A. (2014) "Big C, little c" creativity as a false dichotomy: Reality is not categorical. *Creativity Research Journal*, 26, 131–132.
Runco, M. A. (2017). Active ethical leadership, giftedness, and creativity. *Roeper Review*, 39, 242–249.
Runco, M. A. (2019a). Behavioral view of creativity. In M. A. Runco & S. R. Pritizker (Eds.), *Encyclopedia of creativity* (3rd ed.). Elsevier.
Runco, M. A. (2019b). B. F. Skinner on poetry, fiction, and design: An implicit science of creativity. In V. Glavaneau (Ed.), *Classic readings in the creativity research* (pp. 409–430). Oxford University Press.
Runco, M. A. (2020). Political examples of a dark side of creativity and the impact on education. In C. Mullen (Ed.), *Education under duress*. Springer.
Runco, M. A., & Acar, S. (2019). Divergent thinking. In J. C. Kaufman & R. J. Sternberg (Eds.), *The Cambridge handbook of creativity* (pp. 224–253). Cambridge University Press.
Runco, M. A., & Beghetto, R. (2018). Primary and secondary creativity. *Current Opinion in Behavior Science*, 27, 7–10.
Runco, M. A., & Charles, R. (1997). Developmental trends in creativity. In M. A. Runco (Ed.), *Creativity research handbook* (vol. 1, pp. 113–150). Hampton.
Runco, M. A., & Jaeger, G. (2012). The standard definition of creativity. *Creativity Research Journal*, 24, 92–96.

Runco, M. A., Illies, J. J., & Reiter-Palmon, R. (2005). Explicit instructions to be creative and original: A comparison of strategies and criteria as targets with three types of divergent thinking tests. *Korean Journal of Thinking and Problem Solving*, 15, 5–15.

Runco, M. A., Kaufman, J. C., Halliday, L. R., & Cole, J. C. (2010). Change in reputation as index of genius and eminence. *Historical Methods*, 43, 91–96.

Simon, H. (1988). Creativity and motivation: A response to Csikszentmihalyi. *New Ideas in Psychology*, 6, 177–181.

Simonton, D. K. (1988). Creativity, leadership, and chance. In R. J. Sternberg (Ed.), *The nature of creativity: Contemporary psychological perspectives* (pp. 386–426). Cambridge University Press.

Simonton, D. K. (1995). Exceptional personal influence: An integrative paradigm. *Creativity Research Journal*, 8, 371–376.

Tweney, R. D. (1996). Presymbolic processes in scientific creativity. *Creativity Research Journal*, 9, 163–172.

Undheim, J. O., & Horn, J. L. (1977). Critical evaluation of Guilford's structure-of-intellect theory. *Intelligence*, 1, 65–81.

12

FEMALE TEACHER/RESEARCHER

My Work in Talent Development Education and in Creativity Education

Jane Piirto

Context for My Work

My story is unusual for this anthology. The context for my work is the field of the education of the gifted and talented. I entered this field at the age of 36. I am a retired professor of education and was the Director of Talent Development Education at Ashland University, leading the endorsement and Master of Education programs, whereby teachers obtained state approval to teach identified gifted and talented students. I was in the field from 1977 to 2017—40 years. Before being the lead professor in charge of the gifted endorsement courses at my institution, I worked for 13 years as a high school teacher, college instructor, coordinator of programs at regional education offices, and principal of the oldest school for gifted children in New York City, the Hunter College Elementary School. My shadow self was and is as a published and award-winning poet and novelist.

Influence One

The Federal Report, *National Excellence*, came out in 1993, just as I was writing my synoptic textbook, *Talented Children and Adults: Their Development and Education*, a basic textbook under contract with Merrill, for people studying the education of the gifted and talented. This report famously encountered the use of the term "gifted" and suggested using the term "outstanding talent". The most successful basic textbook author at that time was Barbara Clark, and her book had gone into several editions. My editor at Merrill hoped that my book would do the same. With this influential report, I engaged in a search and replace action for my manuscript and began to name the strengths by domain. I replaced the term "gifted" with "academic talent", "high IQ", "mathematical talent", "verbal talent", "spatial talent", and the like. I changed the title of the book from "Gifted Children and Adults" to *Talented Children and Adults: Their Development and Education*. This report and its suggestion that we drop the term "gifted" was profoundly influential for my work, as it made me think about talent in domains, and to discount the influence of IQ assessment for identifying such.

Influence Two

Another influence in my thinking was my eight years of work with alternative assessment in our field. Mary Meeker (1969) modified the work of J. P. Guilford using 26 of his 120 tests to assess school children. Meeker was my first real mentor in the field. Since I entered the field while doing my PhD in another field, I had no relevant advisers. In 1977, I attended a two-day seminar in Columbus, Ohio, given by Meeker, teaching us to administer and interpret the Structure of Intellect Learning Abilities Test (SOI-LA). I had a background in assessment from my studies to become a guidance counselor, and this test attracted me, because it purported to focus on strengths and to minimize socio-economic differences. It de-emphasized the importance of IQ, and offered diagnosis and remediation for academic weaknesses.

I became an advanced trainer. I conducted many workshops throughout the country, flying to school districts, taking up the slack for Meeker or her husband Robert. I peddled the use of the test with identified gifted populations. I even conducted SOI assessment workshops in my home and at a local Bowling Green motel conference room. Many of my colleagues in gifted education in Ohio and Michigan wanted to find alternative means of finding smart people, means that were not IQ tests. I said I had the answer: the SOI!

But when I used the SOI Learning Abilities Test to test some students in the Hunter College Elementary School who were judged by teachers to be having academic difficulties, the results told us none of the students needed remediation because they were gifted. I realized that the SOI test ceilings were too low for high IQ students. I had been out nationwide in the community of educators of the gifted and talented, propounding an instrument that was not suitable for the population for which it was being touted. Carroll (1993) called Guilford's research methodology "idiosyncratic" and discounted it, saying that it could not be replicated, and the *Mental Measurements Yearbook*'s test evaluation reviews were less than positive. Later, I wrote a biographical study of Meeker for a book about pioneers in our field. I sympathize with the work she tried to do. The pressure on test-makers in validating their work must be extreme.

Influence Three

In creating my research line, I had to figure out how to work alone, without graduate-student help, while teaching 12 hours a semester. My graduate students were full-time employed teachers and school administrators, taking courses to add to their credentialing. Who could I do research with? Or on? I had colleagues in the field at other universities and in schools with whom I could collaborate, and I did (*pace* Diane Montgomery, John Fraas, Barry Oreck, F. Christopher Reynolds, David Feldman, Kari Uusikyla, Susan Keller-Mathers, Karen Micko), but mostly I worked alone. I continued to write and receive grants for Summer Honors Institutes from the State of Ohio, so I had a population upon which I could collect personality assessment data—and I did. I am still sitting on much data.

I had to create a line that engaged me. What would inspire me to have the self-discipline to continue? I like to invent. I like assessment. I like textual analysis and I am also curious about and find pleasure in reading biographical materials. These were the lines I tried to merge.

Genesis of the Piirto Pyramid of Talent Development and My Work on Creativity

As I was writing the textbook (Piirto, 1994, 1999, 2007) under contract for Merrill (later Prentice Hall, Pearson, and then Prufrock), I was also simultaneously reading for and writing a book on creativity under contract for Ohio Psychology Press (later Great Potential Press). It was called *Understanding Those Who Create* (Piirto, 1992, 1998), and the third edition was renamed *Understanding Creativity* (Piirto, 2004).

After doing the wide and intense writing and reading for both books, I thought and thought. I wanted to synthesize the material into a theory of talent development. I walked around my life, in a process of incubation, seeking insight, thinking "What does it all mean?" "What does it mean?" I lived alone with my cat—my children were grown and gone—and so the general practices of silence, exercise, and writing ritual were easy companions.

Fortuitously for my simultaneous work on the creative process, as it gave me a story to tell during lectures, I was driving on I-80 through Pennsylvania, the beautiful scenery unfolding, music on the stereo in my car, weather perfect, meditating. It came to me: "It's personality. It's not IQ, it's personality!" I drove to my daughter's and her husband's new apartment in Brooklyn and slept in a sleeping bag on their newly carpeted floor, the fumes rising as if this were Delphi, and I were the oracle, the middle-aged woman in the tent sitting on a tripod, sniffing the gas rising from the chasm in the earth, making prophecies.

In the middle of the night, I had a dream of Greek gods shooting arrows. Apollo evoked. I got up and sketched three figures—the god of genetics, the god of personality, the god of cognition, all shooting arrows into an amorphous cloud I called "talent". This imaginative dream was natural for me, as a former English major with a master's degree in literature, who had taught Greek mythology to undergraduates in the 1960s. I have been a frequenter of Jungian dream workshops and keep notebooks of my dreams. Creating to me has its mystical side, and as a writer of poems and stories, I embrace this wholeheartedly. My practical side embraces statistical proof, but my inner self listens to emotion, ambiguity, and the enigmatic.

The Piirto Pyramid of Talent Development

When I got back to Ohio, teaching my first class of the semester in 1992, I passed out xeroxed copies of the first chapter of the manuscript, as Merrill was going to field test it on my students. I explained the intuitive drawing of the arrow-shooting gods, emphasizing my insight that talent is developed through force of personality. My students were compliant and nodded their heads. This was their first class in their endorsement sequence and they had never heard of nor did they understand what I was talking about.

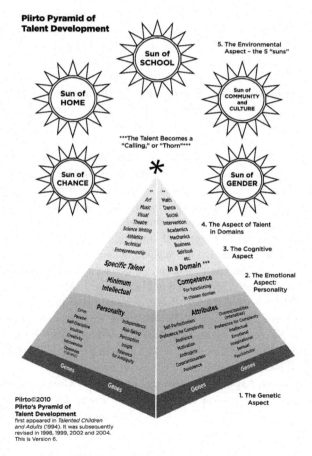

FIGURE 12.1 Piirto Pyramid of Talent Development

But one student stayed after class. She bravely said, "I am a graphic designer. Maybe I can help you with your image. It's kind of a mess, and confusing. You might want to think of a ziggurat". I drove the 75 miles north to my home in the college town I lived in, thinking, "Confusing". "A mess". In my mailbox was a magazine I have subscribed to for a long time—*Vanity Fair*. I like to read the articles and look at the glossy ads. I love the perfume bottles. I poured wine and thumbed through the magazine, with the late news on the television, relaxing after my long day. There in the magazine was a pyramid-shaped form in one of the ads. I tore out the ad and glued it to a piece of paper (Piirto, 2011a).

1. **The Genetic Aspect: Sub-terrestrial.** In its first iteration I had the genetic aspect as an environmental Sun, but in the second edition of the book, I moved it where it belongs—beneath. Fascinated by the work of the Minnesota Studies of Twins Raised Apart, and the work of Bouchard and Plomin and the popularity of genetic theory, I thought about the pervasiveness that we do not even know and are now discovering, of genetic influences. This includes genetic manipulation, according to my nephew, who is currently doing his PhD working on CRISPR at the University of California.

2. **The Emotional Aspect: Personality Attributes.** In my literature review for *Talented Children and Adults*, I accumulated a long list of personality attributes found in various studies. The index for the textbook listed many personality attributes, and in the first edition, I made the list into a chart that summarized their strength among the many studies. Germinal was the Institute for Personality Assessment and Research (IPAR) studies conducted by Barron, MacKinnon, Helson, and others, of practicing writers, architects, inventors, mathematicians, and scientists. The beauty of these studies was that they had comparison groups, conducted much assessment with various instruments, and used Q-sorts and other instruments when they invited the talented people to campus for a weeklong visit. I also was influenced by the proceedings from the Utah creativity conferences in the 1950s and 1960s and by their books published by small publishers and hard to find. Now, with the advent of the Big Five (NEO-PI-R), personality studies can continue with a base instrument and theory. So far, the more current studies have yielded the stronger presence of Openness to Experience among the talented (Kaufman, 2012; Vuyk, Kerr, & Krieshok, 2016), which is one of my Five Core Attitudes for the Creative Process in my work on creativity.

3. **The Cognitive Aspect: Minimum Intellectual Competence.** The main influence on this band on the Pyramid of Talent Development was Dean Keith Simonton (1984), who listed the minimum intellectual capacities necessary for achievement in domains. Linda Gottfredson's work also was influential (Gottfredson, 2001). I was interested in doing away with cutoff scores for inclusion in programs, and although the checklists of Feldhusen

and colleagues, Johnsen and colleagues, and Renzulli and colleagues were important, I also knew that the wheel has already been invented, as elite programs in the arts, sciences, mathematics, and literature, social sciences, and physical performance already had sophisticated criteria that they used to evaluate talent.

4. **The Aspect of Talent in the Domain.** The disappointment of strivers who feel called to do work in one domain or another, but who don't have the mysterious "talent", is important here. I subscribe to the definition of talent that is in the dictionary: "natural aptitude or skill". The expertise researchers and some who insist that talent comes after giftedness, have unnecessarily complicated the problem (Ericsson, Krampe, R. & Tesch-Romer, 1993; Gagné, 1985). It's unfair, but some people are better able to do some things than others. Domains shift according to the Zeitgeist—there is little need for the hunting talent nowadays, and the coding talent has come to the forefront.

5. **The "Thorn".** However, some of those with talent do not want to do the work of refining and developing that talent, and that is OK. In insisting that the thorn is a psychological impetus, that people cannot do the work when they are so motivated, I follow Jung (1965) and Hillman, among others. The archetypal psychologist James Hillman (1996) described the presence of the *daimon* in creative lives. In *The Soul's Code*, Hillman (1996) described the talents in a way similar to Plato's and Jung's: "The talent is only a piece of the image; many are born with musical, mathematical, and mechanical talent, but only when the talent serves the fuller image and is carried by its character do we recognize exceptionality" (p. 45). The thorn is similar to the "call", but without the religious overtones.

Environmental Suns. Then I drew the "suns", the environmental influences on talent development. I had consulted with the American schools in Cairo, Egypt, and had visited the pyramids. I had also noticed how, when you look up at the blue sky from the Nile River in a felucca, it seems as if the sky is full of many suns.

6A **Sun of Chance:** I had used Tannenbaum's (1983) book, *Gifted Children*, as a basic text. I admired his starfish model, and especially his inclusion of the influence of chance in the lives of all of us, including the talented. I made Sun of Chance as an environmental influence, influenced by Tannenbaum.

As a working-class daughter of a welder for a mining company in a northern rural town in the Upper Peninsula of Michigan, I know how important the Sun of Chance is. When I was the principal in New York City, I received many calls from casting agents and producers wanting to look at our bright children for possible roles in movies, television, and theater. These children had the luck of being born in and living in a center for theatrical activity. The inclusion of the Sun of Chance as an environmental factor was also influenced by the work of Simonton (1984) on *proximity* and its importance in the development of talent.

The Sun of Chance has clouds over it when a talented adolescent in a rural high school does not get the counseling needed to make a college choice that will enhance a career. In high school, I didn't even get information on how to sign up for the SAT, and I have never taken the test. My whole entrance into academe as a career had been influenced by my professors at Northern Michigan University nominating me for the editorship of the university student newspaper and for the Woodrow Wilson Graduate Fellowship. I was shocked. I didn't even know what you had to do to get a PhD and I had never thought of going to graduate school. But I took their word and applied for the fellowship and also to graduate schools. They raised my aspirations with their confidence in a shy commuter student.

6B **The Sun of Home.** This was apparent as an influence—I was doing heavy reading of biographies for *Understanding Those Who Create* (1992, 1998), which I had proposed as a book with separate chapters on talented people in domains: visual artists/architects; creative writers; mathematicians/scientists/; musicians/composers; actors/dancers/physical performers. I was finding different themes in the various domains about their family dynamics—for example childhood trauma in writers and rock musicians. I also admired Bloom's (1985) edited book, which included a lot about the families of the talented people he and his colleagues studied.

6C **The Sun of School.** I am an educator, teaching teachers how to teach talented youth. The Sun of School had been very important in my own life, as with the story above about how my professors influenced my life. My parents were not college graduates and while they were avid supporters of me and my sisters, they did not have the tacit knowledge touted by Sternberg in his model, to advise us about choice of college, though my father, when he was in his cups, would urge me: "You're smart. A teacher? You want to be a teacher? Go to the University of Michigan and be a doctor. Go for the money".

6D **The Sun of Community and Culture**. It became apparent in the biographies, interviews, and memoirs I was reading that all of the people were influenced by their friends and colleagues. The myth of the lonely creator in his garret scribbling or painting alone is just that. In my own artistic life, I was also a member of a community of creative writers—the Toledo Poets Center and other writing groups. My comrades in writing poetry and fiction were dear to me. As soon as I began to write literature and to send out my work, I reached out to others doing the same thing. I wrote fan letters to writers whom I admired. I sent work out to my friends to be critiqued, and I critiqued their work. I gave readings. I attended conferences and workshops. I published my friends in the poetry postcards of my small press, and in chapbooks.

The Sun of Community and Culture was illustrated also in my work as a professional in the community of educators of the gifted and talented. I had lunch with, traveled with, and talked to fellow coordinators of programs for the gifted and talented in both states where I was initially employed as a coordinator—Ohio and Michigan. When I went to New York City, Hunter College hired a young researcher who had attended the school where I was principal, Hunter College Elementary School—Rena Subotnik, who was working on a follow-up study of her schoolmates of the 1960s. She hired two students to search for addresses in the banged-up old metal boxes in the basement of the school. The kids worked in my office before school. Rena and I became friends, influencing each other. One of her findings in this longitudinal study was surprising. A common trope in our field is that the high IQ students called "gifted" are our "future leaders". Subotnik, Kassan, Summers, & Wasser (1993) found the opposite. Like the Terman study participants, who had not attended a special school, few, if any of the students who had attended this special school did anything extraordinary in their lives. The researchers said, "Like the Terman group, none of the members of the Hunter group has [yet] achieved the status of a revolutionary thinker" (p. 143). Such innovative and radical thought usually emerges out of obsession and idealism, and the Hunter group expressed wistfulness for lost idealism, but they remained relatively conservative and pleased with their conformity. The belief, or charge, that high-IQ students are our "future leaders", seems not to have been supported by either the Terman or the Hunter group. This study later led me (Subotnik was also doing separate but parallel paths of thought) to add the "thorn" to the Piirto Pyramid.

I joined professional associations, ran for state and national offices, and was appointed to task forces and the like. Colleagues and I enjoyed discussing our work and we influenced each other. We gradually built up a lot of group trust and I still attend certain conferences just so I can see them annually. When the Piirto Pyramid was first published, in 1994, John Feldhusen of Purdue wrote me a congratulatory letter and published my first article on the Pyramid in a journal issue he was editing. Frank Barron wrote and said "The 'Pyramid' is excellent—a compact, eloquent, graphic synthesis". Franz Monks, of the European Council for High Ability, asked me to speak about the Pyramid at the 1994 meeting. Such attention steadily continued, both nationally and internationally.

6E **The Sun of Gender.** Like other young intellectual women of the late 1960s and early 1970s, I had belonged to consciousness-raising groups. I did my PhD in educational leadership at Bowling Green State University. My interest in women led me to focus on a qualitative historical dissertation called *The Female Teacher: Teaching as a "Women's Profession"*. I had read about Catherine Beecher (Sklar, 1973) and her attempt in the nineteenth century to have single women not be spinsters in the attics of their brothers-in-law, but to be out in the communities teaching young children. My own aunts had been female teachers—and they had to quit when they got married—and I dedicated the dissertation to my aunt Lynn, who taught for 40 years.

While working on my dissertation, I came to love archival research. I visited the archives of many of the female seminaries at the numerous small colleges in Ohio, perusing teenage diaries and autograph books, letters to parents, and female seminary charters. My background in literature and my constant, continuous life as a reader of many books led me naturally to qualitative research. This choice to do qualitative research led me to be appointed the qualitative research methodologist for our doctoral program in leadership. In the mid-1990s, while on a visiting professorship at the University of Georgia, a hotbed of qualitative research, I audited courses with prominent qualitative research thinkers—for example, Judith Preiss.

Another influence on gender was more formal. Bowling Green State University began a women's studies program in 1979 and needed an adjunct professor. I sent my resume; they called it "pretty", and I began to teach basic women's studies courses. In 1980 I published my first article about gifted girls in *Roeper Review*. I have continued to publish and present about gender. My most recent was a chapter on the Sun of Gender in 2019.

The Piirto Pyramid seems to be a rarity in its emphasis on gender as an environmental factor. Noble, Subotnik, and Arnold (1996), Kerr and McKay (2014), and others have models of female talent development but in general models, the environmental influence of gender on *both* males and females, does not seem to be emphasized.

Impetus

The Piirto Pyramid of Talent Development created the framework around which my work would be organized. I wrote a book on creative writers using the Pyramid as a framework. It is called *"My Teeming Brain": Understanding Creative Writers* (Piirto, 2002). I organized the second and third editions of both the textbook and the creativity book using the Piirto Pyramid.

In order to confirm the emotional aspect on the Pyramid, I began to assess personality attributes in identified gifted teenagers. We spent an hour and a half twice annually, administering assessments to students who attended the Summer Honors Institute I directed. Over 19 summers, I administered them the Myers-Briggs Type Indicator (MBTI), the High School Personality Questionnaire (HSPQ), the Overexcitabilities Questionnaire I & II (OEQ I & II), the Adjective Checklist (ACL), the BEM Sex-Role Inventory (BEM), the Multidimensional Perfectionism Scale (MPS), the Bar-On Emotional Quotient Inventory (BAR-ON EQ-i), and the full Revised NEO Personality Inventory, Adult form (NEO-PI-R).

These personality attributes were confirmed: Intuition, Androgyny [Tender mindedness (M); Tough mindedness (F)]; Perceiving; Introversion; Thinking;

Emotional Intelligence (self-esteem); Openness to Experience; Conscientiousness; Resilience; Perfectionism (Self); OE's (Intellectual, Emotional, Imaginational). I collected data until I had numbers of at least 200 per instrument. Several studies ensued.

Work on Creativity and the Creative Process

Besides thinking up the Pyramid, I seem to have become known for my work on creativity. The impetus was this: I was troubled by the emphasis in our field on divergent production, and on the positivistic creative problem-solving hegemony, as no creators whom I knew nor whom I had read about used either in their creative processes. I have a high tolerance for ambiguity, but these exercises taught in most programs for teacher training in gifted education seemed to be simplistic and, while fun, to have no relationship to what really happened while creating. I decided to go my own way, to do a little risk-taking, and began to teach an interdisciplinary studies class to undergraduates, revising the course subsequently for the graduate students, using a set of exercises I designed that imitated what real creators really do while creating. My teaching motto is "What is the Image?" and these exercises use a lot of imagery (Piirto, 2016).

The books, *Understanding Those Who Create* (1992, 1998), and *Understanding Creativity* (2004) were received quite well, and I was invited to give keynotes, workshops, presentations, and to contribute chapters to edited books. I derived, from the biographies, interviews, and memoirs, three categories of themes:

1. **The Five Core Attitudes for Creativity** (Risk-Taking; Group Trust; Openness to Experience—originally called Naivete after Jung—Self-Discipline; and in 2004 I added Tolerance for Ambiguity.)
2. **The Seven Is** (Improvisation, Insight, Imagination, Intuition, Imagery, and Inspiration). I am contemplating adding another "I"—Intentionality—to go along with the "Thorn".
3. **General Practices for Creativity** (Exercise, Ritual, A Creative Attitude, Study of the Domain, Meditation, Divergent Production practice).

I have files of examples and direct quotations from real creators in various domains of how they use these in their own creative practice and process, so when I am asked to write a chapter or to give a speech, I can use different examples from different domains. I continue to read authorized and unauthorized biographies, memoirs, and interviews, and continue to collect, classify, and categorize these, gaining insight into the lives and practices of creators.

Another impetus: A professor teaching teachers is required by the teachers' needs, to be practical, and so I also made a book of these exercises emphasizing what real creators do while creating—*Creativity for 21st Century Skills* (Piirto, 2011b). I have field-tested these exercises for 26 years.

Evolution

The Piirto Pyramid experienced a shift in 1997. I had genes as an environmental sun, and I moved it to the structure of the Pyramid, beneath the ground. The concrete memory for this was a tour of one of the pyramids in Giza, where we scrambled on stone paths in dark corridors beneath the surface.

The creativity work evolved from Four Core Attitudes to Five, and the Six Is evolved to Seven Is—and probably, soon, an eighth.

Hindsight

Forty-two years ago, in 1977, when I prepared for an interview to be a coordinator of programs for the gifted in a rural county nearby, I had no idea what would ensue. I entered the field blind and I was not sure I even believed in a differentiated education for bright students, though I was always in the "A" class in junior high and high school, during the early days of tracking. I became an advocate for very practical reasons. It was my job. My job put food on the table for my children and me, and bought furniture, gas, and books. Even when I entered higher education as a professor teaching teachers for an endorsement, I was writing these books because I wanted tenure, and at my small university, textbooks count for tenure and for a full professorship. Receiving a trustees' distinguished professorship was totally surprising, since two of the previous three recipients attended there as undergraduates. I was an outsider and they were good to me.

When I worked directly with bright students, getting to know them, I saw the dire need for special programs. Special programs might not be necessary in schools that already have advanced course options, and highly intelligent, skilled teachers who know their subject matter, but they are drastically necessary in smaller rural schools, and in urban areas—where poverty limits the choices and educations of all students—but especially for bright students. My five years working with the students at Hunter College Elementary School, and 19 years working with rising sophomores and juniors at a grant-funded summer honors institute convinced me that we were helping, and that our work in writing and researching about these students had merit.

I write easily and have a pretty good memory. These helped me in doing research. My background as an English major and literature teacher helped me with critical thinking. Not having studied with a mentor helped me to be a maverick, as I didn't have to please or further the work of anybody. I was free to carve my own path. Besides talent development, creativity, and creative writers, I have also published work about curriculum theory (thought pieces, arts-based inquiry); the Dabrowski theory (autoethnography, mixed methods, MANOVA); subcontinent Indian education (portrait, textual analysis, poetic inquiry); and depth psychology (thought pieces). And I have been rewarded with lifetime achievement, creativity, and distinguished scholar awards—even an honorary doctorate. As my mother would say, "The world is so full of a number of things, I'm sure we should all be as happy as kings", quoting Robert Louis Stevenson. It's been a good run.

References

Bloom, B. S. (Ed.) (1985). *Developing talent in young people*. Ballantine.
Carroll, J. B. (1993). *Human cognitive abilities: A survey of factor-analytic studies*. Cambridge University Press.
Ericsson, K. A., Krampe, R. T., & Tesch-Romer, C. (1993). The role of deliberate practice in the acquisition of expert performance. *Psychological Review*, 100, 363–406.
Gottfredson, L. S. (2001). Intelligence and the American ambivalence toward talent. In N. Colangelo & S. G. Assouline (Eds.), *Talent development IV: Proceedings from the 1998 Henry B. and Jocelyn Wallace National Research Symposium on Talent Development* (pp. 41–58). Great Potential Press.
Gagné, F. (1985). Giftedness and talent: Reexamining a reexamination of the definition. *Gifted Child Quarterly*, 29, 103–112.
Hillman, J. (1996). *The soul's code: In search of character and calling*. Random House.
Jung, C. G. (1965). *Memories, dreams, reflections*. Vintage.
Kaufman, J. C. (2012). Counting the muses: Development of the Kaufman Domains of Creativity Scale (K-DOCS). *Psychology of Aesthetics, Creativity, and the Arts*, 6(4), 298.
Kerr, B. A., & McKay, R. (2014). *Smart girls in the 21st Century: Understanding talented girls and women*. Great Potential Press.
Meeker, M. (1969). *The structure of intellect*. Charles Merrill.
Noble, K.D., Subotnik, R.F, & Arnold, K.D. (1996). A new model for adult female talent development: A synthesis of perspectives from *Remarkable Women*. In K. D. Arnold, K. D. Noble and R. F. Subotnik (Eds.), *Remarkable women: Perspectives on female talent development* (pp. 427–440). Hampton Press.
National excellence: A case for developing America's talent. (1993). U.S. Department of Education. Office of Educational Research and Improvement.
Piirto, J. (1992). *Understanding those who create*. Dayton, OH: Ohio Psychology Press.
Piirto, J. (1994). *Talented children and adults: Their development and education*. New York: Macmillan/Merrill.
Piirto, J. (1998). *Understanding those who create*, 2nd ed. Tempe, AZ: Great Potential Press.
Piirto, J. (1999). *Talented children and adults: Their development and education*, 2nd ed. Columbus, OH: Prentice Hall/Merrill.
Piirto, J. (2002). *"My teeming brain": Understanding creative writers*. Cresskill, NJ: Hampton Press.
Piirto, J. (2004). *Understanding creativity*. Scottsdale, AZ: Great Potential Press.
Piirto, J. (2007). *Talented children and adults: Their development and education*, 3rd ed. Prufrock Press.
Piirto, J. (2011a). *The Piirto Pyramid*. E-book on Kindle and Nook. Sisu Press. Also online at https://janepiirto.com/?page_id=626
Piirto, J. (2011b). *Creativity for 21st century skills: How to embed creativity into the curriculum*. Rotterdam, The Netherlands: Sense Publishers.
Piirto, J. (2016). The five core attitudes and seven Is for enhancing creativity in the classroom. In J. Kaufman and R. Beghetto (Eds.), *Nurturing creativity in the classroom*, 2nd ed. (pp. 142–171). Cambridge University Press.

Simonton, D. K. (1984). *Genius, creativity, and leadership: Historiometric inquiries.* Harvard University Press.

Sklar, K. K. (1973). *Catharine Beecher: A study in American domesticity.* Yale University Press.

Subotnik, R. F., Kassan, L., Summers, E., & Wasser, A. (1993). *Genius revisited: High IQ children grown up.* Ablex.

Tannenbaum, A. J. (1983). *Gifted children: Psychological and educational perspectives.* Macmillan.

Vuyk, M. A., Kerr, B. A., & Krieshok, T. S. (2016). From overexcitabilities to openness: Informing gifted education with psychological science. *Gifted and Talented International,* 31(1), 59–71.

13

BUSINESS AS UNUSUAL

From the Psychology of Giftedness to Changing the World via Innovation

Larisa Shavinina

Context

When I was 7 years old, I asked my father: "Where is America?" He put me on his shoulders and said, "Over there". I was impressed by the beauty of what I saw: blue sky and red poppies. It was one of those wonderful sunny days in the Ukrainian countryside where I spent summers with my grandparents. "When I grow up, will I go to America?" was my second question. "Yes, of course", answered the father. From that moment on, I fell in love with America. I could not understand why some people around me did not love America and my grandmother was not happy when she spoke about Ronald Reagan and heard news about Star Wars. I did not understand, either, why TV presented mostly homeless people in my beautiful America. Fortunately, our family was far away from the Communist Party and nobody explained to me what the Soviet propaganda was all about during the period of the Cold War. As a result, the wonderful blue sky and gorgeous red poppies prevailed in my version of America and the Soviet reality could not crush them at all.

From that sunny day in June, I somehow knew that from now on everything what I was going to do meant the preparation for my adult life in America. I liked learning and was the best in the school. I loved the school enormously: the teachers were excellent! Their teaching was amazing! Every morning I wanted to go to the school, to learn something new, to discuss with my dear teachers a wide range of subjects, and happily rushed home at two or three p. m. to do homework for tomorrow. My self-esteem and self-confidence went up every day, feeling that I would achieve everything in my life because everything is possible if someone works hard. My ten years in the Soviet school in a small town in Ukraine were like a paradise.

By the age of 15 I realized that psychology was my domain after reading the book about the Psychology Department at Moscow State University. I then told everyone that the area of giftedness is exactly what I wanted. I wanted to understand how people can be genius as Albert Einstein. (Sadly, more than 30 years later, at the opening of the second edition of *The Canadian National Conference on Innovation* I admitted that it was my huge professional and ethical mistake to study the so-called Einstein's giftedness; to be described below.)

My parents did whatever possible to encourage and support my education. At 17, I was admitted to the Psychology Department at the Kiev State University. None of my University courses was about giftedness and talent. I studied high ability from the library books. I also asked Paul Torrance, Joseph Renzulli and Harriet Zuckerman to send me their publications; which I quickly absorbed. This is how I started.

After receiving the PhD degree at 24, I moved to England for five months. Then I lived four years in Paris, France. At the age of 29 I immigrated to Canada and five years later got professorship at the University of Quebec in Outaouais (UQO) where I have been since.

Impetus: Unique and Objective Type of Representation as the Basis of Giftedness

> We have to find a new view of the world.... If you can find any other view of the world which agrees over the entire range where things have already been observed, but disagrees somewhere else, you have made a great discovery. It is almost impossible, but not quite.
>
> Richard Feynman, Nobel Laureate in Physics

My PhD was about intellectual giftedness: specifically, on the nature of cognitive experience of mathematically talented teenagers. I was greatly inspired by the research of Professor Marina Kholodnaya, the greatest expert on human intelligence, who supervised my thesis. She influenced my professional development to a great extent by "embedding" the main concepts underlining the nature of high ability, and thus shaped my vision of the field. The main finding of my PhD research was that an individual's cognitive experience of the gifted, which expresses itself in their specific kind of representations of reality or in their unique point of view or vision, is the cognitive foundation for their intellectual giftedness. "Unique" means that the gifted see, understand, and interpret everything that is going on around them differently from other people (Shavinina & Kholodnaya, 1996). Their cognition is also highly objective: they see, understand, and interpret everything in an exceptionally objective manner. As Kholodnaya put it, "they see the world as it was, as it is, and as it will be in its objective reality" (Shavinina, 1996).

Later, I reconfirmed this finding in my research on the child prodigy phenomenon, scientific talent of Nobel laureates, entrepreneurial giftedness, managerial talent, as well as innovation talent and innovation leadership of the outstanding innovators with longstanding records of breakthrough innovations such as Edison, Branson, Jobs, Musk, Morita, Bezos, and others (Shavinina, 2004, 2006, 2013c). The bottom line is this: it does not matter what type of talent these individuals demonstrate—what they have in common is a unique point of view of everything. The nature of giftedness, its fundamental mechanisms, became my main interest in the psychology of high ability.

My PhD and subsequent research on the above-mentioned types of talent further confirmed Kholodnaya's model of intellectually creative giftedness. According to the model, a person's cognitive experience—manifested itself in a unique type of representation—is the cognitive foundation of giftedness. There are the three levels of the manifestations of giftedness, which are based on this foundation: the level of intellectually-creative manifestations, the level of metacognitive manifestations, and the highest level: "specific intellectual intentions" (the concept was coined by Kholodnaya; see Shavinina, 2007).

"Specific intellectual intentions" can be defined as "subjective, internally developed standards of performance" and "norms of intellectually creative behavior" such as the feeling of direction in one's own professional life, the feeling of truth, beliefs (e.g., faith in the power of ideas), preferences (e.g., aspiration to harmony and beauty), and so on. This is also the intellectual impetus, one of the main components this volume emphasizes. Intellectual intentions as a whole and especially beliefs determine the self-confidence of the gifted and the extraordinary stability of their creative work (i.e., that famous "never give up"). Because of highly developed standards of performance and specific ethical norms of intellectually creative behavior it is almost impossible to manipulate by intellectually talented individuals and they have been a "threat" to bad politicians at all times (Shavinina, 1994). This is one of the most important roles of the gifted—especially intellectually gifted—in the global society: to be the guarantor of the best. Years later Michel Ferrari and I edited a volume on this subject (Shavinina & Ferrari, 2004).

As specific intellectual intentions are not only about the unique mind of the gifted, but also about their personality, my next research question was: whether the personality traits of intellectually gifted individuals determine their unique mind or vice versa. My answer was that the unique and objective type of representation as the foundation of giftedness determines the specificity of their personality (Shavinina, 1995).

Child prodigies have always been very attractive to me as an extreme case of giftedness. Trying to explain the essence of the child prodigy phenomenon, I came to the realization that, in fact, this is for most part a developmental phenomenon. It means that sensitive periods for these children lay the foundation for this phenomenon. The concept of sensitive period refers to the periods of heightened sensitivity in child development when children are maximally open to everything around them and easily absorb any new information. This is why learning is exceptionally fast and productive during sensitive periods, which greatly accelerate the cognitive, intellectual, creative, and emotional development of some children and thus advance them as a whole. The explanation of the child prodigy phenomenon as a special case of the intellectually-creative giftedness thus required adding the very basic level—the developmental foundation—to the model of giftedness mentioned above (Shavinina, 1999).

The topic of human potential is presented in a very interesting light in the case of child prodigies. The fact that child prodigies are able to do something amazing—which is typically accomplished only by adults—means that their potential has already been significantly developed. When I studied the famous musical prodigies, I found that their families played an important role in their accelerated development (e.g., Mozart, Mendelssohn). And what is the most interesting is that their parents had already developed their own potentials in other, quite remote domains and then used it for developing their children's potential. In the case of Mozart, it was the entrepreneurial talent of his father; Leopold Mozart greatly contributed to Wolfgang's accelerated development. For instance, he planned the Grand Tour to expose the young Wolfgang to the styles of leading European composers and personal encounters with them. Wolfgang was highly productive during the Tour. By its end, Mozart the authentic performer-composer was born. Beethoven did not have such an entrepreneurial father and later regretted that he did not travel during early childhood years (Shavinina, 2016).

The next research step was scientific talent. Nobel Prize winners have been attracted my attention since the age of 15. Winning a Nobel Prize represents the pinnacle of accomplishment possible in one's field of expertise. Despite the ever-increasing role of science in society, and the quite evident importance of Nobel laureates in contemporary science, one should acknowledge that their childhood and adolescent education has never been studied. Nobel laureates during their childhood encompassed a wide range of abilities, including the gifted but learning disabled, gifted underachievers, the gifted, and children without any special talents. Their divergent trajectories of talent development ultimately led to the same result: amazing scientific discoveries, which attest to the outstanding minds of those who made them. Eventually, all the trajectories led to the same point: zenith in science. In 2006 I proposed a research project aimed at understanding how and why this happened, and what lessons can be derived for the education of today's children. The discovery of the principles involved in the educational development of Nobel laureates should allow educators to accordingly improve, develop, modify and transcend areas in the current curriculum in an attempt to cultivate scientific talent to fruition, even of Nobel caliber, in future generations.

My answer to the question, "Where did all great scientific innovators come from?" was: they came from their early childhood and adolescent education. The main results reveal the exceptional role of parents and teachers in developing innovators—creators of Nobel caliber. I found that family played the most important role in the development of their scientific and innovative talents.

Specifically, Nobel laureates had encouraging and supporting parents, who valued education and loved to read to children. The professional occupations of many parents were related to science. Usually, Nobel laureates grew up in homes full of books and scientific toys/kits that allowed scientific experimentation at home. The early childhood and adolescent education of each Nobel Prize winner was thus characterized by at least one of the above-mentioned three factors, which greatly accelerated the development of their abilities. Each Nobel laureate also had at least one unique teacher during their school years. This uniqueness consisted in the fact that those teachers loved the subjects they were teaching and provided advanced, enriched, and accelerated instruction. They were gifted and excellent teachers with a playful spirit. Teachers manifested interest in students and encouraged them to succeed by inspiring and challenging them. Teachers went beyond the classroom practice and did many extra things for their students, which had great impact on their lives. This is what made them special teachers. Taken together, a good family milieu and special teachers greatly influenced the development of scientific talents of future Nobel laureates. These findings have important educational implications for today's children. They reveal what parents and teachers should and can do if they are concerned with nurturing scientific talents (Shavinina, 2013a).

While in Paris, I became interested in the psychological evaluation of then emerging education multimedia technologies and soon introduced the concept of "high intellectual and creative educational multimedia technologies" (HICEMTs; Shavinina, 2001a). The first publication on this subject attracted the attention of Larry Vandervert from the American Nonlinear Systems who invited me to co-edit a volume on cyber education (Vandervert et al., 2001). Larry was the first person who brought to my attention the idea of publishing edited volumes, and I am very grateful to him for that. I am also indebted to Larry for his confidence that my "time will come" and I will get professorship. He never ever had any doubt in my successful professional future. From then on, I try to live up to Dr. Vandervert's high standards so that he could be proud of me and I hope he is.

Evolution: When Intuition Leads to Innovation

> I do not believe there would be any science at all without intuition.
> *Reta Levi-Montalcini, Nobel Laureate in Medicine*

I became especially interested in publishing handbooks and my first *International Handbook on Innovation* was published in 2003. I remember sometimes "escaping" my full-time maternity leave with the first son Alexander, who was born in 1999. When I had those rare moments, I went to the University of Ottawa Library. Being once there I told myself: "Look, Robert Sternberg edited the *Handbook of Human Intelligence*; Kurt Heller et al. edited the *International Handbook of Giftedness and Talent*, and so on. However, there is no any *Handbook on Innovation*. I must do it". It was my "crystallizing experience". I do not remember that I researched the existing literature on the topic. It was my intuition that led me to the field of innovation.

My goal with the *International Handbook on Innovation* was to unify the field of innovation, because by 2000 it was studied in many different disciplines as an important components. Nevertheless, the urgent demands on innovative ideas, solutions, products, and services required a special multifaceted and multidimensional discipline: the science of innovation. By identifying over 90 leading world experts in various areas of innovation, responsible for much of the current research in the field at that time, inviting them to contribute their comprehensive chapters, and working at nights (Alexander took all my day time), I achieved that goal by putting all perspectives on innovation together in one volume. It is interesting to note that every prospective contributor accepted the invitation to contribute, probably because it was the very first handbook on innovation (Shavinina, 2003).

The *International Handbook on Innovation* thus became the beginning of a unified science of innovation as it provided the most comprehensive account available of what innovation is, how it is managed, how it is developed, how it is measured, and how it affects individuals, companies, societies, and the world as a whole. In brief, the *Handbook* served as an authoritative resource on all facets of theory, research, and practice of innovation. This unique compendium was published by Elsevier Science and became a bestseller.

The second edited handbook, *The International Handbook on Giftedness* went beyond the existing handbooks: it analyzed, integrated, and presented research on giftedness that has not been considered elsewhere (e.g., neuropsychology of giftedness, managerial talent, entrepreneurial giftedness, and so on). I wanted to extend the field of giftedness (Shavinina, 2009c). The handbook also discussed the latest advances in the fast-developing areas of talent research and practice (e.g., gifted education and policy implications). It presented fresh ideas and new directions of research (e.g., polymathy and talent of computer hackers). "It will be a necessary reference for all in the gifted field", predicted Robert Sternberg at that time.

My contributions to this *Handbook* consisted in the introduction of the concept of entrepreneurial giftedness, the discussion of managerial talent as a special type of giftedness, and the further development of new intelligence testing for the identification of the gifted. The chapter on entrepreneurial giftedness focused on early development of gifted entrepreneurs. The cases of Richard Branson, Warren Buffett, Steven Case, Michael Dell, Bill Gates, and Sam Walton were analyzed, which demonstrated that the trajectories of their entrepreneurial giftedness originated from childhood. These cases also show that an early developmental path is common for these gifted entrepreneurs. I further discussed the impact of early manifestations of entrepreneurial giftedness on the subsequent development of their entrepreneurial talent. It is interesting to note that entrepreneurial giftedness is almost synonymous with achievement and success in business (Shavinina, 2009a).

The third handbook, *The International Handbook of Innovation Education* was published by Routledge in 2013 and it opened an entirely new area in education in general and in gifted education in particular, as well as in innovation: innovation education. I was inspired by the universal need to develop innovators identified in 2009–2010. The governments of many countries around the world wished to develop innovators, but they did not know how. *The International Handbook of Innovation Education* provided a clear answer: via innovation education specifically suited for both children and adults (Shavinina, 2013b). Contributors presented many various facets of innovation education and thus defined this new and exciting area of scientific inquiry and practical intervention.

I outlined the structure of innovation education with such important components as: learning from Nobel laureates in science; lessons from eminent innovators with longstanding records of breakthrough innovations; learning from the trajectory of early development of prominent entrepreneurs; lessons on how to implement an individual's ideas into practice in the form of new products, processes, and services and thus avoid the "abortion" of new ideas; and so on. These components of innovation education shed light on how can we teach today's children, adolescents, and adults to make innovations happen (Shavinina, 2013b). I also wrote on how to not overlook innovators and considered the "silent" issues of the assessment of innovative talents in today's children—tomorrow's innovators. This was a logical continuation of my interest in the development of new tests for the measurement of intellectual and creative abilities (Shavinina, 2001b).

I could not imagine that I would love editing handbooks with the five to nine pages of comments on the first drafts of each of the 65+ chapters, plus numerous comments on the subsequent drafts, as well as writing my own chapters, proofreading, dealing with publishers, and so on. I remember sitting in my office in January 2012 overwhelmed with the received manuscripts for *The International Handbook of Innovation Education*, which required my immediate attention. The only image came to my mind then: I am in the sea, the water covers my head, and I do not know how to jump for air. I was saying to myself that day: "there is no fresh air for me in the near future and it does not matter how many jumps I do these days: just endless work". We really do not know our potential.

It turned out that, happily, I published each of the three handbooks after the birth of each of my three sons.

Further Evolution: Innovation Research

> Study hard what interests you the most in the most undisciplined, irreverent and original manner possible.
>
> *Richard Feynman, Nobel Laureate in Physics*

By introducing innovation talent as a special type of giftedness to the field of high ability studies, I was especially interested in research on outstanding innovators with longstanding records of breakthrough innovations, especially when it coincides with innovation leadership as in the cases of Steve Jobs, Richard Branson, Akio Morita, Herbert Kelleher, Jeff Bezos, and others (Shavinina, 2011). Here we are dealing with the phenomenon of individual innovation, which I identified and described in 2007. In sharp contrast to the conventional wisdom of innovation science emphasizing that (1) innovation is a team sport, and (2) people are good either in generating ideas (i.e., creativity) or in their implementing into practice (i.e., innovation), just to mention a few dogmas, I found that there is a rare group of individual innovators. They possess a unique ability to both generate great ideas and to implement them into practice in the form of new products, services, and processes by putting into place all the necessary organizational (e.g., founding Virgin, a group of companies, as Branson did), human (i.e., hiring the best talent possible), and "environmental" (e.g., changing the traditional Japanese work culture as Morita did at Sony) structures. This is what the phenomenon of individual innovation is all about. Studying prominent innovators, I found that this phenomenon is characterized by a rare combination of highly developed creative abilities, innovation leadership, applied wisdom, practical intuition, managerial talent, entrepreneurial giftedness, excellence, and courage, which are based on a unique objective vision—these function jointly and compensate for one another. Compensatory mechanisms are exceptionally well developed in outstanding innovators/leaders with longstanding records of breakthrough innovations (Shavinina, 2013c).

From all my research in the field of giftedness, I can conclude that innovation talent is most related to the maximum realization of human potential due to that rare combination of exceptional abilities. Any of them is already a great accomplishment in its own right, to be it creativity, wisdom, intuition, and so on. Nonetheless, one or two of them is not enough for innovation talent to flourish. Their joint functioning and compensatory mechanisms are the essence of innovation talent. It also explains why innovation does not happen often and why people like Thomas Edison, Steve Jobs, Richard Branson, Herbert Kelleher, and Elon Musk are few and far between. In this light the most interesting research question for me is: when Richard Branson or Elon Musk made any innovative decision, was it based on his wisdom, creativity, intuition, or another talent? I cannot answer that question today. This is the research agenda for the future.

Innovation-based economy became also one of my research interests as a logical continuation of the earlier focus on the impact of the gifted and talented on the global economy (Shavinina, 2009b). Usually, people are concerned with abortion killing potential human beings. However, I observed that nobody appears to be concerned with the "abortion" of new ideas resulting in the killing of potential scientific, technological, and societal innovations. Being implemented into practice in the form of innovative products, processes, or services, creative ideas thus lead to enhanced economic growth and competitiveness by increasing employment and prosperity for all. Accordingly, the "abortion" of ideas is dangerous for any society. All means should, therefore, be used to develop and implement ideas into practice.

While the traditional practice of economic and innovation sciences focuses on implemented scientific and technological innovations (such as, for example, iPad or iPhone, just to mention a few) and their financial profits, I found that neglecting "killed" ideas and, consequently, the costs of lost innovations represents a huge gap in research. When people intentionally or unintentionally abandon their ideas without any desire to further develop them and to eventually implement them into practice, they also abort potential innovations. This is the phenomenon of the "abortion" of new ideas (Shavinina, 2012).

During my work on the *International Handbook on Innovation*, I discovered that no one teaches people how to implement their ideas into practice in the form of innovative products, processes, and services. I also saw that today nobody evaluates the potential impact of "killed" ideas and, therefore, unborn or lost innovations on the economy. It has never been studied. The world can recover from an economic recession and avoid future economic downturns only through innovation, and every effort should be made to prevent the "abortion" of ideas and to ensure their implementation in practice. After the invited presentation on how to develop the next generation of innovators in science, technology, engineering, and mathematics (STEM) disciplines at a special panel at the US National Science Board (with a subsequent report to Congress and President Obama in August 2009) I came to believe that the time was right for initiating this new research direction.

I thus introduced the phenomenon of the "abortion" of new ideas and described the impact of "saved" ideas and implemented innovations on the economy in the renowned case of distinguished innovators. I studied prominent innovators who resisted abandoning their great ideas and eventually implemented them. Akio Morita, Fred Smith, Richard Branson, Herbert Kelleher, Bill Gates, Michael Dell, and Jeff Bezos, just to mention a few, are among them. I roughly estimated the impact of their "saved" ideas and, therefore, implemented innovations on the economy (Shavinina, 2012).

Further research is definitely needed. It should be related to the evaluation of the potential value of innovators' abandoned or aborted ideas (they all had such ideas in addition to the implemented ones) by estimating the possible profit from them and then counting the potential impact of "killed" ideas and, consequently, lost innovations on the economy. This is new, groundbreaking research with a great potential to advance knowledge in innovation science, education, economy, entrepreneurship, business, and public policy. The "abortion" of ideas is a matter of "death and life" for the whole world. By saving many potential innovations, we will thus fuel the global innovation-based economy.

Applied and Multidisciplinary Innovation Research

In the same vein as I could not think of me liking to edit handbooks, I could not imagine that I became the Founding President of *Canada 150+: The Canadian National Conference on Innovation*, which was first organized in 2017 to celebrate the 150th anniversary of Confederation (https://uqo.ca/innovation). My goal has been to make Canada the most innovative country in the world in 20 years from now by developing a new generation of Canadian innovators. I am thus planning to initiate *the National Innovation Talent Search*: a purposeful search for potential innovators among children and adolescents and the versatile development of their innovative abilities. It will be similar to what Julian Stanley pioneered with the *Johns Hopkins Talent Search Model* for identifying exceptional mathematical abilities. The difference consists in identifying and nurturing innovation talents.

The 2017 Innovation Conference was the first time I organized such an event, but I wanted it to become an annual one to track the national progress towards the fulfillment of the 20-year innovation vision by pushing many new directions of innovation inquiry. For instance, asking myself how to actualize and develop everyone's innovative potential and thus make Canada the most innovative country in the world, I proposed to create the "Blue Zone" of innovation nationwide. (The concept of "Blue Zone" in longevity studies refers to those places around the world where there are a high percentage of people who live until the age of 100 or more.) My concept of the "Blue Zone" of innovation implies that every Canadian should be involved in the innovation process: from early childhood until 100+ This new direction of my research—centered on innovation talent—is at the intersection of high ability studies, gifted education, innovation science, economy, public policy, and technology.

Before the third Innovation Conference, I thought about making the whole world the most innovative civilization by unifying all innovators on the globe. It was a significant shift in my vision of innovation research and practice: from the "Blue Zone" of innovation nationwide to the "Blue Zone" of innovation worldwide. I am thus supervising the creation of the social media platform—INNOCREX (www.innocrex.com)—that will connect all innovators. I am, therefore, becoming more and more interested in interdisciplinary and multidisciplinary research and practice.

Breakthrough Evolution or Revolution: Women in Innovation—Do Not Allow "Einsteins" to Ruin Your Lives

> Never give up! Never, never, never, never, never, never, never!
> *Sir Winston Churchill*

Another new addition to my research interests—women in innovation—was inspired by Dr. Tatiana Kirilova, my colleague and friend from the Academy of Sciences of Ukraine. We have been studying the importance of spousal support for women in innovation, and specifically how Pierre Curie's inspiration led Marie Curie to two Nobel Prizes in science, and how Albert Einstein ruined the life of Mileva Marich, his first wife, who made him famous. At the opening of the second edition of the Innovation Conference in 2018 I stated that my previous research on Einstein's hidden giftedness was a professional error. His exceptionally talented first wife, Mileva Marich, wrote the first articles, which created the "genius" of Einstein. Whereas "he treated her as a slave", noted Dean K. Simonton, when we discussed this issue at Stanford University on September 5, 2019.

At the third Innovation Conference we went further with Dr. Kirilova in addressing this important subject by analyzing what today's women can do—and what they should do—to escape the sad destiny of Mileva Marich. Also, how can women model their professional careers after the brilliant career of Marie Curie, whose husband's support helped her receive the two highest honors in science, two Nobel Prizes? This line of research is an exceptionally important endeavor: it sheds light on the role of woman in innovation and on how to encourage the rise of the next generation of female innovators.

Hindsight

Looking back at my career and asking myself what I would want to do differently, I have the only answer: I could do the most important, big things first. That is, to publish the most interesting ideas first, to write the most desirable books first, to create whatever I wanted—but first things first, do not wait for the best time to present the most important idea. This time is today. I could not predict what I could accomplish, but, as was mentioned a few times above, we do not know our full potential. I did not know anything about my ability and love to edit handbooks and to organize conferences. So, I am wondering what the next frontier in my career is.

Acknowledgments

This research was supported by the Social Sciences and Humanities Research Council (SSHRC) of Canada, the Fonds Quebecois de la Recherche sur la Societe et la Culture (FQRSC) under the Support for Innovative Projects grants AN – 129135 and AN-143064, and the Templeton Foundation / The Institute for Research and Policy on Acceleration of the Belin-Blank International Center for Gifted Education and Talent Development of the University of Iowa. The findings and opinions presented in this chapter do not reflect the positions or policies of the granting agencies. I wish to thank Marina Kholodnaya for shaping my vision of the field of high ability studies. I am very grateful to Larry Vandervert for bringing to my attention the idea of publishing edited volumes. Special thanks to David Dai for his review of this chapter and useful suggestions for its improvement. I owe my biggest debt of gratitude to my parents, Anna Shavinina and Vladimir Shavinin, who aroused a passionate curiosity in me. I am particularly grateful to my sons for their patience with me. Finally, I also wish to thank my friends—Elena Avdienko, Tatiana Kirilova, Valentina Levyshkina, Tatiana Ratyshna, Radmila Traiberg, Nicolas Vinette, and Evgenia Yakovleva—for their inspiration and encouragement when I worked on this chapter.

References

Shavinina, L. V. (1994). Specific intellectual intentions and creative giftedness. *European Journal for High Ability*, 5(2), 145–152.

Shavinina, L. V. (1995). The personality trait approach in the psychology of giftedness. *European Journal for High Ability*, 6(1), 27–37.

Shavinina, L. V. (1996). The objectivization of cognition and intellectual giftedness. *High Ability Studies*, 7(1), 91–98.

Shavinina, L. V. (1999). The psychological essence of the child prodigy phenomenon: Sensitive periods and cognitive experience. *Gifted Child Quarterly*, 43(1), 25–38.

Shavinina, L. V. (2001a). A new wave of innovations in psychology: High intellectual and creative educational multimedia technologies. *Review of General Psychology*, 5(3), 291–315.

Shavinina, L. V. (2001b). Beyond IQ: A new perspective on the assessment of human abilities. *New Ideas in Psychology*, 19, 1–25.

Shavinina, L. V. (Ed.) (2003). *The international handbook on innovation*. Oxford: Elsevier Science.

Shavinina, L. V. (2004). Explaining high abilities of Nobel laureates. *High Ability Studies*, 15(2), 243–254.

Shavinina, L. V. (2006). Micro-social factors in the development of entrepreneurial giftedness: The case of Richard Branson. *High Ability Studies*, 17(1), 225–235.

Shavinina, L. V. (2007). What is the essence of giftedness? An individual's unique point of view. *Gifted and Talented International*, 22 (2), 35–44.

Shavinina, L. V. (2009a). Entrepreneurial giftedness: Where did all great entrepreneurs come from? In L. V. Shavinina (Ed.), *The international handbook on giftedness* (pp. 793–807). Dordrecht: Springer Science.

Shavinina, L. V. (2009b). On giftedness and economy: The impact of talented individuals on the global economy. In L. V. Shavinina (Ed.), *The international handbook on giftedness* (pp. 925–944). Dordrecht: Springer Science.

Shavinina, L. V. (Ed.) (2009c). *The international handbook on giftedness*. Dordrecht: Springer Science & Business Media.

Shavinina, L. V. (2011). Discovering a unique talent: On the nature of individual innovation leadership. *Talent Development and Excellence*, 3(2), 165–185.

Shavinina, L. V. (2012). The phenomenon of the "abortion" of new ideas and the impact of "saved" ideas and thus implemented innovations on the economy in the case of gifted innovators. *Talent Development and Excellence*, 4(2), 171–179.

Shavinina, L. V. (2013a). The role of parents and teachers in the development of scientific talent: Lessons from early childhood and adolescent education of Nobel laureates. *Gifted and Talented International*, 28(1), 11–24.

Shavinina, L. V. (Ed.) (2013b). *The Routledge international handbook of innovation education*. London: Routledge/Taylor & Francis.

Shavinina, L. V. (2013c). What can innovation education learn from innovators with longstanding records of breakthrough innovations? In L. V. Shavinina (Ed.), *The Routledge international handbook of innovation education* (pp. 499–512). London: Routledge/ Taylor & Francis.

Shavinina, L. V. (2016). On the cognitive-developmental theory of the child prodigy phenomenon. In G. E. McPherson (Ed.), *Musical prodigies: Interpretations from psychology, education, musicology, and ethnomusicology*. Oxford: Oxford University Press.

Shavinina, L. V., & Ferrari, M. (Eds.) (2004). *Beyond knowledge: Extracognitive aspects of developing high ability*. Mahwah, NJ: Erlbaum Publishers.

Shavinina, L. V., & Kholodnaja, M. A. (1996). The cognitive experience as a psychological basis of intellectual giftedness. *Journal for the Education of the Gifted*, 20(1), 3–35.

Vandervert, L. R., Shavinina, L. V., & Cornell, R. (Eds.) (2001). *CyberEducation: The future of long distance learning*. New York: Liebert Publishers.

14

CREATIVITY AND CITIES

A Personal and Intellectual Journey

Richard Florida

I was born in 1957 in Newark, New Jersey. The Newark of my childhood was a lively, diverse, and thriving city. Most of my extended family, on my mother's and father's sides, lived there—my grandparents and seven sets of aunts, uncles, and cousins. We spent Sunday afternoons at my grandmother's house, where I was surrounded by extended family and friends. Newark at that time was the energetic and vibrant place Phillip Roth writes about, packed with shops and large department stores, great museums and libraries, a mosaic of ethnic neighborhoods, and the incredible industrial complex of the iron-bound or "downneck" section of the city, where thousands of blue-collar workers made their livings.

My interest in work and creativity was shaped by the factory my father worked at—Victory Optical, also in Newark's iron-bound section. He started there in his teens and, except for stints spent fighting in many of the great battles of World War II, worked at Victory Optical until the day he retired. He labored his way up the ladder from factory worker to foreman to one of the plant managers. I was fascinated by his workplace, and always wanted to know more about it. He would take me there sometimes on Saturdays, and I was drawn into this incredible world. My father would tell me about the products the factory made, about the machines that did the work, and—most importantly, he always said—about the men on the factory floor, who provided the talent it needed to keep running. In his eyes, it was their knowledge, intelligence, and creativity that made the plant special. He knew a little bit of each language spoken on that factory floor—from Spanish to German to Polish. His respect for the men was boundless. Not as hard-working cogs in a wheel, either, but as knowledgeable and contributing partners to the intricate processes of the shop floor. Connecting with them—not keeping the machines well-oiled or the company bosses happy—was his first priority on the job. The factory declined in the late 1960s and 1970s, finally closing its doors in the late 1970s—a product of the deindustrialization of America, something that clearly sparked my youthful curiosity and would shape my later interests in innovation and the nature of work and production.

It wasn't just the world of my father's factory captured my imagination. A child of the 60s, I was strongly influenced by that decade's music and popular culture, the British invasion of The Beatles, The Rolling Stones, and the cultural explosion that went along with it. My father bought me my first guitar when I was seven. He also bought my brother a small drum kit. My father had always wanted to play the trumpet. His idols were big band musicians like Tommy Dorsey, Artie Shaw, Gene Krupa, and, Frank Sinatra. But his family didn't have the time or the money to allow him to take up music—he had to work. But he wanted us to have the on the shot at artistic exploration he had never experienced.

My interest in cities was also shaped early on by my experience of Newark. One hot July day in 1967, I saw the city overtaken by turmoil. As my father drove us into the city, the air grew thick with smoke: Newark was engulfed in its infamous riots, and police, National Guardsmen, and military vehicles lined its streets. Eventually, a policeman flagged us down to warn us about "snipers". As my father anxiously turned the car around, he instructed me to lie down on the floor for safety.

I didn't realize it at the time, but I was grappling with the original urban crisis. For all of my life up to that point—and, as I would later learn, for all of modern history—cities had been centers of industry, economic growth, and cultural achievement. But now people—and industry and jobs were fleeing the city for the suburbs. By the time I entered high school in the early 1970s, huge stretches of Newark had fallen victim to economic decay, rising crime and violence, and racially concentrated poverty. The year I graduated from high school, 1975, New York City teetered on the brink of bankruptcy.

Looking back on it, I realize it was there critical events of my youth—the wrenching urban turmoil of Newark and the heartbreaking decline of my father's factory—that shaped my life-long interest in creativity and cities. I wanted—I *needed*—to know why such things were happening; what broader forces were propelling them. Why did my father's factory, which was once so vibrant, shutter and close? Why was Newark, which was also once so vibrant and diverse, erupt into violence and decline? What was producing such racial and class inequality? I sought answers from adults, from my teachers, and ultimately, the world of books. Noticing my precarious nature, on Saturdays, my father would often take me to the Newark Public Library. Sometimes, we'd go to the factory first; sometimes we'd also go to my guitar lessons. Often, we got lunches of pizza and Italian hot dogs. But I immersed myself in those magnificent stacks, searching through all sorts of books on urbanism, social science, public policy, and social commentary.

In the mid-1970s, when a Garden State Scholarship took me to Rutgers College, I found myself drawn to courses in political science, economics, sociology and urban studies. Rutgers was an amazing place at the time, filled with the carried-over energy of the 1960s and boasting incredible professors in the social sciences and especially in urban planning as well as a world class program in jazz and popular music. For the first time, I found a group of peers who also had an interest in intellectual pursuits. After class, we would all retire to the local bars and pubs, where we discussed economic, social, and political issues, as well as popular culture and music, late into the night. When I was a sophomore, my urban geography professor at the time gave us an assignment to tour Lower Manhattan and chronicle what we saw. I was transfixed by the incredible urban change that was under way in SoHo, the East Village, and surrounding areas, captivated by the energy of the streets and of the artists, musicians, designers, and writers who lived and worked there. Old industrial warehouses and factories were being transformed into studios and living spaces. Punk, new wave, and rap were electrifying the area's music venues and clubs—the first tender shoots of what would later become a full-blown urban revival.

I discovered something about my interests in those formative years. They were both intellectual and pragmatic. I was interested in the abstract, to be certain, and took courses in social theory. I read classical political and social theory. But I was also drawn to the real-world problems of actual cities and communities. I took a job in a research center working on a large-scale research projects on the transformation of cities and suburbs and wrote my senior thesis on housing and urban policy.

I went off to study political science and urban planning at MIT and later took a PhD in Urban Planning at Columbia University. At Columbia, I delved into housing and urban issues. I gazed ever more deeply into theories of political economy, economic transformation, place, and the city, meanwhile deepening my historical understanding by reading urban history, labor history, and economic and business history. At the same time, I continued to form bands and seriously follow music throughout most of college and graduate school. My deepest interest was in the punk and new wave movements, which to me seemed to bring smarts to popular music—bands like the Talking Heads, The Clash, Gang of Four, X, and The Jam. To this day, I carry an intense interest in music and popular culture and continued to do research on music, which I view as a veritable fruit fly industry to better understand the intersection of creativity and cities.

Around this time, I came across the emerging theory of economic transformation laid out by the European "regulation school" of political economy, which argued that capitalism was undergoing an epochal turn from what was termed a Fordist economic system to a post-Fordist one. The Fordist system was based on the advances of Frederick Taylor and Henry Ford in building new assembly-line frameworks of mass production, which realized incredible output efficiencies by breaking tasks down into their elemental components. It used the technique of scientific management to allocate tasks and organize the division of labor, combining these divisions with the moving assembly line in order to control and accelerate the pace of work. What really made the Fordist system tick was a complementary system for organizing demand based on mass consumption. And in such mass consumption, half of the equation was related to a whole series of policies and social innovations, many of which had a huge impact on the structure of urban areas. Unionization, for example, made possible by the Wagner Act, enabled workers' wages to rise, and then set in motion a system of wage increases tied to productivity increase. Suburbanization fueled mass consumption. And this suburbanization was based on federal initiatives in housing finance, which ushered in long-term mortgages. There was the interstate highway system, too, which allowed for still more suburban development. These innovations created the wage base and the demand required to stimulate and reproduce the mass production economy.

This system, which worked so well during the 50s and 60s, had begun to break down by the 1980s. But what would replace it? For scholars working on these questions at the time, the key issue was to try to identify new and emerging Post-Fordist models of economic and social organization. One influential line of theory and research pulled together in a book by Michael Piore and Charles Sable, two professors I encountered in my time at MIT, called attention to the flexibly specialized networks of small and medium-sized firms that could be found on the industrial districts model of the "Third Italy".

When I took my first faculty position at Ohio State University in the mid-1980s, I met my colleague and collaborator Martin Kenney. Kenney had just completed a dissertation at Cornell on the biotechnology industry. Kenney and I were both interested conducting research on the nature and trajectory of Post-Fordist capitalism. We put together a research project on venture capital and high-technology capitalism, conducting field research and interviews with dozens of venture capitalists in Silicon Valley and the Route 128 area around Boston. Ultimately, we built a large database from these sources on venture capital investments, flows, and networks of co-investment. We developed the idea that high-tech innovation took place in regionally defined *social structures of innovation*, in which locally embedded venture capitalists played a critical gate-keeping role by identifying and monitoring investments and attracting outside sources of capital (Florida & Kenney, 1988). Yet, the venture-capital model of high-tech economic organization was not a full-blown economic system on the order of Fordism. It was, we concluded, an early and incomplete response to the emerging Post-Fordist age.

Around this time, Honda opened a plant—the first major Japanese automotive plant on American soil—in Marysville, Ohio, a suburb of Columbus near Ohio State. Equipped at first only with our interest in Japanese economic organization, we immediately launched a small research project, collecting background data and visiting the Marysville plant. We quickly geared up a major research effort on the Japanese system and its transfer abroad to America.

Kenney and I argued that the Japanese system represented a more systematic advance over Fordism in that it more fully tapped the intrinsic capabilities of shop-floor workers through comprehensive workplace interaction. We saw in this system a new and more advanced model for harnessing the intellectual and creative energy of *workers*. It was a system of production that channeled workers' natural energy through the use of *kaizen* techniques, suggestion systems, worker involvement in quality circles, team-based work, rotation, and supplier involvement. We built a huge data set of hundreds of firms, detailed the location of the firms and their characteristics, and then conducted a sizeable survey of their operations. We found that these companies were in fact transferring core elements of their production system to the United States (Kenney & Florida, 1988).

We ultimately wrote two books addressing the natures of both of these transformative economic approaches and their spatial implications. In *The Breakthrough Illusion* (Florida & Kenney, 1990), we outlined the US mode of high-tech innovation premised upon venture capital and entrepreneurial startup companies and organized in geographically concentrated networks such as Silicon Valley. That book delved at length into the limits and tensions of this model, for it was our belief that it was a partial and somewhat elitist response. We dealt with the hyper-mobility of high-tech labor, the downsides of the high-tech age, and the problems of failing to integrate larger segments of the workforce or society into the "overall" picture. Our second book, *Beyond Mass Production* (Kenney & Florida, 1993), took up the Japanese response to post-Fordism in earnest. We analyzed the mechanisms that Japanese companies used to harness the knowledge and intelligence of factory workers and examined the cross-national transfer and adaptation of the Japanese model to the United States. We also considered the model's downsides: its limits as a full-blown production system, the way that it continued to exploit workers, and its dependence upon a highly structured system to bind workers' energies to companies.

But it was my years in Pittsburgh, where I relocated in 1987 and taught for almost 20 years at Carnegie Mellon University (CMU), that represented perhaps the biggest intellectual turning point for me, the place where I was able to bring together my interest in capitalist development, innovation (or creativity), and cities. Pittsburgh had been devastated by deindustrialization, losing hundreds of thousands of people and considerable numbers of high-paying factory jobs. Thanks to its world-class universities, medical centers, and corporate research and development units, as well as its major philanthropies, the city was able to stave off the worst. Its leaders were working hard to change its trajectory. Yet, for all its leading-edge research and innovation potential, the talent at Pittsburgh's universities was not staying in the region; my computer science and engineering colleagues and my own students were leaving in droves for high-tech hubs like Silicon Valley, Seattle, and Austin.

A great "aha" moment occurred when of the startup companies that had been launched from Carnegie Mellon abruptly announced that it was moving from Pittsburgh to Boston; all at once a lightbulb seemed to go off in my head. The traditional thinking that people followed companies and jobs, it seemed to me, was not working. Following the established economic-development wisdom, Pittsburgh's leaders had attempted to lure companies by offering them tax breaks and similar incentives: they'd poured money into subsidized industrial and office parks; they'd built a state-of-the-art convention center and two gleaming stadiums. But companies weren't looking for those things, and neither were my students or the other talented people who were leaving. Boston had not offered Lycos any tax breaks or other bribes; in fact, the costs of doing business in Boston, from rents to salaries, were much higher than in Pittsburgh. Lycos was moving because the talent it needed was already in Boston.

It was with all these issues swirling in my head that I wrote *The Rise of the Creative Class* in the summers of 2000 and 2001 (Florida, 2002). My main objective was not to write about high-technology industry or the so-called "new economy", but to track the more fundamental and enduring economic—and especially social and cultural—forces at work in American society. The book went through several iterations and many titles. It took a long time to form in my mind. Fortunately, I had an editor at Basic Books, Bill Frucht, who pushed me to do it. After looking an early draft of the book, Bill said to me: "You've identified a new class. Why are you afraid to call it one?" "Bill", I said, "'class' is a loaded term in the social sciences—I'm not sure I can do that". But when I looked at the data my team was turning up, I became more convinced. The techies, knowledge workers, professionals, and cultural creatives that made up the creative class had grown from five percent of the workforce in 1900, when the US was still primarily an agricultural nation, to ten percent of the workforce in 1950, when the US was primary an industrial nation, to roughly a third of the workforce by the late 1990s. Between 1980 and 1999, the US alone added some 20 million new creative-class jobs.

By the turn of the twenty-first century, the ranks of the creative class had surged to 40 million plus members. It was the advantaged and dominant class of our time, I argued, and its members' tastes, preferences, and proclivities were reshaping not just our cities but our culture, workplace practices, and society at large. I also identified two less advantaged classes that together made up the rest of the workforce: the larger and much-lower-paid service class, roughly 60 million workers, about half of the workforce, who toiled in low-paid food prep, retail, and personal service jobs, and the shrinking ranks of the blue-collar working class, who worked in factories, construction, the trades, transportation, and logistics, and constituted about one-fifth of the workforce.

The cities and the larger metropolitan areas that were most successful economically, I argued further, were those that excelled at what I called the "3Ts of economic development": technology, talent, and tolerance. They had clusters of technology industry; they had great school systems and research universities that produced talent; and they were open-minded and tolerant, which allowed them to attract and retain talent, regardless of gender, race, ethnicity, and sexual orientation.

The third T was the controversial one. A graduate student at Carnegie Mellon at the time, Gary Gates, who would go on to become one of the leading students of gay and lesbian demography, had developed a "gay index" based on data which allowed him to identify the location of gay male households. When we met, he asked me to name the top five locations of my creative class. When I fired back cities like San Francisco, Boston, Austin, Seattle, and Washington DC, he said: "You've also just named five of the gayest cities in the country". We started to work on looking at the intersection of the two and uncovered a striking correlation. Places that had a large gay population also had a large creative class and high-levels of high-tech innovation and startup companies. Later my team and I identified a "bohemian index", and found much the same thing.

When the book was published, it was this part of the analysis that generated controversy. I was taken to task for arguing that diversity—openness to all kinds of people, across gender, race, nationality, and sexual orientation—was an economic driver as well as a moral imperative. Social conservatives derided my research that showed the connections between a city's vibrant music scene, visible gay presence, and its bohemian index and its level of innovation, high-tech industry, and overall wealth. One leading urban economist pointed to "poor but sexy" Berlin, with its bohemian vibe but little in the way of high-tech high-growth industry, as the ultimate contradiction of my creative class theory. But, by 2018, Berlin ranked among the world's twenty leading high-tech startup cities, second only to London in Europe. Outraged by the very notion that diversity could be connected to economic success, some social conservatives accused me of promoting a gay agenda, threatening the conventional nuclear family, and even undermining the foundations of Judeo-Christian civilization.

But none of this is very controversial nowadays. Today, gay marriage is the law of the land in the United States and virtually all of the advanced nations, and a growing body of research confirms the connection between diversity, innovation, and economic growth. When conservative politicians propose and pass discriminatory legislation against gays, business people, who are trying to attract talent to their communities, are among the first to protest. Looking back, it's hard to see what all the fuss was about: As time has gone on, what seemed so controversial, even outlandish then has become conventional wisdom.

For me, cities are the containers of the creative economy—the places that bring together these 3Ts. Indeed, they have come to replace the large industrial corporations as the fundamental organizing units of the Post-Fordist economy. Place itself has become the central organizing unit of the new knowledge-based economy—the basic platform for attracting talent, for matching people to jobs, and for spurring innovation and economic growth.

In time, my work generated a considerable following among mayors, arts and cultural leaders, and urbanists who were looking for better ways to spur urban development. But my message also generated a backlash on both sides of the ideological spectrum. Some conservatives questioned the connection I drew between diversity and urban economic growth, countering that it was companies and jobs, not the creative class, that moved the economy forward. Others, mainly on the left, blamed the creative class and me personally for everything from rising rents and gentrification to the growing gap between the rich and the poor. Although some of the more personal attacks stung, this criticism provoked my thinking in ways I could never have anticipated—I always say I learn a great deal from my critics—causing me to reframe my ideas about cities and the forces that act on them.

Truth be told, the inequality at the heart of the urban revival had captured my attention fairly early on. Back in 2003, well before Occupy Wall Street drew attention to the rise of the "one percent", or Thomas Piketty's (2014) *Capital in the Twenty-First Century* opened our eyes to global inequality, I warned that America's leading creative cities were also the epicenters of economic inequality. I also pointed a second even more vexing dimension of inequality: geography.

> [O]ur society is being divided along class lines—divides that are being etched ever more deeply into America's economic landscape as a result of geographic segmentation. In every region across the country, cities and suburbs are increasingly balkanized into communities of haves and have-nots.

In the introduction to the first paperback edition in 2004, I continued to voice such concerns.

> There is growing evidence from many sources that the U.S. is splitting into two separate and distinct nations, economically, culturally, and politically. The people in these different nations read different newspapers, watch different television shows, vote for different leaders, go about their work differently, and hold mutually incompatible views on almost every subject. (Florida, 2004, p. xxv)

As part of the empirical research I originally conducted in the late 1990s for *Rise of the Creative Class* (Florida, 2002), my team and I ranked and rated all 300-plus US metros on a new measure of wage inequality—the difference or gap in wages between the creative class and the two less-advantaged classes. And we uncovered a strikingly close connection between this wage inequality and creative class concentrations of metro regions. Leading creative class hubs—metros like San Jose, the veritable heart of Silicon Valley, San Francisco, New York, Boston, Washington, DC, and the North Carolina Research Triangle—all numbered among the most unequal places in the country.

But my publisher was concerned that the book was already too bulky, so I instead published those findings in *Washington Monthly,* in March 2003 (Florida, 2003). I later incorporated this analysis into the revised edition that was published for the book's tenth anniversary. In my 2005 follow-up book, *The Flight of the*

Creative Class, I identified such geographic inequality as the key factor in America's growing political polarization (Florida, 2005). While I could never have imagined the virulence of the populism that would come to the surface a decade or so later, I noted then that growing geographic inequality was generating a deepening political divide and prompting a burgeoning backlash against immigration, globalism, science, and education in left-behind places. I warned that it could threaten America's long-held advantages in innovation and high-tech.

Later, when researching the connection between creativity and inequality across roughly 140 nations, I made a more heartening discovery (Florida et al., 2015). Across most of the advanced nations, greater concentrations of the creative class seemed to go along with *less* inequality. The United States was an outlier from this more general pattern. Along with the United Kingdom and a few other nations, the US exemplifies what I dubbed a "low-road path", where higher levels of innovation and higher concentrations of the creative class go along with higher levels of inequality. The Scandinavian and Northern European countries charted an alternative "high-road path", in which higher concentrations of the creative class go along with lower levels of inequality. The reason is not just their large concentrations of the creative class, which makes up as much as 45 or 50 percent of the workforce in these nations, but the fact that they have much stronger social safety nets, national health-care systems, and that they pay working and service class members better, and give them greater job protections. A creative economy can be, and across the advanced nations more generally is, associated with less economic inequality. In other words, it is not the creative economy or the creative class per se that is to blame for America's high level of inequality, or its high levels of concentrated disadvantage or poverty. These things stem from our lack of commitment to a robust safety net and broader attack on the welfare state, tax cutting that has functioned as veritable austerity causing insufficient spending on necessary social services, and on attacks on unions and workers' protections and rights, which have undermined wages, salaries, and job security for service and blue-collar workers.

Slowly but surely, my understanding of cities started to evolve. I realized I had been overly optimistic to believe that cities and the creative class could, by themselves, bring forth a better and more inclusive kind of urbanism. Even before the economic crisis of 2008, the gap between rich and poor was surging in the cities that were experiencing the greatest revivals. As techies, professionals, and the rich flowed back into urban cores, the less advantaged members of the working and service classes, as well as some artists and musicians, were being priced out. In New York's SoHo, the artistic and creative ferment I had observed as a student was giving way to a new kind of homogeneity of wealthy people, high-end restaurants, and luxury shops.

But even as I was documenting these new divides which I wrote about in my book, *The New Urban Crisis* (Florida, 2017), I had no idea how fast they would metastasize, or how deeply polarized these cities would become. In little more than a decade, the revitalization of our cities and our urban areas that I had predicted was giving rise to rampant gentrification and unaffordability, driving deep wedges between affluent newcomers and struggling long-time residents. What troubled me most of all was the decline of the great middle-class neighborhoods that had formed the backbones of our cities and broader society for most of my life. This was the kind of neighborhood I'd been born into, in Newark, and grown up in, in North Arlington. This was the kind of neighborhood I had hoped the new creative class was bringing back to our cities. But now, these once sturdy middle-class neighborhoods were disappearing right before my eyes.

I entered into a period of rethinking and introspection, of personal and intellectual transformation. I began to see the back-to-the-city movement as something that conferred a disproportionate share of its benefits on a small group of places and people. I found myself confronting the dark side of the urban revival I had once championed and celebrated. As I poured over the data, I could see that only a limited number of cities and metro areas, maybe a couple of dozen, were really making it in the knowledge economy; many more were failing to keep pace or falling further behind. Many Rustbelt cities are still grappling with the devastating combination of suburban flight, urban decay, and deindustrialization. Sunbelt cities continue to attract people to their more affordable, sprawling suburban developments, but few are building robust, sustainable economies that are powered by knowledge and innovation. Tens of millions of Americans remain locked in persistent poverty. And virtually all our cities suffer from growing economic divides. As the middle class and its neighborhoods fade, our geography is splintering into small areas of affluence and concentrated advantage, and much larger areas of poverty and concentrated disadvantage.

It became increasingly clear to me that the same clustering of talent and economic assets was generating a lopsided, urban revival—which I dubbed "winner-take all" urbanism—in which a relative handful of superstar cities, and a few elite neighborhoods within them, benefit while many other places stagnate or fall behind. Ultimately, the very same clustering of people and talent that drives the growth of our cities and economy broadly also generates the divides that separate us and the contradictions that hold us back.

My perspective on cities and urbanism was also deeply affected by what I saw happening in my adopted hometown of Toronto. I had moved there in 2007 to head up a new institute on urban prosperity at the University of Toronto. For me, the city was a bastion of the very best of progressive urbanism. Toronto had as diverse a population as can be found anywhere in North America - a thriving economy that was barely dented by the economic crisis of 2008; safe streets, great public schools, and a cohesive social fabric. Yet, somehow, this progressive, diverse city—a place that Peter Ustinov had famously dubbed "New York run by the Swiss"—chose Rob Ford as its mayor. While his personal foibles and dysfunctions may have endeared him to his Ford Nation of supporters, he was, to me, perhaps the most anti-urban mayor ever to preside over a major city. Once elected, Ford went about tearing down just about everything that urbanists believe make for great cities. He ripped out bike lanes on major thoroughfares in his quest to reverse what he called a "war on the car". He developed plans to turn a prime stretch of the city's downtown lakefront into a garish mall, complete with a giant Ferris wheel. Ford had become mayor, it seemed, because he wanted to make the city more like the suburbs.

Ford's rise was the product of the city's burgeoning class divide. As Toronto's once sizable middle class declined and its old middle-class neighborhoods faded, the city was splitting into a small set of affluent, educated areas packed in and around the urban core and along the major subway and transit lines and a much larger expanse of disadvantaged neighborhoods located far from the city center and transit. Ford's message resonated powerfully with his constituency of working people and new immigrants, who felt that the benefits of the city's revitalization were being captured by a downtown elite and passing them by.

I came to see this mounting class divide as a ticking time bomb. If a city as progressive, diverse, and prosperous as Toronto could fall prey to such a populist backlash, then it could happen anywhere. At the time I said Ford was just the first signal of this brewing backlash: more and worse would follow. It did. In short order came England's stunning and wholly unexpected decision to leave the European Union with the Brexit vote. Vehemently opposed by affluent, cosmopolitan London, it was backed by the struggling residents of working-class cities, suburbs, and rural areas who were being left behind by the twin forces of globalization and re-urbanization.

But what came next was even more unanticipated—the election of Donald Trump to the presidency of the United States. Trump rose to power by mobilizing anxious, angry voters in the left-behind places of America. Hillary Clinton took the dense, affluent, knowledge-based cities and close-in suburbs that are the epicenters of the new economy, winning the popular vote by a substantial margin. But Trump took everywhere else—the farther-out exurbs and rural areas—which provided his decisive victory in the Electoral College. All three—Trump, Ford, and Brexit—reflect the deepening fault lines of class and location that define and divide us today.

These political cleavages ultimately stem from the far deeper economic and geographic structures of the New Urban Crisis. They are the product of our new age of winner-take-all urbanism, in which the talented and the advantaged cluster and colonize a small, select group of superstar cities, leaving everybody and everywhere else behind. Much more than a crisis of cities, the New Urban Crisis is the central crisis of our time.

Across my intellectual career I have tried to make sense of and to marry three strands of theory—Marx's theories of class (Marx, 1990; Marx and Engels, 2012), Joseph Schumpeter's concepts of disruptive innovation (Schumpeter, 1943), and Jane Jacobs' ideas on the centrality of cities in our society and economy (Jacobs, 1961; 1965; 1984). My interest in updating and adapting Marx's basic categories of class for the new knowledge economy dates all the way back to my undergraduate and graduate school days in the late 1970s and 1980s. My thinking was greatly influenced by Daniel Bell's (Bell, 1973) theories of post-industrialism and the rise of a new scientific, technical and managerial class, Peter Drucker's writing on the knowledge economy (Drucker, 1967), and the economic sociologist Erik Olin Wright's work on what he dubbed "new class locations" (Wright, 1985).

By the late 1990s, as the economy continued to shift towards knowledge and innovation, I got more and more interested in how to better identify and statistically measure this changing class structure. I started digging into the data, it became evident to me that a new class structure had come into being and that is was organized into three major classes, based on workers' relationships to the means of production. These three classes are all "working" classes—in the sense that they do work for a living. The more fundamental division in society remains between these three working classes and the ultra-advantaged capitalist class, which continues to own and control the means of production. But the *kinds of work* these three classes do differ in a fundamental way. The working class, as Marx defined it, used their physical labor in production. But the creative class is the class of workers who draw principally upon their knowledge or mental labor to engage in research, innovation, product design and development, to manage people or engage in artistic and cultural production. Here, I was particularly taken by and drew explicitly from Marx's about thinking about knowledge work laid out in *The Grundrisse*. "Nature builds no machines, no locomotives, railways, electric telegraphs, self-acting mules, etc"., he wrote a century and a half before the rise of what we now think of the knowledge economy.

> These are products of human industry; natural material transformed into organs of the human will over nature, or of human participation in nature. They are organs of the human brain, created by the human hand; the power of knowledge, objectified. (Marx, 1973, p. 706).

The other even larger new class is the service class whose members engage in the production of routine services, like home health care, food service, and clerical jobs, which in many ways are the support structure required to maintain and reproduce the modern knowledge. Both of these new classes have grown considerably larger than the blue-collar working class, Marx's famed proletariat of manual workers, which has shrunk to just a fifth of the workforce, with only six percent of the entire US workforce engaged in direct factory production.

The other core element of my work was to place cities at the center of the theory of capitalist development. For Marx, industrial capitalism revolved around the factory and the large industrial corporation. My earliest interest in cities was tied to the original urban crisis of the 1960s and 1970s. As mass suburbanization spurred the expansion of industrial capitalism, stoking the demand for cars, refrigerators, television sets, washing machines and dryers coming off the Fordist assembly lines, once-great urban centers, like my own native Newark, New Jersey, declined.

Now, with the rise of the knowledge economy, some of them were beginning to come back to life. I had long been frustrated by the way that leading theories of industrial and regional development put firms and industries at the center of the story, viewing cities as little more than containers for them, either individually or in networks or clusters. As I began to see it, cities were becoming the basic platforms for innovation and capital accumulation, taking on a role analogous to that of the great factories and giant corporations of the industrial economy. And as more affluent and highly educated people and companies poured back into cities and urban centers, place was becoming the central nexus of political conflict and struggle. In the original edition of this book, I called attention to the heightened conflicts over gentrification in leading high-tech cities like San Francisco and Seattle as indicators of this. Where Marx saw the factory floor as the axis of class conflict, I saw the city itself becoming the new arena of class struggles, something that has only increased since then as conflicts over gentrification and displacement, over class division and inequality, and over the colonization of urban centers by big tech firms as grown and deepened.

Ultimately, even in these seemingly dark times—one of my three intellectual inspirations Jane Jacobs titled her final book Dark Age Ahead—I remain optimistic. That is because I believe we have the logic of history on our side. Now more so than at any other time in human history, our economic and social progress turn on the further and fuller development of human creativity. Marx long ago theorized that what made the proletariat a universal class was the collaborative nature of physical labor. But what truly sets humanity apart from all other species and that what will ultimately draw us together is our shared creativity. Creativity is history's great leveler, annihilating the social categories we have imposed on ourselves, from gender and race, to nationality and sexual orientation. It is a collective resource, shared and cultivated by everyone. Every single human being is creative. Our future turns on unlocking and stoking the great creative furnace that lies within each and every one of us.

References

Bell, D. (1973). *The coming of post-industrial society: A venture in social forecasting.* Basic Books
Drucker, P. (1967). *The effective executive.* Harper & Row.
Florida, R. (2002). *The rise of the creative class.* Basic Books.
Florida, R. (2003). The new American dream. *Washington Monthly*, 35(2), 2005–2009.
Florida, R. (2004). *The rise of the creative class and how it's transforming work, leisure, community and everyday life.* Basic Books.
Florida, R. (2005). *The flight of the creative class: The new global competition for talent.* Collins.
Florida, R. (2017). *The new urban crisis: How our cities are increasing inequality, deepening segregation, and failing the middle class-and what we can do about it.* Basic Books.

Florida, R., & Kenney, M. (1988). Venture capital-financed innovation and technological change in the USA. *Research Policy*, 17(3), 119–137.

Florida, R., & Kenney, M. (1990). *The breakthrough illusion: Corporate America's failure to move from innovation to mass production*. Basic Books.

Florida, R., Mellander, C., & King, K. (2015). Creativity and prosperity: The global creativity index. Martin Prosperity Institute, available online at http://martinprosperity.org/content/the-global-creativity-index-2015/

Jacobs, J. (1961). *The death and life of great American cities*. Random House.

Jacobs, J. (1969). *The economy of cities*. Random House.

Jacobs, J. (1984). *Cities and the wealth of nations: Principles of economic life*. Vintage Books.

Kenney, M., & Florida, R. (1988). Beyond mass production: Production and the labor process in Japan. *Politics & Society*, 16(1), 121–158.

Kenney, M., & Florida, R. (1993). *Beyond mass production*. Oxford University Press.

Marx, K. (2010). *Capital*: Volume I. (B. Fowkes, Trans.). Penguin UK. (Original work published 1867)

Marx, K. (1973). *Grundrisse: Foundations of the critique of political economy* (rough draft) (M. Nicolaus, Trans.). Penguin Books in association with New Left Review. (Original work published 1858)

Marx, K., & Engels, F. (2012). *The communist manifesto* (Isaac J., Ed.). Yale University Press. (Original work published 1948)

Piketty, T. (2014). *Capital in the twenty-first century* (A. Goldhammer, Trans.). Harvard University Press. (Original work published 2013)

Schumpeter, J. A. (1943). *Capitalism, socialism, and democracy*. Allen and Unwin.

Wright, E. O. (1985). *Classes*. Verso.

PART 4
Educational and Social Perspectives

15

EVERYTHING I NEEDED TO KNOW ABOUT HUMAN INTELLIGENCE I LEARNED BEFORE I EVEN WENT TO COLLEGE

Robert J. Sternberg

I seem to have been born to study human intelligence. From early on in my life, events seemed to converge to lead me to a career studying intelligence. As I will explain, when I was young, I thought that there was something magical about IQ and IQ testing. I hoped to learn how to be a magician who understood what it was all about. I have come to realize that there was nothing magical then or now about IQ and IQ testing. I further have come to realize that pretty much anything I have needed to know about intelligence I knew before I even entered college.

I have written in a number of places about my career as a professional psychologist, and how my ideas developed (Sternberg, 2000, 2003, 2012, 2014a, 2014b, 2015a, 2015b, 2016). What I would like to focus on here is what I have come to realize is a defining fact of my career: Virtually everything I needed to know about intelligence I knew before I went to college. I just didn't know I knew it. The remainder of my life, after age 18, was figuring out what I knew.

I was born in, and lived my first three years in Newark, New Jersey. Newark was a city that, for many years, had a thriving middle class, which then began to flee, as my family did, to the suburbs. My first memory is of Dennis. We lived on a street called Tuxedo Parkway. I was walking down the sloping driveway of our house. I saw Dennis running after me, a large clothespin in hand. I had no idea why he was running after me—I cannot remember any particular disagreement or altercation. But I was pretty sure he had no good intentions for me. I ran but I did not run fast enough. He caught up to me. He proceeded to hit me on the side of the head with the clothespin. I cannot remember what happened after that. But I still show the scar where he hit me.

In retrospect, the lesson of the Dennis incident is that what defines who you are in your life is not your IQ but rather how you use your intelligence to make things better, not worse or even just the same, for others as well as yourself.

We all encounter bullies like Dennis. Joseph McCarthy as one of the biggest bullies in the history of this country. He made his name as a "red-baiter", finding Communists and Communist sympathizers everywhere he looked (or didn't look). He was no doubt intelligent—had had an undergraduate degree from the University of Wisconsin—Madison, and a law degree from Marquette University—but did not show much in the way of *successful intelligence*. **Successful intelligence** *is one's skill in planning one's life in a way to achieve goals that are personally and societally meaningful and that fit well into one's present or future sociocultural context*. McCarthy's contributions not only did not fit well into the sociocultural context; they worked toward destroying that context by creating imaginary enemies. McCarthy was one of only many bullies in positions of power. As I write, the President of the United States is an even bigger bully than McCarthy. *People who are successfully intelligent make a positive, meaningful, and hopefully enduring difference to the world, at some level.*

What bullies and others who speak and act before they think have in common is a lack of wisdom. In my augmented theory of successful intelligence, *wisdom* is an element of successful intelligence, broadly defined. **Wisdom** *is the use of your intelligence, creativity, and any other abilities and knowledge you have, toward a common good—to make the world a better place*. If people, and especially our school systems, were more concerned with intelligence broadly defined and less concerned with standardized test scores, we might have leaders we could be proud of rather than the amoral, self-seeking, pusillanimous empty suits who occupy so many positions of power. We all would care less about the institution from which a person got his or her degree and more about whether the person has anything to contribute to make the world a better place.

My first formal encounter with the commercial intelligence industry occurred early in elementary school. As soon as she walked into the elementary-school classroom, I froze like an ice cube. "She" was a school psychologist in the school district in my hometown of Maplewood, New Jersey. To me, she was perhaps the most frightening person in the world. She was like someone out of a nightmare. Mind you, there was nothing at all wrong with her. It was all in my head. But the reason it was in my head was that she entered my classrooms every couple of years for the same reason. She was there to administer a group IQ test called the Kuhlmann-Anderson Intelligence Test. The test probably did not say "intelligence test" on it. But I knew what it was. I was petrified.

The psychologist gave us the test booklets. Then she read us the directions. And then she said "Go!" The other students in the class did "go!" I didn't. Petrified rocks don't solve intelligence-test problems. Neither did I as a petrified child. I would hear other students turning the pages of their booklets. Meanwhile I was still on the first few items of the first page. Perhaps understandably, my teachers thought I was stupid. I thought so too.

My early test anxiety is an anxiety shared by millions of others who are required to take standardized tests. Imagine how much talent is lost to society through the loss of the contributions of youth who are held down and back by a system that relies so very heavily on scores on standardized tests. I have found in my own research that children often do not even know what is expected when they take a standardized test (Sternberg & Rifkin, 1979). Are there other ways to assess intelligence? Sure, lots of them (Sternberg, 2003). But there are still many schools where low standardized test scores preclude admission or financial aid. Such a system is not only unwise and actually contrary to the common good—it is also remarkably lacking in *creativity,* a second element of my augmented theory of successful intelligence (Sternberg, in press).

Creativity is *one's willingness to defy the crowd, but also one's own past ideas and the Zeitgeist—or unconscious presuppositions—of the times* (Sternberg, 2018). We, as a society, could be looking for more innovative ways of unmasking intellect and talent. Instead, we are stuck in the early 20th century. Imagine if medical researchers were as uncreative as psychometric researchers and still were recommending medicines that were largely the same as those of the early 20th century. How many more deaths would we have at an early age? The average age of death has increased from the late 40s to the mid-80s largely as a result of medical advances. What society-transforming innovations has the field of commercial psychometric assessment made? Can you think of even one? I can't.

When I was a child, my father rented space in a second-floor walk-up in downtown Newark. That's where he had his button store. He built a button business largely from scratch, selling both retail and mail-order. Customers could buy pre-made buttons. Or they could buy handmade ones. I learned as a young child how to make custom buttons. I used a button-press machine. It would attach fabrics of different kinds to premade button blanks. I could make beautiful buttons with the machine.

I was learning a kind of *practical intelligence.* **Practical intelligence** *is the use of your intellect to adapt to, shape, and select environments. It comprises the tacit knowledge of how to get on in the world.* But practical intelligence is extremely domain-specific, and what constitutes practical intelligence varies from one time and place to another. Making good buttons does not necessarily translate into making good pottery or making good friends, for that matter. Someone can adapt exquisitely well to one environment but horribly to another. The practical intelligence of making buttons, or of running a button store, for that matter, was for a pursuit that had no future. In some ways, I was like the children in developing-world cultures. Often, they learn skills that fit the world in which they grow up. But the skills do not fit as well the world in which they will reside as adults. Many of the skills we have learned to view as valuable will be, or already have become, obsolete as automation takes over many jobs that once required skilled human workers. Thus, we have to make the most of the skills we have that we can leverage to use in our work and personal lives.

My experiences in early life plus my experiences in my early adulthood with potential graduate students were responsible for the development of my triarchic theory of intelligence, which postulates separate components of creative, analytical, and practical intelligence (Sternberg, 1988b). The idea was that you need creative intelligence to generate ideas, analytical intelligence to discern whether your ideas are good ones, and practical intelligence to implement your ideas and persuade others of their value. Three students who applied for our graduate program in psychology at Yale helped greatly in formulating the ideas for this theory. One, "Alice", was strong in analytical skills but had few good ideas of her own—she was analytical but not very creative. Another, "Barbara", was creatively strong but not as analytically strong as Barbara. She had creative ideas but did not test well on standardized tests. And a third, Celia, was practically intelligent—she got every job she applied for—but lacked Alice's analytical skills and Barbara's creative skills.

In the more recent augmented theory of successful intelligence (Sternberg, in press), a central aspect of *successful intelligence* is *figuring out your strengths and weaknesses, and then capitalizing on your strengths and correcting or compensating for your weaknesses*. This is not a question of IQ. It is a question of surveying all your strengths and weaknesses and figuring out how best to adapt, given what you assess them to be.

During the early 1950s, the ethnic composition of Newark was in the process of changing. My family moved from Newark to Maplewood. I was three years old. Maplewood was a lovely place to grow up. It was picturesque. It was safe. And it had good schools. But schooling presented its own challenges to me. In Maplewood, I attended a public school, Tuscan Elementary School. Years later, my mother told me that I had scored in the 25th percentile on the reading-readiness test. So, I had that score on top of my rotten IQ test scores. No wonder I was treated like a loser.

Are academic tests given to young children really valid? Our society starts administering high-stakes tests too early. Our triplets are taking high-takes tests at the age of seven, in Grade 1. In Grade 1, children often have many issues to deal with. Many children are not really ready for high-stakes tests. The schools receive ready-baked scores. The scores are on fancy-looking official reporting forms. But those scores may be much less meaningful than they appear to be. Many of us, myself included, can remember as children taking tests and reaching the end of the test booklet. It is only then we discover that we were not at the end of a separate answer sheet. Or maybe we were at the end of the answer sheet but not the test booklet. There will be nothing in the score records to show that we actually did fine on the test items. Rather, our problem was coordinating numbered items in the test booklet with numbered spaces on an answer sheet.

My teachers up to Grade 4 were decent. But they were unexceptional. They took test scores seriously. So do most teachers today. In fourth grade, I had a teacher who was different. For whatever reason, she saw more in me than my previous teachers did. The previous teachers had seen a reasonably hard-working but not particularly bright product of the lower middle class. My fourth-grade teacher, Mrs. Alexa, saw a child who had potential not revealed by tests. I now had a teacher who had high expectations for me. I wanted to meet her high expectations. So, I stopped being a somewhat mediocre student. Instead, I became a good or even excellent one. The difference was a single teacher. My interactions with her changed my life. What a difference one teacher could make!

Mrs. Alexa was one of huge numbers of teachers who show every year that one teacher can make a huge difference. Just one teacher, especially but not limited to, early on, can change a student's destiny. Mrs. Alexa changed mine. She also showed that low standardized-test scores do not have to be a kiss of death for children's futures. Neither parents nor teachers should ever give up on a child because of low test scores. Test scores reveal only a fraction of a child's latent potentials.

From this experience I learned the extent to which *successful intelligence always develops in a sociocultural context*. One cannot understand a person's intelligence without understanding that sociocultural context (Sternberg, 1984, 2004, in press). The context of my early life—my uneducated parents, the IQ tests, the teachers who did not believe in me—was not conducive to developing the kind of intelligence one needs to succeed in life by one's own standards. Mrs. Alexa was transformational, in the same way that often there is one teacher in other children's lives who are transformational. She helped me get off a path to nowhere and onto a path to somewhere. But many children never have that teacher.

The assumption of *g* theory and of IQ tests is that intelligence somehow "resides in" the individual—it is an individual characteristic, and often is viewed as an innate characteristic. But my later research would show this not to be true (Sternberg, 2003, 2004, 2011, in press). In fact, children who grow up in the upper middle class, with educated parents, start the race for success way ahead of many other children. But like most of their parents, they do not recognize that they have a different starting line, or if they recognize it, they don't care. The IQ test, to a large extent, "launders" background differences to make it look like it is the individual, working as some kind of sole proprietor, who is responsible for his or her success.

My mother, as I mentioned, was not academically oriented. But she saw my interest in academics. The school did not allow textbooks to go home. But I now became very interested in school. She took me to the original Barnes and Noble in New York. At the time, it was just a single store on Fifth Avenue an Eighteenth Street. She purchased for me my choice of school textbooks. She also encouraged me to buy other books in which I was interested. So, parents do not have to be educated or even particularly interested in learning themselves (she wasn't) to encourage their children to learn and do their best in school. An engaged, supportive parent can change a child's life by creating opportunities for that child. Even an uneducated parent or one not particularly interested in education can make a difference.

By fifth grade, I had acquired an active interest in intelligence and intelligence testing. I found myself debating with my teacher over the value of the tests. She was a true believer.

On the one hand, my teacher, Mrs. Evans, disagreed with me. On the other hand, she was at least willing to debate a fifth grader. In retrospect, that was impressive. Moreover, she was willing to debate a fifth-grader who was on record as having a low IQ.

Mrs. Evans showed the importance of being willing to engage children in intellectual debate. As parents, we need to avoid, especially as children grow older, viewing our role as telling children "how things are" to do. Exceptions are issues of health and safety. Many parents and teachers are authoritarian—they want children to think and do as they are told. They often grow up to be the less than reflective adults who fall for authoritarian leaders who tell them what and how to think. Their minds are those of children—"tell me what to think and do, and I will do it". But they are so un-self-aware that they believe that they come up with the ideas that others skillfully plant inside their heads. It is hard to raise a successfully intelligent child in an authoritarian setting.

When I was young, I saw people divide themselves into tribes—Jews and Christians, Republicans and Democrats, whites and blacks, or whatever. Few human characteristics kill off successful intelligence as effectively as does tribalism. Regrettably, tribalism is as strong today as ever. Independence, initiative, intelligence, and anything else seem to matter little in the face of the sometimes seemingly primitive instincts of people (and of other animals). People band together and attack others who are not perceived as members of their tribe. Intelligence theorists should be more concerned about these issues. What good is intelligence if people don't use it when they most need it? But intelligence researchers obsess over issues that are narrower, easier to study, and more likely to lead to the next quick publication. They will spend literally a century studying what g is. And what it really is. And what it really, really is. They are playing in the band while the Titanic of civilization sinks. Certainly, there are more important problems for intelligence researchers to study. An example is why smart people allow their civilization to fall apart. And what can intelligent people do to save it from itself?

By age 13 (Grade 7), I was passionate about understanding the nature of intelligence. In science class, we had to do a science project. I chose as a topic "Development of the Mental Test". For a 13-year-old, it was an ambitious project.

A first part of my science project was to develop my own intelligence test. I called the *Sternberg Test of Mental Abilities,* or the *STOMA*. My underlying idea for the STOMA was pretty uncreative: The idea was that the reason intelligence tests were not as successful as they could be was because they did not include enough different subtests. That is, I thought the tests needed more different kinds of assessments of mental abilities. So, I put together a series of, I think, 18 or so short subtests. That was many more than in then-current batteries. I gave the assessments to a few friends and to my parents. I discovered that, after a few tests, it really did not matter how many subtests I gave. With just a few of the subtests, one got about as good an idea of the final score as one would get if one gave the entire battery. In other words, just adding more different kinds of conventional tests had no real effect. I had rediscovered Spearman's *g*.

A second part of my science project was my giving the Stanford-Binet Intelligence Scale, which I found in the adult section of my town library, to some friends. Unfortunately, a psychologist in the school system got wind of what I was doing and came to the school to yell at me, threatening to burn the book if I ever brought it to school again. Not exactly encouraging words.

The psychologist showed how someone can get a PhD in psychology, or any field, and yet, put in a practical situation, show an astounding lack of practical intelligence. When we look at how one society after another is falling to fraudulent populist leaders seeking to be dictators, we realize how little the IQ gains of the 20th century have been worth in terms of how wise people are.

Creative people defy the crowd (Sternberg & Lubart, 1995). I always have. But it is not a cost-free ride. If you go your own way, expect others to stand in the way. Anticipate that they will actively resist you and your efforts. That said, one often plants the seeds of one's own troubles. I did in seventh grade. I have done so many times since.

Creativity is not a natural outgrowth of intelligence. Whereas creative people defy the crowd, most merely intelligent people follow it. Intelligent people often become successful by using their intelligence to figure out how to be part of the crowd. Then they join it, as mindlessly as anyone else might. Academics imagine themselves to be different. That is precisely why, perhaps, they are often among the worst, as philosopher Thomas Kuhn pointed out. They are as likely as anyone else to follow whatever the latest fad is. Then they may bask in their elevated view of their own intelligence. This is not necessarily a view that is always widely shared. Many scientists were outcasts as children. As adults, some may overcompensate. They may rush to become part of the crowd. This time, though, it is the scientific crowd. They may become much like the people they always avoided and who avoided them. But of course, they never see it in themselves.

As for me, I had one other experience when I was 13 that, for me, was transformational. It was the first day of social-studies class. Our teacher, Mr. Ast, started off the class in an unusual way. He said: "This is your social-studies class. I know you all have been studying social studies for a long time. But just to make sure, is there anyone who doesn't know what social-studies is?" It seemed like a throw-away question. Everyone in the class merely nodded his or her head. We thereby showed that yes, we all did know what social studies is. And then Mr. Ast asked, "OK, then, what is social studies?" We spent two class periods discussing possible answers to this question. Mr. Ast ran the whole class pretty much this way. For the first time, I had a teacher who truly encouraged us to think reflectively and deeply.

How can teachers best encourage their students to think deeply and reflectively—to use their intelligence in a thoughtful way? I believe that there are three very good ways for teachers to encourage students to think deeply and reflectively. First, model the behavior you want to see in students. Second, give students opportunities to think deeply and reflectively. Third, reward the students when they think well.

Very few teachers are like Mr. Ast, which may be why it is so hard to find students who are eager and able to engage in wide-ranging and deep critical thinking. The educational system in which most students are educated encourages neither wide-ranging nor deep critical thinking. On the contrary, it often emphasizes shallow thinking. This is the kind of thinking in which the students are supposed to guess what the teacher, or test-constructor, wants to hear. If teachers rightfully emphasize critical thinking, their assessments must match their teaching. Otherwise, students end up thinking that the emphasis on critical thinking is merely a game. They will not expect to be rewarded for participating in the game.

I continued to study intelligence testing on my own during my junior-high school years. But I did not actively pursue any research until the summer after Grade 10, when I was 16. I spent the summer at the somewhat pretentiously entitled "National Youth Science Center". It was held at the now-defunct Nasson College in picturesque Springvale, Maine. In a psychology project, I found that listening to music, on average, improved performance on a series of mental-ability tests. But the "on average" was key. It helped some people, was indifferent to others, and was harmful to others. So often, we use averages as though they apply to everyone. We then end up with conclusions that apply to people on average but to no one in particular.

In eleventh grade, I had devised a physics aptitude test. I was trying to salvage my flagging physics grade. I also was trying to figure out why I was not a particularly good physics student. Half the test I constructed consisted of mathematical problem solving. The other half involved spatial and mechanical problem solving. I was good at the first part. But I was truly lousy at the second part. By my senior year in high school, my former physics teacher, Mr. Genzer, allowed me to try out the test on physics students. It ended up having a very respectable validity coefficient of .64 (on a 0=low to 1=high scale). I remember the level of correlation because I was taken aback that the test was quite successful.

My high school used the Physics Aptitude Test for a few years but the personnel changed and the test went by the wayside. This is a theme in education today. It is extremely hard to get lasting change. To get such change, there needs to be serious pressure from multiple pressure points. Otherwise, systems tend to revert to what they have done before and are comfortable with. We end up doing the same things in schools, with minor cosmetic variations, year after year decade after decade, century after century.

Senior year came around. I found myself taking a number of Advanced Placement (AP) courses. These courses were supposed to give us, as students, an edge in college admissions. While taking this array of Advanced Placement courses in twelfth grade, I found myself interviewing for various colleges. I am not sure how my mother engineered my going around to interviews. She was receiving a grand total of $25 a week in combined alimony and child-support payments from my father.

I applied to colleges and ended up deciding to go to Yale. The spring before going to Yale, I took a chance and wrote to a then-prominent testing company, The Psychological Corporation, in New York. I wanted to see whether they might have a summer-job opening for me. I told them in my letter something about my experience in psychological testing. They must have been intrigued. They got back in touch to offer a job interview. I went to New York to interview. Two bigwigs in the corporation, Jerome Doppelt and David Herman, interviewed me. They then gave me—I should have predicted it—an ability test. I guess I passed. I was hired and went to work there in the summer of 1968. In those days, it was a long train commute from New Jersey. But I went for it anyway.

The summer was a blast. I learned a lot about psychological testing. Not all that I learned was exactly what I might have expected. Some of it was downright surprising. Test publishers sometimes convey the impressions that there is some magic in the construction of psychological tests, such as intelligence tests. In fact, there is no magic in the construction of psychological tests. Test publishers try to create a mystique. It is a way to hide just how dicey some of what goes into test construction is. It's a bit like knowing what the actual ingredients are of that sausage you are about to eat. The manufacturer keeps it a secret for a reason.

One of my tasks was to create a classification system for items on a famous and very difficult test of analogical reasoning. This was a test with items such as A is to B as C is to ?. The "?" was replaced by answer choices. This was a daunting task. But eventually it led me to a successful categorization. The corporation actually used what I came up with—at least, then. I noted that the items were very difficult. But in many cases, it was not because of the "analogical reasoning" involved. Rather, it was because of the huge amount of vocabulary and general information one needed to successfully answer the items on the test. I did some research. I then discovered that scores on the test were most highly correlated with the vocabulary and general-information subtests of a famous test of intelligence. What appeared to be a "verbal reasoning" test was actually, to a large extent, a test of knowledge. This would not be a bad thing, in itself, if the users of the test (at the time, mostly graduate schools) had realized that what they were measuring. This was primarily vocabulary and general information rather than verbal reasoning. But that was not the way the test was being pitched at the time. This experience working with the analogies test had a profound effect on my later theorizing and research.

How do you, or how does anyone, know what a particular ability test really measures? Do not assume—ever—that the title of a test tells you what the test really measures. That's like believing that a product advertised on television really will do what it is supposed to do. There are statistical analyses that can help reveal what a test measures. But often they are not purposely done by test publishers in order to obscure what the test actually measures. Sometimes tests are given nondescript names or acronyms to further obscure what the tests measure. It is odd, I believe pathetic, that our society uses large numbers of high-stakes tests where it is not clear what the tests truly measure. What is more pathetic is that people often seem not to care too much.

I had a strange experience that revealed to me just how dicey the whole testing proposition was. I was asked to help proctor a test for entry-level (generally, high-school educated) job applicants. The testing took place on the top floor of the building in which we were housed. So late in the day, I went up to the top floor to help supervise the testing session.

The session used what was then called CAST—Controlled Administration of Standardized Tests. The idea was to have the test administered by a tape recorder so that the conditions of administration would be exactly the same for all test-takers, no matter where or when they took the test. So far, so good, right? After all, we all want to take tests under standardized conditions. But there were three serious problems.

The first problem was the voice on the tape. The president of the company (an executive but also a serious psychologist and a famous constructor of psychological tests) decided that he wanted to be the voice on the test. The president was from Texas. He had a strong Texas drawl. So the first problem was with the test-taker's comprehension. The words the president said might be well understood in Texas, or at least in parts of Texas. But for people in New York, it was a real challenge to understand the accent of the test-administrator.

The second problem was with the effort to make the test to be fully comparable across all test-takers. It was not possible to have one set of questions from test-takers in one setting and another set of questions from other test-takers in a different setting. So far as I can remember, no questions were allowed, at least in that particular testing session.

The third problem was that there was no test-administrator there to match the pacing of the testing to the particular group being tested. The voice on the tape just kept going and going. It read a predetermined sequence of statements. It droned on, regardless of what was happening in the room. It became obvious to me pretty quickly that the result was chaos. Some test-takers were not sure what was being said. Others were not sure where in the test booklet they were. And others were not sure exactly what they were being asked to do. What was supposed to be a highly standardized and highly orderly administration was actually out of control. But the employers who received the test scores would never know that.

So, it often appears that tests are valid because, on average, they predict this or that. But in reality, they may predict well for some people and poorly for others. This was certainly the case in what I saw that summer before college.

So, in 1968 I enrolled in college and learned a lot about psychology and even about intelligence. But pretty much everything I needed to know about intelligence I learned before I even started my freshman year. Ultimately, I would build a career studying intelligence. It did not always seem that way. First, I studied intelligence (Sternberg, 1977). Then I started to study creativity (e.g., Sternberg, 1988a), but eventually realized that creative intelligence is an important part of intelligence, more broadly, just as is practical intelligence (Sternberg, 1988b). Then I studied wisdom, until I realized that that, too, is an important part of intelligence (Sternberg, in press). And now I have come back to realizing that it all fits together into what I call *adaptive intelligence* (Sternberg, 2019), or one's intelligence in creating a better rather than an increasingly degraded world for our children and grandchildren. It is unfortunate that so many scholars studying intelligence have failed to see this. Nature does not care; there are always other species that can take over if and when we human destroy ourselves. We, however, should care. A notion of intelligence that fails to recognize how poorly humans have adapted can stand. The question is whether the world can stand in the face of such a narrow, individualistic, and short-sighted notion.

References

Sternberg, R. J. (1977). *Intelligence, information processing, and analogical reasoning: The componential analysis of human abilities*. Hillsdale, NJ: Lawrence Erlbaum Associates.
Sternberg, R. J. (1984). A contextualist view of the nature of intelligence. *International Journal of Psychology*, 19, 307–334.
Sternberg, R. J. (1988a). A three-facet model of creativity. In R. J. Sternberg (Ed.), *The nature of creativity* (pp. 125–147). Cambridge University Press.
Sternberg, R. J. (1988b). *The triarchic mind: A new theory of human intelligence*. Viking.
Sternberg, R. J. (2000). In search of the Zipperump-a-zoo: Half a career spent trying to find the right questions to ask about the nature of human intelligence. *The Psychologist*, 13(5), 250–255.
Sternberg, R. J. (2003). It all started with those darn IQ tests: Half a career spent defying the crowd. In R. J. Sternberg (Ed.), *Psychologists defying the crowd* (pp. 256–270). American Psychological Association.
Sternberg, R. J. (2004). Culture and intelligence. *American Psychologist*, 59(5), 325–338.
Sternberg, R. J. (2011). The theory of successful intelligence. In R. J. Sternberg & S. B. Kaufman (Eds.), *Cambridge handbook of intelligence* (pp. 504–527). New York: Cambridge University Press.
Sternberg, R. J. (2012). Twelve hundred publications later: Reflections on a career of writing in psychology. In E. Grigorenko, E. Mambrino, & D. Preiss (Eds.), *Writing: A mosaic of new perspectives* (pp. 449–458). Psychology Press.
Sternberg, R. J. (2014a). Coping with a career crisis. *Chronicle of Higher Education*, 60(20), A28–A29.

Sternberg, R. J. (2014b). I study what I stink at: Lessons learned from a career in psychology. *Annual Review of Psychology*, 65, 1–16.

Sternberg, R. J. (2015a). Career advice from an oldish not quite geezer. *Chronicle of Higher Education*, 61(37), A27–A28. http://chronicle.com/article/Career-Advice-From-an-Oldish/230335/

Sternberg, R. J. (2015b). Still searching for the Zipperumpazoo: A reflection after 40 years. *Child Development Perspectives*, 9(2), 106–110.

Sternberg, R. J. (2016). Successes and failures in a sixty-year career trying to understand human intelligence. *International Journal for Talent Development and Creativity*, 4, 175–181.

Sternberg, R. J. (2018). A triangular theory of creativity. *Psychology of Aesthetics, Creativity, and the Arts*, 12, 50–67.

Sternberg, R. J. (2019). A theory of adaptive intelligence and its relation to general intelligence. *Journal of Intelligence*, 7(4), 23.

Sternberg, R. J. (2020). The augmented theory of successful intelligence. In R. J. Sternberg (Ed.), *Cambridge handbook of intelligence* (2nd ed., pp. 679–708). Cambridge University Press.

Sternberg, R. J., & Lubart, T. I. (1995). *Defying the crowd: Cultivating creativity in a culture of conformity*. New York: Free Press.

Sternberg, R. J., & Rifkin, B. (1979). The development of analogical reasoning processes. *Journal of Experimental Child Psychology*, 27, 195–232.

16

REFLECTIONS ON MY WORK

The Identification and Development of Creative/Productive Giftedness

Joseph S. Renzulli

> Any new theory is first attacked as absurd; then it is admitted to be true, but obvious and insignificant; finally, it seems to be important—so important that its adversaries claim that they have discovered it themselves.
>
> *William James*

Most of my work over the past several decades has focused on the four theories depicted in Figure 16.1. The first two theories, the Three Ring Conception of Giftedness and the Enrichment Triad Model, were developed simultaneously, the first one dealing with the interacting characteristics that describe what contributes to creative productivity and second dealing with three types of educational enrichment experiences that promote its development. The context in which they subsequently evolved had its origins in my work in the late 1950s as a junior high school mathematics and science teacher. In the years that followed, I began to pursue graduate work in educational psychology and this work evolved into a specialization that focused on giftedness, creativity, and talent development. The two theories at the bottom of Figure 16.1 emerged in later years and all four theories, taken collectively, subsequently became the foundation for the Schoolwide Enrichment Model (SEM) (Renzulli & Reis, 1985, 1997, 2014). The SEM is a school organization plan that represents an attempt to apply these four theories to total school improvement, both in terms of school achievement and students' creative productivity. The major goal of the SEM is to offer opportunities, resources, and encouragement to any and all students that might be overlooked through traditional cut-off score approaches to determine giftedness. It also recommends strategies for infusing more enrichment experiences into the ubiquitous standards driven curriculum that prevents many students from

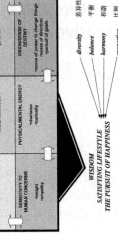

FIGURE 16.1 Theories underlying the development of creative/productive giftedness

experiencing the enjoyment and engagement in learning that should be a hallmark of what effective schooling should be all about.

The realization that the "brand" of learning involved in our approach to total school enrichment programs requires quick and easy access to resources for making curricular modifications to enrich the curriculum and personalized learning. The most recent reiteration of our work is a technology-based program that provides an individual strength-based profile for each student and a data base that contains thousands of enrichment resources that are correlated with student profiles. These theories and the context for their development will be discussed in the sections that follow.

There is a good deal of interaction between and among the four theories in Figure 16.1 and I am certain that more work needs to be done on strategies for implementing practical applications of these ideas. I conclude the chapter with a brief description of some current work and the direction that future theory development and research might take.

The Enrichment Triad Model and The Three Ring Conception of Giftedness

On October 4, 1957, the Soviet Union successfully launched Sputnik 1, the world's first artificial satellite. America's reaction to this historic event was especially impactful on the education establishment and the need to better prepare our students at all levels to improve science education so that our nation could compete with the Russians. This event is probably what "kick-started" what was subsequently the beginning of my career in gifted education and talent development.

My superintendent of schools approached me with a request to develop an after-school science program for our "gifted" students; at that time the standard definition of giftedness was an IQ or 130 or higher. I was provided with a list of these students and began a frantic search for anything I could find on science curriculum for the gifted. Despite my best efforts, there was very little in the literature on recommended curriculum, and I did not find any material focused on Science Curriculum for the Gifted. This lack of prescribed curriculum was fortunate because if such material was available, I would have undoubtedly continued to teach in a didactic and prescriptive manner. I did, however, come across a book by F. Paul Brandwein entitled *The Gifted Student as Future Scientist* (Brandwein, 1955). As a teacher at Forest Hills High School in New York City, Dr. Branden translated theory into practice as he experimented with eyes-on, hands-on, brains-on, minds-on techniques in science. At that time, he had more produced more Westinghouse Science Talent Search winners than any other person in the country.

When I read Brandwein's work, I became acutely aware of his forward-thinking ideas about education and how an inductive, investigative approach to learning differed from a didactic, prescriptive approach, which at the time (and in some cases continues) to be the predominant ways that teachers were trained. His ideas offered me, as a novice teacher, a hands-on investigative approach with all the necessary tools, materials, instructions, rocks, minerals, fossils, chemicals, beakers, plastic tubing, measuring devices, etc. to turn a traditional classroom into a scientific laboratory. The laboratory atmosphere that Dr. Brandwein advocated became the basis for my gifted program and from that time forward I knew that the "canned" lessons I was using in my regular science class curriculum were exactly opposite from the kind of teaching that inspires young minds. My goal became to encourage my students to think, feel, and do like professional scientists, even if at a more junior level from adult scientists; this approach became what in later years what I described as the Type III Enrichment component of the Enrichment Triad Model. This component focuses on individual and small group investigations of real problems, which are characterized by the following four criteria:

1. Personalization of Interest
2. Use of Authentic Investigative Methodology
3. No Existing Solution or "Right" Answer
4. Designed to Have an Impact on an Audience Other Than or in Addition to the Teacher.

These criteria resulted from my reading of Brandwein's work as well as the influences of my fascination with biography and interviews with prominent people that will be discussed below. Again, I remind the reader that the two theories being discussed emerged simultaneously, and over a long period of time. And the two theories are intended to interact with one another to address the questions of: Who are they? and What can we do to develop creative/productive giftedness in young people?

Type I Enrichment (General Exploratory Experiences) and Type II Enrichment (Group Training Activities in areas such as thinking skills, creativity, learning-how-to-learn skills, and the effective use of technology) emerged logically from a need to address the second question above. How do we develop interest in students? And what kinds of creative and investigative skills and resources do they need to follow up on interests in a reasonably professional manner? I also recommended that these two types of general enrichment be made available to all students. The need to deliver effective Type II Enrichment, and especially the skills necessary to carry out authentic investigative methodology, led me to what became my lifelong search for "How-To" books across all areas of knowledge; and in recent years, the meta-cognitive skills in technology that help young people become efficient finders and users of professional investigative skills from the Internet. Even before Triad and Three Ring "went to press", I was teaching in a way that was decidedly different from prescribed curricular units and stipulated lesson plans. And I developed much better relations with my students by encouraging them to experience the experimental nature of science as they selected topics in their own areas of interest, hypothesized, conducted experiments, and submitted their work to science fair competitions. These types of experiences and the four criteria listed above make Type III Enrichment different from today's popular focus on project-based learning.

These early teaching experiences also influenced what later became the Three Ring Conception of Giftedness depicted in the upper left corner of Figure 16.1. Although the superintendent's charge was to establish a gifted science program for 130 IQ students, I quickly realized that several students in my regular science classes had "the right stuff" to benefit from the special program, so I quietly started sneaking them into the special class for high-IQ students. And in many cases, it turned out that the motivation, creativity, and special interests in various areas of science of these below-the-IQ-cut-off-score-students produced as good or better outcomes as the high IQ students. I also started adapting my regular science classes to this "brand" of teaching and found that these classes became more exciting when they went beyond traditional teaching based on unit plans, lesson plans, and whatever was prescribed in science textbooks. This experience produced modifications in my thinking that will be discussed later in the section on the Schoolwide Enrichment Model (Renzulli & Reis, 2014).

In later years, when I began to pursue graduate degrees in educational psychology, my early intuitive decisions about who is best served through special opportunities led me to research studies that supported the direction I was taking. Although the influence of intelligence, as traditionally measured, quite obviously varies with domain-specific areas of achievement, many researchers have found that creative accomplishment is not necessarily a function of measured intelligence (Munday & Davis, 1974). In a review of several early research studies dealing with the relationship between academic aptitude tests and professional achievement (or what I later defined as creative/productive giftedness), Wallach (1976) had concluded that academic assessments are best at predicting the results a student will obtain on other academic assessments. Wallach also pointed out that academic test scores at the upper ranges—precisely the score levels that are most often used for selecting persons for entrance into special programs, do not necessarily reflect the potential for creative/productive accomplishment.

I reviewed numerous research studies that also supported Wallach's finding that there is little relationship between test scores and school grades, on the one hand, and real-world accomplishments, on the other (i.e., Bloom 1963; Harmon 1963; Hudson 1960; Mednick 1963; Wallach & Wing 1969). In fact, another study dealing with the prediction of various dimensions of achievement among college students by Holland and Astin (1962) found that getting good grades in college had little connection with more remote and more socially relevant kinds of achievement.

These early personal experiences and the research I reviewed undoubtedly led to my description of the one component in the Three Ring Conception of

Giftedness as "above average but not necessarily superior ability". Many people still interpret this statement to mean measured academic ability only and frequently ask for a cut-off score or percentile. In the original article on the Three Ring Conception (Renzulli, 1978), I pointed out that there are many other domain-specific areas of human performance that cannot be measured by traditional achievement or cognitive ability tests. A more recent study by Arnold (1995) provides additional support for the need to examine other predictors of creative/productive giftedness. She followed high school valedictorians fourteen years after graduating from high school, finding that although they work hard and follow rules, they are not the creators or transformative leaders.

The creativity component of the Three Ring Conception had its origin when I was a master's degree student in the in the early 1960s. I read a book by Getzels and Jackson (1962) entitled *Creativity and Intelligence: Explorations With Gifted Students* and ran across an article entitled *The Minnesota Test of Creativity Thinking* (Goldman, 1964), later to become the famous *Torrance Tests of Creative Thinking* (TTCT, Torrance, 1966). I was fascinated by this concept and began reading everything I could find on the topic. One article that prompted action on my part was based on Guilford's well know presidential address at the American Psychological Association (Guilford, 1950) in which he expressed concern and dismay about how little attention psychologists and educators had paid to the study of creativity. Armed with copies of the TTCT, which Dr. Torrance personally taught me and my graduate students how to score, I embarked on research (Renzulli & Callahan, 1974; Renzulli, Owen, & Callahan, 1974) that resulted in the development of a five-volume series of creativity training activities entitled *New Directions in Creativity* (Renzulli, 1972a, 1972b; Renzulli & Callahan, 1972; Renzulli, Renzulli, Ford, & Smith, 1976a, 1976b) and conducted a series of studies to determine the effectiveness of these activities on improving TTCT scores in young people (Callahan, & Renzulli, 1974). These experiences, taken collectively, resulted in the inclusion of creativity in the Three Ring Conception.

The task commitment component in the Three Ring Conception is the result of a variety of experiences going back to childhood interests. I loved reading the biographies of famous people and, because of experiences in my own young life, I found that focus and hard work were necessary to achieve desired results. And in 1968 I served as a research consultant to the White House Task Force on Education of the Gifted, a project that subsequently resulted in the publication of the Marland Report (1972). One of my responsibilities on the task force was to interview well known people across a variety of disciplines.[1] The one thing that resulted from these interviews was that highly focused motivation was attributed to *everyone's* success. I didn't want this concept to be confused with general motivation (or what is now popularly being called "grit"). There must be a focus on a specific task, challenge, or enterprise as the outcome of creative/productive enterprises and therefore I came up with the title "Task Commitment" for the third ring in the Three Ring Conception. As I have pointed out in numerous publications, no single ring makes giftedness, or what I prefer to call gifted behaviors. It is all three rings working together that produce the ideas, actions, and finding and using the necessary know-how to develop and apply gifted behaviors to achieve a desired goal.

Curriculum Compacting

Another event from my early experience as a math teacher resulted in what was later to become a major component of my work. Realizing that many of my more able math students were bored in my heterogeneously grouped math classes led me to a teaching strategy that was eventually formalized into a process called Curriculum Compacting. I allowed any interested student to do their seat work by working from the bottom of the worksheet page where the most difficult problems were usually found. They checked their answers at my desk; if all answers were correct, they were given the opportunity to do something else for the remainder of the math class. I quickly realized that just giving student more advanced work sheets would eventually become counter-productive, so I began searching for some high-interest math activities. Unbeknownst to me at the time was that this experience would begin what has been a lifelong search for high interest and high engagement enrichment learning activities.

Research was later conducted on the process (Reis, Westberg, Kulikowich, & Purcell, 1998), now one of the most widely used processes for modifying the prescribed curricular for advanced level students. We also developed a teaching strategy called curricular enrichment infusion (Renzulli & Waicunas, 2016), which provides teachers with a systematic process for examining curricular topics and brainstorming ways in which enrichment experiences could be blended into prescribed curricular material.

The Multiple Menu Model for Developing Differentiated Curriculum

One final aspect related to the two models discussed above is a model I developed for a course on curriculum development for the gifted. The literature on this topic focused mainly on advanced content and thinking skills but often does not have guidance for blending in direction for the *application* of content and thinking skills that develops creative productivity. I believe that application should be the hallmark of any curriculum for high potential students, so I developed a plan that blends content and thinking skill processes with ways that students can use these skills to develop creative and investigative products within the framework of any curricular topic (Renzulli, 1988). A unique aspect of this model is a menu called Artistic Modification. Guidelines for this menu invite teachers to personalize lessons by sharing anecdotes, observations, hobbies, or personal experiences and beliefs about an event, topic, or concept covered in mainly knowledge-based curriculum. As such, it can be used with any instructional strategy and during any point in a prescribed instructional sequence. Personalizing lessons through artistic modification invigorates teachers, demonstrates the relevance of topics to real life situations, and thereby generates interest and excitement among students. Most of all, it gives teachers the license to be playful with any curriculum they are developing.

Operation Houndstooth and Executive Functions

The original graphic for the Three Ring Conception was embedded in a houndstooth background because people frequently asked me where the three rings came from. The black and white houndstooth graphic was intended to convey the interaction between personality and environment, but it wasn't until several years later that I began investigation of this sub-theory. And, as is the case with most starting points, my first motivation came from the activities I observed visiting a Triad-based program in Connecticut, one of the first that had been implemented in the state. A fifth-grade girl observed a primary age student being bullied. Under the direction and encouragement of her gifted program teacher, she began a very passionate year-long Type III Enrichment project to address and bring about changes to this bullying situation by showing videos about bullying and developing simulations in which students could participate in role playing in various hypothetical bullying situations. Wow, I thought! If we truly believe that many high potential young people will eventually assume leadership positions in their chosen career areas, shouldn't we be encouraging them to use their talents to make the world a better place (Renzulli, 2002, 2008)?

Although examining the personality and environmental factors underlying the Three Ring Conception had been on the back burner of my mind for a long time, I reached a point where a scientific examination of these background components was necessary for us to understand more fully the sources of gifted behaviors and more importantly, the ways in which people transform their gifted assets into constructively positive action. My decision was also influenced by the new work on positive psychology that was being done by Martin Seligman and Mihaly Csikszentmihalyi (2000). This movement focuses psychology on enhancing what is good in addition to fixing what is maladaptive behavior. The goal of positive psychology is to create a science of human strengths that will help us understand and learn how to foster socially constructive virtues in young people. Financial and intellectual capital are the well-known forces that drive the economy and result in generating highly valued material assets, wealth production, and professional advancement—all important goals in a capitalistic economic system. Social capital, on the other hand, is a set of intangible assets that address the collective needs and problems of other individuals and our communities at large. I knew that work in this area would deal with less discreet variables than those things that are measured by standardized tests. At the same time, however,

I believed that if gifted education is helping to produce people who will make important changes in the world my interest turned to addressing another series of questions that should be important in gifted education. What causes some people to mobilize their interpersonal, political, ethical, and moral realms of being in such ways that they place human concerns and the common good above materialism, ego enhancement, and self-indulgence? How can we understand the science of human strengths that brings about the remarkable contributions of people like Nelson Mandela, Rachel Carson, Mother Theresa, and even the young girl in the bullying example above? How can we expand the mission of gifted education to include a non-cognitive focus on opportunities, resources, and encouragement to develop talents that are directed toward making the lives of people better?

A confirmatory factor analysis produced an instrument that led to the six factors represented in the lower right hand of Figure 16.1. Research by Sytsma (2003) and subsequent studies (Renzulli, Koehler, & Fogarty, 2006; Renzulli, Sands, & Heilbronnor, 2011) concluded that Houndstooth oriented activities led to the constructive development of gifted behaviors, and the internalization of the co-cognitive factors. It also showed that students became creative producers at the highest level of the Houndstooth Intervention Theory by internalizing a combination of the six co-cognitive traits.

It is my hope that other researchers in the field will use our instrument (and/or other measures) to conduct additional intervention studies about the Houndstooth factors. We very much need to examine the best ways to encourage our most able young people to internalize the factors identified in Operation Houndstooth and to internalize these values as they pursue their adulthood endeavors.

The Executive Functions theory in the lower left corner of Figure 16.1 is a spin-off from the work done on Operation Houndstooth and it also relates to the Task Commitment concept in the Three Ring Conception of Giftedness. In spite of the work in Three Ring, Triad, and Houndstooth, I still felt that "something was missing" from attempts to explain the motivation and skills that were observed in students' work on high quality Type III Enrichment projects. A comprehensive review of both the psychological and business leadership literature led me to countless articles on executive functions. Especially influential was Sternberg's article on successful intelligence and the concept of "tacit knowledge" (Sternberg, 1997). A study was conducted using an instrument entitled the *Scale for Rating the Executive Functions of Young People* (Renzulli & Hartman, 1971) and this study resulted in the identification of the five factors listed in the lower left section of Figure 16.1. An ongoing search was and continues to be pursued for materials and teaching strategies to develop the skills in young people related to these five factors. Also influential in the development of these theories was the groundbreaking work of Howard Gardner (1983), who cast a new light on how we look at the entire concept of intelligence.

The Schoolwide Enrichment Model (SEM)

As indicated above, the development of my work usually has its origins in practical classroom settings. One of the things observed in programs using the Three Ring Conception and the Enrichment Triad Model was that several teachers of the gifted were sharing their materials and teaching strategies with regular classroom teachers. And in more recent years, national reports dealing with 21st Century skills (National Research Council of the National Academies, 2008, 2010) strongly recommended that higher level thinking, once considered to be the "property" of gifted programs, should be made available to all students. Over the years a series of studies summarized by Sally Reis and I (Reis & Renzulli, 2003), a study by Kim (2016) and a study by three Dutch economists (Booij, Haan, & Plug, 2016) provided favorable results regarding the effectiveness of the SEM and the underlying theories that led to this talent development model.

The Renzulli Learning System

One of the things we recognized through extensive involvement with schools and districts using the SEM was that the "brand" of learning recommended places unusual demands on teachers and they simply don't have the time to find the kinds of enrichment-based resources necessary for effective implementation of the model. The Renzulli Learning System (RLS) developed at the University of Connecticut (Renzulli & Reis, 2007) is a research-based enrichment program (Field, 2009) that uses a computer-generated assessment of student strengths in the areas of academic achievement, interests, learning styles, and preferred modes of expression. This first step produces an electronic profile for each individual student. The Profiler has been purposefully designed to personalize a part of every student's school experience.

The second step is an enrichment differentiation search engine then scans through approximately 50,000 resources and sends students to web sites that are based on each student's individual profile. All resources in our 14 categorical databases are high engagement ("hands-on") activities that have been multiply classified by subject matter experts according to topic, age/grade appropriateness, curriculum standards, and that are safely suitable for use by young people. Teachers can use the same system to search the databases for enrichment activities that they would like to infuse into their regular curriculum. Research [Field] shows that the program increases achievement and promotes the three main goals of the SEM—Enjoyment, Engagement, and Enthusiasm for Learning.

The Evolution and Destination

I have always believed that theories and research in an applied field have limited value if they cannot be translated into practical applications that have an *impact* on the work of teachers, administrators, students, and policy makers. Our widely used *Scales for Rating the Behavioral Characteristics of Superior Students* (Renzulli & Hartman, 1971), forms such as the *Curriculum Compactor* and the *Type III Management Plan*, the 250 activities in the *New Directions in Creativity* program, and our recently developed *Renzulli Learning System* are just a few examples of my concern for practical applications. Theories, in and of themselves, cannot be researched. It is the practices that are derivatives of theories that yield data about the value of any given theory. It is for this reason that, over the years, a good deal of my work has been devoted to developing instruments, teaching materials and strategies, and developing tools in technology that provide useful resources for practices carried out in schools and classrooms. The most important consideration guiding my work over the years has been that the theories and research discussed here have had a practical impact on identification, educational practices, and policies that have been adopted in states, school districts, and numerous countries around the world.

Three contributions are special sources of satisfaction from the more than half century of work devoted to this field. First, bringing the concept of creative-productive giftedness (as distinct from lesson-learning giftedness) to its present level of acceptance in the field has been the most important theoretical contribution that my colleagues and I have made over the years. This has not been easy because evaluating creative productivity, social action projects, and executive function skills is not as easy as reporting gains on achievement tests, but many people believe that applicable accomplishments rather than test score gains are what make gifted contributions to societies, economies, and cultures. And to me, great accomplishments range from Nobel Prize winners to the fifth-grade girl mentioned above who started a highly effective anti-bullying program to help one small boy in her school.

Second, extending the pedagogy of gifted education and school wide enrichment to more students than those who achieved an arbitrarily determined cut-off score is also a source of pride. Many young people, especially students from minority and low-income groups, have the potential to develop gifted behaviors if we can make greater strides to close the *opportunity gap* that exists from day care to college admission. These populations are the fastest growing talent pools in our nation and underrepresentation is the greatest challenge facing our field. I hope we can address it because creative human capital is the world's most renewable resource.

Third is the large number of outstanding graduate students that have studied with my colleagues and me, as well as the summer Confratute program at the University of Connecticut that began in 1978 and has trained more than 35,000 teachers and administrators in the pedagogy that develops creative and productive giftedness. This pedagogy differs from traditional lesson learning by focusing on investigative and creative skills and the *application* of knowledge and thinking skills to the development of a product, performance, or other modes of expression that are intended to have an impact on one or more targeted audiences. Again, it is the practical application of this pedagogy in the form of professional development for teachers that has helped to change schools and classrooms in what I believe is a favorable direction.

There are two words that have guided the destination of my work over the years. The first word is *focus*. I have not attempted to be an expert on all the topics in my field and no week goes by when I am not referring requests for information to people in the field with specialties that I do not have. Rather, I have focused my research and practical derivatives on the "big ideas" related to the theories presented in this chapter and the ways in which many of the practices in gifted education can have an impact on general education. Related to focus is what I sometimes call the concept of slow growth. None of our work on the SEM happened overnight. One idea takes time to develop, field test, carry out research, gather numerous examples of best practices, and sell the idea to an always-hesitant-to-change audience. It also requires spending a great deal of time in schools because teachers, not researchers, bloggers, or platform orators, know best what will work in schools and classrooms.

I have resisted getting into prickly squabbles with critics who have concerns about my work. There are and always will be critics, especially for work that has gained a good deal of acceptance and popularity. I am guided by the only quote pasted at the top if my computer by Winston Churchill who said, *"If I stop to throw stones at every dog that barks at me, I will never reach my destination"*.

And my destination relates to the second word, which is *impact*. I do not take issue with the endless flow of research studies, commentary, journalism, and oration about the field of gifted education, but I do consider the value of these contributions in terms of the practical impact they might have on the field. Practical impact in an applied field is everything.

If I were to add a third word to my destination in this process it would be the last word from a cartoon that I have framed on my desk. It shows an ant trying to push a large boulder up a hill. The caption says, "I'll quit when is stops being *fun*". I have thoroughly enjoyed the work and am proud of the many graduate students with whom I have worked and who have gone on to become experts in their own areas of specializations. I am also proud of the many creative and dedicated teachers and administrators from around the world from who I have received countless practical ideas for advancing my work and the many scholars and researchers who participated in various projects during the 22 years when I served as the director of the National Research Center On The Gifted And Talented. I am indebted beyond words to Robert Sternberg and Howard Gardner (I call them my Body Guards), two of the best-known cognitive psychologists in the world, whose support of my work over the years has been a source of strength, especially when critics took issue with my argument against only using IQ scores to determine giftedness and only providing advanced students with accelerated curriculum experiences that focused on the traditional acquisition, storage, and retrieval of information. I am also beholden to Sally Reis, who has contributed to the theoretical and research aspects from the very start; and without whose remarkable teacher's craft knowledge and understanding of what works in schools and classrooms, none of this work would have become so widespread. If I were to summarize in a few words how my career evolved they would surely include an insatiable curiosity to find out about how things work and how we can improve and replicate them in practical ways to make a difference for learners. Also included would be the willingness to put in the time and energy to investigate big ideas, and the ability to surround myself with creative and energetic people who believe as I do *that schools should be places tor talent development*. My only regret is that I don't have another lifetime to work on the several concepts and intriguing ideas and questions that keep piling up in the *Big Idea File* on my computer.

Note

1 Privacy restrictions prevented the publication of the names of these individuals.

References

Arnold, K. D. (1995). *Lives of promise: What becomes of high school valedictorians: A fourteen-year study of achievement and life choices.* Jossey-Bass.

Bloom, B. S. (1963). Report on creativity research by the examiner's office of the University of Chicago. In C. W. Taylor & F. Barron (Eds.), *Scientific creativity: Its recognition and development* (pp. 215–264). John Wiley and Sons.

Booij, A., Haan, F., & Plug, E. (2016). *Enriching students pays off: Evidence from an individualized gifted and talented program in secondary education.* Bonn, Germany, University of Amsterdam, Tinbergen Institute, IZA and UCLS.

Brandwein, P. F. (1955). *The gifted student as future scientist.* Harcourt Brace Jovanovich.

Callahan, C. M., & Renzulli, J. S. (1974). Development and evaluation of a creativity training program. *Exceptional Children, 41,* 44–45.

Field, G. B. (2009). The effects of the use of Renzulli learning on student achievement in reading comprehension, reading fluency, social studies, and science. *International Journal of Emerging Technologies in Learning (iJET), 4*(1), 23–28.

Gardner, H. (1983). *Frames of mind: The theory of multiple intelligences.* Basic Books.

Getzels, J. W., & Jackson, P. W. (1962). *Creativity and intelligence: Explorations with gifted students.* John Wiley and Sons.

Goldman, R. J. (1964). The Minnesota tests of creative thinking. *Educational Research, 7*(1), 3–14.

Guilford, J. P. (1950). Creativity. *American Psychologist, 5,* 444–454.

Harmon, L. R. (1963). The development of a criterion of scientific competence. In C. W. Taylor & F. Barron (Eds.), *Scientific creativity: Its recognition and development* (pp. 44–52). John Wiley and Sons.

Holland, J. L., & Astin, A. W. (1962). The prediction of the academic, artistic, scientific, and social achievement of undergraduates of superior scholastic aptitude. *Journal of Educational Psychology, 53,* 132–133.

Hudson, L. (1960). Degree class and attainment in scientific research. *British Journal of Psychology 51,* 67–73.

Kim, M. (2016). A meta-analysis of the effects of enrichment programs on gifted students. *Gifted Child Quarterly*, 60(2), 102–116.

Marland, S. P. (1972). *Education of the gifted and talented (Vol. 1). Report to the Congress of the United States by the U.S. Commissioner of Education*. U.S. Government Printing Office.

Mednick, M. T. (1963). Research creativity in psychology graduate students. *Journal of Consulting Psychology* 27, 265–266.

Munday, L. A., & Davis, J. C. (1974). *Varieties of accomplishment after college: Perspectives on the meaning of academic talent* (Research Report No. 62). American College Testing Program.

National Research Council of the National Academies (2008). *Research on future skills demands: A workshop summary*. The National Academies Press.

National Research Council of the National Academies (2010). *Exploring the intersection of science education and 21st century skills: A workshop summary*. The National Academies Press.

Reis, S. M., & Renzulli, J. S. (2003). Research related to the Schoolwide Enrichment Triad Model. *Gifted Education International*, 18(1), 15–40.

Reis, S. M., Westberg, K. L., Kulikowich, J. M., & Purcell, J. H. (1998). Curriculum compacting and achievement test scores: What does the research say? *Gifted Child Quarterly*, 42, 123–129.

Renzulli, J. S. (1972a). *New directions in creativity* (vol. 1). Harper and Row.

Renzulli, J. S. (1972b). *New directions in creativity* (vol. 2). Harper and Row.

Renzulli, J. S. (1978). What makes giftedness? Re-examining a definition. *Phi Delta Kappan*, 60, 180–184.

Renzulli, J. S. (1988). *Technical report of research studies related to the revolving door identification model*. The University of Connecticut, Bureau of Educational Research.

Renzulli, J. S. (2002). Expanding the conception of giftedness to include co-cognitive traits and to promote social capital. *Phi Delta Kappan*, 84(1), 33–40, 57–58.

Renzulli, J. S. (2008). Operation Houndstooth: A positive perspective on developing social intelligence. In J. VanTassel-Baska, T. Cross, & F. R. Olenchak (Eds.), *Social-emotional curriculum with gifted and talented students* (pp. 79–112). Prufrock Press.

Renzulli, J. S., & Callahan, C. M. (1972). *New directions in creativity* (vol. 3). Harper and Row.

Renzulli, J. S., & Callahan, C. M. (1974). Evaluating and using creativity development materials. *Learning*, 2, 49–50.

Renzulli, J. S. & Hartman, R. K. (1971). Scale for rating the behavioral characteristics of superior students (SRBCSS). *Exceptional Children*, 38, 211–214.

Renzulli, J. S., & Reis, S. M. (1985). *The Schoolwide Enrichment Model: A comprehensive plan for educational excellence*. Mansfield Center, CT: Creative Learning Press.

Renzulli, J., & Reis, S. (1997). *The Schoolwide Enrichment Model: A how-to guide for educational excellence*, 2nd ed. Creative Learning Press.

Renzulli, J. S., & Reis, S. M. (2007). A technology based program that matches enrichment resources with student strengths. *International Journal of Emerging Technologies in Learning*, 2(3), 1–12.

Renzulli, J., & Reis, S. (2014). *The Schoolwide Enrichment Model: A how-to guide for educational excellence*, 3rd ed. Prufrock Press.

Renzulli, J. S., & Waicunas, N. (2016). An infusion-based approach to enriching the standards-driven curriculum. In S. M. Reis (Ed.), *Reflections on gifted education: Critical works by Joseph S. Renzulli and colleagues* (p. 411–428). Prufrock.

Renzulli, J. S., Koehler, J., & Fogarty, E. (2006). Operation Houndstooth intervention theory: Social capital in today's school. *Gifted Child Today*, 29(1), 14–24.

Renzulli, J. S., Owen, S. V., & Callahan, C. M. (1974). Fluency, flexibility, and originality as a function of group size. *Journal of Creative Behavior*, 41, 225–260.

Renzulli, J. S., Renzulli, M. J., Ford, B. G., & Smith, L. H. (1976a). *New directions in creativity* (vol. 4). Harper and Row.

Renzulli, J. S., Renzulli, M. J., Ford, B. G., & Smith, L. H. (1976b). *New directions in creativity* (vol. 5). Harper and Row.

Renzulli, J. S., Sands, M. M., & Heilbronnor, N. N. (2011). Operation Houndstooth: A positive perspective on developing social intelligence. In A. Ziegler & C. Perleth (Eds.), *Excellence: Essays in honour of Kurt Heller* (pp. 217–244). LIT Verlag.

Seligman, M. E. P., & Csikszentmihalyi, M. (2000). Positive psychology. *American Psychologist*, 55(1), 5–14.

Sternberg, R. J. (1997). The theory of successful intelligence. *Review of General Psychology*, 3, 292–316.

Sytsma, R. E. (2003). *Co-cognitive factors and socially-constructive giftedness: Distribution, abundance, and relevance among high school students* (Doctoral dissertation). University of Connecticut, Storrs.

Torrance, E. P. (1966). *Torrance tests of creative thinking*. Personnel Press.

Wallach, M. A. (1976). Tests tell us little about talent. *American Scientist* 64(1), 57–63.

Wallach, M. A., & C. W. Wing, Jr. (1969). *The talented students: A validation of the creativity intelligence distinction*. Holt, Rinehart and Winston.

17

ACADEMIC ACHIEVEMENT, IDENTITY, AND HOPE

Investing in and Over Time

Frank C. Worrell

When I was in secondary school in Trinidad, my goal was to be an English teacher. Today, I am a Professor. In this chapter, I discuss my early schooling experiences in an education system that was based on the British system, and I highlight aspects of those early experiences that put me on the path to becoming an academic who studies at-risk youth, cultural identities, time perspective, talent development. Although these may seem to be disparate topics, they are all part of an individual's identity constellation, because identity encompasses not just who you are but also what you do and what groups you belong to. Although I did not know it at the time, my secondary school was a gifted program, both for academics and for extracurricular activities like music, and some students were served better than others. The school that I ran as a Principal was a continuation high school serving at-risk youth and dropouts, some of whom had dropped out of the secondary school I attended. These students had beliefs about themselves and their futures that were determined in part by the messages that they received from teachers, parents, and their academic and behavioral difficulties. I have been able to study these topics separately and in relation to each other for 25 years and there are still many questions that have not been answered.

Academic Achievement, Identity, and Hope: Investing in and Over Time

I conduct research in several different areas, and in deciding where my intellectual journey began, I realized that much of what I study originated in events that happened well before I began my doctoral studies. Thus, I started with a section that I have labeled "Before the Academy". This section provides an important, contextual backdrop for my journey to the academy and as an academic.

Before the Academy

I was born in Trinidad and Tobago (T & T). We lived in Port-of-Spain, the capital of T & T, in an area called "behind the bridge". In sociological terms, it was a slum; the house was accessed via a dirt track going up a hillside and the only running water in the house was in the kitchen. T & T's educational system consisted of seven years of elementary school and seven years of secondary school. In the 7th year of elementary school, students wrote the Common Entrance Examination to get into secondary school. If a student failed the Common Entrance Examination, that student remained in elementary school for two more years and then went into vocational training, although they did have the option to try the exam a second time. If a student passed the examination, the student was placed in one of three *tiers* of secondary school, with Tier 1 schools being the most prestigious and the most selective. At the end of Year 5 in secondary school, students took the Ordinary Level Examinations from Cambridge University, and, if they earned high enough grades, they were allowed to continue to the final two years when they took the Advanced Level Examinations, which were a prerequisite for college entrance. Fans of the Harry Potter series will recognize the seven-year pattern of secondary schooling, as Harry and his peers had to take the Ordinary *Wizarding* Level exams (OWLs) in Year 5 and the Nastily Exhausting Wizarding Test in Year 7. The description of the Year 7 tests is quite apt.

Both of my parents had been born to very poor families in rural villages, and the only schools in their area were one-room elementary schools. My father attended the first four years of elementary school, but my mother completed elementary school. Because she was seen to be "bright" by the teacher, she was kept on as his assistant for several years. When she was 15, he helped her study for the entrance examination into the local Teachers' College, where elementary school teachers were trained; she was admitted and received her teacher credential after completing a two-year diploma program, which I think is equivalent to an Associate degree. Although my father only had four years of elementary schooling, he was able to pass a basic skills examination when the Police Force was expanding and became a policeman. He received one promotion in that role from Constable to Corporal, as his lack of education precluded further advancement. Given my parents' background, there were several important themes in our household. These included education as a tool for advancement, the importance of supportive environments, and the possibility of reaching higher through hard work and striving. These themes inform my research agendas to this day.

I began elementary education in a school that was not considered prestigious, and I did well in all subjects except arithmetic. Two years before the Common Entrance Examination, my parents transferred me to an elementary school where a teacher that they knew provided "lessons" in arithmetic after school to help me prepare for my examination. By that time, we had moved into suburbia and the middle class. When I wrote the Common Entrance Examination in Year 7 of elementary school, I passed for the highest ranked Tier 1 school for boys at the time. I was one of 500 students in T & T who received a $24 scholarship, and one of two students from my elementary school to get into my secondary school. Although I did not know it then, this was my first introduction to gifted education, and my secondary school even allowed one class of students to *accelerate* their education by moving from Year 2 to Year 4.

Despite my success at elementary school, I was not a diligent student. My academic success was largely driven by the fact that I attended school regularly and was attentive in class (my parents were a cop and a teacher). I also had a good memory and was able to do well at the end of year examinations, which were the only ones on which grades were based. This strategy became less effective in secondary school and when I wrote the O-Level examinations, I did not obtain high enough grades to get into the A-Level program at the school I attended. I could have gone to a less selective school for A-Levels, but my school was one of the few schools for boys with a choir, an extracurricular activity that was my passion. Thus, I repeated Year 5 at the school and did well enough the second time to be accepted into the A-Level program. I still had not learned the importance of studying and although I passed all of my A-Level examinations, my grades were far from stellar. As chance would have it, many students from much more affluent families did not pass their A-Level examinations in the year that I took them, and an Assistant Teacher position which I had not been initially allowed to apply for, as I was not expected to pass my exams, was offered to me, as several of the students who had signed up for it did not pass their exams and could not accept the posting.

My secondary schooling yielded several personal and academic lessons that continue to guide me. The first had to do with schools as communities. The group that I hung out with was not comprised of the more affluent students and my friends and I were not welcome in certain circles. The school was public but Catholic, and I was not accepted into the Scout troop that my Catholic friends were in; the priest in charge suggested that I "try the other Scout troop". And I was not a jock, a prized identity in an all-male secondary school. The lack of a jock identity was exacerbated by my name. My parents had named me after the first Black captain of the West Indies cricket team knighted by Queen Elizabeth, the second, for his contribution to cricket (Google "Sir Frank Worrell"). My apparent lack of natural ability in sports, generally, and in cricket, particularly, alongside of my love of singing and growing recognition in secondary school that I was gay made identity and community a very salient issue for me throughout my eight years of secondary school. I was lucky in that I had the choir and the drama club as places where I belonged.

There were also academic lessons. One of these is that a good memory is not sufficient for academic success. Another involves expectations. I am the third of four siblings and was the only one to get into A-Levels. After the A-Level results came out, my mother told my father she could not drink a toast in my honor as

I "had not done [my] best". The third was that my parents' emphasis on task commitment was correct. I had given far more attention to choir than I had to my core subjects. I received a General Merit Medal for my contribution to the choir based on the music teacher's recommendation. Many years later, my former music teacher loaned me the money to pay for my first year of my doctoral program at Berkeley from her husband's life insurance. Fourth, I learned that achievement is relative. I was awarded the A-Level History Prize, despite the fact that my grade in A-Level History was a "C". Because I knew far less history material than my classmates, I had attempted every question on the examination, whereas my peers who knew much more history than I did had spent so much time on the earlier questions, they did not get to all the questions.

I taught for a year as an Assistant Teacher, entered university in Canada with the intention of majoring in English—I planned to be a teacher—and minoring in Psychology, as a student had gone "berserk" at a concert in secondary school and I had become intrigued in understanding why. My father had told me to find a university that would accept me and he would find the money. Canada was more affordable than the United States or the United Kingdom and psychology was not yet offered at the University of the West Indies. In the fall of my sophomore year, on my father's prodding (he had retired from the police force and was working two jobs to put me through college), I applied for and, to my surprise, received a Commonwealth Scholarship granted by Canada to Trinidad. I excelled in college—it helped that every assignment counted toward the final grade unlike Trinidad—and completed Bachelor's and Master's degrees in Psychology. I returned to Trinidad to repay my service for the fellowship. I first taught at my former secondary school as an English teacher and then became Principal of another school that set the stage for my doctoral studies.

Doctoral Studies

When I applied to doctoral programs, I had a clear idea of what I wanted to study. I was serving as Principal of a private secondary school in Trinidad. In the United States, this school would have been called a continuation high school, as the students who were attending it had dropped out of, or been expelled from, other secondary schools. Having attended a highly selective secondary school, I had seen many of my classmates, who had done extremely well in elementary school, fail to succeed in secondary school. I, myself, had repeated Year 5 of secondary school, and was one of the few students that repeated who had been able to continue to A-Levels. Thus, I was interested in studying *dropouts* and *pushouts* from the school system.

And the decision to focus on dropouts led directly to my current interests. In reading the literature on dropouts, I learned about the achievement gap among ethnic-racial groups and I was also reintroduced to Erikson's (1968) psychosocial theory. Upon reading Erikson's books, I became fascinated with identity in adolescence. Erikson contended that hope from Stage 1 (Infancy) became *time perspective* in adolescence and that competence from Stage 4 (School Age) became *anticipation of achievement* in adolescence. Erikson also pointed out that African Americans and American Indians would have identity challenges in the United States, given that identity achievement "required reclaiming an identity that had been stripped away by their social and historical experiences" (Worrell & Gardner-Kitt, 2006, p. 294). My core research interests—at-risk youth, temporal constructs, cultural identities, and talent development—all originated in the intersection of my interests in dropouts and psychosocial theory. Moreover, these interests have continued throughout my career. Although all of them are not always center stage, they have been omnipresent, so I have not had to make difficult decisions.

Integrating Risk Status and Time Constructs

My doctoral program emphasized prevention, and the concepts of risk factors and protective factors became a critical framework for my studies. This framework often referenced Erikson's notion of developmental tasks. I did my doctoral qualifying examination on three topics—(a) university teacher effectiveness, (b) Black education, and (c) dropout prevention—and opted for dropout prevention for my dissertation work, as this topic subsumed African American underachievement but also allowed me to use the risk-resiliency model as my theoretical framework. I had a teaching assistantship during my first year in the doctoral program, but to pay my rent in the summer, I had to find a job. As a foreign student, I was not allowed to work off campus and I got a job as an instructor with UC Berkeley's Academic Talent Development Program—previously called the Gifted Program—which served students with strong academic records. In my dissertation work, students attending the talent development program served as "not-at-risk" comparison groups.

At the time I was completing my dissertation, school climate was considered a key factor in a student's decision to drop out. Although I agreed with the premise that different students could experience the same school context quite differently, I was also convinced that students' perception of school climate was determined in part by the psychosocial lens through which they viewed schooling. My dissertation work yielded several findings supporting this hypothesis. It showed that students assigned to a continuation school reported substantially higher scores on risk factors than students in the talent development program (Worrell, 1997a). I also showed that at-risk students who were resilient had more risk factors than not-at-risk students, but were similar on protective factors (Worrell, 1997b). In another study (Worrell et al., 1999), we showed that although self-esteem did not differ among a vulnerable at-risk group, a resilient at-risk group, and a not-at-risk group, their beliefs that *the future would work out* distinguished the resilient at-risk group and not-at-risk group from the vulnerable at-risk group. Finally, school climate did not predict dropout status, prospectively, but believing that the future would work out did distinguish between at-risk youth who dropped out and at-risk youth who completed their high school diplomas (Worrell & Hale, 2001). In other words, *believing in a positive future* predicted resilience in at-risk groups and this belief in the positive future was present both in the resilient groups (as a protective factor) and in the not-at-risk groups (as a promotive factor).

My work on time would have continued with a focus on future-oriented constructs such as hope and perceived life chances. However, in 1999, Zimbardo and Boyd introduced the Zimbardo Time Perspective Inventory (ZTPI) to the literature and argued for the importance of looking at the past and present, in addition to looking at the future. As luck would have it, ZTPI scores did not work well in adolescent samples (Mello & Worrell, 2007), but the insight about the multiple time periods proved to be an important catalyst in my research, resulting in the development of the Adolescent and Adult Time Inventory (Mello & Worrell, 2007, 2015). The AATI assesses the past, present, and future in several domains: time meaning, time frequency, time relation, time orientation, and time attitudes. Although there have been interesting findings in all of the domains, the AATI time attitudes are the most frequently used. Scores on these constructs are robust and the subscales have yielded generalizable profiles. These scores have now been validated in 12 countries. In a recent study (i.e., Worrell & Andretta, 2019), we found time attitude profiles predict other time constructs, well-being, academic constructs, and past and expected discrimination, confirming the hypothesis that students' *temporal lenses* play an important role in determining *how* they see and interpret the world.

Cultural Identities

My interests in dropouts had led me to research on the achievement gap, and one of the more compelling theoretical explanations for the achievement gap was Ogbu's (1978) cultural ecological theory. In this model, Ogbu articulated the role of identity in an individual's cultural ecological context, reminding me of Erikson's (1968) writings on minority identity achievement. Moreover, Ogbu's model explained achievement gaps not just in the United States, but in several other countries (e.g., Japan, the United Kingdom, New Zealand), and the model also provided an explanation for why immigrant groups might be more or less successful in a host country. Ogbu's theory sparked my interest in being able to examine the role of cultural identities in academic achievement. At the time, the Multigroup Measure of Ethnic Identity (Phinney, 1992) was the only measure of cultural identity that could be used across groups. Using this measure, I was able to show that ethnic identity predicted achievement differently for different groups of academically talented students (Worrell, 2007).

Specific to looking at identity in African Americans, in 1995, I accepted an invitation to participate in developing a scale to measure racial identity based on

Cross' (1991) revised nigrescence model. The scale development process, which took five years, resulted in the Cross Racial Identity Scale (CRIS; Vandiver & Worrell, 2001), which assesses six different attitudes: assimilation, miseducation, self-hatred, anti-White, Afrocentricity, and Multiculturalist. In keeping with the idea of psychosocial lenses, I led a study to see if we could identify racial identity profiles, and our team was the first to identify *generalizable* Black racial identity profiles in African Americans. These profiles predict differential levels of psychopathology and other psychological constructs in African American adolescents and adults (Worrell et al., 2006; Worrell et al., 2014). In ongoing work, we have modified the CRIS to assess ethnic-racial identity attitudes (the Cross Ethnic-Racial Identity Scale [CERIS]) in African Americans, Asian Americans, Latinx, and European Americans (Worrell, Mendoza-Dento et al., 2019). The CERIS will allow researchers to see if similar profiles can be found in different ethnic-racial groups and if the correlates of these profiles are the same across groups. Recent work has also shown that these attitudes can be measured outside the United States, which will allow for cross-cultural and cross-national research on these constructs.

Talent Development

When I began teaching in the Academic Talent Development Program in 1989, my goal was to pay the rent. However, as I continued to work with these students, I became interested in how much they differed from the at-risk youth that I was studying. The students in the talent development program had strong academic identities and sought out extra work if they thought they might get less than an A on an assignment, whereas students in the continuation schools resisted doing extra work to move their grade from a C to a B. This observation piqued my interest in the factors beyond intellectual ability that resulted in outstanding performance.

In reviewing the literature on gifted and talented youth, two things stood out. First, there was the large number of theoretical perspectives on what was giftedness, most of which focused on one or a few aspects of the phenomenon. Second, although there were numerous papers on the underrepresentation in gifted education of the subgroups that were overrepresented in the dropout statistics (e.g., Latinx, African American, Native American), the explanations for underrepresentation (a) focused on important but distal variables such as racism and discrimination, and (b) invoked test bias as a primary cause of underrepresentation without engaging the countervailing evidence in the measurement literature. Moreover, the achievement gap, which was highlighted in the literature on dropping out, was not mentioned in the literature on gifted and talented, although the lower distributions of the underrepresented groups on achievement tests provided a compelling explanation for the disproportionality in gifted and talented education programs.

Moving beyond using academically talented students merely as comparison groups, I started looking at identification practices for gifted education as well as issues of competence, identity, and other psychosocial constructs. Combining my interest in minority education and talent development also resulted in a series of papers on these topics (e.g., on the underrepresentation of African Americans, and on ethnic identity's differential associations with achievement in different ethnic-racial groups; Worrell, 2007). I had started presenting on gifted and talented education at the American Educational Research Association in the mid-1990s and Paula Olszewski-Kubilius invited me to speak on a panel she was chairing at the National Association for Gifted Children's annual conference in 2002. I got along well with Paula and a colleague, Rena Subotnik, both of whom have become major collaborators.

In 2009, Rena was invited to contribute a review piece on gifted education to *Psychological Science in the Public Interest*, and she invited Paula and me to co-author it with her. The resulting monograph, in which we introduce the talent development megamodel (Subotnik et al., 2011), has become a widely cited piece in the literature. The megamodel became the basis of a special issue of *Gifted Child Quarterly* in 2012, with responses from a number of leading scholars in the field, including researchers from Australia and from Germany. This engagement pushed our thinking and, in addition to a variety of papers in which we flesh out aspects of the megamodel, we have published works in which we apply the megamodel to gifted education in schools (Olszewski-Kubilius et al., 2018; Worrell et al., 2019) and to high performance across a range of domains (Subotnik et al., 2019).

In the talent development megamodel, we attempt to capture the complexity of giftedness as a phenomenon across domains. We define giftedness developmentally, beginning with potential in the childhood, which becomes outstanding achievement and sometimes, eminence in adulthood. We acknowledge the role of general and domain specific abilities, psychosocial and mental skills, opportunities, appropriate coaching, and chance, as well as the domain differences in talent development trajectories. In some of our most recent work in this area, we have engaged with scholars from several countries in Europe to review and adapt the megamodel into a framework that facilitates the development of testable hypotheses and empirical investigations. Called the talent achievement in domains (TAD) model (Preckel et al., in press), we look forward to continuing to work on the megamodel and TAD within and beyond the United States.

Measurement Research: A Side Benefit

My training is as a school psychologist, and one of the aspects of school psychology training that is stressed is the importance of using reliable scores that yield valid inferences. School psychologists contribute to classification decisions that have very high stakes across the lifetime (e.g., autism, gifted, learning disability). In assessment circles, a distinction is frequently made between scores on research instruments or instruments used for group decisions and scores on instruments used for individual decisions, with the level of evidence being considerably higher for individual decision making (American Educational Research Association et al., 2014). In much of my research journey, I have been confronted with operationalizations of constructs that did not hold up to psychometric scrutiny. Moreover, whereas constructs used in research were usually limited to the sphere of other researchers, the 24-hour news cycle, the presence of the internet, and the press of universities to be relevant in the public eye has led to research being translated into the popular media.

Thus, grit, growth mindsets, and the power pose are not only written about in academic journals; these constructs are discussed on National Public Radio and morning television shows, written about in popular books for the public, and discussed in TED talks. And this exposure leads to a translation from research to practice at a speed that does not allow for the usual academic vetting. If research constructs are going to be used in practice and public policy decisions, the instruments measuring these constructs need to be held to the same standard that we hold assessments that are used for individual decision making. In both the cultural identity and time perspective literatures, questions were being raised about the validity of the constructs being measured. Thus, in doing research in these areas, it was important to examine the psychometric properties of scores on the instruments that purported to measure the constructs my colleagues and I were interested in studying.

And in fact, the development of the AATI, the CRIS, and the CERIS, were all inspired, in part, by the fact that instruments in the extant literature were not measuring the constructs with the level of integrity that was desired. In the process of examining scores on existing scales and developing scales for use, scale development and validation became another tool in my academic toolkit. This tool proved to be useful beyond learning *how* to engage in the process. It highlighted the important interplay between theory and empirical research and rejected a false distinction held by some of my colleagues that empirical research and theoretical advancements were done in different papers. My work over the years has shown quite clearly that these two aspects of scholarship are intimately intertwined.

Conclusion

The topics that I study all have their history in my early schooling experiences: talent development from the secondary school that I attended and my days as a choir boy; dropouts, from the school that I served as principal for; time perspective from my parents' lessons about working toward the future; and identity, from not living up to my name and wanting to choose a different path. These research threads have been with me throughout my career, although some may get more attention in some years than others. I am still involved in music, which kept me connected to school, even when I was not doing well academically, and provided a strong sense of belonging to and an identity in my secondary school. I understand how an activity that provides an identity and a community can be a critical protective factor for at-risk youth.

Cultural identities can be framed as "either/or" or "both/and", and the latter framing is more useful in helping individuals from minority and marginalized groups develop a sense of belonging and a recognition that cultural and academic identities do not have to be incompatible. I have learned a lot about what it takes to develop talent, and I have also argued that talent development can go beyond gifted education to serve students who are disenfranchised by our education system (Weinstein & Worrell, 2016; Worrell & Dixson, 2018). I have been able to give back to T & T, which gave me so much, by validating instruments that allow T & T's Ministry of Education to diagnose reading and behavioral problems (Watkins et al., 2014). Finally, my work has highlighted the importance of viewing the world through a temporal lens that focuses on the positives in the past, present, and future. One of the things that my mother always said, was, "Aim for the stars. If you miss, you can still land in the treetops".

References

American Educational Research Association, American Psychological Association, & National Council on Measurement in Education (2014). *Standards for educational and psychological testing*. American Educational Research Association.

Cross, W. E. Jr. (1991). *Shades of black: Diversity in African American identity*. Temple University Press.

Erikson, E. H. (1968). *Identity: Youth and crisis*. Norton.

Mello, Z. R., & Worrell, F. C. (2007). *The Adolescent and Adult Time Inventory—English*. Authors.

Mello, Z. R., & Worrell, F. C. (2015). The past, the present, and the future: A conceptual model of time perspective in adolescence. In M. Stolarski, N. Fieulaine, & W. van Beek (Eds.), *Time perspective theory: Review, research, and application. Essays in honor of Phillip G. Zimbardo* (pp. 115–129). Springer. https://doi.org/10.1007/978-3-319-07368-2_7

Ogbu, J. U. (1978). *Minority education and caste: The American education system in cross-cultural perspective*. Academic Press.

Olszewski-Kubilius, P., Subotnik, R. F., & Worrell, F. C. (Eds.) (2018). *Talent development as a framework for gifted education: Implications for best practices and applications in schools*. Prufrock Press.

Phinney, J. S. (1992). The Multigroup Ethnic Identity Measure: A new scale for use with diverse groups. *Journal of Adolescent Research, 7*(2), 156–176.

Preckel, F., Golle, J., Grabner, R., Jarvin, L., Kozbelt, A., Müllensiefen, D., Olszewski-Kubilius, P., Subotnik, R. F., Schneider, W., Volk, M., & Worrell, F. C. (in press). Talent development in achievement domains: A psychological framework for within and cross-domain research. *Perspectives on Psychological Science*.

Subotnik, R. F., Olszewski-Kubilius, P., & Worrell, F. C. (2011). Rethinking giftedness and gifted education: A proposed direction forward based on psychological science. *Psychological Science in the Public Interest, 12*(1), 3–54. https://doi.org/10.1177/1529100611418056.

Subotnik, R. F., Olszewski-Kubilius, P., & Worrell, F. C. (Eds.) (2019). *The psychology of high performance: Developing human potential into domain-specific talent*. American Psychological Association. http://dx.doi.org/10.1037/0000120-000.

Vandiver, B. J., & Worrell, F. C. (Eds.) (2001). Psychological nigrescence revisited. [Special issue]. *Journal of Multicultural Counseling and Development*, 29(3).

Watkins, M. W., Hall, T. E., & Worrell, F. C. (2014). From Central Guidance Unit to Student Support Services Unit: The outcome of a consultation process in Trinidad and Tobago. *Journal of Educational and Psychological Consultation*, 24(4), 283–306. https://doi.org/10.1080/10474412.2014.929962

Weinstein, R. S., & Worrell, F. C. (Eds.) (2016). *Achieving college dreams: How a university-charter district partnership created an early college high school*. Oxford University Press. https://doi.org/10.1093/acprof:oso/9780190260903.001.0001

Worrell, F. C. (1997a). Academically talented students and resilient at-risk students: Differences on self-reported risk and protective factors. *The Journal of At-Risk Issues*, 4(1), 10–18.

Worrell, F. C. (1997b). Predicting successful or non-successful at-risk status using demographic risk factors. *The High School Journal*, 81(1), 46–53.

Worrell, F. C. (2007). Ethnic identity, academic achievement, and global self-concept in four groups of academically talented adolescents. *Gifted Child Quarterly*, 51(1), 23–38.

Worrell, F. C., & Andretta, J. R. (2019). Time attitude profiles in American adolescents: Educational and psychological correlates. *Research in Human Development*, 16(2), 102–118. https://doi.org/10.1080/15427609.2019.1635860

Worrell, F. C., & Dixson, D. D. (2018). Retaining and recruiting underrepresented gifted students. In S. I. Pfeiffer (Ed.), *Handbook of giftedness in children*, 2nd ed. (pp. 209–226). Springer. https://doi.org/10.1007/978-3-319-77004-8_13

Worrell, F. C., & Gardner-Kitt, D. L. (2006). The relationship between racial and ethnic identity in black adolescents: The Cross Racial Identity Scale (CRIS) and the Multigroup Ethnic Identity Measure (MEIM). *Identity: An International Journal of Theory and Research*, 6, 293–315. doi:10.1207/s1532706xid0604_1

Worrell, F. C., & Hale, R. L. (2001). The relationship of hope in the future and perceived school climate to school completion. *School Psychology Quarterly*, 16(4), 370–388. https://doi.org/10.1521/scpq.16.4.370.19896

Worrell, F. C., Andretta, J. R., & Woodland, M. H. (2014). Cross Racial Identity Scale (CRIS) scores and profiles in African American adolescents involved with the juvenile justice system. *Journal of Counseling Psychology*, 61(4), 570–580. https://doi.org/10.1037/cou0000041

Worrell, F. C., Latto, I. K., & Perlinski, M. A. (1999). The relationship of risk status to self-esteem and perceived life chances. *The Journal of At-Risk Issues*, 5(2), 33–38.

Worrell, F. C., Mendoza-Denton, R., & Wang, A. (2019). Introducing a new assessment tool for measuring ethnic-racial identity: The Cross Ethnic-Racial Identity Scale-Adult (CERIS-A). *Assessment*, 26(3), 404–418. https://doi.org/10.1177/1073191117698756

Worrell, F. C., Olszewski-Kubilius, P., & Subotnik, R. F. (2019). The psychology of high performance: Overarching themes. In R. F. Subotnik, P. Olszewski-Kubilius, & F. C. Worrell (Eds.), *The psychology of high performance: Translating human potential into domain-specific talent* (pp. 369–385). American Psychological Association. http://dx.doi.org/10.1037/0000120-018

Worrell, F. C., Subotnik, R. F., Olszewski-Kubilius, P., & Dixson, D. D. (2019). Gifted students. *Annual Review of Psychology*, 70, 551–576. https://doi.org/10.1146/annurev-psych-010418-102846

Worrell, F. C., Vandiver, B. J., Schaefer, B. A., Cross, W. E., Jr., & Fhagen-Smith, P. E. (2006). Generalizing nigrescence profiles: A cluster analysis of Cross Racial Identity Scale (CRIS) scores in three independent samples. *The Counseling Psychologist*, 34(4), 519–547. https://doi.org/10.1177/0011000005278281

Zimbardo, P. G., & Boyd, J. N. (1999). Putting time in perspective: A valid, reliable individual-difference metric. *Journal of Personality and Social Psychology*, 77, 1271–1288. https://doi.org/10.1037/0022-3514.77.6.1271

18

INTELLECTUAL ROOTS AND PATHS

Sally M. Reis

Context

As a bright child growing up in a working-class town, my relationship with learning and schooling were at odds. Although I loved learning, I disliked school, where I was unchallenged and where being creative often meant getting into trouble. I experienced a more challenging education in junior high school, and subsequently worked for 13 years as a school teacher and administrator. During that time, I encountered students who, like myself, enjoyed learning in a more creative way and tried to improve their schooling experiences. This work eventually inspired me to return to graduate school to investigate how to make education better—especially for talented, creative students. My research career began with investigations of Joe Renzulli's (1977) Enrichment Triad Model and its extensions to a broad pool of students.

Joe and I turned out to be excellent collaborators, and I soon took on a lead role in developing and conducting research on school structures that applied to the model. Our research demonstrated that these methods could benefit students of all achievement levels, and these ideas emerged into the Schoolwide Enrichment Model, explained in this chapter (Renzulli & Reis, 1985; 1997; 2014). Along with this collaborative work, I have followed my interests to conduct research in three major areas during my career. First is conducting research about the Schoolwide Enrichment Model, explained briefly in this chapter; second, using strength-based teaching methods to support high-potential students with unique needs; and third, describing the life paths and decisions faced by talented and eminent women. I also pursued academic administration, serving as a department head, the vice provost for academic affairs, and a president of one of my professional organizations. I began to understand the importance and impact of positive, supportive leadership and these experiences enhanced my research on talented women.

Early Life

Neither of my parents graduated from college and my childhood was not one that included many intellectual opportunities and insights, but I was always eager to learn. The school district I attended was in a blue-collar factory city and was not a good place for smart students. Beginning in fourth grade, I was often excused from class and tasked to serve as a "helper" to whatever adult needed mainly office-type support. My father used to joke that I deserved a paycheck for time that I spent in my elementary school office answering the phone and doing odd jobs for teachers. This work cemented my commitment to avoid clerical duties in the future and was probably the reason I was drawn to the work of my future partner and husband, Joseph Renzulli, in curriculum differentiation and compacting. The other way I survived those boring years was reading, often times by hiding a more advanced book inside the cover of our basal reader. I was an early and passionate reader, a habit that has sustained and enriched my life. Books have been my lifelong companion and this definitely was the impetus for my research about advanced readers.

On October 4, 1957, the Soviet Union successfully launched Sputnik and the world's first artificial satellite, the size of a beach ball, took only 98 minutes to orbit the Earth. I was six years old and distinctly remember standing in our front yard, staring into the sky watching in vain for a tiny streak of light. That satellite became a metaphor for what was to happen in American education. By the time I entered junior high school in September 1963, Sputnik had begun to change our educational landscape. I was placed in an accelerated program beginning in seventh grade, one of 20 elementary school students who entered the accelerated program, from 400 students who came together from across the district entering my junior-high class.

By 1963, and thanks in no small part to SPUTNIK, my school district and many others across the USA had awakened to the idea that American advanced learners needed more stimulation to compete with the Russians. They launched various types of accelerated and advanced programs to address this need. I initially loved my accelerated class but over time I began to understand the cadences of my classmates' responses and boredom set in again. While some of my classmates were destined to be valedictorians, I had a more creative side. I became the class problem solver, and was perhaps, the least diligent homework completer in the group.

I achieved As with minimal effort, despite the accelerated options. In retrospect, I understand that I was an intellectually lazy student. As the oldest of six children, I worked a few nights and every weekend at a local department store to help my family financially. It had become apparent to me that I was only going to be able to attend college if I earned a full academic scholarship. None of the most competitive colleges were accepting women at that time and I had little academic guidance in my application process. Without any guidance, I decided to apply primarily to women's colleges, potentially foreshadowing my interest in smart women. I desperately wanted to attend Smith College, but promised my parents that I would go where the financial-aid package was best. And so, I found myself heading to Pittsburgh's Chatham University as a psychology and English major in 1969.

This was also the height of the Vietnam War Protest movement and a heady and amazing time to be a student. My college was exhilarating. I joined every protest I could, was elected president of my class, and drank the intellectual Kool-Aid of my generation. I listened to and met Margaret Mead, attended classes and lectures at Carnegie Mellon and the University of Pittsburgh, and spent every free minute I had reading all that was assigned and more. I was intellectually challenged in small classes of smart women and learned, at that point, to speak out as often and as much as I wanted, without fear of appearing "too smart". My happiest hours were spent at the beautiful Chatham library, where I read for hours, sometimes daydreaming that I was occupying the same chair used by Rachel Carson, my college's most famous alum.

On May 4, 1970, my life changed. The Kent State shootings, also known as the May 4 massacre, resulted in unarmed, protesting college students being killed by members of the Ohio National Guard, happened only a short distance from my campus. Simultaneously, mass protests ignited our nation in response to the bombing of Cambodia by the United States military. I spent my junior year studying in London and continued to protest the war. I became immersed in travel, theater, and acquired a broader knowledge of the world and when I returned, was changed in ways that I can hardly describe.

Chatham required an honors type thesis of every senior and in an English class there, I met one of the intellectual loves of my life, English Professor Cummins, who served as my thesis advisor and intellectual guide. I was teeming with ideas about psychology and English and looking for a thesis idea about which I could feel some intellectual passion when Professor Cummins gave a lecture on the last months of Charles Dicken's life. I had found my topic. Dickens, nearly always short of the funds he needed to take care of his large family and expenses, was the most popular author in England. Enter Wilke Collins, who became his rival. Collins published *The Moonstone,* which is widely considered to be the first detective novel and the grandfather of one of the most popular genres in the English language. The novel (like most books of the time) was originally serialized in Dickens' own magazine, and it became so popular that Collins became a household name.

Charles Dickens was complicated, driven, obsessed, and usually ego-centric. He was also committed to social change. *The Mystery of Edwin Drood*, his final novel, was only half finished when Dickens died in 1870. He left no detailed notes or plan for the ending of the novel, due to his competition with Wilke Collins who was racing into stardom for *The Moonstone*. For my senior thesis, I became one of many Dickens scholars to try to finish the novel. I felt like a *practicing professional* and a literary scholar, and that feeling was one I remembered when I began to advocate for academically talented students' right to choose their advanced interest-based projects to complete in school. I learned to be a young scholar by my work to create an original ending to the *Mystery of Edwin Drood* and Professor Cummins' refusal to accept work that was beneath his standards and my potential. It was the first time that I had been intellectually challenged on my first creative productive writing. This project exposed me to the joy of intellectually rigorous work as well as the perseverance necessary to excel.

Early Teaching Career

Following college, I became a teacher in the public-school system in Pittsburgh. At the time, I thought that my next step would be law school but during that first year of teaching (six 9th-grade English classes of 30 students daily) I became interested in and curious about my students, especially the smart ones who were lazy and unmotivated. I also began to understand the work and effort required to be an effective teacher. It was in my first year of teaching that I met Chris, an academically talented, underachieving, turned-off gifted girl, who was angry and negative toward school, her teachers, and the other students in her classes. I eventually achieved success with her after eliminating her regular work and engaging her in independent study that she selected, based on her interests. This experience made me want to learn more about academically talented students, the choices they made, the reasons they underachieved, and what I could do to motivate and engage them. That in turn led me to coursework at the University of Pittsburgh about gifted education, gifted and creative students, and John Dewey, E. Paul Torrance, James Gallagher, and the continuation of my intellectual journey toward the practical scholar I have become.

I met Joe Renzulli, who became my intellectual partner and husband, soon after I moved back to my Connecticut hometown from Pittsburgh to teach in my hometown. He sent me an early draft of an article he had written on The Enrichment Triad Model (Renzulli, 1977). This was my first exposure to his work and the ideas that would influence the rest of my professional and personal life. As I had already taken some classes about academically talented students and was interested in learning more, I became friendly with the emerging leaders of gifted education in Connecticut. We were a young, irreverent, and creative group who eagerly sought interaction with scholars in the field. My interactions with gifted-education experts from the National Leadership Training Institute were intellectually and personally stimulating and life changing. These pioneers, including Sandy Kaplan, James Gallagher, and Harry Passow, were among my earliest intellectual influencers.

My superintendent of schools asked me to start a gifted program and I used the opportunity to directly experiment with some of Joe's ideas. I first implemented an enrichment program for talented students in middle school, then elementary, and finally, high school. Frustrated by the requirement to administer individual IQ tests to select students for these gifted programs and the time and expense this incurred, I began thinking deeply about broadening the notion of who was gifted and who was not. I also thought about who else could be served by enrichment, which seemed to benefit a much broader pool of students. That journey became my life's work.

Transition to Research Faculty

After I finished graduate school and became a professor, I constantly questioned why gifted-education pedagogy could not be extended to more students. This basic idea is the basis for the Schoolwide Enrichment Model (SEM), which I developed in partnership with Joe Renzulli. The SEM is widely used in schools and provides three types of services: identifying students' strengths and interests, modifying their curriculum to eliminate work they already know and replacing that with more exciting work. This enrichment includes exposing them to new ideas and topics of interests, teaching them different types of creative thinking skills and also how to do advanced work, and finally, letting them choose projects and products of their own interest. In the highest level of enrichment, students write novels, create science projects, conduct historical research and develop inventions that are in their areas of personal interest. The SEM is used around the world as a magnet theme, a school-based program, and an enrichment program for academically talented students. It provides opportunities for students to become involved in learning about areas of their own interest and substitutes more exciting and creative work for the regular curriculum work that they have already mastered.

Impetus and Logic of Expanding Enrichment Opportunities

My first publication, based on my doctoral dissertation, was related to Joseph Renzulli's Three Ring Conception of Giftedness. This definition expands the concept of who is gifted to a broader pool of students, identified by three clusters of abilities, creativity, and task commitment. We were granted permission from the state of Connecticut to increase the number of students served in gifted programs in 12 school districts. We included the top 15 percent of academically talented students, instead of the top 3–5 percent as state guidelines recommended at the time. I was most interested in creative-productive giftedness, and whether these top academic students could also produce creative products. In this journey, I was also influenced by the expanding conceptions of intelligence of in the pioneering work of Robert Sternberg (1985) and Howard Gardner (1993). Their work was, and continues to be, both inspiring and influential for us. My dissertation research influenced much of my later school-based practitioner work conducted in schools on educational practices. We argued against using a single criterion, an IQ test, to identify students, and instead, for the creation of talent pool of high-potential students that could benefit from enrichment. This study resulted in more flexible identification criteria and local norms being used to identify more students across our state, an effect that was particularly noticeable for culturally diverse and poor students in urban and suburban districts across our state. It expanded the more conventional selection and identification processes that had largely excluded students of poverty from gifted programs in prior years.

Research on the Schoolwide Enrichment Model (SEM)

I have been the primary researcher on the SEM (https://gifted.uconn.edu/schoolwide-enrichment-model/), the school-based talent development approach described above that the product of four decades of research and field-testing, since its first edition was published in 1985 (Renzulli & Reis, 1985; 1997; 2014). We have worked in over 25 countries and all 50 states and the SEM is currently used in thousands of school districts. Also based on this work, I have become increasingly interested in how enrichment pedagogy can be used to provide engaging and interesting learning experiences for all students. Enrichment pedagogy includes different ways of teaching, for example, using creativity training, problem solving, and opportunities for project-based learning for all students in school. This brand of teaching emphasizes that all students should have opportunities to pursue and develop their interests in school and that educators should differentiate and personalize instruction whenever possible to enable students to have more creative, self-selected interest-based experiences in school.

Talented Readers and the Schoolwide Enrichment Reading Model (SEM-R)

In some of my favorite work, I led a team of colleagues to conduct research on using enrichment strategies to challenge and engage readers of all achievement levels, especially talented readers. This work was actually a culmination of previous work as it combined my love of reading, my background as a language arts and reading teacher, previous work in the SEM, and curriculum compacting. The premise of SEM-R is that students' school-based experiences with reading should be joyful, and the first goal of reading experiences, after students learn to read, should be that they enjoy reading. The more pleasurable reading experiences they have, the more likely it is that students will want to read independently and develop the self-regulation necessary to remain lifelong readers. In the SEM-R, we expose students to many different books in which they can become interested and then give them time in class to select and read these high-interest books that are slightly to moderately above their current reading levels. We then provide independent and differentiated reading instruction based on their individual needs, eliminating grouped reading instruction in favor of differentiated reading instruction and more time to read in class. Our goal is to create independent, lifelong readers who read challenging text with pleasure.

This research, which was funded by two federal grants, provides support for applying enrichment and differentiation theories to reading (https://gifted.uconn.edu/semr-pubs/). The major result of this empirical work was that teachers using SEM-R could eliminate most of group-reading instruction (up to 4–5 hours weekly) and replace it with targeted differentiated reading instruction applied to interest-based books that students selected and actually wanted to read—all with no loss of reading achievement. This research demonstrated that it is possible to save students from hundreds of hours of basic, whole-group instruction when we substitute self-selected, pleasurable independent reading paired with differentiated instruction and still meet or exceed achievement goals.

Research on Curriculum Differentiation and Compacting

Perhaps due to the time I spent being bored in school, and definitely due to my interactions with and advocacy for students as a teacher, I became interested in studying how differentiated teaching strategies could work. Differentiated instruction involves identifying what students already know and eliminating what they have already mastered. Teachers then assign different work and opportunities to students based on their strengths and interests. Imagine being in a classroom where you did not have to repeat work that you already know! Curriculum Compacting enables teachers to streamline the regular curriculum, ensure student mastery of basic skills, and provide time for challenging enrichment activities or acceleration activities. My team's research on compacting demonstrated that academically talented students can be have 40–50 percent of regular curriculum eliminated without any decrease in scores on their achievement tests (Reis, Westberg, Kulikowich & Purcell, 1998). This is a frequently cited research study in our field. Bob Sternberg, another of my intellectual heroes and influences, once asked after a presentation about compacting, "Why can't all teachers do this every day?" Indeed, that is the goal.

Research on Students with both Academic Talents and Disabilities

My research about the challenges and problems faced by academically talented students who also have learning disabilities (called twice-exceptional or 2E) was inspired by my colleague, collaborator and friend Dr. Susan Baum. Many educators simply don't understand that students with disabilities such as dyslexia and autism can also have academic talents. Their disabilities usually mask their talents while their talents simultaneously mask their disabilities. After my first study of this population and the challenges they face revealed educational lives both heartbreaking and inspiring (Reis, Neu, & McGuire, 1997), I was motivated to identify appropriately challenging, academic compensation strategies that helped 2E students to be successful.

My research in this area over the last two decades will be boosted by a recent federal grant that will enable me to continue learning more about how to help students with Autism Spectrum Disorder (ASD) learn the academic and social skills to succeed in college. Creating opportunities for educators to provide enrichment and talent development opportunities to these 2E students who have both extreme talents and deficits is an ongoing interest and the current focus of my work. In addition to helping students with strategies to compensate for their weaknesses, such as by providing extra time on tests and instructing them in learning strategies, educators need to help 2E students develop their academic talents. Their talents are where we can ignite their interests, fuel a passion for learning, and help them find future work that is engaging and fulfilling.

Research on Talented and Eminent Women

Following the broad path of my intellectual journey, some of my favorite, and perhaps best-known work, is my research on talented women and girls and why so many still underachieve at the highest levels of accomplishment. Perhaps, the most glaring example of the "why so few" phenomenon occurred recently, when the Forbes 2019 list of America's 100 Most Innovative Leaders included only one woman. This shocking oversight demonstrates that the absence of women at the top of many professions continues to exist. It is long past time for change, and we need more women and diverse leaders in every profession to bring their varied voices and ideas to solve the problems facing our society. I have loved the longitudinal research I conducted on talented, eminent women (Reis, 1998; 2005) and the opportunities I have had to give speeches about this group across the world. The eminent women I studied all encountered blocks to their talent development by negative stereotyping but excelled in their areas. They were all characterized by a strong belief in self and a desire to develop their talents. They all focused on the contributions they could make that were meaningful and that would improve our society. The opportunity to conduct this research and propose new theories about women's talent development and creativity has been a highlight of my intellectual journey.

My interviews with older, highly eminent women for the first volume of this work was an illuminating first step in understanding the choices and obstacles faced by eminent women. I also wanted to better understand the reasons that some decide not to pursue the highest level of accomplishment in their fields. Some women chose simpler lives that gave time for family, children, or spouses, or chose more private lives to enable a focus on their work, later understanding that this decision caused their work to be less known. The environment they selected to be able to do their work, as Sternberg (2002) suggested, was critical, but so was their determination and motivation to succeed.

In my current work, I am interviewing a second group of eminent women. My focus this time is on their creativity and creative processes, but I am also interested in what drives them and the obstacles they encounter. This research about 15 highly creative women from different domains will enable me to study their beliefs about their own creativity and talents. Each has acknowledged that they are highly creative and explained what inspired their work. Most are primarily motivated by their passion for their discipline and their desire to make a creative impact in their domain. They acknowledge experiencing various blocks to their creative work and encountering gender stereotyping, but each ignored these, focusing more on their work, as opposed to the obstacles that they encountered. Most were married and had children, but those who chose not to marry or have partners were no more or less successful or creative than those who did.

Evolution

My early research on expanding conceptions of giftedness, and my decisions to study school-based practices are examples of applied research that is challenging to conduct. In addition to concerns about student and teacher privacy and changing the status quo, it is increasingly difficult for educators to participate in research. School-based research is, however, critically important for educators and policy makers who want "evidence-based practices" to make decisions about what is best for students. It is challenging to evaluate best practices in enrichment and gifted education in rapidly changing schools where laws and funding for services are declining by the year. Educational research is critically important for research-based practices that improve engagement and achievement.

I believe that my most important scholarly and intellectual evolution has been on expanding gifted-education strategies and work to benefit more students, including those with disabilities. The research that we conducted on the SEM-R, for example, was applied to all students in the school who could already read, and we found that below average and readers with disabilities also relished the opportunity to select their own high interest books. These students did better, with far less whole group instruction, than did their peers in the control group that received regular grouped reading instruction.

Other research conducted on the SEM in one large urban school investigated providing Enrichment Clusters, one specific type of SEM pedagogy, to all students. Enrichment Clusters are non-graded opportunities for highly engaging, self-selected activities that meet for about an hour a week, such as creating an invention, and completing a product or service. During Clusters, students select the activities they want to pursue, such as performing plays, investigating local history, helping others, writing short stories, or making movies. We found that during the 90 minutes weekly that students enjoyed clusters, there were significantly fewer absentees, and almost no behavioral problems in a school of almost 700 students, with 90 who were identified as having behavior disorders (Reis, Gentry, & Maxfield, 1998). It was easy to see that students with disabilities—indeed, all students—deserve opportunities to pursue their interests and learn the strategies they need to succeed in school while also doing enjoyable, creative work. This research brought me back to the beginnings of my intellectual journey and the influential work of Renzulli, Sternberg, and Torrance, which expanded my views on giftedness and the ways it develops over a lifetime.

Hindsight

Given my success at leading research teams and conducting research, I wish I had spent more time conducting more research on talented women. Even today, many smart women are plagued by feelings that they are not talented enough, or good enough to be top scholars or leaders. Too few women are emerging as leaders across domains. I hope my current work will help some of them to understand that a lack of confidence can hold back even those who appear to be successful. That is the reason I continue to study eminent women, almost all of whom have self-doubts at various times in their careers. They overcome this doubt, as I did, by years of effort and good work, but for some, it delays their progress over time and remains an obstacle to reaching the highest levels of their goals and aspirations.

Since the beginning of my research career, my years as a public-school teacher remained an influence. Most of the researchers whom I most admire, including Renzulli, Sternberg, Torrance, and Gallagher, have conducted applied and/or school-based research and contributed theories that were practical for teachers. In hindsight, I wished I had arrived earlier at the importance of gifted-education pedagogy and the difference these could make for all students. The time in the intervening decades, however, was most likely necessary to better understand the power and the importance of these paths. Also, educational change has resulted in the standards movement, that has now overtaken American education, and which has had a negative impact on many high-potential and gifted students. Too many smart students are stuck doing work that they already know—over and over again—in school, even though we have developed the tools and strategies to change this.

Also, in reflecting on my career, I benefited from decades of experience and the funded research opportunities I had to experiment with applications of gifted-education pedagogy on all students, including those with disabilities. Understanding that all students should have some opportunities to develop their talents and interests has been essential to my development as a scholar over time. The research I have conducted on these intellectual ideas has demonstrated that what has historically been gifted-education pedagogy should be driving educational practice for all students. All students should be given the opportunity to develop their creativity, to work in areas of interest, to have personalized and differentiated instruction, and to develop their talents. In some schools, the talent pool should be much, much larger, and in some schools, all students should be considered a talent pool, and receive regular enrichment opportunities.

More students will be engaged and fulfilled in school if we plan educational experiences around enrichment opportunities. Interests guide much of what students want to do in school, and creative accomplishments completed in school are important guiding forces for one's future. Just as my own opportunity to complete self-selected, highly creative work in college started me on an intellectual journey in a way that my elementary school office staff might never have predicted, more creative work in schools can result in a larger pool of creative and fulfilled adults whose work makes a difference in the world.

References

Gardner, H. (1993). *Frames of mind: The theory of multiple intelligences*. Basic Books.
Reis, S. M. (1998). *Work left undone: Compromises and challenges of talented females*. Mansfield Center, CT: Creative Learning Press.
Reis, S. M. (2005). Feminist perspectives on talent development: A research based conception of giftedness in women. In R. J. Sternberg & J. Davidson (Eds.), *Conceptions of giftedness* (2nd ed., pp. 217–245). Cambridge University Press.
Reis, S. M., Gentry, M., & Maxfield, L. R. (1998). The application of enrichment clusters to teachers' classroom practices. *Journal for Education of the Gifted*, 21(3), 310–324.
Reis, S. M., Neu, T. W., & McGuire, J. M. (1997). Case studies of high-ability students with learning disabilities who have achieved. *Exceptional Children*, 63, 463–479.
Reis, S. M., Westberg, K. L., Kulikowich, J. M., & Purcell, J. H. (1998). Curriculum compacting and achievement test scores: What does the research say? *Gifted Child Quarterly*, 42, 123–129.
Renzulli, J. S. (1977). *The Enrichment Triad Model: A guide for developing defensible programs for the gifted and talented*. Creative Learning Press.
Renzulli, J. S., & Reis, S. M. (1985). *The Schoolwide Enrichment Model: A comprehensive plan for educational excellence*. Creative Learning Press.
Renzulli, J. S., & Reis, S. M. (1997). *The Schoolwide Enrichment Model: A how-to guide for educational excellence*, 2nd ed. Creative Learning Press.
Renzulli, J. S., & Reis, S. M. (2014). *The Schoolwide Enrichment Model: A how-to guide for educational excellence*, 3rd ed. Prufrock Press.
Sternberg, R. J. (1985). *Beyond IQ: A triarchic theory of human intelligence*. Cambridge University Press.
Sternberg, R. J. (2002). Raising the achievement of all students: Teaching for successful intelligence. *Educational Psychology Review*, 14, 383–393.

19

LEARNING FROM LIFE

How I Became a Wisdom Researcher

Judith Glück

The Early Days: Unlimited Ambition

I became a wisdom researcher by chance. At least, I never planned to become a wisdom researcher. Like many people, I originally studied psychology because I wanted to be a psychotherapist. However, in my first semesters at University of Vienna, I was fascinated by statistics. Gerhard H. Fischer, then chair of the methods department at University of Vienna, is a renowned expert on item-response modeling. I had always liked math, and I enjoyed the courses taught by Fischer and his colleagues. During my studies, I gravitated more and more toward the general issue of how to measure psychological constructs in valid and reliable ways. I was lucky to work with Georg Gittler, a spatial-ability researcher from whom I have adopted an almost-compulsive attention to the smallest details of any study that we do—as any member of my research team will confirm. For my diploma thesis, I developed an item pool for assessing spatial cognition. Shortly after I got my diploma, a colleague in the developmental-psychology department quit his job, and Brigitte Rollett, the department chair, asked me if I wanted to be the department methodologist. So, my first job brought me into developmental psychology—something I had never expected to happen. My husband-to-be, a cognitive psychologist/neuroscientist, was also working at the university. At one point, both of us were interviewed for the student union's newsletter. Their long list of questions included our career plans and with which psychologist we would most like to have dinner. I said, essentially, that I wanted to be a very successful researcher and that I would like to have dinner with Robert J. Sternberg.

While I worked on my dissertation, which tested whether gender differences in spatial ability could be explained by strategy use (they couldn't), I was accepted into a summer school at the Max Planck Institute (MPI) for Human Development in Berlin on new methods for analyzing change. As is the way of Max Planck Institutes, the list of speakers was pretty much the crème de la crème. At the summer school, I had two of those random encounters that can shape people's lives. The first was a dinner with pre- and postdocs working at the MPI. One guy constantly bragged about how cool it was to be working for "Uncle Max", how they got to meet all those superstars, Uncle Max paid for all their travel expenses, even doctoral students had research assistants working for them, and so on. At the end of that dinner, I knew I wanted to be a Max Planck researcher, if only to prove that that guy wasn't the only big shot around. The second encounter was much nicer: Another summer-school participant named Eva Lankes (now a professor of education at Munich University) invited me to join her and Kai Schnabel (now Kai S. Cortina, professor at the University of Michigan) on a sailing trip on the Havel. Enjoying the sun in Kai's boat, we chatted about people at the MPI. Kai mentioned that Paul Baltes, the director of the Lifespan Development Group, probably didn't even talk to people who had not published in *Psychological Review*. I guess he didn't really mean this as a compliment, but in my youthful overambition, what I took away was that I wanted to be someone that Paul Baltes talked to. I didn't know anything about lifespan development, but how hard could that be?

I often gave methods talks at developmental-psychology conferences—the topic of item response models for measuring change generally sounded impressive enough to get me on the program. So, I often met people working in Paul Baltes' group, especially Ulman Lindenberger (now Baltes' successor at the MPI), who was and is a bit of a methods geek as well. At one conference, Ursula Staudinger (now a professor at Columbia University) gave a talk about the wisdom conception that she, Baltes, and Jacqui Smith had developed. I remember that I found the issue of measuring such a complex and elusive construct quite interesting. But that interest was easily outstripped by the question how men and women solved cube-comparison tasks.

The sky crashed down on me (in a good way) at the 1998 conference of the German Psychological Society in Dresden. Nine years after the German wall came down, at first the conference seemed remarkable mostly for the ugliness of Dresden and the inedibility of the food in the university cafeteria, both of which have changed a lot since then. From our hotel room in a suburb, our view of the city was dominated by white steam emerging from an enormous smoke stack. We wondered whether it could be a nuclear power plant but didn't dare to ask the staff for fear of being rude. On the third day of the conference, I saw Paul Baltes walking toward me with a smile on his face. I turned around to see whom he meant, but he actually meant me. "Frau Glück", he said (I can still hear his voice), "do you have a minute?" I never really found out how he even knew my name. In hindsight, I guess that Ulman Lindenberger had asked him to offer me a job because he was interested in item-response modeling. At the time, it felt like being struck by lightning: Baltes asked me if I was interested in a postdoc position at the MPI. I stammered that I certainly was, but that I was going to need a few more months to finish my doctorate. No problem, Baltes said. Just send me an application letter and we'll invite you for a job talk. Then we can discuss all the details.

I didn't sleep much the next night. Obviously, this was an offer that I couldn't turn down. Technically, it was possible to take a two- or three-year leave from my position in Vienna. On the other hand, I had never lived anywhere else than in Vienna and I was quite scared. But, of course, thinking of the Uncle Max guy and Kai Schnabel's sailboat, I had to say yes. In April 1999, I moved to Berlin.

The Berlin Years: Finding My Field (Or Being Thrown into It)

I did not exactly thrive at the MPI. This was probably due to a core characteristic of the Max Planck system, the so-called Harnack Principle. Wikipedia says that the Harnack principle "is one of several closely related theorems about the convergence of sequences of harmonic functions", but the Harnack Principle of the Max Planck Society

> represents a traditional policy of appointing the brightest minds as Scientific Members [...], and building whole departments around these exceptional individuals when they become departmental directors. [...] The Scientific Member alone decides on his or her research objectives and methods. [...] Once appointed, the heads of department or Max Planck Research Groups do not follow a curriculum or research programme determined by the organization or by market requirements. Instead, they rely on their own intuition, which allows them as researchers to transform and advance the cause of science. (www.mpg.de/39596/MPG_Introduction.pdf)

This is certainly cool when you are a "Scientific Member", that is, director of a Max Planck Institute (note, however, that Max Planck directors are regularly evaluated against extremely high standards). It can be a bit less cool for the members of the departments built around scientific members. I certainly would not say that Paul Baltes was not a good director. But working at the MPI made me realize what had most attracted me to academia: the freedom to choose my own "research objectives and methods", which I had been granted right from the start. Now, at the MPI, Baltes assigned me to the wisdom project. I never really found out why. Ursula Staudinger was leaving for a professorship, so someone needed to take over. But in addition, he may have seen something in me that I definitely did not see at the time. The ways of Paul Baltes were often mysterious—people who worked with him still sometimes spend hours talking about things he did and said. Someone once told me he thinks Baltes intentionally assigned people to topics completely new to them, so that they would not get too confident. A friendlier interpretation would be that he wanted to open up new perspectives for them. In my case, I never would have thought that he was essentially setting the foundation for my whole career.

Before I moved to Berlin, I read what the group had published on wisdom. They had been the first researchers who developed both a theory of wisdom and a method to measure it. Their original idea, typical for the 1980s, was to define wisdom as a form of expertise—expert knowledge not about chess or music, but rather about the fundamental issues of the human existence (see, e.g., Baltes & Smith, 1990). Defining wisdom as expertise had several implications, some of which have been heavily criticized (e.g., Ardelt, 2004). One implication is that wisdom is essentially a quality of the mind—a cognitive competence. The Berlin group soon clarified that what they focused on was *wisdom-related knowledge*, not wisdom—a disclaimer that still often goes unmentioned when they are cited by others. Another implication is that wisdom-related knowledge is acquired by deliberate practice. Chess players on the way to becoming a grandmaster play many hours a day, deliberately focusing on their weaknesses, working with coaches and mentors to optimize performance. This idea has never really rung true to me with respect to wisdom. Does a person on the way to wisdom work hard, strive for excellence, and practice advice-giving with a focus on eliminating weaknesses? I do believe that the road to wisdom is unpaved and steep and requires in-depth self-examination (Weststrate & Glück, 2017), but the idea of a person working very hard on becoming ever wiser does not fit my inner picture of a truly wise person.[1] The wisest people I met in 20 years of wisdom research were certainly experts on the human existence, but they had not acquired their expertise through goal-driven daily practice. They were just deeply curious, fascinated by the "big questions" of human life to an extent that, even when something terrible happened to them, somewhere in the back of their minds they would be observing the experience with a kind of scientific interest. They became wise without consciously striving for wisdom. (I should probably note that Buddhists would disagree with me here.)

In our first meeting, Baltes told me that he wanted me to investigate his idea of wisdom as a meta-heuristic—a kind of knowledge system that makes people choose the right way of dealing with difficult situations (Baltes & Staudinger, 2000). He was a bit vague, but I understood that I should study how wisdom was related to problem-solving strategies. I designed a study to do that, but it didn't quite hit the point of what Baltes wanted. (That happened a lot, to almost everyone.) Over time, it became clear that as a first test of the meta-heuristic idea, I should study whether people could intentionally become wiser. The 1990s were the heyday of priming research, showing (sometimes in ways that could not be replicated) that people scored higher in knowledge tests after thinking about university professors (Dijksterhuis & Van Knippenberg, 1998), or that people walked more slowly after being primed with faces of old people (Bargh, Chen, & Burrows, 1996), and so on. My study built on that research: Would people give wiser responses to difficult life problems if they first spent some time thinking about wisdom? Baltes thought they would, assuming that the concept of wisdom activates certain attitudes, thinking strategies, and bodies of knowledge.

To measure wisdom, we used the Berlin wisdom paradigm (BWP). Typical for research on expertise, the BWP is a think-aloud method: participants are presented with brief descriptions of a difficult life problem and asked what one could consider and do in such a situation. Notably, the question is not "what should be done?" or "what would you do?" in order to invite participants to think about different possible perspectives. A participant whose response indicates rich knowledge about life as well as an awareness of the relativity of values, the context-dependence of human behavior, and the uncertainty of life will receive a high wisdom score (see, e.g., Baltes & Staudinger, 2000).

As per the Harnack principle, Max Planck Institutes have almost unlimited resources, so my experiment was *big*. After a baseline wisdom problem, participants in the three "wisdom conditions" were first asked to think about wisdom (in three different ways) and then to try to give a wise response to two more wisdom problems. Combined with two intelligence and two control conditions, there were seven groups, each including about 45 participants. In addition, we measured predictor variables, including life experience, intelligence, and personality. Four research assistants interviewed the participants, and ten highly educated raters evaluated all 3 x 318 transcripts—Uncle Max at his best. Finally, the study was completed and the research assistant sent me the data. I remember sitting in front of my computer, carefully clicking myself through the commands for an analysis of variance and hitting "OK".

Well ... the p value was something like .85. There was no difference whatsoever between the seven groups. Nothing came even close to a significant difference. One year of data collection, 318 participants x 2 interview sessions, and the effect of the wisdom conditions was zero.

It has been a rather important insight for me that null effects often tell far more interesting stories than expected effects. Especially with complex constructs like wisdom, it is relatively easy to set oneself up for the findings one wants by choosing the most suitable measures and experimental manipulations. Therefore, data that clearly say "no" to your hypothesis teach you so much more than data that say "yes" or "maybe" or "probably, with a few more older participants". However, on that sunny day in Berlin, the question was how that insight would go down with Paul Baltes. Finally, I had an idea: could the wisdom instructions at least have had an effect on *some* participants? Perhaps participants who were somewhat closer to wisdom—higher in, say, life experience, intelligence, or openness to experience—would profit from an instruction to give a wise response, whereas participants low in those resources might actually be so distracted or confused by the instruction that their wisdom actually declined? That idea pretty much saved my life, or at least my sanity: the data's response to it was quite a clear "yes" (Glück & Baltes, 2006).

The idea that certain resources shape how wisely we can respond to challenges became an important part of my thinking about wisdom. In a way, this is Baltes' meta-heuristic at work: There are certain qualities, such as openness, intelligence, or compassion, that are not per se part of wisdom—people can have them without being wise. A wise person, however, will utilize these qualities optimally both in dealing with difficult situations and in reflecting from experiences in order to learn from them. In the MORE Life Experience model (Glück & Bluck, 2013), we proposed that wisdom develops as people learn from life challenges and that certain psychological resources help them to do so. Susan Bluck, who developed this model with me, is my longest-term collaborator. We first met at the MPI, where Susan was a postdoc as well. I was fascinated by her research, which covers the whole range from individual autobiographical memories to how people make sense of their lives and everything in between. While I loved to read diaries and memoirs, I had never known that life stories actually were a field of psychological research. I'll never forget our first long chat in the MPI cantina (although autobiographical-memory research tells me I probably have most of the details wrong by now: I believe it was afternoon and the cantina was empty, but we may well have been having lunch in the MPI's crowded but beautiful garden). We both were not quite satisfied with the Berlin wisdom paradigm. Training interviewers for my study, I got the impression that even smart students could talk very wisely about theoretical wisdom problems because they could imagine what psychologists want to hear. This does not mean, however, that they would deal half as wisely with the same problem in their own life. Susan and I felt that actual wisdom manifests itself in how people deal with real-life challenges outside the lab. We came up with a little study of this idea, and Baltes allowed us to add it to my project. At the end of the interview, participants were asked when they had done something wise in their life.

The paradigm became the basis of many future studies: participants first made a list of events where they thought they had been wise. Then they picked the one where they had been wisest. They narrated the event freely and answered some questions about it. We found that most people talked about really difficult situations—we don't need wisdom to decide between walking and taking the bus. We need it to make big decisions, deal with bad events, or learn to navigate long-term challenges (Bluck & Glück, 2004). Participants' self-perceived wisdom took different forms in different age groups (Glück, Bluck, Baron, & McAdams, 2005). The idea that wisdom manifests itself in how people think about their own experiences has been a building block for much of my subsequent research. In 2002, Susan moved to the University of Florida, but we collaborated intensively for ten years and then somewhat less intensively, because we are both just too busy, until now. Bluck and Glück are still a great team, as proficient at developing creative ideas as they are at giggling like teenagers.

When I look back on my three years in Berlin, I think I owe them most of my career and many of my best friendships. Paul Baltes was a master networker and strategist. Countless superstars gave talks at the MPI, and the doctoral students and postdocs had dinner with them afterwards. I actually got to have my dinner with Bob Sternberg! And from that first dinner grew, much later, the *Cambridge Handbook of Wisdom* that he and I co-edited last year and other book projects. I learned a lot from my colleagues in the department—Ursula Staudinger, Ute Kunzmann, Jutta Heckhausen, and others. Being part of the Baltes family could be weird—the master strategist was also a master manipulator. But I learned more than at any other time in my career. I learned things that I try to reenact with my own research groups and things that I never ever want to reenact. In many ways, Paul Baltes has become an important inner voice for me—all these years later, and more than 13 years after he passed away, I can still imagine what he would say about some issues, and although I do not always agree, I am deeply grateful to him.

Back Home: Learning About Uncontrollability

In the summer of 2001, my husband and I got married—he had been working in Gerd Gigerenzer's group since 2000. We had a big party in the garden of the MPI. In early 2002, we moved back to Vienna, and in April, our son Jonas was born. He is now a wonderful young man of almost 18 years, and he has taught me some of my most important insights about life—and about wisdom. Having kids was a full-immersion course in uncontrollability. That course began before Jonas was even born. For some reason, I was certain my baby was going to be a girl. When a Turkish woman in my gym in Berlin told me (based on belly shape plus the way I held out my hand) that it would be a boy, I didn't listen. I often talked to Leonie, the little girl inside my womb—until I had my first high-resolution ultrasound examination. This was definitely not a girl ... so much for little Leonie. I had gotten a first glimpse of how children refuse to be shaped by their parents' fantasies.

Things continued along these lines after Jonas was born. The limits of control became part of my thinking about wisdom. Most people overestimate their control over what happens in their lives. Some people underestimate their control and view themselves as helpless victims. Wise people know a lot about uncontrollability—many have been through very bad times. But they are not helpless; they know they can deal with whatever happens. One of our study participants had a child born with severe brain damage. She said about that experience,

> I've grown up, really grown up in a positive sense, I've lost many fears. I've really begun to have trust in life. That's strange, because I often see the exact opposite happening—that people lose trust when they are confronted with a handicapped life. But I simply know that nothing can happen to us— everything has already happened! And I continue to learn. (Glück, in press)

Klagenfurt: Learning from Life and from Great People

When Jonas was four, I got a developmental-psychology professorship in Klagenfurt, where my husband was professor of cognitive psychology. Around the same time, I got pregnant again. Thus, in early 2007, we moved to Klagenfurt with baby Lena (this time, I learned that even uncontrollability is uncontrollable: I had hoped for a girl, therefore expected a boy, but a girl it was). After my first year there, I got my first large grant from the Austrian Research Fund to study the developmental model of wisdom that Susan and I had been discussing for a long time. I also got a grant from the Defining Wisdom Project initiated by John Cacioppo and Howard Nusbaum at the University of Chicago—a great opportunity to discuss wisdom with researchers from various fields. Together with some fantastic doctoral and master's students—Lara Dorner, Susanne König, Katja Naschenweng, and Uwe Redzanowski—I started our first large wisdom study. It tested the basic assumption that the resources of the MORE Life Experience Model (mastery, openness, reflectivity, and empathy/emotional regulation) would be cross-sectionally correlated to wisdom. As part of the sample, we looked for wisdom nominees—an interesting endeavor that got us in touch with some fascinating people, but also taught us that not everyone whom one person considers as wise is necessarily wise (see also Redzanowski & Glück, 2013). Building on Susan's and my paradigm, participants were interviewed about two challenges in their life—an unspecified difficult life event and a serious conflict. They narrated each event freely and then answered questions about it. We also administered all available measures of wisdom and measures of the MORE resources. As expected, the resources were related to wisdom across assessment methods (Glück, Bluck, & Weststrate, 2018).

The greatest thing, however, was that the data also taught us things we had not expected. Early on, Susanne König noticed that wisdom nominees seemed to be talking about gratitude a lot. Following up on this idea, she found systematic relationships between wisdom and gratitude (König & Glück, 2014). Katja Naschenweng did an ethnographic study of the "rare species of the truly wise", observing five of our wisest participants as they lived their everyday lives. She found that they all lived the life that was right for them. None of them cared about wealth, fame, or power. They cared about interesting conversations, art, science, and philosophy, and the beauty of nature. Together, Susanne's and Katja's studies taught me that wisdom does not arise within a person alone. Wise people are wise because they truly listen to others—not just to give good advice, but to learn, to understand different perspectives and broaden their own.

I also learned from those findings that wisdom research needs qualitative as well as quantitative methods. Susanne's strongest finding was not the significant correlation between wisdom and gratitude—it was the fact that wisdom nominees *spontaneously* talked about gratitude far more often, and in different ways, than control participants. Katja's study, with only five participants, drew large crowds at conferences because even quantitative psychologists are interested in how people actually live. Qualitative methods can teach us many things that statistics can't, and vice versa.

Another unexpected finding was how much participants' wisdom varied across narratives. We interviewed them about both a conflict and a difficult event only because we were not sure which would work better. However, when they were coded for wisdom dimensions, correlations between the two narratives were not much larger than .30. In other words, participants who talked quite wisely about one event could be unwise about another. This fits well with a new way of thinking propagated by Igor Grossmann, a young and energetic social psychologist whose work has considerably enriched and broadened wisdom research over the last decade. Igor has demonstrated in various ways that people's wisdom varies across situations (overview in Grossmann, 2017). Grossmann and colleagues found that an "ego-decentered" perspective makes people reason more wisely. Therefore, it would seem important to create structures that induce ego-decentered reasoning in, say, politicians, judges, or teachers. We are currently investigating conditions that foster or hinder wisdom in professional contexts: how is teachers' or managers' professional wisdom influenced by the structures they are working in? Teachers' main job is to teach kids math or Latin—how should they deal with a struggling adolescent? Should a manager focus on maximizing profit even at the cost of some people's jobs?

Another topic that still intrigues me is how we can better measure wisdom. In my early days in Klagenfurt, I gave a presentation about our research. Afterwards, my colleague Axel Krefting, a clinical psychologist and psychoanalyst, asked me whether wisdom-related knowledge is necessarily verbal or even verbalizable. He was thinking about psychotherapy sessions where there had been some kind of breakthrough—where he said something that actually changed his patient's perspective. Reflecting back on such moments, he never really knew why he had said that particular thing—he certainly had not mentally selected it from a list of possibilities. He felt that it was mostly nonverbal, based on intuitions that had been honed in 30 years of therapeutic practice. Wisdom-related knowledge is not necessarily explicit and verbal. It can be implicit and intuitive, which renders purely verbal measures questionable.

There is another way in which wisdom goes beyond verbal knowledge. When we ask participants what they have learned from an experience, many responses sound trivial—"you can't always get what you want", "life is short", and so on. But there is an enormous difference between theoretically knowing these things, and a hundred other truisms, and *really* knowing them—having experienced them in one's own life. We all know that we are going to die—why does a serious accident or illness often change someone's life completely? Because they realize that they *really* are going to die—in fact, they could be dead already. This kind of experience-based knowledge can change us; theoretical knowledge cannot. Ardelt (2004) argued that methods like the Berlin wisdom paradigm assess what people know theoretically and not what knowledge they have internalized.

This is why intelligent but unwise people can sound so wise in the Berlin wisdom paradigm. I have come to believe that to measure wisdom well, we need to look at people's own experiences and how they make sense of them. I am still struggling, however, with how to practically distinguish between theoretical and internalized insights. More broadly, the question of how we can devise measures of wisdom that are as close as possible to real life, without actually putting people in difficult situations, keeps intriguing me.

An important co-struggler with such questions has been Nic Weststrate. When he first visited us for a semester, he was still a doctoral student with Michel Ferrari in Toronto. Later, he did a postdoc here, which was unfortunately cut short when he got—way too early, at least for me!—an assistant-professor position at the University of Illinois at Chicago. Nic is an incredibly smart and creative researcher interested in narrative psychology, wisdom, and storytelling—how people make sense of experiences. Among many other things, he reanalyzed our interview data, showing that growth-oriented reflection about life challenges is related to wisdom, while closure-oriented reflection is related to well-being (Weststrate & Glück, 2017). How wise people manage to be happy and at peace with life while being fully aware of the "dark side" of our existence is a question that still fascinates me. I think we are really privileged to be able to investigate such questions! A few years ago, I taught a course on wisdom together with Ursula Renz, a philosophy professor. In one class, she taught us how to read and understand Aristotle. Afterwards, I told her this had been fascinating. She said, "Can you believe that we actually get paid for this?"

One internalized insight of my own—truism warning!—is that time is a one-way street. Seeing one's kids grow is one way to learn this—another is seeing one's parents age. My father is 90 and struggling with an unfortunate mix of depression and early dementia. He was always a strong personality and a role model for me in many ways. Seeing him so much changed and knowing that at some not-so-distant time he will be gone, shows me how much real meaning there is to such trivialities as "Carpe diem". The strong ambition that drove my early career waned a lot after I had kids, and now that I am entering the second half of my life (as my mother optimistically told me on my 50th birthday), other things, such as strong relationships to family and friends and enjoying nature, become more important. I still couldn't live without my work, however. I am in the lucky position to work with a team of great, creative, fun people, and I've learned to manage my schedules better and actually be much more productive in less time. Maybe I'm finally becoming a bit wiser.

Acknowledgments

I would like to end this chapter by acknowledging the many people from whom I've learned. My family taught me the most important lessons—my kids and nephew taught me about uncontrollability and unconditional love, and my husband taught me that long-term love is possible. Most of my more academic insights about wisdom emerged from conversations with colleagues and co-workers. In alphabetical order (I hope I'm not forgetting anyone!): Monika Ardelt, Irina Auer-Spath, Paul B. Baltes, Susan Bluck, Eva Beichler, Sarah Campill, Lara Dorner, Michel Ferrari, Igor Grossmann, Imke Harbig, Dominik Holzer, Ingrid Koller, Susanne König, Ute Kunzmann, Michael R. Levenson, Katja Naschenweng, Howard C. Nusbaum, Michaela Pötscher-Gareiss, Stefanie Rappersberger, Uwe Redzanowski, Ursula Renz, Andreas Scherpf, Barbara Sobe, Nicola Spannring, Ursula M. Staudinger, Robert J. Sternberg, Irene Straßer, Valerie Tiberius, and Nic M. Weststrate. I hope I'll never stop learning from others.

Note

1 It does, however, fit my inner picture of Paul Baltes, who was an extremely smart and self-controlled strategist constantly monitoring himself and others. I could probably fill pages with anecdotes about how different authors' conceptions of wisdom are related to their personalities …

References

Ardelt, M. (2004). Wisdom as expert knowledge system: A critical review of a contemporary operationalization of an ancient concept. *Human Development*, 47(5), 257–285.

Baltes, P. B., & Smith, J. (1990). Toward a psychology of wisdom and its ontogenesis. In R. J. Sternberg (Ed.), *Wisdom: Its nature, origins, and development* (pp. 87–120). Cambridge University Press.

Baltes, P. B., & Staudinger, U. M. (2000). Wisdom: A metaheuristic (pragmatic) to orchestrate mind and virtue toward excellence. *American Psychologist*, 55(1), 122–136.

Bargh, J. A., Chen, M., & Burrows, L. (1996). Automaticity of social behavior: Direct effects of trait construct and stereotype activation on action. *Journal of Personality and Social Psychology*, 71, 230–244.

Bluck, S., & Glück, J. (2004). Making things better and learning a lesson: Experiencing wisdom across the lifespan. *Journal of Personality*, 72, 543–572.

Dijksterhuis, A., & Van Knippenberg, A. (1998). The relation between perception and behavior, or how to win a game of trivial pursuit. *Journal of Personality and Social Psychology*, 74(4), 865–877.

Glück, J. (in press). How MORE Life Experience fosters wise coping. In M. Ferrari & M. Munroe (Eds.), *Post-traumatic growth to psychological well-being: Coping wisely with adversity*. Springer.

Glück, J., & Baltes, P. B. (2006). Using the concept of wisdom to enhance the expression of wisdom knowledge: Not the philosopher's dream, but differential effects of developmental preparedness. *Psychology and Aging*, 21, 679–690.

Glück, J., & Bluck, S. (2013). The MORE Life Experience Model: A theory of the development of personal wisdom. In M. Ferrari & N. M. Weststrate (Eds.), *The scientific study of personal wisdom* (pp. 75–98). Springer.

Glück, J., Bluck, S., & Weststrate, N. M. (2018). More on the MORE Life Experience Model: What we have learned (so far). *The Journal of Value Inquiry*, 53, 349–370.

Glück, J., Bluck, S., Baron, J. & McAdams, D. (2005). The wisdom of experience: Autobiographical narratives across adulthood. *International Journal of Behavioral Development*, 29, 197–208.

Grossmann, I. (2017). Wisdom in context. *Perspectives on Psychological Science*, 12, 233–257.

König, S., & Glück, J. (2014). "Gratitude is with me all the time:" How gratitude relates to wisdom. *The Journals of Gerontology, Series B: Psychological Sciences*, 69, 655–666.

Redzanowski, U., & Glück, J. (2013). Who knows who is wise? Self- and peer-ratings of wisdom. *The Journals of Gerontology, Series B: Psychological Sciences*, 68, 391–394.

Weststrate, N. M., & Glück, J. (2017). Hard-earned wisdom: Exploratory processing of difficult life experience is positively associated with wisdom. *Developmental Psychology*, 53, 800–814.

EPILOGUE

The Past, Present, and Future of (Research on) Human Potential

David Yun Dai

> The aim of science is to secure theories with a high problem-solving effectiveness.
>
> Larry Lauden (1981, p. 145)

That all history is contemporary may not be agreed upon by all historians. However, the history of the intellectual and scientific inquiry into any topic can be seen as contemporary in the sense that historical views and perspectives are intricately connected to contemporary endeavors. To be sure, some ideas are "dead" or getting "shelved"; but others are alive and well in the minds and ongoing work of living researchers and scholars. The historical and contemporary perspectives, highlighted in the title of the book, are deeply connected.

One may ask why we should care to find a deep historical current (or undercurrent) of understandings if in fact we are still wrestling with issues debated more than a hundred years ago regarding human accomplishments, and when we are still searching for tools and methods that will allow us to know better about developmental possibilities and limits of a particular individual, or evolutionary possibilities and limits of the human race. The answer is that we are working on human potential, a topic with much uncertainty. The magnitude of this topic is no less than that encountered by physicists who are fathoming the depth of the universe.

This volume of contributions is about the narrative of scientific inquiry into human potential. According to a purely technical view of science (i.e., technical rationality), narrative is too literary and altogether unnecessary if all problems, arguments, and discrepancies can be resolved analytically with technical rationality. From this view, one need only apply rigorous scientific procedures to find clear-cut answers and perfect predictions. Unfortunately, truth cannot be delivered merely through technical rationality in human science, and sometimes even in physics. You cannot accurately measure the velocity of an electron without compromising the measurement of its position, and vice versa, according to Heisenberg's *uncertainty principle*. Uncertainty will remain no matter how sophisticated our analytic apparatus becomes.

When Einstein argued that living knowledge in the mind of a scientist is more important than knowledge documented or codified in books or articles (see the quotation in the Introduction chapter), he meant something deeper than just an issue of formality: Scientific knowledge is fundamentally creative because knowing is a subjective act of meaning-making (Bruner, 1990; Polanyi, 1958), albeit constrained by evidence. Einstein even saw science as a form of rhetorical persuasion with the totality of evidence; therefore, rhetorical structure and device (e.g., the logic of argumentation I use in this epilogue) will always be present in scientific discourse (Holton, 1981; see also Abelson, 1995). It makes perfect sense to look into the lived experiences of the intellectual journeys of most established contemporary scientists and scholars. We need to know why they felt compelled to pursue specific lines of work and what they think of as viable arguments about the nature and cultivation of human potential. In short, Einstein's remarks were echoed by Schön's (1983) argument that truth lies in our reflective rationality (i.e., the truthfulness or validity of a claim is a matter of human judgment), more so than in technical rationality (i.e., the truthfulness or validity of a claim can be determined by infallible analytical tools and methods).

Context: Historical Connections and Positional Identity

When we look at the careers of the contributors to this volume, we cannot help but find the backdrop of their work: the significant people they came across in their early careers, the ideas they stumbled upon that later became important in their inquiry, the Zeitgeist of their times. Understanding this "cohort effect" becomes important. (Note that throughout this epilogue, any mention of names without citation refers to respectively authored chapters in this volume.)

Zeitgeist

We witnessed an unwavering belief prevalent in the early 20th century following the ideas of Galton (1869)—that human potential is *quantifiable* or measurable (e.g., Terman, 1925, or Thorndike, 1938, 1943). Consequently, the basic script is that human potential is some sort of capacity unleashed or transformed through various nurturing circumstances (e.g., Gagné, 2005). This script starts to change when human potential is seen as shaped and revealed by significant person-environment interaction (Bronfenbrenner, 1989; Bronfenbrenner & Ceci, 1994) and demonstrated in adaptive acts in functional contexts, be it practical or intellectual (Sternberg, 1985, 2019; see also Dai, 2019), or as growing with the extended mastery of a specific task or domain (Ceci & Liker, 1986; Feldman, 2003; Subotnik et al., 2011; see also Ericsson, 2006). The changes in Zeitgeist are palpable.

Intersubjectivity and Intellectual Lineage

We can see in the preceding autobiographic accounts how intellectual interests and ideas have taken shape through *intersubjectivity* of a social network; ideas were seeded, spread out, and grew. The contributors to this volume have had deep intellectual lineage with luminaries from older generations, such as Lewis Terman, Jean Piaget, Adriaan de Groot, Jerome Bruner, Urie Bronfenbrenner, J. P. Guilford, Paul Torrance, Lee Cronbach, Herbert Simon, Benjamin Bloom, Paul Baltes, Julian Stanley, Abe Tannenbaum, to name a few. In a sense, all intellectual inquiries into human potential documented by the authors in this volume were in one way or another triggered by social encounters in their early careers, resulting in potent ideas and visions through *crystallizing experiences* (Walters & Gardner, 1986), pursued to fruition in the past three or four decades.

Positional Identity

Greeno (2002) borrowed the term *positional identity* in describing how individuals position themselves in a social and intellectual activity. It is particularly interesting to see how the authors entered their respective fields of study and how they engaged in specific issues of human potential from their unique angles or vantage points. Serendipity or chance encounter seems prevalent (e.g., Ceci, Glück, Winner), but so is self-direction (e.g., the nature of topics that piqued a particular interest, thus betraying one's disposition and positional identity). Some inherited a positional identity (e.g., Glück), but others carried a strong one throughout their careers (e.g., Florida, Geary, Simonton). Some are psychometrically oriented (e.g., Ackerman), others, developmentally oriented (e.g., Feldman), and still others teachers turned scholars (e.g., Piirto, Reis, Renzulli, Worrell). Different entry points led to different developmental trajectories. For example, Reis (this volume) discovered the issue of *talent loss* in her encounters with students, unlike those who started purely out of intellectual curiosity (e.g., Simonton); Piirto, Reis, Worrell have a distinct focus on gender and ethnic minority issues as they relate to the realization of human potential. Different positional identities add cognitive (and social) diversity and richness to the mix of scientific discourse and enhance its dynamics.

Emergence of Novelty

Related to positional identities, novelty in the discourse arose from the individuality of the participants. Some could not find a fit and had to create their own niches, conceptually as well as methodologically (e.g., Feldman, Simonton, Sternberg), and others, by inventing new instruments and procedures, broadened the scope of inquiry (e.g., the Kanfer-Ackerman Air Traffic Control Task; Ackerman). Still others, driven by equity concerns over opportunities for gifted and talented girls and minority students, broadened conceptions of how human potential can be hindered as well as facilitated (Reis). Thus, new developments in the issue of human potential are highly related to context (e.g., social and intellectual connections, positional identity, and individuality).

Constraints

Related to the historical context, a major constraint is the prevalent conceptual and methodological apparatus available and used at the time. For example, the authors' inquiries span across a half century. What tools and resources were available determined in part how far they could go in scientific inquiry. It is probably unfair to be overly critical of early generations of scholars and researchers for being unable to conceptualize human potential through the lens of dynamic systems theory or for the failure to computationally simulate with any technical sophistication the emergence of novelty or complexity. In the science of human potential, as in other fields, constraints can be technical as well as conceptual.

Impetus: The Deep Logic that Drives the Research Agenda

While context and positional identity discussed above reveal the entry point of a particular line of work, the question of impetus has to do with the deep logic of understanding human potential with various foci and in various ways. Although human potential of any sort does not lend itself easily to objective determination (see Runco), we can identify recurrent themes (Holton, 1981) regarding human potential and its realization through human development. Examples of such themes are the nature-nurture issue, the malleability of human potential, the domain-specific issue, and various facets of human agency (self) underlying developmental potential. These themes constitute a web of concepts or a rhetorical structure guiding research. How researchers situated themselves in this rhetorical context reveals their *ontological commitments* (Lakatos, 1978).

The Nature-Nurture Debate and the Issue of Malleability

The psychometric conceptions of intelligence and creativity, which implicitly hold a static capacity view of human potential, still loom large in scientific discourse on human potential. The nature-nurture issue concerns the extent to which individual differences in psychometrically defined intelligence can be attributed to natural endowment or environmental experience. Some biologically oriented researchers naturally tend to trace the origins of human potential all the way back to the evolution of homo sapiens (e.g., Geary; Feldman). More socially oriented researchers would focus on experiential and social-contextual factors (e.g., Ceci & Williams, 1997). Defined more broadly, the nature–nurture issue concerns whether and to what extent human potential is fixed or malleable (Ericsson et al., 2007; Howe et al., 1998; Gagné , 2009). While a fixed-capacity view of human potential (e.g., Francis Galton's view of ability) is increasingly seen as untenable, the argument for human malleability does not negate individual differences in rates of learning, and even a significant Matthew effect, namely, cognitive and learning advantages getting amplified over time (see Ceci & Papierno, 2005; Simonton, 1999; see also Gobet, this volume). Therefore, both extreme nature and extreme nurture arguments are untenable (Ackerman, 2014, this volume). Significant progress beyond the nature–nurture debate is a new direction sampled from this volume toward a more dynamic construal of human potential:

- Ackerman's notion of investment, highlighting the role of motivation and long-term dedication;
- Renzulli's view of emergence of creative productivity through educational experiences;
- Subotnik and her colleagues' effort to chart a new path toward talent development.

The field has gone beyond the nature–nurture debate to deal with more subtle issues of how nature and nurture interact, for instance, how *nurture changes nature*, quantitatively as well as qualitatively, as in the case of structural and functional changes of the brain as the result of extended musical training (Schlaug, 2001), or the extent to which *nature constrains nurture* in a fundamental manner, as in the case of differential rates of learning and asymptotic performance given the same task environment (Howard, 2009; Shiffrin, 1996) and differential selective affinity (Dai & Renzulli, 2008). These seemingly contradictory arguments are in fact complementary rather than antithetical. It is not the issue of which is true, but that of when and where each claim holds.

Beyond the issue of whether nature or nurture carries more weight, the epigenetic and nature–nurture reciprocal interaction approaches (Dai & Coleman, 2005; Gottlieb, 1998, 2007; Horowitz, 2000) go far beyond the issue of malleability to seek a deeper understanding of how the biological and the social-cultural interact in a relational developmental system (Overton, 2014), resulting in various forms of personal excellence (Piirto, 1994).

The Domain-Specific and Boundary-Crossing Nature of Human Endeavor

Is the human brain fundamentally shaped through evolution to be an all-purpose powerhouse, or is it designed to deal with specific situations, conditions, and kinds of input (Geary and Gardner)? Tensions can be found between those who tends to emphasize the domain-specific nature of manifested human potential (see Gardner, Piirto, and Subotnik), and those who consider intellectual potential for learning and transfer across domains and activities as quite versatile (Geary, 2005, this volume; Robinson, this volume; Robinson, Zigler, & Gallagher, 2000). Ceci and Liker (1986) was a pivotal study not just putting the capacity view to question but also showing how one, regardless of IQ performance, can tune into a cultural domain and achieve expertise through devotion and extended experience (see also Ericsson, 2006; Ericsson et al., 1993).

The distinction between potential and achievement highlighted by Runco (this volume) when defining creativity is instructive. *Potential* by nature is fluid, thus not entirely confined to particular set of constraints, rules, and boundaries; in contrast, achievement or developmental outcomes are always more subject to differential control parameters for different domains of activity. Several contributors (e.g., Ackerman, Feldman, Winner, Sternberg) seem to entertain a more eclectic view in this regard. Sources of domain specificity can come from biologically based constraints, for instance, numerical, verbal, and spatial cognitive apparatuses (Lubinski & Benbow, 2006), as well as the cognitive and social complexity of a cultural domain in question (Simonton, 1999; this volume). Nevertheless, humans are by nature creative in the sense of inventing new conceptual and technical tools and artifacts that enhance their adaptations to specific task conditions (Gould, 1991). In short, the boundary of a human endeavor can be created, narrowed or broadened, and broken. In this regard, what Murray (2003) called *meta-invention* (p. 209) becomes relevant: Human beings are capable of not only creating rules and boundaries, but also of changing them. Thus, it makes sense to think that creative potential is by nature fluid and boundary-crossing (Runco).

The Multifaceted Nature of Human Agency: Which Part of the Elephant?

Deeply embedded in the notion of human potential is human agency for effecting changes in oneself as well as in the environment. Piaget (1950) was one of the earliest psychologists to point out the multifaceted nature of human agency by specifying a cascade of developmental changes in human adaptive capability, some embodied, and others, symbolic, and still others formal and hypothetical-deductive. Human agency can also be viewed from different *epistemic stances*: whether the nature of human agency is sheer physical capacity, or some kind of biologically or socially designed adaptive functions, or by nature reflecting the working of human desires and intentions to effect certain changes (Dennett, 1987; see also Dai, 2010). One of the reasons for the controversies regarding the malleability and domain-specificity of human potential is the selective focus or the chosen epistemic stance. The history of conceptions of human potential is imbued with concepts with different levels of organized complexity, for example, neural efficiency (Jensen, 2001), reasoning ability (Kyllonen & Christal, 1990), emotional intelligence (Mayer & Salovey, 1997), delay of gratification (Mischel et al., 1989), mindset (Dweck, 2006), grit (Duckworth, 2016), deliberate practice (Ericsson, 2006), synergy of cognitive diversity (Page, 2008), or a community of committed learners or professionals (Scardamalia & Bereiter, 2006; Florida, this volume). Many explorations represented in this volume encompass multiple levels of human agency:

- Situated cognition in the wild, be it race track gambling or street peddling (Ceci);
- The Piirto Pyramid of talent development, with purpose on top (Piirto, 1994);
- Developmental orchestration of abilities, psychosocial skills, mentorship, and social support (Subotnik) for reaching eminent performance or productivity.

Horowitz (2000) pointed out the tendency in developmental psychology of creating "single-variable stories" (p. 3), which, due to their simplicity, are appealing to social media and lay audience, but often falling short of taking into account the working of the entire developmental system. To be sure, some concepts, such as neural efficiency, may provide a reductionistic explanation for a phenomenon (e.g., the rate of learning; Haier & Jung, 2008). However, what is worth noting is the issue of timescale of a phenomenon: to the extent to which a human endeavor involves a significant amount of individual learning and development over time, the human agency involved must be complex and multifaceted, not reducible to one simple component. Single-variable stories, be they Spearman's g, or growth vs. fixed mindset (Dweck, 2006), are also easily reified as material or structurally permanent, whereas human agency is fundamentally adaptive and *enactive*. For example, Ackerman (this volume) distinguishes between typical engagement and maximal performance (see also the distinction I make between characteristic and maximal adaptation; Dai, 2017, or between effective and optimal functioning; Fischer & Pipp, 1984). The distinction suggests significant intraindividual variability in terms of exercising human agency, which is likely sensitive to specific social and developmental contexts. Such a trend toward a more fine-tuned understanding of human potential, epitomized in Ackerman, among others, reflects a more general tendency to move away from single-variable stories (e.g., Spearman's g), to embracing more complex levels of developmental processes and changes.

Evolution: Continuities and Discontinuities

When we consider the evolution of our understandings of human potential in a large timescale of multi-generational efforts since Galton (1869), we will realize that the evolution of ideas must be gradual and incremental, only sometimes appearing more radical (e.g., Ericsson et al., 2007) in light of Sternberg's (1999) propulsion model of creativity.

Integration of the "Being" and "Doing" Accounts of Human Potential

There is a clear indication of a trend toward the theoretical integration of individual differences into otherwise developmental process models (Horowitz, 2000, 2009; Ackerman, Feldman, Gobet, Shavinina, Subotnik, and Winner). Research on expertise is moving in the same direction (Gobet, this volume; Ullén et al., 2016). This trend holds promise for the change of mindset in the field (see Dai, 2019).

The methodological indication of the integration of the "being" and "doing" accounts of human potential is the integration of psychometric and cognitive traditions in research (Ackerman, 1988). A telling example is Gobet's recent research. After collaboration with De Groot and Herbert Simon and following a more cognitive tradition, Gobet felt compelled to integrate the psychometric approach into a cognitive approach, just as Ackerman (1988) felt compelled to integrate the cognitive tradition into a predominantly psychometric approach. These efforts to integrate person and process accounts help resolve discrepant findings between differential and cognitive research, a conundrum Cronbach (1957) identified decades ago. The integration is also a way to go beyond "single-variable stories" (Horowitz, 2000).

Resolving the Tension between the Nomothetic (Quantitative) and the Idiographic (Qualitative) Approaches

One can always start investigation with a nomothetic assumption of human development as following universal laws and regularities (e.g., most people will follow the same developmental path, sooner or later, or have more or less of the same thing, thus subject to the isolation of variables and quantification). Historically, quantitative approaches seek to identify critical dimensions of individual differences and determine their long-term predictive power regarding their life achievements and contributions. This tradition continues to date and has made some important strides (e.g., Lubinski & Benbow, 2006; Terman, 1925; see also Ackerman and Simonton). Neo-Piagtian researchers started to pay attention to domain-specific cognitive development in formative years (e.g., Porath, 2006). Expertise research also aims to determine, quantitatively, the amount of deliberate practice that will lead to high-level expertise (e.g., the ten-year rule; Simon & Chase, 1973). However, this normality may not hold when a range of phenomena especially pertinent to high potential (child prodigies, polymath, unique individuality, etc.) seems to be more of outliers and exceptions. Feldman (1994) was probably the first to point out this "Piaget's error" and proposed the continuum along which different developmental phenomena can be properly placed: from universal to unique (Feldman, this volume, Figure 7.1). Feldman's (2003, this volume) notion of *nonuniversal development* provides rationale for a more idiographic approach (see Molenaar, 2004, for a more technical argument for pursuing an idiographic research). Indeed, many contributors to this volume advocate qualitative methods because the targeted phenomena lean toward the unique end, be it child prodigies (Feldman), "rage to master" in art (Winner, 1996), gifted girls and women (Piirto and Reis), a unique representation of the world as foundation for giftedness (Shavinina, 1999).

However, developmental uniqueness is not the only reason to use qualitative methods. While objective measurements and quantified predictions are always held in high esteem in psychology, a legacy of Galton and Thorndike, Terman recalled that Stanley Hall, his advisor, "gave me his blessing and some advice on the danger of being misled by the quasi-exactness of quantitative methods (quoted in Winkler & Jolly, 2014, p. 67). The nomothetic-idiographic tension identified by Allport (1937) was evident even at the inception of psychology: when Spearman (1904) declared success with "objectively" defined and measured intelligence, Binet, the pioneer of intelligence tests, was preoccupied by "*idiographic complexity*" (Brody, 2000, p. 19). Indeed, in Terman's (1925) landmark longitudinal study of 1500 high-IQ children, a large amount of work to identify "success" factors was inductive and interpretive in nature (Terman & Oden, 1959). Ceci and Liker's (1986) study of professional gamblers was in large part a detailed task analysis of expert performance. The nature of human science almost dictates that a large chunk of inquiry is *interpretative* in nature; even neural and physiological evidence in psychology demands functional interpretations, which are not always clear-cut. Stanley Hall apparently was wary of *physics envy* (see Koch, 1992), a tendency to make psychology (or economics) look more mathematical, and to treat human interpretation as precariously subjective, something to be minimized for the sake of objectivity (which partly explains the rise and popularity of behaviorism). This is why Runco (this volume) feels that creativity research is going too far in seeking the status of "hard" (or harder) science, why Piirto (this volume) went out of her way to study the lives of those who create, or why Glück (this volume) argues for more qualitative research and careful interpretation of the human mind, wise or not so wise. Cognitive, affective, and social complexities of expertise, creativity, and wisdom call for a new human science that can distinguish itself from physical science and even the rest of natural science (see Bruner, 1990).

From a Patched Quilt to Seamless Fabric

Snow (1992) described theory development as initially looking like a patched quilt, lacking in coherence and elegance, gradually growing to be a piece of seamless fabric, with no apparent loose ends and glaring patched-up holes.

Understanding human potential for high accomplishments may also follow this path, with some concepts or pieces of evidence falling into place later, what might be called theory-data asynchrony: a special case of developmental *decalagé*. Science, to use the metaphor of *Neurath's boat* (Neurath, 1952), is constantly under construction, retaining some old parts while building new ones and functioning as a temporary, functional structure (e.g., floating and moving). To pursue the metaphor of Neurath's boat further, initially there are many well-made pieces of the boat yet to be put to functional use for the floating device; likewise, early theories of giftedness, talent, polymathy, or creativity tended to be component theories (see Ziegler & Phillipson, 2012 for a critique). Gradually, components so identified become functional within a system, and the nature of their dynamic interaction becomes clearer and well-articulated over time. In this sense, we might see the contributors to this volume as representing scholars from biological, psychological, and sociological disciplines who are working on several fronts to build their respective pieces of the Neurath's boat of how humans develop their talent and achieve significant feats. As indicated by the integration efforts discussed earlier, the patched work will look more seamless over time.

Essentialism vs. Developmental Contextualism: A Watershed?

Discontinuities may also prevail in that we might never have a unified theory of human potential, given the heterogeneity of phenomena under investigation as well as researchers' different worldviews (Pepper, 1942) and ontological commitments (Lakatos, 1978). Regarding human potential, the nature vs. nurture biases will likely persist. Those who have a bias toward nature are more likely to seek essentialist explanations, and those who have a bias toward nurture lean toward explanations that are developmental and contextual. Metaphorically, essentialists tend to see human potential working like a volcano: there are *basic elements or driving forces* from within that ultimately explains relevant accomplishments; environmental conditions are just a facilitator. The volcano metaphor seems to better fit with some phenomena, such as child prodigies as having a unique vision or representation of the world early on (Shavinina, 1999; but see Feldman, 1986, for a co-incidence theory of child prodigy), or creativity as consisting of a relatively few basic elements, all manifestations being derivatives (Runco, 2010). Essentialists have a deep ontological commitment to the person in question. When everything is said and done, nature (the person) prevails over nurture (the environment) (Gagné, 2005; Tannenbaum, 1983; Lubinski & Benbow, 2006). Methodologically as well as theoretically, essentialists seek *parsimony*. This helps explain why Runco keeps fighting the trend toward using creative productivity as the sole criterion for creative expression because it risks losing the essence of creativity (see Runco, 2010). The volcano metaphor is the right heuristic for building a theory of giftedness and talent (e.g., Gagné, 2005; Tannenbaum, 1983). From an essentialist point of view, those who seek developmental contextualist explanations are doomed to get lost in the sea of chaos, complexity, and randomness that characterize much of our real-life circumstances.

Developmental contextualists, in contrast, do not believe that some sort of exceptionality is necessary for great accomplishments; nor do they believe that there is an essential force driving the entire developmental process of achieving great feats. Metaphorically, the contextually bound developmental process is like river formation, which enjoys many "degrees of freedom", with no pre-ordained destiny, as it were. To be sure, water seems to have a disposition to run in a certain direction (which, by the way, is also an illusion as it is mainly a gravity pull), but the shape and direction of a river is "developmentally" shaped over time, subject to the contextual influence of natural elements as well as "disturbance" of human intervention. If so, a reductionist strategy of collapsing the complexity of talent and creative accomplishments into a limited number of essential elements would miss critical turning points and critical events in one's development. Even physical science treats the formation of snow crystals (snowflakes), rivers, or hurricanes as the ever-complex self-organization of a dynamic system (Libbrecht, 2004). Likewise, the evolving nature of human individuality through social-cultural experiences warrants a detailed analysis in light of a relational developmental system (Overton, 2014); it is even more true when the development of talent, polymath, expertise, or creativity is concerned (Dai, 2019; Dai & Renzulli, 2008; Sawyer, 2002, 2003).

In this regard, Gardner's hindsight (this volume) is instructive. We can see his initial formulation of "frames of the mind" (Gardner, 1983) as *essentialist* in nature, especially regarding the modularity of the brain/mind. However, decades later, Gardner (this volume) sees more value in considering how cultural forces shape the human mind through development, an apparent move toward recognizing the viability of developmental contextualism. To be sure, there are theories of human potential that fall between the extreme forms of essentialism and developmental contextualism.

Hindsight

Have we made some progress and achieved some deep insights since Galton (1869), or Plato, conceptualized the nature of human potential for great accomplishments? Although the progress is obvious, the game seems still wide open. The reasons seem to have to do with the nature of the topic of human potential: Know thyself. It imposes epistemological challenges as well as normative ones.

Epistemological Side of Understanding Human Potential

When we tackle so many phenomena, child prodigies, precocity, talent, polymath, varied domains of expertise and creativity (art, science, technical invention, etc.), it is apparent that they may not conform to a single "grand theory" of human potential for great accomplishments. It seems problematic to use Einstein or Mozart as a "fruit fly" of human potential, and it is also problematic to think that everyone can become an Einstein or a Mozart. It is probably wise to embrace a more circumscribed, middle-range theory approach (Merton, 1996), recognizing that our arguments are at best conditional knowledge, tied to a specific set of observations and the phenomena we are dealing with, which have much heterogeneity, to begin with.

The more we learn about human development, the less likely it is that we will succumb to the kind of temptation for radical or "greedy" reductionism as Galton did. Or more broadly, we are less likely to appeal to single-variable stories (Horowitz, 2000) and more likely to embrace models that match the level of complexity we see in a phenomenon, be it child prodigies, highly refined artistry, or scientific creativity (not to mention that each of these phenomena has its own heterogeneity!). Epistemologically as well as strategically, we still have to decide how far *analytic science* can lead us, and at what point we would have to resort to *integrative or synthetic science*. For example, we might have to eventually use developmental science (Cairns et al., 1996) as a multi-disciplinary framework to understand human potential because the framework encompasses developmental biology and psychology as well as cultural artifacts such as information technology systems and social structures, which are deeply ingrained in education and human development. We still have to reckon with the paradoxical nature of human agency (means-ends capabilities) as capable of effecting changes in oneself, yet significantly constrained by its environments as well as its biology.

Regardless of what epistemic stances we take, we will do well to be intellectually honest and open to new evidence and alternative explanations. Combating dogmatism and absolutism (Ambrose, Sternberg, & Sriraman, 2012) and encouraging open conversation is especially needed when a theory of human potential can have the ethical and social consequence of either cultivating and facilitating or stifling and killing human potential.

The Normative Side of Understanding and Harnessing Human Potential

Rather than being value-neutral, human science (e.g., psychology, medicine, economics) involves a distinct concern over improving natural and human conditions. The argument that creativity can be put to destructive rather than constructive use (Cropley et al., 2010) is not just stating a possibility; it is part of the reality. It is quite telling that Gardner, Renzulli, and Sternberg, among others, have investigated the nature of human intelligence and creativity for most part of their careers, only to finally reach the same point of contemplating how to make good use of the human potential (e.g., Gardner, Csikszentmihalyi, & Damon, 2001; Renzulli, 2005; Sternberg, 2017). Sternberg's question of why smart people do stupid things and Glück's pursuit of wisdom and ego-decentered reasoning make it clear that understanding of human potential misused and abused is also an important topic for research.

Herbert Simon (1969) views human science as *the sciences of the artificial*, concerned with "what ought to be", though constrained by natural science, which is mainly concerned with "what is". An urgent issue relevant to the science of human potential now is how human talent will be cultivated and used in the age of artificial intelligence (AI).

- We have already witnessed a changing landscape of how human potential is developed and expressed, for better or for worse. Inevitably, many scientists and engineers will lose their jobs to AI. Artificial talent is already replacing human talent. In the meantime, many new niches will be created and new forms of talent will emerge. To guide talent development, we need to explore the talent demand and supply in the foreseeable future (Zhao, 2012), which is going to be quite different from what Tannenbaum (1983) envisioned 40 years ago.
- We have witnessed vast technological advances to a point when chip-enhanced talent is not a remote pipe dream but an imminent reality (e.g., Elon Musk's neuralink). What does it say about the prospects of talent development and competition, and for that matter, the issue of equity when only the rich can afford such an enhanced mind? What should education look like with the prospects of human-machine interface, and how can we cultivate and maximize human potential (e.g., creativity) in a way that can work optimally with the power of AI?
- Harari (2017) warned about a possible future when a few super-humans (intelligent minds coupled with cutting-edge technology) rule the world, and the majority of people, instead of finding and realizing their own niche potential, become puppets and fools. Indeed, technocratic celebrities are seeking hegemony and embrace the vision of *technological singularity* (Kurzweil, 2006). This happens in a time when the world powers are craving dominance by luring scientific and inventive talents for that purpose. Can a science of human potential provide pathways to wisdom and sanity to save homo sapiens from self-destruction (including weaponizing AI along with bio-agents, and the decoupling of intelligence and consciousness; Harari, 2017)? Can it help people go beyond a narrow vision of technocracy to embrace a world where we can still enjoy and draw meaning from the creations of civilization accumulated over the last four or five thousand years (Gardner)?

Conclusion

This volume presents lived experiences of a group of distinguished scholars who have been for decades on an intellectual journey that is of critical importance in understanding how human accomplishments come about, and how the human civilization is made possible through human development. The volume provides a glimpse of how much progress has been made; when we look at where we are now, it is a far cry from the times when Galton, Terman, and Thorndike were trying to conceptually and empirically handle the topic. However, we are still far away from making definitive claims on many issues, partly due to the equifinality and multifinality of human development, and partly because we are not coordinating our efforts as much as we should. This edited volume, with a wide representation of topics and foci, helps place each author's work in a larger fabric of collective efforts and indicates what can be done in the future. Last but not least is the autobiographic nature of the narratives—how Simonton as a young boy got fascinated with great people in history, and how Gobet's interest shifted from science to chess, and back to science again, or how Nancy Robinson picked up what Hal Robinson left and moved on to build a brand of her own contributions, and how Sally Reis transformed from a teacher to a researcher. The narratives make this volume a precious source for contemplating the nature of human potential in its own right. As a whole, they constitute a collective memory of an extended intellectual journey, a journey spanning over the last five decades, a journey (apologies to Abraham Lincoln) of which new insights are gained, for which these scholars are known, and by which the new comers are inspired. With salute and admiration, and with a poem, I conclude this epilogue:

Volcano and River: Of Human Potential

 Silent for decades and centuries
  Sneaking, simmering, snarling
 Hungry for space, air, and breathing room
  Boom, busted!
 Splendid, a wave of heat shooting to the sky
  Dazzling and shining
 Snakes of flame, lava, and ashes
  Encroaching, engulfing, entrenching
 A new landscape
  in the making

 Drops, gazillions of drops, made of water molecules
  Of apparent insignificance
 Merging, meshing, meandering
  A flow of melody made of random notes
 Whirling, falling, rushing to the sea
  Sound and fury, and heavenly lullaby
 The tireless cutting, eroding, and molding
  Seamless and unrelenting
 A secret path unfolding, and
  A new horizon emerging

Acknowledgments

Thanks are due to David Henry Feldman, Bob Sternberg, and Jessica Murray for their helpful comments on an early version of this article. This work was partly supported by a grant to the author from Army Research Institute for Behavioral and Social Sciences (Grant No. W911NF-17-1-0236). The author was encouraged to freely express his opinions. Ideas presented here, therefore, do not necessarily represent those of the funding agency.

References

Ambrose, D., Sternberg, R. J., & Sriraman, B. (Eds.) (2012). *Confronting dogmatism in gifted education*. Routledge.

Abelson, R. P. (1995). *Statistics as principled argument*. Lawrence Erlbaum.

Ackerman, P. L. (1988). Determinants of individual differences during skill acquisition: Cognitive abilities and information processing. *Journal of Experimental Psychology: General*, 117, 288–318.

Ackerman, P. L. (2014). Nonsense, common sense, and science of expert performance: Talent and individual differences. *Intelligence*, 45, 6–17.

Allport, G. W. (1937). *Patterns and growth in personality*. Holt, Rinehart & Winston.

Brody, N. (2000). History of theories and measurements of intelligence. In R. J. Sternberg (Ed.), *Handbook of intelligence* (pp. 16–33). Cambridge University Press.

Bronfenbrenner, U. (1989). Ecological systems theory. In R. Vasta (Ed.), *Annals of child development, Vol. 6: Six theories of child development*. Greenwich, CT: JAI Press.

Bronfenbrenner, U., & Ceci, S. J. (1994). Nature-nurture reconceptualized in developmental perspective: A bio-ecological model. *Psychological Review*, 101, 568–586.

Bruner, J. (1990). *Acts of meaning*. Harvard University Press.

Cairns, R. B., Elder, G. H., & Costello, E. J. (Eds.) (1996). *Developmental science*. University Press.

Ceci, S. J., & Liker, J. (1986). A day at the races: A study of IQ, expertise, and cognitive complexity. *Journal of Experimental Psychology: General*, 115, 255–266.

Ceci, S. J., & Papierno, P. B. (2005). The rhetoric and reality of gap closing: When the "have-nots" gain but the "haves" gain even more. *American Psychologist*, 60, 149–160.

Ceci, S. J., & Williams, W.M. (1997). Schooling, intelligence, and income. *American Psychologist*, 52, 1051–1058.

Cronbach, L. J. (1957). The two disciplines of scientific psychology. *American Psychologist*, 12, 671–684.

Cropley, D. H., Cropley, A. J., Kaufman, J. C., & Runco, M. A. (Eds.) (2010). *The dark side of creativity*. Cambridge University Press.

Dai, D. Y. (2010). *The nature and nurture of giftedness: A new framework for understanding gifted education*. Teachers College Press.

Dai, D. Y. (2017). Envisioning a new foundation for gifted education: Evolving Complexity Theory (ECT) of talent development. *Gifted Child Quarterly*, 61, 172–182.

Dai, D. Y. (2019). New directions in talent development research: A developmental systems perspective. *New Directions for Child and Adolescent Development*, 168, 177–197.

Dai, D. Y., & Coleman, L. J. (2005). Epilogue: Conclusions and implications for gifted education. *Journal for the Education of the Gifted*, 28, 374–388.

Dai, D. Y., & Renzulli, J. S. (2008). Snowflakes, living systems, and the mystery of giftedness. *Gifted Child Quarterly*, 52, 114–130.
Dennett, D. (1987). *The intentional stance.* Bradford Books/MIT Press.
Duckworth, A. (2016). *Grit: The power of passion and perseverance.* Scribner.
Dweck, C. S. (2006). *Mindset: The new psychology of success.* Random House.
Ericsson, K. A. (2006). The influence of experience and deliberate practice on the development of superior expert performance. In K. A. Ericsson, N. Charness, P. J. Feltovich & R. R. Hoffman (Eds.), *The Cambridge handbook of expertise and expert performance* (pp. 683–703). Cambridge University Press.
Ericsson, K. A., Krampe, R. T., & Tesch-Romer, C. (1993). The role of deliberate practice in the acquisition of expert performance. *Psychological Review*, 100, 363–406.
Ericsson, K. A., Nandagopal, K., & Roring, R. W. (2007). Misunderstandings, agreements, and disagreements: Toward a cumulative science of reproducibly superior aspects of giftedness. *High Ability Studies*, 18, 97–115.
Feldman, D. H. (1986). *Nature's gambit: Child prodigies and the development of human potential.* Basic Books.
Feldman, D. H. (1994). *Beyond universals in cognitive development*, 2nd ed. Ablex.
Feldman, D. H. (2003). A developmental, evolutionary perspective on giftedness. In J. H. Borland (Ed.), *Rethinking gifted education* (pp. 9–33). Teachers College, Columbia University.
Fischer, K. W., & Pipp, S. L. (1984). Process of cognitive development: Optimal level and skill acquisition. In R. J. Sternberg (Ed.), *Mechanisms of cognitive development* (pp. 45–75). Freeman.
Gagné, F. (2005). From gifts to talents: The DMGT as a developmental model. In R. J. Sternberg & J. E. Davidson (Eds.), *Conceptions of giftedness* (2nd ed., pp. 98–119). Cambridge University Press.
Gagné, F. (2009). Debating giftedness: Pronat vs. antinat. In L. Shavinina (Ed.), *International handbook on giftedness* (pp. 155–198). Springer Science.
Galton, F. (1869). *Hereditary genius: An inquiry into its laws and consequences.* Macmillan.
Gardner, H. (1983). *Frames of mind.* Basic Books.
Gardner, H., Csikszentmihalyi, M., & Damon, D. (2001). *Good work: When excellence and ethics meet.* Basic Books.
Geary, D. C. (2005). *The origin of mind: Evolution of brain, cognition, and general intelligence.* American Psychological Association.
Gottlieb, G. (1998). Normally occurring environmental and behavioral influences on gene activity: From central dogma to probabilistic epigenesis. *Psychological Review*, 105, 792–802.
Gottlieb, G. (2007). Probabilistic epigenesis. *Developmental Science*, 10, 1–11.
Gould, S. J. (1991). Exaptation: A crucial tool or an evolutionary psychology. *Journal of Social Issues*, 47(3), 43–65.
Greeno, J. G. (2002). Toward the development of intellectual character. In E. W. Gordon & A. B. L. Bridglall (Eds.), *Affirmative development: Cultivating academic ability* (pp. 17–47). Rowman & Littlefield.
Haier, R. J., & Jung, R. E. (2008). Brain imaging studies of intelligence and creativity: What is the picture for education? *Roeper Review*, 30, 171–180.
Harari, Y. N. (2017). *Homo deus: A brief history of tomorrow.* HarperCollins.
Holton, G. (1981). Thematic presuppositions and the direction of scientific advance. In A. F. Heath (Ed.), *Scientific explanation* (pp. 1–27). Clarendon Press.

Horowitz, F. D. (2000). Child development and the PITS: Simple questions, complex answers, and developmental theory. *Child Development*, 71, 1–10.

Horowitz, F. D. (2009). Introduction: A developmental understanding of giftedness and talent. In F. D. Horowitz, R. F. Subotnik, & D. J. Matthews (Eds.), *The development of giftedness and talent across the lifespan* (pp. 3–19). American Psychological Association.

Howard, R. W. (2009). Individual differences in expertise development over decades in a complex intellectual domain. *Memory and Cognition*, 37, 194–209.

Howe, M. J. A., Davidson, J. W., & Sloboda, J. A. (1998). Innate talents: Reality or myth? *Behavioral and Brain Sciences*, 21, 399–442.

Jensen, A. R. (2001). Spearman's hypothesis. In J. M. Collis & S. Messick (Eds.), *Intelligence and personality: Bridging the gap between theory and measurement* (pp. 3–24). Lawrence Erlbaum.

Koch, S. (1992). The nature and limits of psychological knowledge: Lessons of a century qua "science". In S. Koch & D. E. Leary (Eds.), *A century of psychology as science* (pp. 75–97). American Psychological Association.

Kurzweil, R. (2006). *Singularity is near: When humans transcend biology*. Penguin Books.

Kyllonen, P. C., & Christal, R. (1990). Reasoning ability is (little more than) working-memory capacity? *Intelligence*, 14, 389–433.

Lakatos, I. (1978). *The methodology of scientific research programs*. Cambridge University Press.

Lauden, L. (1981). A problem-solving approach to scientific progress. In I. Hacking (Ed.), *Scientific revolutions* (pp. 144–155). Oxford University Press.

Libbrecht, K. (2004/2005, Winter). Snowflake science. *American Educator*, 20–25, 48. (Originally in *The snowflakes: Winter's secret beauty*, 2003, Voyageur Press).

Lubinski, D., & Benbow, C. P. (2006). Study of mathematically precious youth after 35 years. *Perspectives on Psychological Science*, 1, 316–345.

Mayer, J. D., & Salovey, P. (1997). What is emotional intelligence? In P. Salovey & D. Sluyter (Eds.), *Emotional development and emotional intelligence: Educational implications* (pp. 3–31). New York: Basic Books.

Merton, R. K. (1996). *On social structure and science*. University of Chicago Press.

Mischel, W., Shoda, Y., & Rodriguez, M. I. (1989). Delay of gratification in children. *Science*, 244, 933–938.

Molenaar, P. C. M. (2004). A manifesto on psychology as idiographic science: Bringing the person back into scientific psychology, this time forever. *Measurement*, 2, 201–218.

Murray, C. (2003). *Human accomplishments: The pursuit of excellence in the arts and sciences, 800 B. C. to 1950*. HarperCollins.

Neurath, O. (1952). *Foundations of the social science*. University of Chicago Press.

Overton, W. F. (2014). Relational developmental systems and developmental science: A focus on methodology. In P. C. M. Molenaar, R. M. Lerner, & K. M. Newell (Eds.), *Handbook of developmental systems theory and methodology* (pp. 19–65). The Guilford Press.

Page, S. E. (2008). *The difference: How the power of diversity creates better groups, firms, schools, and societies*. Princeton University Press.

Pepper, S. C. (1942). *World hypotheses*. University of California Press.

Piaget, J. (1950/2001). *The psychology of intelligence*. Routledge.

Piirto, J. (1994). *Talented children and adults: Their development and education*. Macmillan.

Polanyi, M. (1958). *Personal knowledge: Towards a post-critical philosophy*. University of Chicago Press.

Porath, M. (2006). The conceptual underpinnings of giftedness: Developmental and educational implications. *High Ability Studies*, 17, 145–158.

Renzulli, R. S. (2005). The three-ring conception of giftedness: A developmental model for promoting creative productivity. In R. J. Sternberg & J. E. Davidson (Eds.), *Conceptions of giftedness* (2nd ed., pp. 98–119). Cambridge University Press.

Robinson, N. M., Zigler, E., & Gallagher, J. J. (2000). Two tails of the normal curve: Similarities and differences in the study of mental retardation and giftedness. *American Psychologist*, 55, 1413–1424.

Runco, M. (2010). Education based on a parsimonious theory of creativity. In R. A. Beghetto & J. C. Kaufman (Eds.), *Nurturing creativity in the classroom* (pp. 235–251). Cambridge University Press.

Sawyer, R. K. (2002). Emergence in psychology: Lessons from the history of non-reductionist science. *Human Development*, 45, 2–28.

Sawyer, R. K. (2003). Emergence in creativity and development. In R. K. Sawyer, V. John-Steiner, S. Moran, R. J. Sternberg, D. H. Feldman, J. Nakamura, & M. Csikszentmihayi (Eds.), *Creativity and development* (pp. 12–60). Oxford University Press.

Scardamalia, M., & Bereiter, C. (2006). Knowledge building: Theory, pedagogy, and technology. In R. K. Sawyer (Ed.), *The Cambridge handbook of the learning sciences* (pp. 97–115). Cambridge University Press.

Schlaug, G. (2001). The brain of musicians: A model for functional and structural adaptation. In R. J. Zatorre & I. Peretz (Eds.), *The biological foundations of music* (Annals of the New York Academy Sciences, Vol. 930, pp. 281–299). New York Academy of Sciences.

Schön, D. A. (1983). *Reflective practitioner*. Basic Books.

Shavinina, L. (1999). The psychological essence of the child prodigy phenomenon: Sensitive periods and cognitive experience. *Gifted Child Quarterly*, 43, 25–38.

Shiffrin, R. M. (1996). Laboratory experimentation on the genesis of expertise. In K. A. Ericsson (Ed.), *The road to excellence: The acquisition of expert performance in the arts and sciences, sports, and games* (pp. 337–345). Lawrence Erlbaum Associates.

Simon, H. A. (1969/1996). *The sciences of the artificial*. The MIT Press.

Simon, H. A., & Chase, W. G. (1973). Skill in chess. *American Scientist*, 61, 394–403.

Simonton, D. K. (1999). Talent and its development: An emergenic and epigenetic model. *Psychological Review*, 3, 435–457.

Snow, R. E. (1992). Aptitude theory: Yesterday, today, and tomorrow. *Educational Psychologist*, 27, 5–32.

Spearman, C. (1904). "General intelligence", objectively determined and measured. *American Journal of Psychology*, 15, 201–292.

Sternberg, R. J. (1985). *Beyond IQ: A triarchic theory of human intelligence*. Cambridge University Press.

Sternberg, R. J. (1999). A propulsion model of types of creative contributions. *Review of General Psychology*, 3, 83–100.

Sternberg, R. J. (2017). ACCEL: A new model for identifying the gifted. *Roeper Review*, 39, 152–169.

Sternberg, R. J. (2019). A theory of adaptive intelligence and its relation to general intelligence. *Journal of Intelligence*, 7(4), 23. Available online at https://doi.org/10.3390/jintelligence7040023

Subotnik, R. F., Olszewski-Kubilius, P., & Worrell, F. C. (2011). Rethinking giftedness and gifted education: A proposed direction forward based on psychological science. *Psychological Science in the Public Interest*, 12(1), 3–54.

Tannenbaum, A. J. (1983). *Gifted children: Psychological and educational perspectives*. Macmillan.

Terman, L. M. (1925). *Genetic studies of genius: Vol. 1, Mental and physical traits of a thousand gifted children*. Stanford University Press.
Terman, L. M., & Oden, M. H. (1959). *Genetic studies of genius: The gifted group at mid-life*. Stanford, CA: Stanford University Press.
Thorndike, E. (1938). Great abilities, their frequency, causation, discovery, and utilization. *Scientific Monthly*, 47(1),59–72.
Thorndike, E. (1943). The origins of superior men. *Scientific Monthly*, 56(5), 424–433.
Ullén, F., Hambrick, D. Z., & Mosing, M. A. (2016). Rethinking expertise: A multifactorial gene-environment interaction model of expert performance. *Psychological Bulletin*, 142, 427–446.
Walters, J., & Gardner, H. (1986). The crystallizing experience: Discovering an intellectual gift. In R. J. Sternberg & J. E. Davidson (Eds.), *Conceptions of giftedness* (pp. 306–331). Cambridge University Press.
Winkler, D. L., Jolly, J. L. (2014). Lewis M. Terman: A misunderstood legacy (1877–1956). In A. Robinson, & J. L. Jolly (Eds.), *A century of contributions to gifted education: Illustrative lives* (pp. 64–78). Routledge.
Winner, E. (1996). *Gifted children: Myths and realities*. Basic Books.
Zhao, Y. (2012). *World class learners: Educating creative and entrepreneurial students*. Corwin.
Ziegler, A., & Phillipson, S. N. (2012). Toward a systemic theory of gifted education. *High Ability Studies*, 23(1), 3–30.

LIST OF CONTRIBUTORS

Phillip L. Ackerman is Professor of Psychology at the Georgia Institute of Technology. He received a BA with Honors from the University of Virginia (1979), AM (1981) and PhD (1984) degrees from the University of Illinois, Urbana-Champaign. He has conducted basic and applied research in cognitive psychology, individual differences, psychological testing, and human abilities. He has written extensively on the nature of adolescent and adult learning, skill acquisition, selection, training, abilities, personality, and motivation. He has co-edited three books on individual differences and is the editor of a book on cognitive fatigue. Dr. Ackerman's main contributions involve integration across multiple fields of psychological inquiry, specifically related to individual differences. Noteworthy contributions include integration of information processing and ability approaches to individual differences in skill learning; integration of ability and motivational determinants of learning and performance; integration of ability, personality, and interest traits; and explication of an integrated approach to adolescent and adult intellectual development. He is a Fellow of six divisions of the American Psychological Association; Human Factors & Ergonomics Society, American Educational Research Association, Psychonomic Society, and he is a Charter Fellow of the Association for Psychological Science. In 1992, he was the recipient of the American Psychological Association's *Distinguished Scientific Award for Early Career Contribution to Psychology* for his work on the determinants of individual differences in skill acquisition. In 2014, he received the *Franklin V. Taylor Award for Outstanding Contributions in the Field of Applied Experimental/ Engineering Psychology*.

Stephen J. Ceci is the H. L. Carr Chaired Professor of Developmental Psychology at Cornell University. He is the author of approximately 500 articles, chapters and books. Ceci has been the recipient of lifetime achievement awards from the American Psychological Association, the Association for Psychological Science, and the Society for Research in Child Development as well as a number of other recognitions such as a senior Fulbright-Hayes invitation to think tanks around the world. He is listed among the most eminent psychologists of the modern era. Currently, Ceci is president of the Society for Experimental Psychology and Cognitive Science. In recent years he has been inducted into the American Academy of Arts and Sciences and the National Academy of Education. He received his baccalaureate degree from the University of Delaware, his Master's degree from the University of Pennsylvania, and his doctorate from the University of Exeter, UK.

David Yun Dai, PhD, is Professor of Educational Psychology and Methodology at University at Albany, State University of New York. Dr. Dai was born and raised in Shanghai, China. He earned his BA in Chinese Language and Literature (1983) and MA in comparative literature (1988) from East China Normal University (Shanghai), and worked as an instructor of literature in the College of Liberal Arts at Shanghai University (1988–1991) before he went to the United States in 1991. He received his doctoral degree in psychology from Purdue University (1998) with John Feldhusen as his advisor (1992–1998), and worked as a post-doctoral fellow at the National Research Center on the Gifted and Talented, under the tutelage of Joe Renzulli at the University of Connecticut (1998–1999). Dr. Dai has published ten authored and edited books, and over 100 journal articles, book chapters, and encyclopedia entries in educational psychology, gifted and talented education, and creativity. Dr. Dai was the recipient of the Early Scholar Award in 2006 and the Distinguished Scholar Award in 2017 conferred by the National Association for Gifted Children (NAGC) in the United States. He was a Fulbright Scholar twice, to China for educational research during 2008–2009, and to Germany for lecturing and research on the cultivation of talent and creativity during 2015–2016.

David Henry Feldman is Professor and former Chair of the Eliot-Pearson Department of Child Study and Human Development at Tufts University. Professor Feldman has also held faculty appointments at the University of Minnesota and Yale University as well as visiting appointments at Tel Aviv University, Harvard University, the University of California at San Diego and the University of California at Berkeley. He has been a Fulbright Scholar, Scholar of the Year of the National Association of Gifted Children, and President of the Society for the Study of Human Development. He is author or coauthor of six books and hundreds of articles, including *Changing the World* (with Mihalyi Csikszentmihalyi and Howard Gardner) and *Nature's Gambit: Child Prodigies and the Development of Human Potential* (with Lynn Goldsmith). His macro theory of cognitive development is presented in *Beyond Universals in Cognitive Development* and several other chapters and articles. Professor Feldman was educated at the University of Rochester, Harvard University and Stanford University where he received his PhD in 1969.

Richard Florida is a University Professor at the University of Toronto's Rotman School of Management and School of Cities. He is also a Distinguished Fellow at New York University's Schack Institute of Real Estate where he helped to create its Urban Lab. One of the world's leading urbanists, Florida has written several global bestsellers, including *The Rise of the Creative Class* (2002) and *The New Urban* Crisis (2017). He is author of over 100 peer-reviewed articles and book chapters. He writes frequently for media outlets like the *New York Times*, the *Wall Street Journal*, the *Financial Times* and *The Atlantic* and helped to found *CityLab*, the world's most influential publication devoted to cities and urbanism. Florida previously taught at Carnegie Mellon University, George Mason University, and Ohio State University, and has been a visiting professor at Harvard and MIT as well as a Non-Resident Fellow of the Brookings Institution. Born in Newark, New Jersey, he earned his bachelor's degree in political science from Rutgers College and PhD in urban planning from Columbia University.

Howard Gardner is the Hobbs Research Professor of Cognition and Education at the Harvard Graduate School of Education. He is a leading thinker about education and human development; he has studied and written extensively about intelligence, creativity, leadership, and professional ethics. He has received honorary degrees from thirty-one colleges and universities, including institutions in Bulgaria, Canada, Chile, Greece, Hong Kong, Ireland, Israel, Italy, South Korea, and Spain. Gardner's most recent books include *Good Work, Changing Minds, The Development and Education of the Mind, Multiple Intelligences: New Horizons,* and *Truth, Beauty and Goodness Reframed*. A recent book, co-authored with Katie Davis, is *The App Generation*, published in the fall of 2013. In 2020, MIT Press will publish his intellectual memoir *A Synthesizing Mind*. He is the winner of the 1990 Grawmeyer Award in Education, 2011 Asturias Prize in Social Science, and the 2015 Brock International Prize in Education. A Festschrift marking Gardner's 70th birthday is available online at howardgardner.com. as is further information about this unique text. With Wendy Fischman, he has recently completed data collection for a national study of higher education. Emerging findings are available on the blog Life-Long Learning at howardgardner.com.

David C. Geary received a BS in psychology from Santa Clara University in 1979 and a PhD in developmental psychology from the University of California, Riverside, in 1986. He's currently a Curators' Distinguished Professor in the Department of Psychological Sciences and Interdisciplinary Neuroscience Program at the University of Missouri. His work spans topics ranging from children's mathematical cognition to the evolution of sex differences. He's written four sole authored books: *Children's Mathematical Development* (1994), *Male, Female* (3 editions, 1998, 2010, 2021), *Origin of Mind* (2005), and *Evolution of Vulnerability* (2015). He also co-authored one book, *Sex Differences* (2008), co-edited a five-volume series on Mathematical Cognition and Learning, and a volume on evolution and human development. He has published more than 300 articles and chapters across the fields of psychology, education, and biology, and has had extensive funding from the National Institutes of Health and the National Science Foundation. He served on the President's National Mathematics Advisory Panel from 2006 to 2008, and was appointed by President G. W. Bush to the National Board of Advisors for the Institute of Educational Sciences, US Department of Education (2007 to 2010). Among other honors, he is a fellow of the American Association for the Advancement of Science and the Association for Psychological Sciences and is a recipient of a MERIT award from the National Institutes of Health.

Judith Glück has been full professor of developmental psychology at University of Klagenfurt, Austria, since 2007. She completed her diploma (comparable to a master's degree) in psychology in 1995 and her doctoral degree in 1999, both at the University of Vienna, Austria. From 1999 to 2002, she was a postdoctoral research fellow at the Max Planck Institute for Human Development in Berlin, Germany. From 2002 to 2007, she was an associate professor of developmental psychology at University of Vienna. She is married with two children, born in 2002 and 2007.

Judith's main topic of research is wisdom psychology. She is interested in the development of wisdom through an interplay of life experiences and internal and external resources, new methods of measuring wisdom, situational predictors of wisdom, wisdom in professional contexts, and people's conceptions of wisdom across different cultures. Her research has been funded by several grants from the Austrian Science Fund (FWF). She has published in renowned outlets including *Annual Review of Psychology*, *Developmental Psychology*, and *The Journals of Gerontology: Psychological Sciences*. She is co-editor of the *Cambridge Handbook of Wisdom* (2019).

Fernand Gobet is a Professor at London School of Economics and Political Science. Dr. Gobet earned his PhD in psychology in 1992 at the University of Fribourg, Switzerland. After a six-year stay (1990–1995) at Carnegie Mellon in Pittsburgh, where he worked on chess expertise with Nobel Prize winner Herbert Simon, he held positions at the University of Nottingham (Senior Research Fellow and Allan Standen Reader in Intelligent Systems, 1996–2003), Brunel University (Professor of Cognitive Psychology, 2003–2012), University of Liverpool (Professor of Decision Making and Expertise, 2013–2019), and the London School of Economics and Political Science (2019–present; Professorial Research Fellow). His main research interests are (a) the psychology of expertise and talent,

(b) cognitive training, (c) the development of computer models of expertise and the acquisition of first language, and (d) in artificial intelligence, the use of genetic programming to automatically generate scientific theories. He is the designer of CHREST (Chunk Hierarchy and REtrieval STructures), one of the few cognitive architectures in the world. He has over 350 scientific publications, including ten books. His recent books include *Understanding Expertise: A Multi-Disciplinary Approach* (London: Palgrave, 2016) and *The Psychology of Chess* (London: Routledge, 2019). He is an International Chess Master since 1985 and in 1984 was made Honorary Citizen of Montpellier (France).

Jane Piirto is Trustees' Distinguished Professor Emerita at Ashland University. Selected awards include the Mensa Education and Research Foundation Lifetime Achievement Award (2007); the NAGC Distinguished Scholar (2010); the E. Paul Torrance Award for Creativity (2014); the WCGT International Creativity Award (2017); and an Honorary Doctor of Humane Letters (2004). Jane has 100 + scholarly publications in peer-reviewed journals and edited books. As a creativity researcher, in the spirit of having expertise in a recognized creative artistic domain, she has also published 225+ separate poetry, fiction, and creative nonfiction works in literary venues. Jane has 12 single-authored books: *Creativity for 21st Century Skills; Understanding Creativity; "My Teeming Brain": Understanding Creative Writers; Understanding Those Who Create* (2 editions); *Talented Children and Adults* (3 editions); *The Three-Week Trance Diet; A Location in the Upper Peninsula; Saunas*. She has edited one book, *Organic Creativity*, and coauthored one book: *Luovuus*. Since 1974, Jane has presented 300+ keynotes, scholarly studies, workshops, readings, and consultations on 6 continents. Jane has a BA in English (Northern Michigan University, 1963); an MA in English (Kent State University, 1966); an MEd, Counseling (South Dakota State University, 1973); and a PhD in Leadership (Bowling Green State University, 1977).

Sally M. Reis holds the Letitia Neag Chair in Educational Psychology, is a Board of Trustees Distinguished Professor, and the former Vice Provost for Academic Affairs at the Neag School of Education at University of Connecticut. She served as Principal Investigator of the National Research Center on the Gifted and Talented and Department Head of the Educational Psychology Department. She was a classroom teacher and administrator in public education before her work at UConn. She has authored and co-authored more than 270 articles, books, book chapters, monographs and technical reports, and worked in a research team that has generated over 60 million dollars in grants in the last 15 years. Her scholarship on academically talented students and strength-based pedagogy is diverse and broad, as summarized by her numerous articles, books, book chapters, monographs, and technical reports. Her specialized research interests are related to diverse populations of talented students, education of students with both talents and disabilities, gifted females, and using enrichment and strength-based pedagogy to enhance education for all students. She has won multiple awards, including being named a UConn Board of Trustees Distinguished Professor and a fellow of Division 15 of The American Psychological Association.

Joseph S. Renzulli received his doctorate in educational psychology at the University of Virginia in 1966 and is a Distinguished Professor of Educational Psychology at the University of Connecticut, where he also serves as Director of the Renzulli Center for Creativity, Gifted Education, and Talent Development. He is an international leader in gifted education and applying the pedagogy of gifted education teaching strategies to *total school improvement*. His work on the Schoolwide Enrichment Model, and the use of instructional technology to assess student strengths and match resources to students' electronic profiles were pioneering efforts to make the field more flexible and to place the focus on talent development in *all* students. He has obtained more than 50 million dollars in research grants and the American Psychological Association named him among the 25 most influential psychologists in the world. In 2009 he received the Harold W. McGraw, Jr. Award for Innovation in Education, and he was recently listed as one of the world's top 30 international education professionals by the Global Guru Annual Survey.

Nancy M. Robinson (Stanford BA, 1951; PhD, 1958, Developmental and Clinical Psychology) is Professor Emerita of Psychiatry and Behavioral Sciences at the University of Washington and former Director of the Halbert and Nancy Robinson Center for Young Scholars. The Center, established by the Robinsons in 1975, is best known for its pioneering program of radical acceleration for young gifted students who skip several years of secondary school. From 1959 to 1988, her first career dealt with intellectual disability, beginning at the University of North Carolina (1959–1969); her second career, in the field of giftedness, began in 1981. Her research interests in the latter focused on marked acceleration, intellectual assessment of children and youth, and precocity in very young children. Among her honors are the Distinguished Scholar Award and Ann Isaacs Founders Memorial Award, National Association for Gifted Children. Her contributions to the field of giftedness include a successful model of radical acceleration to college of very bright students provided a social cohort, the importance of extremely early intervention in the equitable realization of promise in children of marginalized families, and demonstration through parental observation that, indeed, standardized measures do reflect "real life."

Mark A. Runco earned a PhD in Cognitive Psychology from the Claremont Graduate School. He studied creativity as a student and has kept at since graduating in 1984. He has published over 300 books, articles, and chapters on creativity and closely related topics and has developed a variety of courses and seminars on creativity and Innovation. He earned tenure at the University of Hawaii, Hilo, and then moved to California State University, Fullerton, where he directed the Creativity Research Center of Southern California. Next was an Endowed Professorship at the University of Georgia, where he was also Director of the Torrance Creativity Center. In addition, he has held adjunct positions at Buffalo State University and the Norwegian Business School. He is currently the Director of Creativity Research at Southern Oregon University (www.sou creativityconference.com), as well as a Fellow and Past President of Division 10 of the APA. He is Founding Editor of the *Creativity Research Journal*. His creativity textbook has been translated into ten languages. The third edition of that text and third edition of the Encyclopedia of Creativity, which he co-edited, are being released in 2020 (www.markrunco.com). He remains CEO of Creativity Testing Services, LLC (www.creativitytestingservices.com). His various awards and grants (e.g., Spencer Foundation, Creative Education Foundation) and further details on his career can be found, along with his CV, at www.ma rkrunco.com.

Larisa Shavinina is Professor at the Université du Québec en Outaouais and the Founding President of Canada 150+: The Canadian National Conference on Innovation. Her research focuses on innovation talent, women in innovation, intellectually creative giftedness, child prodigy, scientific talent of Nobel laureates, entrepreneurial giftedness, innovation leadership, managerial excellence, and wisdom. Dr. Shavinina introduced innovation education as a new direction in education in the *International Handbook of Innovation Education* (Routledge, 2013), which she edited. Innovation is an important element in her research on talent and economy. She introduced the phenomenon of the "abortion" of new ideas. Dr. Shavinina is especially interested in research on outstanding innovators with longstanding records of breakthrough innovations. She edited the bestselling *International Handbook on Innovation* (Elsevier, 2003), which is considered the beginning of innovation science. It was aimed at unifying the field of innovation, merging business, management, and psychological perspectives. Dr. Shavinina also edited the *International Handbook on Giftedness* (Springer, 2009) that set a new standard for the field of high ability studies. Dr. Shavinina received her Bachelor's degree (1990), Master's (1991) in psychology, and PhD in psychology (1993), with specialization in Psychology of Giftedness and Talent from Kiev State University, Ukraine.

Dean Keith Simonton earned his 1970 BA in psychology from Occidental College and his 1973 MA and 1975 PhD in social psychology from Harvard University. In 1976 he joined the faculty at the University of California, Davis, and retired 50 years later as Distinguished Professor Emeritus of Psychology. His more than 500 single-authored publications focus on various aspects of genius, creativity, leadership, talent, and aesthetics—most commonly using historiometric methods. His honors include the William James Book Award, the George A. Miller Outstanding Article Award, the Theoretical Innovation Prize in Personality and Social Psychology, the Sir Francis Galton Award for Outstanding Contributions to the Study of Creativity, the Rudolf Arnheim Award for Outstanding Contributions to Psychology and the Arts, the Henry A. Murray Award for "distinguished contributions to the study of individual lives and whole persons," the Joseph B. Gittler Award for "the most scholarly contribution to the philosophical foundation of psychological knowledge," the Distinguished Scientific Contributions to Media Psychology Award, the E. Paul Torrance Award for Creativity, three Mensa Awards for Excellence in Research, and the Mensa Lifetime Achievement Award. His 14 books include the 2014 *Wiley Handbook of Genius* and the 2018 *Genius Checklist*.

Robert J. Sternberg is Professor of Human Development at Cornell University and Honorary Professor of Psychology at the University of Heidelberg, Germany. Sternberg's BA is from Yale University and his PhD from Stanford. He also has 13 honorary doctorates. He is past-president of the American Psychological Association, the Federation of Associations in Brain and Behavioral Sciences, and of the International Association for Cognitive Education and Psychology. Sternberg is past winner of the Grawemeyer Award in Psychology, and the Williams James and James McKeen Cattell Awards from the Association for Psychological Science. He is a member of the US National Academy of Education and American Academy of Arts and Sciences, as well as a Fellow of the American Association for the Advancement of Science. Formerly, he was treasurer of the Association of American Colleges and Universities. He has been cited over 180,000 times and has a Google h index of 205. He has appeared in various listings of most cited psychologists. Sternberg's main interests are in intelligence, creativity, wisdom, love, and hate. He is the author of a number of books, including *What Universities Can Be* (2016, Cornell University Press) and *Adaptive Intelligence* (in press, Cambridge University Press). Sternberg is married to Karin Sternberg and has five children, Seth, Sara, Samuel, Brittany, and Melody.

Rena F. Subotnik, PhD, is Director of the Center for Psychology in Schools and Education at the American Psychological Association (APA). One of the Center's missions is to generate public awareness, advocacy, clinical applications, and cutting-edge research ideas that enhance the achievement and performance of children and adolescents with gifts and talents in all domains. She has been supported in this work by the National Science Foundation, the American Psychological Foundation, the Association for Psychological Science, the Camille and Henry Dreyfus Foundation, and the Jack Kent Cooke Foundation. Before she came to APA in 2001, Dr. Subotnik was a Professor of Educational Psychology at Hunter College in New York City, and Research Coordinator for the

Hunter College Campus Schools (K–12 laboratory school for 1600 gifted children). Dr. Subotnik received her PhD from the University of Washington, her Master's from Teachers College, Columbia University and her BA from the City College of New York. She is a Fellow of AERA, two Divisions of APA, and a Distinguished Scholar of the National Association for Gifted Children. Her work (with Paula Olszewski-Kubilius and Frank Worrell) is published in *Scientific American, Scientific American Mind, Annals of the New York Academy of Sciences, Frontiers in Psychology, Psychological Science in the Public Interest* and the *Annual Review of Psychology*.

Ellen Winner is Professor of Psychology at Boston College and Senior Research Associate at Project Zero, Harvard Graduate School of Education. She received her BA in English Literature from Radcliffe College and her PhD in Psychology from Harvard. Her work specializes in the psychology of the arts. At Boston College she directs the Arts and Mind Lab, which focuses on cognition in the arts in typical and gifted children as well as adults. She has written over 200 articles and is author of four books and coauthor of three: *Invented Worlds: The Psychology of the Arts* (1982); *The Point of Words: Children's Understanding of Metaphor and Irony* (1988); *Gifted Children: Myths and Realities* (1996); *How Art Works: A Psychological Exploration* (2018); and co-author of *Studio Thinking: The Real Benefits of Visual Arts Education* (2007); *Studio Thinking 2: The Real Benefits of Visual Arts Education* (2013); *Studio Thinking from the Start: The K-8 Art Educator's Handbook*. She served as President of APA's Division 10, Psychology and the Arts in 1995–1996, and received the Rudolf Arnheim Award for Outstanding Research by a Senior Scholar in Psychology and the Arts from Division 10 in 2000. She is a fellow of APA Division 10 and of the International Association of Empirical Aesthetics. A 2020 special issue of *Empirical Studies in the Arts* honored her work.

Frank C. Worrell received his Bachelor's (1985) and Master's (1987) degrees in Psychology from the University of Western Ontario and his PhD in Educational and School Psychology (1994) from the University of California, Berkeley. He is currently Professor and Director of the School Psychology Program at UC Berkeley, where he also serves as Faculty Director of the Academic Talent Development Program and the California College Preparatory Academy. His areas of research include at-risk youth, cultural identities, gifted education/talent development, scale development, and time perspective. A former co-editor (2012–2014) and editor (2015–2016) of *Review of Educational Research*, Dr. Worrell was also a Member at Large on the Board of Directors of the American Psychological Association (APA; 2016–2018). Dr. Worrell is a Fellow of the American Educational Research Association, the Association for Psychological Science, and five divisions of APA, and an elected member of the Society for the Study of School Psychology and the National Academy of Education.

Dr. Worrell is a recipient of the Distinguished Scholar Award from the National Association for Gifted Children (2013), the Distinguished Contributions to Research Award from Division 45 (the Society for the Psychological Study of Culture, Ethnicity, and Race; 2015) of APA, the Outstanding International Psychologist Award from Division 52 (International Psychology; 2018) of APA, and the Palmarium Award in Gifted Education (2019) from the University of Denver's Morgridge College of Education.

SUBJECT INDEX

A the achievement gap 215, 217–18
adaptive intelligence 195–96, 264, 273;
  Successful intelligence 186–190,
  195–96, 205, 211, 234
age and achievement 116–17, 123;
archival research 150
artistic development in children 41
at-risk youth 212, 216–218, 221, 274;
  dropouts 212, 215–217, 220;
  protective factors for
at-risk youth 216
asymptote, asymptotic performance
  251

B behavioral ecology 3, 5, 8
behaviorism and Skinner 129;
  observable behaviors 129
beyond Terman 91, 95
Big Five (NEO-PI-R) 146
biologically primary vs. secondary 6
brain damage 41, 46, 241
brain imaging 67, 262

C the capacity view of talent 250–51
chess players' perception and memory
  62, 65; chunking theory & template
  theory 65; *perception and memory in
  Chess* 66, 73
chess players' thinking 62; *see also*
  Adriaan de Groot; Pattern
  recognition and search 62

child prodigy 80, 156–158, 166–67,
  256, 264, 272; *Nature' Gambit* 46,
  79–80, 84, 262, 267
children's memory 55
cognitive development 78–81, 83, 129,
  254, 262, 267; the BEST criteria 81;
  development of expertise 69,
  78–79, 81–82
cognitive diversity 253
cognition in the wild 253
cognitive psychology 60, 68, 71, 74,
  96, 129–30, 135, 242, 266, 269,
  271
collaborative creativity 79
community of committed learners 253
comparative psychology 5
computational modeling 60, 65–66, 71
computer simulations 72, 120
contrarianism 129–30, 132–33, 135,
  137–38
creativity 30, 44, 58, 78–80, 83–87,
  89–90, 99, 101, 107, 111, 113,
  115–117, 120–42, 144, 146,
  150–54, 162, 175–77, 179–81,
  186–87, 191, 195–97, 200–02, 207,
  209–11, 228–29, 231–32, 250, 252,
  254–59, 261–62, 264, 267–68,
  270–73; the *art bias* 130, 138;
creative accomplishments 234, 257;
creative productivity 94, 124, 197,
  203, 207, 251, 256, 264; dark side
  of 131–32, 139–40, 177, 261;

domain-specificity of 252;
intentions 85, 132–35, 157, 166,
185, 252; moral creativity 132–33,
140; personal creativity 128,
133–36, 140; the potential-
performance distinction 127; *primary
vs. secondary* 6; the product approach
to 134; creativity and cities 168–70;
the creative economy 174,
176–177, 179–80; innovation
155–57, 159–67, 169, 171–72, 174,
176–81, 271–73
critical thinking 25, 152, 192
crystallizing experience 76, 84, 160,
265
cultural identities 216–17, 221, 274;
Cross Racial Identity Scale 218,
222–23

D delay of gratification 253, 263
deliberate practice 69–71, 103, 108,
120, 238, 253–54, 262
developmental science 258, 261–63
disruptive innovation 178
distinction between potential and
performance/achievement 127, 252
distributed intelligence 13
dogmatism and absolutism 258
the domain-specific issue 250

E The Early Entrance Program at UW
32, 37
ego-decentered 243, 258
emotional intelligence 47, 151, 253, 263
experimental vs. Correlational 18
expertise 17, 23, 44, 59–62, 65–74, 79,
81–82, 87, 94–95, 120–21, 125,
136, 147, 158, 238–39, 252,
254–55, 257, 261–65, 269–70; *see*
Ericsson; thinking and expertise 61;
verbal protocol 66–67, 71; talent vs.
practice 61
epistemic stances 252, 258
epistemological 257
equity concerns 250
essentialism vs. developmental
contextualism 256
everyday cognition 54, 57, 59;
Brazilian bookies and street vendors
55; *see* Ulric Neisser
evolution 3, 5–11, 14–15, 46, 51,
57–58, 68, 80, 117, 120, 127, 152,
159, 161, 164, 206, 232, 251,
253–54, 262, 268–69; Charles
Darwin 7, 14, 131; *Evolution of
Vulnerability* 9–11, 15, 269; sex-
specific vulnerabilities 4, 8–9, 11;
human evolution 80; mitochondrial
functioning 3, 10–12, 14–15;
mitochondrial energy production
12–13;
exceptionality 147, 257; exceptional
memory 52, 54

F far transfer 70, 74
Frames of Mind 42, 46, 79, 84, 131,
209, 234, 262

G genius 44, 86, 95, 113, 115–16, 118,
124–25, 133, 141, 154, 156, 165,
262, 265, 272–73
gifted education 78, 84–86, 89;
acceleration 36–37, 93, 165, 230,
271; Schoolwide Enrichment
Model (SEM) 206, 228–29
Giftedness 33–34, 38, 78–80, 83–91,
95, 102, 113, 140, 147, 153,
155–60, 162, 165–67, 197,
199–03, 205, 207–08, 210–11,
219, 221–22, 228, 232–34, 255–56,
261–65, 271–72; the rage to master
102–03, 108, 255; academically
gifted children 103; gifted girls
150, 255
grit 13, 138, 202, 220, 253, 262

H habits of mind 105
Harvard Project Zero 41, 103, 108–09
hemispheric specialization 5
human accomplishments 247, 259,
263; possibilities & limits of 247
human agency 93, 250, 252–53, 258
human potential 1, 41–47, 75, 79–80,
82, 84, 93, 113, 116, 158, 162,
247–54, 256–60, 262, 267; as
capacity xvii; as disposition or
propensity xvii, 93, 105, 249, 257;
as capability xix; 24, 252; as
psychosocial phenomenon 218–29,
253; malleability of human potential
250
Human Potential Project 79
Hunter College Elementary School
85–87, 142–43, 149, 152

278 Subject Index

I
historiometric methods 118; historiometry 118–19, 125; significant samples 118, 124
Horsemen of the Apocalypse 9–10

idiographic complexity 255
ill-structured problems 4
individual human genomes 45
information processing tasks 19; automatic (vs. controlled) processing 19
insider knowledge 88–90, 92–94
Institute for Personality Assessment and Research (IPAR) 115
intellectual 3, 16–30, 37–38, 44, 51, 59–61, 64, 80, 84–85, 115, 118–19, 124–25, 146, 149, 151, 156–59, 161, 166–68, 170, 172, 178, 180, 190, 204, 212, 218, 224–27, 229–33, 247–49, 252, 259–60, 263, 265–66, 268, 271–72; disability 30, 271; mental retardation 30, 32, 34, 264
intelligence 3–4, 11–15, 17, 19–21, 23–29, 42–47, 51, 55–57, 59–62, 65, 68–70, 73–75, 78, 81, 84, 87, 95, 118–19, 121–22, 124–25, 129, 131, 139–41, 151, 153, 156, 159–60, 168, 172, 185–93, 195–96, 201–02, 295, 209–11, 228, 234, 239–40, 250, 253, 255, 258–59, 261–64, 268, 270, 273; adult intelligence 19, 23–28, 56; artificial intelligence 60, 65, 74, 129, 259, 270; fluid intellectual abilities (Gf) vs. crystallized intellectual abilities (Gc) 18, 21–22; context-free measures 23; general intelligence 3, 11–12, 15, 42, 51, 55, 57, 59, 131, 262, 264; see Charles Spearman;
intersubjectivity 249
interviews with experts 55
the investment theory; sustained mental effort 25
IQ, constancy of, 16; formal education and IQ performance 56; influence of 69, 143;
intelligence and achieved eminence 118; IQ and expertise 17, 59, 67, 69–70, 72, 74, 81–82, 87, 95, 120–21, 125, 252, 254–55, 261, 264; IQ and exceptional leadership 120

J Juilliard Pre-College 87, 92

K The Kanfer-Ackerman Air Traffic Control Task 20, 250

L leadership 42, 44, 113, 115–17, 119–25, 140–41, 149–50, 154, 157, 162, 166, 204–05, 225, 227, 268, 270, 272; sociocultural leadership 116
learned helplessness 63–64; see Martin Seligman

M mathematically precocious children 35; the Center for Talented Youth, Julian Stanley 32, 34, 164, 249;
Matthew effect 251
Max Planck Institute of Empirical Aesthetics 99
maximal adaptation 253; maximal performance 21; see typical performance
mathematical development 6–7, 14, 269
mathematical model of talent development 120,
meaning-making 248; see also Jerome Bruner
measurement 118; complex task performance 20; domain knowledge 22–24, 26; external validity 24; perceptual speed 19, 27; psychomotor abilities 19–20, 27; sex/gender differences 3–7, 9, 11–15, 22, 27, 235, 268–69; trait complexes 22–23
Megamodel of Talent Development 89, 92–94, 219
mentorship 94, 122, 253
meta-analysis 70, 74, 210
metaphors and symbolic play 100; metaphoric renaming 100–01; metaphoric thinking 101; pretend action metaphors 100
methodology 16–17, 60, 66–67, 73–74, 116, 143, 200, 263, 267; case study methodologies 131; interpretative approaches 66; multi-disciplinary research 60, 72, 164; Neurath's boat 256; quantitative approaches 66, 254
mindset 220, 253–54, 262; growth mindset 220
multiple intelligences 42, 46–47, 81, 139, 209, 234, 268

N National Research Center on the Gifted and Talented 87, 208, 267, 270
the nature-nurture debate 250–51; being" and "doing" accounts 254
neural efficiency 253
the nomothetic-idiographic tension 255; nomothetic assumption 254
Nonuniversal Theory 79, 81–83; culturally constructed domains 81; nonuniversal development 255; the universal-unique continuum 81

O ontological commitments 250, 256, *Origin of Mind* 12, 15, 262, 269
operation Houndstooth 204–05, 210–11
optimal objectivity 135
optimal talent development 37–38

P the paradoxical nature of human agency 258
Piaget 41, 63, 78, 80–82, 129, 131, 139–40, 249, 252, 254, 263
Piaget's error 254
The Piirto Pyramid of Talent Development 144–45, 150, 253
positional identity 248–50
positive psychology 204, 211
post-conventional thinking 138
post-Fordist economy 174
practical intelligence 87–88, 95, 187–88, 191, 195
Project Zero 41, 97–99, 103, 107–09, 274
psychometric approaches to intelligence 69; specific abilities 80, 94, 219; technological advances 24, 259
psychological testing 16, 28, 193, 221, 266;
the psychology of the arts 99, 107–08, 274; abstract expressionist paintings 102; art-making 98, 105; child as artist 99; developmental psychology of the arts 98; art education 78, 103, 108; *How Art Works* 99, 108, 274; thinking like an artist 105
psychosocial skills 85, 90, 92–95, 253

Q qualitative research 70, 150, 255

R racetrack handicappers 55; cognitive complexity 56–57, 59, 261; context-specificity 56
rates of learning 251
reasoning ability 253, 263
relational developmental system 251, 257, 263
remarkable women 92, 94, 153

S the sciences of the artificial 259, 264
selective affinity 251
sex differences 3–7, 9, 11–15, 268–69; sex differences in the nDNA 13; sexual selection 7–8, 10–11, 14–15
single-variable stories 253, 258
scholarly productivity/artistry 87, 92
social recognition 133–135, 138, *social structures of innovation* 171
Sputnik 32, 136, 199, 225
standardized test 186–88, 194, 204, The Structure of Intellect Learning Abilities Test (SOI-LA) 143; *see* J.P. Guilford

T tacit knowledge 148, 187, 205
talent 32, 35, 37–39, 44, 60–61, 65–66, 68–73, 80, 83–95, 102–03, 105, 108, 113, 115, 120, 124, 139, 142–47, 150, 152–53, 156–60, 162, 164–66, 168, 172–74, 177, 180, 186–87, 196–97, 199, 206–07, 209–12, 216, 218–22, 229, 231, 234, 249, 251, 253, 256–57, 259, 261, 263–64, 267, 269, 271–72, 274; talent domains 93
talent achievement in domains (TAD) 92–93, 219
talent development 32, 37–38, 73, 80, 83–85, 87–89, 92–95, 120, 142, 144–147, 150, 152–53, 158, 165–66, 196–97, 199, 206, 209, 212, 216, 218–21, 229, 231, 234, 251, 253, 259, 261, 271, 274; talent trajectories 93–94
talented 40, 55, 76, 78, 87, 90, 94, 107, 130, 137, 140, 142–43, 146–49, 153–54, 156–57, 162, 165–66, 173, 178, 208–11, 217–19, 222, 224–25, 227–31, 233–34, 250, 263, 267, 270; *talented and eminent women* 224, 231; *talented readers* 229
technical rationality 247–48

Subject Index

temporal lenses 217; temporal constructs 216; adolescent and Adult Time Inventory 217, 221; Zimbardo Time Perspective Inventory (ZTPI) 217
3Ts of economic development 173
toddlers with precocious language 35
trait variability 7; condition-dependent traits 8–10, 14; sexually selected traits 8–12, 15; spatial abilities 7–8, 11
tribalism 45, 190
typical vs. maximal performance 21; typical intellectual engagement 21

U uncertainty principle 248
unit of analysis 118, 120
Utah creativity conferences 146
urban planning 170, 268,

V the volcano vs. river metaphor 256

W Wechsler Adult Intelligence Scale 19, 24, 28, 56
Westinghouse (Intel) Science Talent Search 89, 91, 95, 199
wisdom 26, 29, 38, 43, 88, 95, 162, 173–74, 186, 195, 235–46, 255, 258–59, 269, 272–73; the Berlin Wisdom Paradigm (BWP) 239–40, 243–44; the Defining Wisdom Project 242; limits of control 241; uncontrollability 241–42, 244; wisdom as expertise 238; wisdom as a meta-heuristic 238; wisdom and gratitude 242
worldviews 256

Z zeitgeist 4, 25, 55, 123, 127, 147, 187, 248–49

NAME INDEX

A Abelson, Robert P. 248, 261
Acar, Selcuk 129, 137, 139–40
Ackerman, Phillip L. 16, 18–24, 26, 27–28, 249–254, 261, 266
Allport, G. W. 255, 261
Ambrose, Don 258, 261
Angoff, William H. xix
Antonakis, John 120, 122
Ardelt, Monika 238, 243, 245
Arnold, Karen D. 91–92, 94–95, 105, 153, 202, 209
Ashcraft, Mark 5

B Baer, John 130, 139
Baltes, Paul B. 236–41, 245, 249
Bandura, Albert. xix
Bargh, John A. 238, 245
Barron, Frank 130, 138–39, 146, 149, 209
Beier, Margaret E. 22, 27–28
Belsky, J. xviii
Bereiter, Carl 253, 264
Bilalić, Merim 69, 73
Binet, Alfred 21, 24, 26, 28, 255
Bloom, Benjamin 86, 90, 94, 148, 153, 201, 209, 249,
Bluck, Susan 240, 242, 245–46
Booij, Adam S. 206, 209
Bouchard 146
Bronfenbrenner, Urie 32, 57–59, 248–49, 261,

Brown, Roger 98–100, 108
Brandwein, Paul F. 199–200, 209
Bruner, Jerome 80, 83, 96–98, 248–49, 255, 261

C Cairns, Robert B. 258, 261
Callahan, Carolyn M. 202, 209–211
Camp, R. 77, 103, 108
Campbell, Donald T. 120–22, 125
Carroll, John B. 18, 20, 28, 143, 153
Carson, Rachel 205, 226
Ceci, Stephen J. 51, 55–57, 59, 248–49, 251–53, 255, 261, 266–67,
Cerridwen, Anemon 120, 122
Chamrad, Diana L. 39
Chassy, Philippe 69, 73
Clark, Barbara 142
Cohen, Jeffrey E. 119, 122
Cole, Michael 78, 83, 141
Cotton, Samuel 8–9, 14
Cox, Catharine M. 118, 122
Cronbach, Lee J. 18, 21, 23, 28, 249, 254, 261
Cropley, Arthur J. 130, 139–40, 258, 261
Cropley, David H. 132, 139–40, 258, 261
Cross Jr, William E. 218, 221, 223
Csikszentmihalyi, Mihaly 44, 47, 79, 83–84, 130–31, 139, 141, 204, 211, 258, 262, 267

Name Index

D Dai, David Yun 73, 80, 83, 165, 247–48, 251–54, 257, 261–62, 267
Dale, Philip S. 35, 39
Damian, Rodica Ioana 122
Davis, Bridgett M. 53, 59
Davis, K. 42, 46, 268
Davies, Nicholas B. 5, 15
Deary, Ian J. 12, 14–15
de Groot, Adriaan D. 60, 62–64, 66, 73, 249, 254
Demming, John A. 24, 28
Dennett, Daniel 252, 262
Derks, Peter L. 120, 123
Dewey, John 227
Dijksterhuis, Ap 238, 245
Dumas, Denis 137, 139
Dweck, Carol S. 253, 262

E Einstein, A. 116, 156, 164–65, 248, 258
Epstein (chapter 11) 129, 139
Ericsson, K. Anders 66, 69, 73, 103, 108, 147, 153, 249, 251–54, 262, 264
Erikson, Erik H. 77, 215–17, 221

F Feldhusen, John 146, 149, 267
Feldman, David Henry 44, 46, 75, 79–80, 83–84, 144, 249–52, 254–56, 261–62, 264, 267–68
Ferguson, George A. (1956) 26, 28
Field, Gara. 206, 209
Fischer, Kurt W. 253, 262,
Fleishman, Edwin A. 20, 28
Flinn, Mark 6
Florida, Richard 168, 171–73, 175–76, 180–81, 249, 253, 268,
Freudenthal, Daniel 67, 73

G Gallagher, James 227, 233, 252, 264
Gallagher, Jim 31
Gagné, Francoys 80, 84, 147, 153, 248, 251, 256, 262
Galton, Francis 248, 251, 253, 255, 257–58, 260, 262, 273
Gardner, Howard 41–44, 46–47, 76, 79, 84, 97–98, 100–102, 108–09, 131, 139, 205, 208–09, 228, 234, 249, 252, 257–59, 262, 265, 267–68
Gaulin, Steven J. C. 8, 14
Geary, David C 3, 6–9, 11–15, 249, 251–52, 262, 268
Getzels and Jackson (1962) 202, 209

Gladwell, Malcolm xv
Glück, Judith 235–36, 238, 239–242, 244–46, 249, 255, 258, 269,
Gobet, Fernand 60, 62, 65–74, 251, 254, 260, 269
Goleman, Daniel 43, 47
Goldman, R. J. 202, 209
Gottfredson, Linda S. 146, 153
Gough, Harrison G. 119, 123
Gould, Stephen Jay 69, 74, 252, 262
Gottlieb, Gilbert 251, 262
Greeno, J. G. 249, 262
Gresalfi, Melissa xxi
Grossmann, Igor 243, 245–46
Gruber, Howard E. 73, 121, 123, 131–32, 139
Guilford, J. P. 27–28, 128, 136, 139–141, 143, 202, 209, 249, 263

H Haier, Richard J. 253, 262,
Harari, Yuval Noah 45, 47, 259, 262
Harmon, Lindsey R. 201, 209,
Hass, Richard W. 137, 139,
Hawking, Stephen xx
Heller, Kurt A. 87, 95, 159, 211,
Helson, Ravenna 130, 139, 146,
Henry, Rebecca A. 21, 28, 75, 103, 153, 170, 261
Herrnstein, Richard J. xvi
Hetland, Lois 104, 107, 108
Hilgard & Atkinson, 1967 115, 123
Hill, Geoffrey 10, 14–15
Hillman, James 147, 153
Holding, Dennis Harry 64, 65, 74
Holland, John L. 201, 209
Holton, Gerald 248, 250, 262
Horowitz, Frances Degen 251, 253, 254, 258, 263,
Howard, Robert W. 251, 263
Howe, Michael J. A. xviii
Hudson, Liam 201, 209,
Humphreys, Lloyd 17
Hunt, Earl 18
Hutchins, Robert Maynard 114, 123

J Jacobs, Jane 178, 180, 181
Jašarević, Eldin 8, 14, 15
Janos, P. M. 39, 40
Jarvin, Linda 87, 91–93, 95, 221
Jay, E. 134, 139
Jensen, Arthur R. 253, 263
Johnson, Wendy 13, 15
Johnstone, Rufus A. 8, 15

Name Index

K Kanfer, Ruth
Kaufman, James C. 139–141, 146, 153, 264
Kerr, Barbara A. 146, 150, 153, 154
Kim, Mihyeon 206, 210
Kimura, Doreen 7, 15
Klingemann, Hans-Dieter 119, 123
Koch, Sigmund 255, 263
König, Susanne 242, 245, 246
Kornhaber, Mindy L. 42, 43, 47
Kozbelt, Aaron 120, 123, 221
Kratz, Rene Fester 11, 15
Kurzweil, Ray 259, 263
Kyllonen, Patrick C. 18, 28, 253, 263

L Lacey 27, 28
Lakatos, Imre 250, 256, 263
Lane, Nick 11, 15
Lane, Peter C. R. 72, 74
Lauden, Larry 245, 263
Lehman, Harvey Christian 116–117, 123
LeVine, Robert A. 42, 47
Liberman, Alvin 6
Lohman, David F. xix
Lowenfeld, Viktor 103, 108
Lubinski, David 34, 252, 254, 256, 263

M MacKinnon, Donald W. 116, 123, 130, 139, 146,
Mackintosh, 1998 69, 74
Maddow, R. 133, 139
Magnusson, David xx
Marland Jr, Sidney P. 202, 210
Martindale, Colin 120, 123
Marx, Karl 178–181
Maslow, Abraham Harold 82, 84
McLaren, Robert B 131, 132, 139
Meeker, Mary 143, 153
Melton, Arthur W. 27, 28
Meeker, Mary Nacol 143, 153
Mednick, Martha T. 201, 210
Mello, Z. R. 217, 221,
Meredith, Daniel 120, 123
Merrill, Maud 29, 32, 142, 144, 145
Merton, Robert K. 258, 263
Miller, Geoffrey 11, 15
Miller, George 96, 97, 273
Mischel, Walter 253, 263
Miller, Arthur I. 130, 140
Molenaar, Peter C. M. 255, 263
Monks, Franz 87, 149
Moran, Seana 264
Murray, Charles A. 252, 263

N Naroll, Raoul 117, 123
Neisser, Ulric 58
Neurath, Otto 256, 263
Newell, Allen 71, 74, 263
Nisbett, Richard E. xvii
Noble, K. D. 150, 153

O Ogbu, John U. 217, 221
Olszewski-Kubilius, Paula 219, 221, 222, 264
Overton, Willis F. 251, 257, 263

P Page, Scott E. 253, 263
Pardoe, Iain 120, 123
Patrick, Catharine 130, 140
Pepper, Stephen C. 256, 263
Piaget, Jean 41, 63, 78, 81, 82, 129, 131, 139, 140, 249, 252, 254, 263
Piirto, Jane 86, 95, 142, 144–146,51, 153, 249, 251–253, 255, 263
Piketty, Thomas 175, 181
Plomin 146
Plucker, Jonathan A. 95, 130, 136, 140
Pluess, M. xviii
Polanyi, Michael 248, 263
Preckel, Franzis 93, 219, 221

R Redzanowski, Uwe 242, 245, 246
Reis, Sally M. 249, 250, 255, 260
Renzulli, Joseph S. 147, 156, 197, 201–207, 209–211, 224, 225, 227–229, 233, 234, 249, 251, 257, 258, 262, 264
Robinson, Hal B. 29, 40, 260
Robinson, Nancy M. 29, 39, 40, 252, 260, 264
Root-Bernstein, Robert xviii
Rose, Todd 44, 47
Runco, Mark A. 126, 128–130, 132–135, 137–141, 250, 252, 255, 256, 261, 264

S Sala, Giovanni 67, 71, 73,
Salas, Eduardo 94, 95
Sawyer, R. Keith 257, 264
Scardamalia, Marlene 253, 264
Schaefer-Simmern, Henry 104, 108
Schlaug, Gottfried 251, 264
Schliemann, Analúcia D. 55, 59
Scheffler, Israel 42, 47
Schneider, Walter 18, 221
Schön, Donald A. xxiii
Schumpeter, Joseph 178, 181

Name Index

Seligman, Martin E. P. 63, 204, 211
Shavinina, Larisa V. 155–163, 166, 167, 254–256,
Shearer, Branton 262, 264
Shiffrin, Richard M. 251, 264
Siegler, Robert 5
Simon, Herbert A. 60, 62–66, 68, 74
Simonton, Dean Keith 117–125, 127, 133, 141, 146, 147, 154, 165, 249–252, 254, 260, 264
Sklar, Kathryn Kish 149, 154
Snow, Richard Eric. 22, 28, 255, 264
Snyder, Samuel S. 78, 79, 84
Sorokin, Pitirim 119, 123, 125
Spearman, Charles 3, 15, 191, 253, 255, 263, 264
Staff, Toby 69, 70, 74
Sternberg, 2000 69, 185
Sternberg, Robert J. 185, 187–191, 195, 196, 205, 208, 211, 228, 232–235, 245, 248, 250, 252, 254, 258, 261, 262, 264, 265
Stroop, J. Ridley. 23, 28
Subotnik, Rena F. 219, 221, 222, 249, 251–254, 263, 264
Sytsma, Rachel Elizabeth 205, 211

T Tannenbaum, Abraham 85, 86, 95, 147, 154, 249, 256, 259, 264,
Terman, Lewis 32, 86, 87, 91, 95, 115, 118, 125, 149, 248, 249, 254, 255, 260, 265
Thorndike, Edward L. 248, 255, 260, 265

Thurstone, L. L. 17, 19, 28
Torrance, E. Paul 156, 202, 211, 227, 233, 249, 270, 272, 273
Tucker, Ledyard 17

U Ullén, Fredrik 254

V Vandiver, B. J. 218, 222, 223
Vuyk, M. A. 146, 154
Vygotsky, Lev Semenovich 81, 82

W Waber, Deborah P. 5, 15
Wachs, Theodore D. xxi
Wallach, M. A. (1976) 201, 211
Walberg, Herbert J. 118, 125
Walters, Joseph 76, 84, 249, 265,
Watkins, Marley W. 221, 222
Weinstein, Rhona S. 221, 222
Werner, Heinz xx
Weststrate, Nic M. 238, 242, 244–246
Whipple, Guy Montrose. 19, 28
Winkler, Daniel L. 255, 265
Winner, Ellen 255, 265
Witty, Paul xvii
Woods, Frederick Adams 119, 125
Worrell, Frank C. 212, 214, 216–219, 221–223, 249, 264
Wright, Logan. 17, 28

Z Zahavi, Amotz. 7, 15
Zhao, Yong 259, 265
Ziegler, Albert 73, 95, 211, 256, 265
Zimbardo, Philip G. 217, 221, 223